State Environmental Management

Elizabeth H. Haskell
Victoria S. Price

The Praeger Special Studies program—utilizing the most modern and efficient book production techniques and a selective worldwide distribution network—makes available to the academic, government, and business communities significant, timely research in U.S. and international economic, social, and political development.

State Environmental Management
Case Studies
of Nine States

PRAEGER SPECIAL STUDIES IN U.S. ECONOMIC, SOCIAL, AND POLITICAL ISSUES

Praeger Publishers   New York   Washington   London

Library of Congress Cataloging in Publication Data

Haskell, Elizabeth H   1942-
     State environmental management.

     (Praeger special studies in U. S. economic,
social, and political issues)
     Bibliography: p.
     1. Environmental policy—United States—
States—Case studies. 2. Administrative agencies
—United States—States—Case studies. I. Price,
Victoria, 1943-   , joint author. II. Title.
HC110. E5H36   353. 9'3'8232   72-90667

PRAEGER PUBLISHERS
111 Fourth Avenue, New York, N.Y. 10003, U.S.A.
5, Cromwell Place, London SW7 2JL, England

Published in the United States of America in 1973
by Praeger Publishers, Inc.

Printed in the United States of America

CONTENTS

LIST OF TABLES

LIST OF CHARTS

The institutions of government at all levels have lagged behind pressing new social concerns, of which the environment is one. Nineteenth-century organizations frequently do not match twentieth-century problems, and legal authority is sometimes inadequate. This institutional lag has been most acute in state governments that, under our federal system, are the administrative layer between the increasingly powerful federal government and municipalities. In popular thinking, the states are often regarded as the last bastion of reactionary thinking, political corruption, and bureaucratic ineptitude, and some persons believe that this institutional layer has declined in importance.

However, in the environmental field, as in others, the states' potential for effective management is very great indeed. States are neither so parochial nor susceptible of domination by a few large economic and political interests as are local governments. States can plan and administer day-to-day programs, such as the issuance of permits, without the massive red tape and inflexibility that ensnarls the federal bureaucracy. Yet, unlike localities, their perspective for planning and management can often reach throughout whole watersheds, airsheds, or urbanizing regions. They have inherent as well as assigned powers that are vital legal tools to cope with environmental degradation. For example, unlike the federal government, states may restrict uses of privately owned land through such techniques as zoning, although this power has traditionally been delegated to localities. States also have a variety of ways to raise money. They can bring a "close-to-people" perspective to the necessary but centralizing force of the federal government, which must be relied on to raise much revenue and set national goals. They can also provide a consolidating influence to the highly fragmented pattern of local governments.

This is the states' potential. That their performance has been bleak by comparison is not grounds to junk the entire federal system. That the federal government is assuming an even increasingly large role in environmental regulation (see Appendix A) is likewise not grounds to ignore states, for they too have an increasingly valuable part to play. Rather, it is time to focus on the reform of the institutions of state government.

Many states think so too, and some are moving faster and more effectively than their federal partner to streamline governmental organizations and give them new regulatory powers over pollution and land use problems. This book examines some of these state reforms—innovations that can help other state governments understand options for institutional change.

Two types of reforms are covered. The first are new environmental departments created by the reorganization of existing state agencies to give pollution and resource programs a new "ecological" perspective and higher priority in state government. The second set of changes involve new organizations to implement new state strategies for land use control and waste management and an increased role for courts through citizen action. The book is divided into two parts, based on these two types of institutional changes.

Part I covers Environmental Departments Created through Reorganizations:

Chapter 1. Illinois ● Three state agencies—Pollution Control Board, Environmental Protection Agency, Illinois Institute for Environmental Quality—have responsibility for all forms of pollution control, but each in a different functional way.

Chapter 2. Minnesota ● Pollution Control Agency consolidates pollution controls and a part-time board sets policy for the agency.

Chapter 3. Washington ● Department of Ecology consolidates pollution control programs and water resources management. A citizens Ecological Commission and adjudicative Pollution Control Hearings Appeals Board are also created.

Chapter 4. Wisconsin ● Department of Natural Resources consolidates pollution control and resource conservation programs, overseen by a Natural Resources Board.

Chapter 5. New York ● Department of Environmental Conservation consolidates pollution controls and conservation programs, with the advisory guidance of the State Environmental Board.

Part II discusses three New State Strategies:
Land Use Management

Chapter 6. Vermont ● The Environmental Board and five District Commissions have new statewide authority for land use planning and regulation.

Chapter 7. Maine ● The Board of Environmental Protection has new power to regulate large-scale land development, statewide.

Waste Management

Chapter 8. Maryland ● The Maryland Environmental Service can draft regional plans, finance, build, operate, and own solid and liquid wastes treatment and disposal facilities, wholesaling environmental services to local governments and industries.

An Increased Role for State
Courts through Citizen Lawsuits

Chapter 9. Michigan ● Everyone is guaranteed "standing to sue" public or private entities in court to protect the environment and the "public trust" therein; and courts can instruct executive agencies to adopt a particular environment standard.

Chapter 10. Recommendations ● General criteria are outlined for evaluating environmental institutions of government and recommendations are offered for establishing effective and responsive state environmental agencies.

By no means are these the only states in which interesting changes have occurred to improve environmental protection. Rather, we selected these nine states in order to study a range of institutional models, political styles, and environmental conditions. We studied environmental reorganizations because they are not only a sign of government's commitment to the issue, but to differing degrees have increased the ability and desire of government to respond to public wishes. To be sure, organizational structure is no substitute for vigorous law enforcement, adequate funding, and able people, but creaky structures have substantially inhibited effective programs in the past. While many states have undergone recent environmental reorganizations or are thinking of them (see Appendix B), some of the new state strategies examined are particularly novel. Our main focus in most of these cases has been on pollution control and its regulatory aspect, the environmental topic we believe most needs state attention at this time.

The work and its conclusions are not solely intended to be theoretical social science research. They have the practical objective of informing state officials concerned about environmental organizations in terms that are meaningful to them. Furthermore, there is a substantial normative ingredient. Our objective is to increase the responsiveness of governmental agencies to the public's wishes by intensifying their motivation as well as their capability to respond. In general we favor one responsible organization for each major environmental mission. We believe it should be given sufficient program tools to do its job and be directed by a single leader whose decisions are highly visible to the governor, the legislature, and the public. This person should then be held accountable through the political system for his organization's performance.

Most of the state organizations examined in this book were established in 1970, and consequently the performance records that could be examined here are not large and some conclusions are necessarily tentative. No attempt has been made to study the role of the federal government and local government comparatively as they relate to the states. While such intergovernmental analyses are important, they exceeded this study's limit of time and funds.

This book is the product of two years' research on state governments, funded by the Ford Foundation. The project was initially directed by Elizabeth H. Haskell, who was a 1970-71 Fellow of the Woodrow Wilson International Center for Scholars at the Smithsonian Institution, Washington, D.C. Victoria S. Price was research associate on the study. This book is an evaluative study and builds on the first report of this project, entitled *Managing the Environment: Nine States Look for New Answers*, published by the Woodrow Wilson Center in April, 1971.

The work was conducted by means of field research, examination of the products and processes of the organizations, and a review of literature in the fields of political science, public administration, and environmental management. We have depended heavily on personal interviews with the individuals who had key roles in the creation of their state's governmental system and those who now direct the organizations. As time permitted, we sought persons who represented many different points of view in order to balance our understanding. In Appendix C we list the individuals who have taken time from their busy schedules to share their knowledge and experience with us. We thank each of them for their contribution to our study. We would also like to acknowledge the assistance of Nancy Carson Shirk, Rebecca Cook, Louise Platt, John Davidson and Richard Booth, who contributed to the preparing of this manuscript.

ENVIRONMENTAL DEPARTMENTS CREATED THROUGH REORGANIZATIONS

INTRODUCTION

Illinois is attacking its pollution control problems with a unique, three-agency institutional structure and some of the most comprehensive regulatory authority in the country.

The Illinois Environmental Protection Act of 1970[1] reorganized the state's pollution control division located in the health department and two part-time, antipollution boards into three new, full-time agencies. The same act enlarged the state's antipollution regulatory authority and assigned significant new powers over air, water, land, radiation,* and noise pollution and public water supplies to each of the three new organizations, giving each unit a different primary function to perform. These units are the Pollution Control Board, the Environmental Protection Agency, and the Illinois Institute for Environmental Quality.

The five-member Pollution Control Board (PCB) sets environmental standards and regulations and adjudicates enforcement proceedings. This is the only appointive antipollution board in the country that works full time and has its own staff and funds. The Environmental Protection Agency (EPA) recom-

---

*In the May 8, 1972 Pollution Control Board Newsletter (No. 47), the PCB stated that "it no longer has any authority over radiation and may no longer require permits for the operation of nuclear facilities, under Title 6(a) of the Environmental Protection Act. . . . The Supreme Court's recent decision in the Northern States Power case, originating in Minnesota, deprived the States of jurisdiction over radiation discharges, thereby leaving the Atomic Energy Commission as the sole agency empowered to regulate the field."

CHART 1.1

Illinois Environmental Quality Institutions

	Environmental Protection Agency	Pollution Control Board	Illinois Institute for Environmental Quality
Officer	Director 1. Appointed by governor, advice and consent of Senate 2. 2-year term 3. Salary: $35,000 a year	Chairman 1. Appointed by governor, advice and consent of Senate 2. Serves at governor's pleasure, but a member of the board for 3 years. All 5 members serve 3-year terms. 3. Salary: $35,000 a year; board members, $30,000	Director 1. Appointed by governor 2. Cannot be removed except for cause 3. Salary unspecified in law; current salary, $23,000
Appropriation (in thousands of $, fiscal years)	1970[2] 3,250[3] 1971 5,785.9[4] 1972 8,230.4[5] 1973 6,859.9[6]	1970 — 1971[7] 525 1972[7] 968.3 1973[8] 1,107.3	1970 — 1971[9] 2,000 1972[10] 2,000 1973 2,000
Staff Size (end of fiscal year)	246 333 462 632	— 18 21 20	— 9 20 22
Jurisdiction	Air pollution, water pollution, solid wastes, public water supplies, noise	Air pollution, water pollution, solid wastes, public water supplies, noise	All pollution, as well as all other aspects of environmental quality such as land use, resource conservation, reuse of wastes

Functions

Environmental Protection Agency	Pollution Control Board	Illinois Institute for Environmental Quality
1. Monitor noise, land, air, and water quality and investigate violations of rules and standards.	1. Hear and adjudicate cases of violations of rules, standards, or act. Set fines.	1. Sponsor applied research.
2. Authorized to prosecute enforcement cases before board but in fact refers actions to attorney general.	2. Set standards and regulations for pollutants, permit systems, inspection and monitoring systems, and operator licensing.	2. Initiate rulemaking hearings before board, suggest standards to board.
3. Initiate rule-making hearings before board, recommend standards.	3. Grant variances to standards after hearings.	3. Perform environmental resource planning.
4. Investigate and recommend action to the board on variance applications. *Must* testify on permit denials, or validity or regulations. *May* testify at all other board hearings.	4. Hear appeals of EPA's denial of permits.	4. Act as technical staff PCB, EPA, other state agencies on request.
5. Issue permits for (a) incinerators, (b) public water supply systems, (c) wastewater treatment works in industry and municipalities, (d) waste discharges to air and water, (e) solid waste disposal sites, (f) any others board designates as facilities that cause or control pollution.		5. Do program planning and evaluation for EPA, PCB.
6. Train operators of solid waste disposal sites.		6. Evaluate curricula for all levels of education; instructors.
7. Train and certify municipal treatment plant operators.		7. Store and retrieve environmental data gathered by state.
8. Train and certify public water supply facility operators.		
9. Give grants of federal and state funds to communities to build wastewater treatment works and to do solid waste planning.		
10. Give technical aid to municipalities and industry, perform lab analyses.		
11. Collect and disseminate data and conduct experiments.		
12. Develop and operate electronic data processing system.		
13. Declare pollution emergencies and seal pollution sources.		

[1] Actual expenditures were less. (See later in chapter for expenditure figures.)
[2] For Divisions of Sanitary Engineering and Laboratories, transferred to EPA later in fiscal year.
[3] General revenue appropriation: excludes federal program grants, as well as federal and state funds for construction of municipal wastewater treatment plants.
[4] State general revenue appropriation. This figure includes $1,000.0 to construct a new Chicago laboratory. Excludes $726.9 of federal program grants and municipal construction.
[5] State general revenue appropriation, including a reappropriation of $1,409.3 for Chicago lab. Excludes $986.7 in federal program grants and municipal construction money.
[6] State general revenue appropriation. Excludes $2,626.5 in federal program grants and municipal construction funds.
[7] Original and supplemental general revenue appropriations.
[8] Original appropriation.
[9] $200.0 of IIEQ's funds allocated to PCB's use. Actually expended $816.0.
[10] $200.0 of IIEQ's funds allocated to PCB's use.

mends standards, investigates variances, initiates enforcement actions, identifies polluters, issues permits and financial aid, and extends technical assistance. The third agency, the Illinois Institute for Environmental Quality (IIEQ), conducts environmental planning and research and acts as analytical staff to the PCB in support of its standards-setting function. (See Chart 1.1 for a summary of data about the three organizations.)

The Illinois system is designed to separate certain functions seen as conflicting for a single agency. The major division of authority sought is between prosecution and adjudication of disputes. These responsibilities are divided between the EPA and the PCB. Since standards-setting is considered to bias the task of bringing suit to enforce regulations, these two functions are divided between the PCB and EPA. The PCB's two jobs of adopting standards and adjudicating disputes were not thought to conflict, although some parties who come before the PCB now believe that they do. Research and planning are handled by a separate institute because they are viewed as unable to compete favorably for funds and staff with the crisis-oriented abatement work of EPA. Functional separation is expected to increase the overall level of antipollution activity and to reduce bias.

While the main assignments of the three agencies differ, some jobs are intentionally duplicated among them and the attorney general's office, particularly planning, drafting of environmental standards, and initiating enforcement suits. (See Chart 1.2 for a complete listing of duplicated functions.) Duplication of functions was intended to step up regulatory work, but another effect has been interagency competition. A "healthy spirit of competition" was intended between the EPA and the attorney general, when both were assigned the responsibility of prosecuting alleged law violators. Although unintended, competition also resulted between EPA on the one hand, and PCB and IIEQ on the other, in the initial period. Conflicting styles and strategies of the three agency leaders contributed to this situation. In each case, competition proved counterproductive since the agencies depend greatly on one another to achieve effective environmental controls, and no one agency has sufficient power or staff to implement its assignment independently.

Illinois solved this conflict of competition and interdependency of organizations in a practical way—by eliminating competitive aspects through an informal agreement between the attorney general and EPA and the appointment of a new director to EPA.

The Illinois logic of functional separation, as well as intentional overlap of some jobs, sharply contrasts with other states, which consolidated all antipollution functions into one agency in an effort to achieve administrative efficiency and eliminate program duplication.

The Illinois experience already shows some of the advantages and disadvantages of a multiagency system for pollution control. The new organizations with specific, narrow missions got off to a fast start on tough, legal regulation of pollution. Some of the strictest environmental clean-up standards in the country are being set. Functional specialization has also broken up what used to be a regulatory monopoly in the executive branch. The number of enforce-

CHART 1.2

Duplicated Environmental Functions

A. *Recommend Standards*

1. Pollution Control Board sets standards on own initiative or acts upon request as below.
2. Illinois Institute for Environmental Quality can require PCB to hold a hearing on its proposal to set, amend, or repeal standards; technical staff to PCB in drafting standards.
3. Environmental Protection Agency proposes standards and can require PCB to hold a hearing on them.
4. 200 citizens can petition PCB and require a hearing on their standards proposal.

B. *Prosecute Enforcement Cases*

1. EPA is authorized to initiate enforcement proceedings before PCB, but in fact refers cases to the attorney general for his prosecution.
2. Any private citizen can initiate enforcement proceedings before the PCB to enforce the Environmental Protection Act and standards set under it, or can initiate a suit in lower courts to protect his constitutional right to a "healthful environment." A citizen can also sue in lower court to enforce the Environmental Protection Act, but if he loses he must bear all court costs.
3. Attorney general can initiate enforcement action in circuit court to abate air, water, and land pollution under his own authority,* or initiate action before the PCB, like any citizen, to enforce the Environmental Protection Act. Also handles appeals to the appellate courts under the Environmental Protection Act, collects fines through civil action in circuit court, and brings actions in circuit court under the EPA in emergencies.
4. All state and local law enforcement officers have the "duty" of enforcing the act and regulations and officers have authority to issue citations for such violations.

C. *Conduct Research, Planning, and Evaluation*

1. IIEQ conducts and sponsors research, does long-range program planning, policy and land use planning, conducts evaluations of EPA's and PCB's programs.
2. EPA collects and disseminates information and technical data, conducts experiments, does laboratory work, conducts its own program planning, as well as policy planning and evaluation relating to its own programs.
3. PCB conducts ad hoc research in proposing its own standards.

D. *Carry Out Intergovernmental Relations*

1. EPA represents the state in dealing with federal government, except for standards setting, research, and some planning.
2. PCB represents the state for matters of standards-setting.
3. IIEQ represents the state on research and some planning matters.

---

*76th General Assembly, House Bill 3793, as approved.

ment actions has increased, fines are higher, and research has been strengthened. But the Illinois experience also indicates that when several agencies operate in a popular field such as the environment, competition is likely to result. This rivalry can be counterproductive if agencies are highly interdependent, as they are in Illinois. Even when competition is eliminated, a multiagency system to implement one set of policies requires some mechanism to coordinate the work, plan comprehensive environmental strategies, and evaluate the total effect of the several agencies' policies and programs. When functions overlap, some means is needed to allocate efficiently workloads and funds among all agencies.

The Illinois experience is important in that private citizens are empowered to participate actively in the administrative processes of government. They can recommend antipollution standards and initiate enforcement suits against polluters before the PCB. Contrary to industry fears, no rash of lawsuits has resulted. Only a few citizen actions have been initiated, and these have resulted in significant pollution abatement orders. The participation of environmentalists continues to be limited by the need for funds and lawyers to present their cases to the PCB in the required adversary proceedings.

THE PROCESS AND OBJECTIVES OF REORGANIZATION

Governor Richard B. Ogilvie recommended to the 76th Illinois General Assembly in April, 1970 the creation of the new three-part environmental structure. He and his advisors were generally displeased with the rate of antipollution progress in the state and wanted to be able to say the governor had turned Illinois around on this popular political issue.

The proposal for reorganization and regulatory reform was preceded by analysis within the Bureau of the Budget. House Bill 3788 was drafted and shepherded through the legislature by the governor's environmental coordinator, David Currie, then a professor of environmental law at the University of Chicago and now chairman of the new Pollution Control Board. Currie, who was then a close advisor to the governor, is the principal designer of the administrative and legal system that emerged.

Previous Structure

The previous institutional set-up in Illinois had come under attack for producing inadequate air and water quality standards and ineffective enforcement. Air pollution control had been lodged in the Air Pollution Control Board and the water pollution control in the Sanitary Water Board. Solid waste management, a smaller program, was administered by the Department of Public Health. The two boards were staffed by the Department of Public Health's

Division of Sanitary Engineering, which operated quite independently within the health department. The division was directed by the chief sanitary engineer, who served as technical secretary to both boards. Clarence Klassen held this position from 1935 until 1970 when he was appointed director of the Environmental Protection Agency.

In theory the boards had the power to set pollution control standards and conduct hearings in order to determine violations to be turned over to the attorney general for prosecution. In reality these groups usually rubber-stamped the recommendations of the technical secretary and the Department of Public Health. Board members were unpaid, had no staff of their own, and met only occasionally. Many members of these policy-making bodies were directors of state departments whose main constituencies were groups responsible for pollution or private citizens selected to represent special interest groups.

While these boards had no staff of their own, met only occasionally, and did not have the capability to draft effective standards, they could veto any aggressive action on the part of the health officials to set and enforce strong regulations. Conservation interests were often outvoted. Enforcement procedures called for the boards to refer violations of standards and law to the attorney general for his prosecution in circuit courts, but few such requests were ever made. Court action generally resulted in fines that were too low to have a deterrent effect on future polluters.

Reorganization Aims

There were five main reasons behind Governor Ogilvie's recommendation of three new pollution agencies:

1. *Consolidate pollution control programs.* The governor criticized the separation of pollution controls in two boards reasoning that "environmental protection cannot with safety be so artificially categorized. What is done to the air may affect the water. Disposal of solid wastes may cause air and water pollution problems. Care *must* be taken so that efforts to improve one resource do not worsen another. We live in one unified environment and we need one unified program."[2]

2. *Separate conflicting and competing functions.* The old structure combined the two conflicting functions of prosecutor and judge of air and water pollution enforcement cases, in effect, in the Department of Public Health, a situation called "not consistent with the impartiality expected of an arbiter under the rule of law."[3] For drafters of the new plan, the experience of the federal independent regulatory agencies, such as the Federal Trade Commission, was used as a model of what not to do. Such federal agencies set standards, prosecute alleged violators of the rules, and adjudicate the disputes, thus providing a regulatory monopoly. By contrast, the new Illinois Pollution Control Board cannot initiate enforcement proceedings, but can only

adjudicate cases referred to it. Nor can EPA, which acts as a policeman by identifying polluters and initiating suits, set environmental rules and standards.

Some functions, if not directly in conflict, were thought at least to compete unfavorably for time and funds when carried out by the same agency. The health department staff, which had responsibility for all antipollution tasks, had neglected research and long-range planning, and a new institute just for that purpose was created to concentrate on these jobs and produce more results.

3. *Generate increased regulatory action.* While each agency has a distinct primary responsibility to perform, various regulatory and planning responsibilities are shared with other units as a secondary task. Some of the functional overlap was intended to increase regulatory activity by increasing the number of responsible parties. Some was simply unavoidable. For instance, EPA has to perform some research and planning relating to its programs. In at least one instance—the sharing of prosecutorial powers by the EPA and attorney general—the overlap was designed to create interagency competition.

The theoretical logic for authorizing the agency to share the attorney general's formerly exclusive power to prosecute pollution violators was that competition would generate twice as much enforcement. Unlike traditional public administration systems, which are designed to eliminate overlap, duplication, and friction, this system was purposely built on calculated tensions.

But there was also a more practical, political logic in Illinois for giving some of the attorney general's powers to EPA. Attorney General William J. Scott was considered in 1970 as a possible Republican gubernatorial primary opponent of Governor Ogilvie in 1972. In 1969, the General Assembly had specifically authorized the attorney general to move on his own without waiting for cases to be referred to him by the state's pollution control boards. With his new authority, Scott was getting a great deal of favorable publicity for bringing lawsuits against several large companies, such as U.S. Steel in Chicago. He brought more than 200 lawsuits against polluters between July, 1969 and January, 1970.[4] A great many of these, however, were never carried through to a successful conclusion. The governor's spokesmen who drafted the Environmental Protection Act did not want to see their proposed step-up in pollution enforcement turned into an increased publicity program for the attorney general. They felt that if EPA shared his "pollution fighter" role, this situation might be avoided.

4. *"Professionalize" the PCB.* The Environmental Protection Act consolidated previously part-time air and water boards into one full-time board composed of five "technically qualified" people. They earn $30,000 a year, except for the chairman who earns $35,000. Financial disclosure is required of members. No more than three board members may be of the same political party and all are appointed by the governor to serve staggered three-year terms. The board hires its own staff and is declared to be "independent."[5] Full-time attention to its environmental work was expected to make standards-setting more effective and to make the body more expert and less dependent on the health department officials who would staff the new EPA. These features were

10

intended to eliminate the conflict of interest that had occurred previously when board members served the state part time and held some other full-time job that prejudiced their public responsibilities.

This full-time, appointive board is a unique institution among state governments, where policy boards and commissions traditionally serve only part time and rely on an administrative agency for staff and technical aid. Previous Illinois boards like those in other states were, by statute, composed of representatives of regulated interests.

The new board is the functional equivalent of a trial court, as the adjudicative role has been shifted to the board to decide facts and set fines in pollution abatement cases. Illinois' reorganization aimed to create an administrative body that would develop environmental expertise and be tough on polluters. Appeals from board decisions by-pass the circuit courts and go directly to the appellate courts, where no new trial is held.

5. *Move the pollution programs out of the health department.* In the health department, pollution control had to compete for funds, staff, and public attention with many unrelated types of health programs that distorted the state's decision-making. Furthermore, degradation of the environment was thought to be more than a health problem. Legislation drafters felt that the health department staff was too sympathetic to polluters and that the state's regulatory role suffered as a result. Also, moving the pollution control people— the sanitary engineering division and the laboratories division—into a new EPA was expected to make their job more visible to the public and gain more widespread support. The staff could devote its full attention to environmental problems. Establishing a new agency was seen as necessary to weaken the existing client relationship between state regulators and polluters.

The three-agency structure recommended by the governor was adopted virtually unchanged by the legislature. While industry opposed the structure, its real objections to House Bill 3788 were not with its reorganization provisions, but with the increase in state regulatory power that is authorized. These provisions were the target of intense industrial lobbying and several features were stricken or revised in the final bill in line with industry objections.*

---

*In the House, the bill passed overwhelmingly, with two amendments of significance:

1. Changed from the original bill was the guarantee that citizens had the right to sue in courts for violation of a newly declared right to a "clean environment." Under the original proposal, money damage could be claimed against polluters or the state. While leaving intact the right to sue, the House eliminated the ability to secure money damages from the state, arguing that this provision would endanger the state's ability to sell its bonds.

2. The original bill provided that 25 private citizens could secure a hearing from the Pollution Control Board on their proposal to set or revise pollution control standards or regulations. The House raised this number of citizens required to petition to 200. This would keep trivial matters from occupying the board's attention, it was argued.

Industrial lobbyists focused their attention on the Senate, aiming to emasculate the bill. The Senate, like the House, was then controlled by the governor's party—the Republicans. To counteract the industrialists' pressures for crippling amendments to the bill, the governor's spokesmen called for public and press support. Up to that point, proenviron-

THE REGULATORY SYSTEM

The regulatory work as specified by the Environmental Protection Act includes (1) setting standards; (2) enforcing standards and the act; (3) reviewing and issuing variances; (4) issuing permits; and (5) acting upon private citizens' initiatives.

Setting Standards

The Pollution Control Board has great leeway to set standards and define the nature and extent of the pollution control program in Illinois, limited only by the general categories of outlawed pollution. This policy-making power is a delegation of legislative authority from the General Assembly to the PCB. The PCB's jurisdiction includes air pollution, water pollution, land pollution and refuse disposal, noise, public water supplies, and, at one time, atomic radiation.* Within these broad areas the Environmental Protection Act suggests

---

mental citizen groups had demonstrated no active support for the measure, believing that the overwhelming House passage meant the bill would sail through the Senate. Now citizens groups launched into action. Groups such as the Clean Air Coordinating Committee from the Chicago area, the Illinois Wildlife Federation, and the League of Women Voters contacted state senators; and over 200 citizens traveled to Springfield to testify for the bill.

The Senate committee and the full Senate had yet to act, and it was the last week of the special session of the General Assembly. Representatives of the governor and the attorney general met in a midnight session with industrial spokesmen and agreed on certain amendments. These agreed-upon changes were then approved by the Senate Executive Committee and the full Senate. The House agreed to the Senate versions in the waning hours of the session, time allowing no further negotiations.

The Senate made these significant changes in House Bill 3788:

1. Emasculated the provisions for citizens' standing to sue in court, by adding the requirement that "no action shall be brought under this Section until 30 days after the plaintiff has been denied relief by the Board. . ." and more importantly, "The prevailing party shall be awarded costs and reasonable attorneys' fees." This last provision made citizen suit too risky financially.

2. Dropped a provision for effluent charges, i.e., money charges to be imposed on waste discharges, which increase with the pollution potential of the waste.

3. Dropped the proposed board power to outlaw nonreturnable bottles and other items that create disposal problems.

4. Dropped the requirement that industry would purchase monitoring devices that would be placed on their smokestacks and pipes to measure the quality of discharges to the environment.

5. Added the requirement that the board members must be "technically qualified."

6. Changed the provision that a variance application would be denied if the board did not act on it in 45 days. As enacted, an applicant for a variance from standards would automatically receive approval if the board refused to. act on the petition within 90 days.

7. Dropped language requiring that all pollution control standards be set high enough to eliminate health hazards, as a minimum requirement.

*See note on page 3.

12

those standards listed in Chart 1.3. It is not a binding list and the PCB may set fewer or more standards and regulations at its discretion.

The broad delegation of legislative authority to the PCB is predicated upon what Governor Ogilvie called "the impracticability of seeking detailed and sharply defined pollution control standards from a legislative body."[6] This authority has been challenged as an unconstitutional delegation of legislative authority that violates the separation of powers. The courts have not ruled on any of the constitutional challenges to the Illinois Environmental Protection Act.

The PCB has taken its role so seriously that on one occasion when a bill[7] was introduced in the General Assembly to set specific standards for noise—a proper exercise of legislative power—the PCB objected strongly. It wrote the General Assembly opposing the legislation, contending that "in essence it deprives the board of authority to determine noise standards for the state,"[8] a power it only holds on delegation from the legislature. The Illinois administrative agencies, like many states' agencies, believe that the legislature should only adopt broad policies by authorizing sets of standards, leaving to the agencies the task of drafting specific controls.

The PCB is required to hold a hearing before adopting any standard. Once standards are set, every public and private entity in Illinois must comply, as well as persons or entities outside the state when their pollution crosses into Illinois. All state agencies must comply with standards or be subject to prosecution for violations before the PCB. No state department may license any vehicle, vessel, or aircraft for operation in Illinois until the applicant has proof of pollution controls required by the PCB.

The chairman has declared rule-making, or the adopting of environmental standards, to be the "Board's first priority,"[9] and most of PCB's time has been spent on this function. The strategy was to adopt by early 1972 a completely revised and updated set of regulations governing air and water pollution, emphasizing emission and effluent standards rather than merely ambient air and water quality standards. These were completed by April, 1972. Then the PCB shifted its rule-making focus to noise, solid wastes, and other newer state concerns.

During the first year of operation, the PCB drafted and advocated environmental standards. It also heard testimony on the proposals and formally adopted them. In the first 11 months, members of the PCB initiated 25 of the 35 rule-making proceedings.* Although the Environmental Protection Agency had a division assigned the job of drafting standards within each of its five bureaus, these were largely unstaffed. Consequently EPA proposed only three sets of standards in the first 11 months. The IIEQ formally proposed none, but served actively as technical staff to the PCB in rule-making, particularly by funding needed research and analysis and providing witnesses for PCB proceedings.

---

*Not all of these 35 rule-making proceedings are significant, since some relate to such trivial matters as the formal repeal of obsolete provisions and corrections of typographical errors.

CHART 1.3

Standards Specifically Authorized
by Illinois Environmental Protection Act

Air Pollution[a]

1. Ambient air quality
2. Emissions
3. The issuance of permits by the agency to facilities, vehicles, etc., that cause or control air pollution
4. Conditions of sale of any fuel, vehicle, or article that the PCB thinks is an air pollution hazard
5. Air pollution emergencies or episodes
6. Inspection and surveillance requirements and procedures that the EPA follows
7. Monitoring equipment procedures

Water Pollution[b]

1. Water quality
2. Effluents
3. Issuance of permits for equipment, facility, vessel, or aircraft that causes or controls water pollution
4. Certification of sewage treatment plant operators by EPA
5. Filling or sealing abandoned waterwells
6. Sale of detergents, pesticides, and whatever else the PCB deems a water pollution hazard
7. Water pollution emergencies
8. Inspection and surveillance by the EPA
9. Monitoring equipment and procedures used by EPA

Public Water Supplies[c]

1. Location, design, construction, and continuous operation and maintenance of public water supply installations, changes or additions

Noise[d]

1. Limitations on noise emissions beyond the boundaries of the property of any person
2. Monitoring equipment standards and collection and reporting of data from monitoring

Land Pollution and Refuse Disposal[e].

1. Location, design, construction, operation, maintenance, and discontinuance of the operation of refuse collection and disposal sites and facilities
2. Certification by EPA of personnel to operate disposal facilities or sites
3. Dumping of any refuse
4. Equipment and procedures for monitoring contaminant discharges at their source; collection of samples; collection, reporting, and retention of data resulting from such monitoring.

Atomic Radiation[f]

1. Radiation
2. Permits are also issued by the PCB, not the EPA; this permit specifies the maximum allowable level of radioactive discharge as determined by the PCB

---

[a]Title II, secs. 8-10, Ill. Rev. Stat. secs. 1008-10.
[b]Title III, secs. 11-13, Ill. Rev. Stat. secs. 1011-13.
[c]Title IV, secs. 14-19, Ill. Rev. Stat. secs. 1014-19.
[d]Title VI, secs. 23-25, Ill. Rev. Stat. secs. 1023-25.
[e]Title V, secs. 20-22, Ill. Rev. Stat. secs. 1020-22.
[f]Title VI-A, sec. 25a, Ill. Rev. Stat. sec. 1025a (PCB has declared this matter no longer in their jurisdiction).

Some PCB and IIEQ spokesmen feel that the IIEQ and EPA should draft standards and advocate them before the PCB, allowing the board to adopt standards as a type of adjudicative process, with members weighing and resolving alternative proposals as expressed by others.

The agencies have moved in this direction during the second year of operations, with IIEQ and EPA drafting more standards, sometimes on their own initiative and sometimes at the PCB's request. Jointly, EPA and IIEQ have had responsibility for preparing the air quality implementation plans, noise standards, and solid waste regulations. In some instances, such as water effluent standards, first proposed by the PCB, EPA assigned technical staff to the job, and IIEQ funded the needed outside research. In other cases, such as solid waste only, IIEQ organized task forces, on which EPA played an active part. Both EPA and IIEQ are now drafting or studying additional regulations. Chart 1.4 lists the most significant antipollution standards considered by the PCB or actively pending as of May, 1972, along with the source of the original proposal.

The PCB has established a reputation for setting strong standards, which reinforces its image as environmental advocate. For example, while rewriting the air quality regulations, the PCB, in effect, outlawed coal or residual fuel oil for residential or commercial use in the Chicago region by May 20, 1975. The restriction cannot go into effect yet because the Circuit Court of Cook County has issued a temporary restraining order in *Roth-Adam Fuel Company* v. *Pollution Control Board.* The case is being appealed.

The PCB tightened by 30 percent the former federal-state phosphorus water quality standard for Lake Michigan. Also adopted was a 1 mg/1 effluent standard for phosphorus discharged into the lake by the end of 1971 to reduce eutrophication. This effluent limit has also been extended to the Fox River. Also, the deadline for secondary sewage treatment along the Mississippi and Ohio rivers was moved up to 1973 from 1977 and 1978.

On another occasion the PCB adopted a strict 0.5 parts-per-billion limit on mercury discharges as both an effluent standard and a water quality standard, applicable to all Illinois waters, and required reporting of substantial mercury uses. This is substantially lower than the 2 parts-per-billion proposed by the federal government. The PCB says the level is the lowest that present measuring devices can reliably report and some industry spokesmen question whether it can be measured at all. The standard has the effect of forbidding all mercury discharges. Commenting on this mercury prohibition in relation to the state law's requirement that standards be "technically feasible" and "economically reasonable," the PCB said in its newsletter: "As to the question of the balancing of the technical feasibility and economic reasonableness of the strict effluent standard, the opinion (of the board accompanying the standard) stated that it is almost always feasible to terminate discharges by going out of business and if the pollution is devastating enough it may be economically reasonable to require it."[10] Tough language to accompany a tough standard.

Using its power to write regulations in another way, the PCB has encouraged the communities in DuPage County, adjacent to Chicago, to move

CHART 1.4

Major Antipollution Standards Considered
by Illinois Pollution Control Board as of May, 1972

Standard	Status
Water	
Phosphorous water quality standards and effluent standard for Lake Michigan	Adopted, 1971
Mercury water quality and effluent standard	Adopted, March, 1971 Being appealed
Effluent standards and chemical constituents including zinc, arsenic, cyanide, flouride, and mercury, statewide	Adopted, January, 1972
Water quality and domestic sewage treatment plant standards, statewide	Adopted, March, 1972
Plant nutrient regulations, limiting phosphorous, sewage sludge, and nitrogen on agricultural lands	PCB requested IIEQ to study
Phosphate detergent ban	Rejected proposal by private citizens, 1971
Regulation that calls for hearings in DuPage County to implement regional wastewater treatment facilities	Adopted, 1971
Deep well disposal regulations	IIEQ drafting following a citizen's petition
Septic tanks location regulation, including a permit system	EPA and HEQ drafting
Regulation of sewer connections to inadequate plants	Under consideration
Air	
Air pollution episodes regulations	Adopted, 1971
Open burning regulations, including a permit system	Adopted, September, 1971
Asbestos emission standards	Adopted, January, 1972
Air emission standards statewide for SO_2, NO_x, Co, hydrocarbons, and particulates, including operating permits	Adopted, April, 1972
Revision of air quality standards to complement new air emission standards	Hearings completed
Air quality standards for trace metals such as lead, cadmium, asbestos, beryllium, hydrogen sulfide, hydrogen cyanide, flourides, chlorine gas, hydrogen chlorides	PCB asked IIEQ to draft
Other	
Beverage container regulations to require a 5¢ deposit on all beverage containers to consumer	IIEQ proposed; Cook County Court enjoined PCB hearings
Radiation from nuclear reactors	IIEQ developing standards. PCB jurisdiction unclear following Supreme Court decision upholding federal preemption
Mine-related pollution regulations for opening, operating, and abandoning mines, including effluent standards for drainage	Adopted
Public water supplies regulations	PCB asked EPA to draft
Noise from stationary sources	PCB considering IIEQ and citizens proposals
Airport noise, statewide	Under consideration, IIEQ revising a citizens' proposal
Solid waste (landfill) regulation	Drafted by IIEQ at PCB request
Feedlot regulations	Published; hearings scheduled

toward a regional wastewater treatment system for the area. In line with the Regional Wastewater Plan approved by the Northeastern Illinois Planning Commission,[11] the PCB required that plans be drafted that provide for 9 sewage treatment plants by 1975 to replace over 90 plants now operating in the county.

The PCB also challenged the federal government's preemption of the field of regulating radioactive discharges from nuclear facilities by setting standards stricter than the federal ones. In this case, involving the Commonwealth Edison Company Dresden Unit 3 near Morris, the PCB set an ultimate emission limit of 1/1,800 of the Federal Atomic Energy Commission standard.[12] However, the Supreme Court upheld the federal preemption, and the PCB has subsequently ruled that it no longer has jurisdiction over radiation.

Enforcement

Enforcement of the PCB's rules and the Environmental Protection Act involves three state organizations and private citizens.* The Environmental Protection Agency identifies polluters through surveillance, inspection of waste sources, and review of data presented with permit or variance applications. Then EPA refers cases for prosecution to the attorney general who prosecutes all violators for the state before the PCB and in court. The third organization, the Pollution Control Board, adjudicates the complaint as the "court" of first resort.

In addition, any private citizen in Illinois can initiate enforcement proceedings before the PCB by filing a formal complaint that is not declared by the board to be "duplicitous or frivolous." Informal complaints are referred to EPA for investigation. The burden on a citizen when bringing an enforcement action is less stringent than that required for proposing rules or regulations, since any one citizen may file a complaint. While this encourages public participation, the private citizen still must comply with the same notice provisions required of the EPA, which requires 21 days' notice to the violator, telling him of the manner and extent to which he violates a rule and which specific rule.[13]

The current division of enforcement responsibilities between EPA and the attorney general is an administrative/political agreement and not one envisioned by the Environmental Protection Act. The 1970 act authorized EPA to prosecute its own complaints before the PCB, by-passing the attorney general altogether, if it chose. Initially, the EPA proceeded to do just that, hiring attorneys, staffing, and presenting most of its own legal cases before the PCB, although some cases were still referred to the attorney general. However,

---

*Suits can be initiated to enforce the pollution prohibited by the Environmental Protection Act, whether or not particular standards have been adopted governing that form of pollution.

the attorney general, in addition to some referrals, also had authority to initiate his own suits without EPA, either before the PCB or in court. Furthermore, the Environmental Protection Act states that the attorney general shall represent the Pollution Control Board in appeals to the appellate courts, collect fines from polluters as assessed by the PCB, and halt discharges that create an "extreme emergency creating conditions of immediate danger to the public health" by instituting a civil action for an immediate court injunction.

Competition and tension between EPA and Attorney General William Scott began to mount. The latter contended that he should handle all litigation from the start, that he was the official, elected legal officer for the people of Illinois. In fact, he said, the Illinois Constitution prohibited any other state agency from even hiring attorneys. Scott claimed that his office had the necessary legal expertise and that it was wasteful and inefficient for the Environmental Protection Agency to try to duplicate it. The attorney general also felt that he would eventually have to handle any case that was appealed, and that a "client" should not have two attorneys.

Both organizations tried to acquire the expertise they lacked to become more autonomous. In some cases, the attorney general contracted with private firms for the scientific and engineering expertise his office lacked. EPA sought to expand its legal staff, projecting an increase to 35 staff members by July 1, 1972.

In February, 1971, the competition among these state organizations was undercut by an agreement between spokesmen for the governor and the attorney general, both of whom were of the same political party. EPA would, as before, refer all its enforcement cases to the attorney general for prosecution before the Pollution Control Board and in the courts. However, EPA retained exclusive jurisdiction over variance applications and used these for enforcement purposes, recommending that the PCB fine applicants for past noncompliance with state regulations. Then, in October, 1971, EPA agreed to refer all variance recommendations to the attorney general for hearing before the PCB.

Why did the Illinois officials revert to the old prosecution system? It can only be presumed that at the time the 1970 act was drafted and passed the governor's people underestimated the opposition the attorney general would pose to sharing his pollution-prosecutorial authority. When faced with the reality of a possible public fight with the attorney general, they saw the political costs to the governor of their original competitive strategy much higher than the benefits. The political environment was such that a quiet, informal agreement could dissolve competitive aspects.

Despite the administrative agreement, some tension persists between the EPA and the attorney general on legal strategies. The attorney general's office complains that the EPA is doing too much preliminary legal work on cases, sorting out a great many possible violations and not referring them to the attorney general. The attorney general and his staff would like to receive a great number of referrals, even those not appropriate for suits, so that they could try to negotiate some compliance without prosecuting every case. EPA, on the other hand, feels that the attorney general's negotiations might let polluters off too easily. It prefers that each case be litigated, unless the alleged polluter agrees fully to EPA's control program and often to a fine and performance bond. In at least one instance, the attorney general negotiated a settlement of a case and presented it to the PCB for approval, despite the opposition of the EPA director. The PCB backed up EPA and refused to accept the settlement. In August, 1972, the board publicly announced its refusal to accept two other settlements recommended by the attorney general, calling them "inadequate and insufficient."[14]

As of August 1, 1972, EPA had initiated 383 complaints of violations, considerably more than EPA's predecessor. (Only 16 of these cases were filed in the year 1970.) In the same 1971-72 period, the PCB held hearings on 14 citizen-initiated complaints, including one from a local control agency. The EPA director indicates that his agency would file even more enforcement complaints with the attorney general, except that there is already a backlog in that office and with the Pollution Control Board. In the first year of EPA operations no cases were filed before the PCB against polluters in the City of Chicago, although EPA contends that it referred Chicago cases to the attorney general.

The Pollution Control Board decides whether an alleged violator is guilty of illegal pollution. Procedural checks on the PCB are like those on the courts. Public notice must be given on the hearing of a complaint, which is conducted by a hearing officer and may be attended by a member of the board.[15] Both parties may be represented by counsel and may cross-examine witnesses. The burden of proof is on the complainant to show that the defendant violated a standard of pollution. Once this burden is met, the burden shifts to the defendant to prove that it would be an arbitrary or unreasonable hardship to comply with the rule. After the hearing, the PCB must issue a final order and write and publish its opinion.

The PCB can order violators to cease and desist, revoke permits, or fine offenders. Appeals from all PCB decisions are to the appellate courts, which consider only the record established by the Pollution Control Board. Two dozen board decisions had been appealed to the appellate courts as of July, 1972, but no decisions were made on PCB actions.

The penalties set by the PCB have been stiffer than court actions—the highest amounting to $150,000 assessed against the Granite City Steel Company and $149,000 against GAF Corporation, a Joliet roofing manufacturer who was applying for a variance after violating state regulations for years.[16] Fines in 144 cases from July, 1970 to November, 1972 amounted to $611,861, not all of which had been collected.

In several instances, the PCB has prohibited any new sewer connections when a community's sewage treatment plant is overloaded and violating state standards.

The most significant enforcement case was brought by the League of Women Voters and other private citizens against the suburban Chicago North Shore Sanitary District for polluting Lake Michigan and the Skokie River.[17] The EPA subsequently joined in the action. The PCB ordered the district to proceed immediately with a $90-million construction program involving five plants that had been delayed by litigation and lack of funds. The PCB ordered the issuance of additional bonds without referendum and banned all new sewer connections until the treatment facilities were installed. The ban produced a raft of variance applications, many of which the PCB denied. The goal is the complete diversion of all sewage effluents from the lake by 1974, with advanced waste treatment and stormwater retention at three large plants to produce an effluent with only 4 part-per-million of biochemical oxygen demand.

The North Shore case was also significant because the PCB issued cease and desist orders to the Committee to Save Highland Park to stop its further prosecutions that had held up the sewage district's expansion program. It also demonstrated the usefulness of the PCB handling both air and water pollution cases. A second suit was filed contending that the sewage facilities were polluting the air. The PCB combined these two complaints to take a complete look at the pollution problem.

Variances

Ironically, the variance—official permission to violate the law for up to one year on grounds of hardship—has been a key enforcement device in Illinois. EPA investigates a variance application and recommends an action based on both the technical and legal facts. Compliance schedules have been written into the variances, performance bonds required, and fines attached to variances for past failures to comply with state regulations. In fact, most of the money penalties in the first 11 months of operation were connected with variance rather than enforcement cases. Since October, 1971, variance cases have been presented to the PCB by the attorney general; prior to that time they were EPA's responsibility. As of August 1, 1972, EPA had initiated 545 variance recommendations, as compared to 383 public and 14 private enforcement complaints filed with the board.[18]

Performance bonds required of variance applicants have been in an amount high enough to make it more expensive to default than to comply. In one instance a bond of $2,600,000 was required, which will be forfeited if the asphalt roofing manufacturing firm in question does not install the required treatment facility.[19] In fact, the 1970 law *requires* that a performance bond or other such security be posted if the hardship complained of in the variance application is just the need for more time.

Permits

Permit powers are assigned to the Environmental Protection Agency, with review by the PCB. Anyone intending to construct or operate equipment or facilities that might emit pollutants must first secure a permit from EPA. EPA has 90 days to review the permit application, and if no final action is taken in that time the application is automatically approved. If EPA denies the permit, the applicant may petition for PCB review, where the burden of proof is on him. The PCB has another 90 days to act on this petition, or the permit is issued. Permit systems are required for construction of air, wastewater, and public water supply treatment facilities; operations of wastewater, public water supply, and solid waste disposal facilities; mine water drainage; construction of solid waste facilities; and, as of December, 1972, for operations of air emission equipment.

Citizen Controls and Other Checks on the Agencies

The Environmental Protection Act intends that private citizens supplement state action and also become a prod or watchdog for better public programs. The following is a listing of the major powers given to private citizens and requirements placed on the environmental agencies to protect citizens' rights.

Open Meetings, Notice

1. The PCB must meet at least once a month. All PCB meetings are open to the public, and notice of each must be given at least 24 hours in advance, except in emergencies. At all hearings, the public must be given reasonable opportunity to be heard.

2. Whenever the PCB schedules a hearing to set standards or rules, adjudicate enforcement cases, or consider variance applications and appeals of permit applicants, it must (a) give notice of the meeting at least 21 days in advance (20 days for standards-setting), giving the time, date, and purpose of the hearing in a newspaper of general circulation in the area affected; (b) given written notice to any person in the area concerned who has in writing requested such notice; and, (c) if the hearing is to set standards or regulations, the PCB must make these available on request, together with summaries of the reasons supporting their adoption.

3. Any person heard or represented at a PCB's hearing or requesting notice shall be given written notice of the PCB's final decision to set standards or a decision on enforcement, variance, or permit appeals case.

4. The PCB must issue notice of proposed adoption of procedural rules, and any person can submit written statements regarding those proposals.

5. When the EPA identifies a pollution violation and the PCB schedules an enforcement hearing, the violator must be notified in writing and sent a formal complaint, and a copy of both are sent to the person who has complained about the pollution and to any other person in the county in which the offending activity occurred who has requested notice of enforcement proceedings.

6. When the EPA receives a variance application it must (a) notify in writing any person in the county in which the installation is located who has

requested in writing notice of variance petitions, and (b) publish notice of such petition in a newspaper of general circulation in the county.

Open Records

7. The PCB must keep a complete and accurate record of all its meetings. A newsletter of PCB activities is published bi-weekly. EPA also publishes a newsletter. Most testimony must be recorded stenographically, and these records, along with written submissions to the PCB, IIEQ, and EPA files must be open to public inspection and copying at cost. The only exceptions are trade secrets, material relating to court actions, or "internal communications."

Right to Initiate Public Action

8. Two hundred or more citizens can petition the PCB to set, revise, or repeal standards and rules, and the PCB *must* hold a public hearing if the proposal is "not plainly devoid of merit" and has not been considered by the PCB within the preceding six months.

9. Any person may file a formal complaint of violation of the act or regulation, and if it is not "duplicitous or frivolous," the PCB *must* hold hearings. Additionally, anyone can submit written statements to the PCB, and the PCB may permit any person to offer oral testimony.

10. Any person may file an informal complaint with the PCB, which is then referred to the Environmental Protection Agency, which *must* investigate it.

11. The PCB *must* hold a hearing on an application for a variance if anyone objects to its approval within 21 days of when the application is filed.

Public Hearings

12. The PCB must hold at least one public hearing in the affected area before adopting standards or regulations. If the regulation is statewide in effect, hearings must be held in at least two areas of the state. However, the PCB may revise the proposed standard that was the subject of the hearing, without holding a further hearing.

13. Enforcement proceedings require a public hearing, as do permit appeals.

14. The PCB must hold public hearings prior to issuing a permit for an atomic power plant.

15. Hearings must be held before a qualified hearing officer (an attorney licensed to practice in Illinois).

16. Any party to an enforcement, variance, or permit appeals hearing before the PCB may be represented by counsel, make oral or written arguments, offer testimony, and cross-examine witnesses.

Written Opinions

17. When the PCB issues an enforcement order, or acts on a variance application, power plant permit request, or permit appeals, it must file and publish a written opinion stating the facts and reasons leading to its decision, and notify respondent of such order in writing by registered mail.

Appeal

18. Any person adversely affected or threatened by any rule of the PCB may seek judicial review in the appellate courts.

THREE-AGENCY STRUCTURE

Pollution Control Board

The PCB has been very active and the most visible of the three environmental agencies. As of August, 1972, it had adopted over ten sets of standards and drafted many of them, including complete revisions of air and water quality standards, which have been federally approved with only two and three exceptions respectively. It has received over 900 variance, permit, and enforcement cases. Only 1 percent of the filed cases remained to be decided by April, 1972.

Because of the level of activity and the "toughness" of their decisions, the PCB is considered by environmentalists and regulated parties to be the strongest antipollution advocate of the three new Illinois agencies. The advocacy approach of the PCB results partly from the personalities selected for membership. PCB members were selected, just as they are for other states' boards, in part to represent special interest groups. One member was selected to speak for agriculture, Dr. Samuel Aldrich of Urbana, Professor of Agriculture at the University of Illinois. He resigned July 1, 1972 and was replaced by State Representative Donald A. Henss, who was named outstanding legislator by the Illinois Agriculture Association. Another was supposed to represent local government, Samuel T. Lawton, Jr., former mayor of Highland Park and chairman of the old Air Pollution Control Board. A third member was selected to please industry, Richard Kissel of Lake Forest, formerly attorney for Abbott Laboratories and a spokesman for industrial interests during the legislative enactment of the Illinois Environmental Protection Act. Kissel resigned in the summer of 1972 and was replaced by John L. Parker, a patent attorney. A fourth member was selected who is knowledgeable about federal programs and satisfactory to conservationists, Jacob Dumelle of Oak Park, an engineer and former director of the Lake Michigan Basin Office of the Federal Water Quality Administration. The chairman, David P. Currie, was selected to represent environmental interests. He was formerly the governor's Coordinator of Environmental Quality and Professor of Environmental Law at the University of Chicago, and is known as an outspoken advocate of vigorous public controls on pollution. Spokesmen for the business community complain that the board's, and particularly Chairman Currie's, vigorous environmentalist posture conflicts with the adjudicative function of that body. They objected when the chairman one day made antiindustry speeches and the next day sat in judgment at a standards-setting, enforcement, or variance proceeding. This occurred in the early period of his tenure and subsequently Currie stopped making public statements altogether. PCB newsletters, also tough-sounding initially, moderated over time. However, some alleged polluters still do not feel they get a fair hearing.

Contributing to the PCB's lack of credibility as an objective body has been its actual solicitation of enforcement cases. While the PCB is supposed to await

23

cases brought by others, members have felt frustrated by the lack of effective enforcement suits. Chairman Currie, writing in his second report in June, 1971, solicited cases in this way:

> We should be happy to receive a great many more agency complaints. Moreover, not one enforcement case so far has concerned a polluter in the City of Chicago. One of the most important changes wrought by the Environmental Protection Act was to abolish local exemptions from state law in order that we might have a unified statewide program. It is high time the intended statewide program became a reality. . . . : In my opinion, too few citizen complaints are being filed. There must be hundreds of violations, such as open burning or dumping, smoky chimneys, or egregious discharges to streams that can be established by simple eyewitness testimony; without technical expert knowledge; this kind of case seems ideally suited to citizen proceedings. . . . In the hope of encouraging more enforcement efforts, we expect to utilize coming board meetings around the State to explore local pollution problems, inviting citizens to tell us of their complaints and the agency to describe for us the condition of the local air and water and the compliance status of local pollution sources.[20]

The PCB has conducted hearings throughout Illinois, inviting citizen and environmental action groups to describe their complaints, and requesting the EPA to report on the compliance status of local pollution sources.

As testimony to the PCB's tough reputation, regulated parties have repeatedly sought legislation to limit its powers. All attempts either failed in the legislature or were vetoed by the governor.

A second technique of private parties opposed to the agency's performance has been to attack its appropriations. In January, 1972, when it became apparent that the PCB's fiscal 1972 appropriation would not be adequate to conduct the many required hearings and publish the transcripts (the bulk of PCB operating costs), the board requested supplemental funds. The General Assembly held up the appropriations until the very end of the legislative session. PCB proceedings had to be postponed for lack of funds. However, the PCB then received the money and hired twice as many officers to remove the backlog of cases.

In both attacks on the PCB's authority and appropriations, the legislature was split more along interest-group lines than along political party lines. Spokesmen for regulated entities from both parties led the attack.

The usual lobbying that occurs in state agencies and part-time pollution control boards in other states is relatively absent from Illinois PCB dealings. Industrialists no doubt expected the Pollution Control Board to behave much like previous Illinois commissions, meeting and negotiating abatement agreements privately. Similarly, environmentalists expected the new PCB to allow them to participate more informally than has occurred, particularly since citizen participation was a major goal of the act and the PCB chairman was known as a strong supporter of private action. Citizen groups complain it is still necessary to hire attorneys and scientists in order to make as valid a technical record as would be necessary in a regular court. They say that formal proceedings may be appropriate to the PCB's adjudication of disputes, but should not apply to standards-setting, variance, and permit hearings. The problem is that formal citizen access—requiring lawyers and environmental specialists —tends to produce a record that favors the polluter who has more funds, full-time technical staff, and tax advantages working for him. By contrast, environmental citizen groups work part time and depend on donations of funds and expertise.

The PCB describes its own problems as lack of time and funds to carry out all assignments. The staff consists of just six legal assistants, six secretaries, a clerk, and her five assistants. The fiscal 1972 budget was $968,300. The initial appropriation was for $828,300, of which $673,300 was for staff and operating expenses and $155,000 for board members' salaries. The supplemental appropriation to cover the deficit in operating expenses was $140,000.

The work load expands almost daily, as more standards are set and more variances are requested and must be acted upon in 90 days. The PCB has requested that the legislature extend this consideration period to 120 days.[21]

Illinois Institute for Environmental Quality

Intended as the analytical and scientific component of the three environmental agencies, the IIEQ's major role to date has been as technical staff to the Pollution Control Board. The close relationship of the two organizations results partly from the close friendship of the two agency leaders, David Currie and Michael Schneiderman, director of the IIEQ. Proximity reinforces the IIEQ/PCB relationship, for both are housed in the same quarters in Chicago. Although the Environmental Protection Agency also has an office in the same building in Chicago, EPA top management spends most of its time in Springfield. The PCB has never been given adequate funds or technical staff to do its own fact-gathering and research. The act intended that the PCB would depend on the IIEQ, as well as EPA, for technical expertise. The IIEQ and EPA would make proposals and justify them before the PCB, so that the basis for regulatory decisions would be a matter of public record. This would both inform private citizens and maintain a separation of powers. However, this approach assumes that the PCB will perform in a purely adjudicative role, which has not been the case to date.

In fiscal 1971 and 1972 the IIEQ allocated $200,000 of its budget to the PCB to be used as it wished. In addition, most of the IIEQ's current research and planning relates to PCB needs.

The IIEQ's principal power is its authority to propose standards as specific statements of long-range objectives. It does not investigate particular enforcement cases unless long-range goals are at stake. The IIEQ's long-range planning activity has been slight because most work is in reaction to immediate PCB needs. However, the IIEQ's director believes his agency's main contribution in the future will be planning and hopes to give this function increasing emphasis. The IIEQ, like many state planning offices, has no implementation authority of its own.

The division of work between the IIEQ and EPA, both of whom are assigned the task of drafting standards, gathering data, and planning, is very informal. The two directors simply get together and agree on program assignments. Most IIEQ work is contracted to universities and private groups.

Unlike EPA and the PCB, the IIEQ's jurisdiction is not limited to pollution control. It can initiate studies and conduct planning for land use, conservation of resources, reuse of waste products, environmental impacts of development projects, and any other topic that might come within the statute's definition of "environmental quality and recycling, reuse and conservation of natural resources and solid wastes."[22] With this authority the IIEQ has sponsored an evaluation of environmental impacts of transportation plans and is sponsoring a computerized land use data system effort.

The IIEQ is criticized by some scientists who say its work is too legally oriented and overemphasizes the regulatory aspects of the state's pollution control at the expense of scientific and management needs and long-range planning requirements. Some environmental groups have charged that the IIEQ has not geared up quickly enough, pointing out that it actually spent only $816,000 of its fiscal year 1971 appropriations of $2 million, and returned the remainder to the state treasury. The fiscal year 1972 appropriation again was $2 million, with $200,000 of this allocated to the PCB's exclusive use. Spokesmen for industrial interests contend that while the IIEQ was set up, in part, to research better and cheaper solutions to industrial waste problems, little attention has been devoted to these matters to date. Furthermore, some contend that the IIEQ is too closely tied to the PCB and is intended to be an independent research agency.

Environmental Protection Agency

The Illinois Environmental Protection Agency is the more traditional type of state pollution control agency. Its assignments include issuing permits, making recommendations to the PCB on variance applications, drafting standards, preparing enforcement cases, monitoring for pollution, planning, and granting technical and financial aid.

EPA's public image is of a slower-moving, more bureaucratic organization than the other two environmental agencies, and it is considered to be less of a tough environmental advocate than the PCB. In part, this results from its year and one-half transition period, when it was considered to be "struggling." While the PCB and IIEQ were new organizations with new people and fresh missions, the EPA began its life with virtually the same staff, performing much the same jobs, in the same way, as the previous Sanitary Engineering and Laboratories Divisions of the Department of Public Health.

Since it was created in 1970, EPA has undergone three fundamental changes: a replacement for the first director and completely new top management, a revised organizational structure, and an increased emphasis on regulatory responsibilities.

The most significant of these changes was in EPA leadership, since this precipitated the other revisions. Clarence Klassen, the state's chief sanitary engineer since 1935, was appointed EPA's first director and served until early 1971, when the governor asked him to retire. Klassen represented the older style of pollution control administration, preferring to work out incremental compliance with industry and local officials in closed-door meetings rather than prosecuting polluters. Klassen's strategy, common to both federal and state programs until the late 1960s, emphasized voluntary compliance, technical aid to industries and municipalities, grants to localities, and engineering solutions rather than legal ones. It was a policy encouraged by legislators and governors since there was little voter support for active court-enforced abatement before 1970.

This style and Klassen, personally, clashed with the new activist, legally oriented leadership of the PCB and IIEQ. These and other state officials saw Klassen as unwilling to give sufficient attention to regulatory matters (such as drafting standards and generating enforcement cases), unresponsive to the needs of the PCB, and unsympathetic to environmental citizen groups. Klassen, who had been the only state pollution control leader for many years, now had to share significant power with the other two agency directors. He was accustomed to dealing informally with "his" old air and water pollution boards, which followed his lead, and so he objected to the new PCB's insistence that all testimony and negotiations including his own be conducted in public. Klassen objected to being cross-examined by private citizens at such public hearings. He felt his many years of service to the state and experience in pollution control warranted different treatment.

Klassen was replaced by William Blaser, a close ally of the governor and the industrial management consultant who had conducted the study that established EPA's new internal organization. Blaser's appointment was confirmed by the legislature in February, 1971, but not without opposition both from political partisans and environmentalists who objected to his lack of experience in the pollution control field.

Blaser is an increasingly active public spokesman for the state's antipollution program, making about 100 speeches a year. But he sees his agency's role as environmental advocate only on enforcement prosecution matters. In this instance, EPA gathers evidence against alleged polluters for submission to the PCB. On all other matters, such as drafting standards, making recommendations on variances, issuing permits, and surveillance, he sees EPA's role as a type of adjudicator of the varied interests in the state. He describes his own role as that of balancer of the two extremes—those who want no pollution and those who

27

want no regulation—for the purpose of serving the broader middle public. Consequently, Blaser says environmentalists think EPA is moving too slowly, and many of them do. On the other hand, the director thinks industries and local governments feel EPA is moving too fast on pollution control.

In his public statements, Blaser frequently combines a call for environmental protection with vocal support for economic development. Describing his agency's enforcement role, Blaser says "an effective, yet reasonable course of operation in the area of law enforcement requires balance, particularly when a limited staff is involved."[2][3]

Despite criticism, EPA has received sizable budget and staff increases from the legislature. In fact, in contrast to the PCB, EPA has had only one serious program battle with the General Assembly. That body, particularly its Democratic members, proposed to cut from $200 million to $80 million EPA's fiscal year 1972 request to sell clean water bonds approved by the voters in 1970. These funds cover the 25 percent state share of construction costs for municipal wastewater treatment plants. Ultimately, the legislators approved the full amount, after receiving a flood of angry communications from local officials whose construction dollars would have been cut. The following year the legislature approved the full $200 million requested without a fight. EPA says this amount is enough to fund fully the state's share of every grant application.

Since taking over EPA, Blaser has hired new people to fill nearly all top jobs and reorganized the existing staff. Both moves were intended to give the new director firmer control of the agency, revitalize the organization, and improve its regulatory output. Between February, 1971 and August, 1972, Blaser filled 79 of the top positions with 62 new people recruited from outside the state government. The total personnel in the agency will increase from 454 in fiscal year 1972 to 632 in fiscal year 1973. Thus, with resignations, retirements, and these increases, two-thirds of EPA's positions will be filled by new people by the end of fiscal year 1973.[2][4]

The director and his personal staff have given much time and attention to the internal reorganization, which helped clear top positions for the new personnel and also broke up the fiefdoms that had existed in field offices. In the past, the head of each field office reported only to the director of the agency, which had the effect of making him virtually autonomous. The new organization sets up five divisions for pollution control and public water supplies and two support divisions. This pattern is similar to that under the previous director. However, the second-level jobs are now substantially changed—from a geographical breakdown to functional bureaus. Field personnel must now report through their respective pollution control divisions (see Chart 1.5 and Table 1.1).

Blaser prefers the "program"-oriented internal organization for his agency, rather than one based on functions. He believes it makes one person accountable to him for each form of pollution control. Blaser sees no need for integrating air pollution, water pollution, solid waste, and noise programs, so there is no staff for this purpose in the director's office. While he recognized that such integration was a key objective of the Environmental Protection Act

CHART 1.5

Organization Chart of the Illinois Environmental Protection Agency,
Effective August, 1972

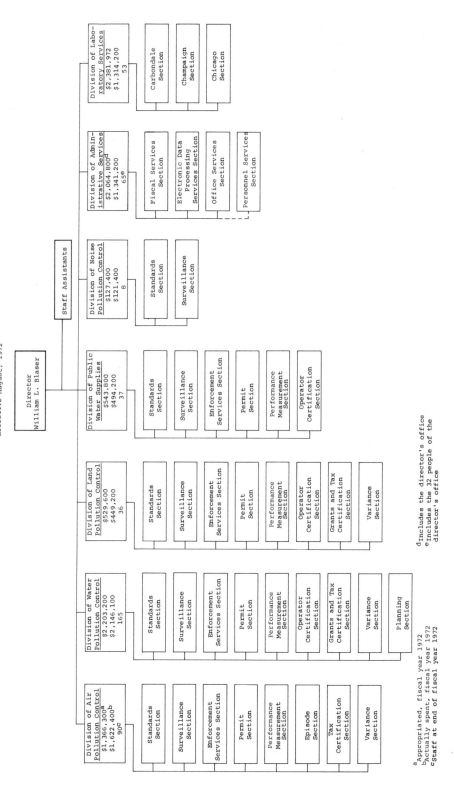

aAppropriated, fiscal year 1972
bActually spent, fiscal year 1972
cStaff at end of fiscal year 1972

dIncludes the director's office
eIncludes the 32 people of the
director's office

TABLE 1.1

Budget and Staff Size of
Illinois Environmental Protection Agency, 1970-73
(fiscal years)

		Budget (in thousands of $)	
1970	1971	1972	1973
3,250.[2]	5,785.9[2] (state funds)	8,230.4[2] (state funds)	6,859.9[2] (state funds)
	726.9 (fed. program grant)	986.7 (fed. program grant)	2,626.5 (fed. program grant)
	6,512.8 (total approp.)	9,217.1 (total approp.)	9,486.4 (total approp.)
	4,443.5 (actual expend.)	7,661.8 (actual expend.)	
		Staff Size (by end of fiscal year)	
246	333	462	632

Source: Environmental Protection Agency, August, 1972.

[1] This is an estimate of expenditures by EPA's predecessor, the Division of Sanitation Engineering, Department of Public Health.

[2] Excludes state funds to localities to construct wastewater treatment works.

and the reorganization it set in motion, he believes that experience has proven such integration unnecessary and unworkable. All that is needed, Blaser believes, is to standardize from division to division the treatment and procedures for those persons dealing with EPA.

The main functional objective of the reorganization and new staff is to increase regulatory activity, and regulatory outputs are accelerating. However, even if variances are considered enforcement devices, the case load is still light compared to the number of likely violations. For example, Blaser indicated in October, 1971 that 82 percent of the state's municipal wastewater treatment plants would not meet deadlines that year for further treatment required years ago by the Sanitary Water Board.[25] A lesser percentage of industries is thought to be out of compliance with water quality regulations. Blaser's enforcement strategy has been to delay enforcement prosecutions against municipalities until water quality standards were revised and state money available to fund the state's share of local construction costs. The overall enforcement strategy now is to go after the largest sources of pollution of every type, on an ad hoc basis.[26]

Director Blaser indicates that his agency would file more enforcement cases to the attorney general, but that a backlog of cases is already pending there and before the PCB. Indeed, a backlog or sizable dropping of cases from prosecution is occuring somewhere between the EPA surveillance staff and the PCB (see Table 1.2). The number of permits is

TABLE 1.2

Violations of State Law Identified by Illinois EPA Surveillance Staff and
Forwarded to Enforcement Services Division, Compared to Number of
Prosecutions before PCB Brought by Attorney General
(fiscal years)

	EPA Surveillance Cases, 1971	AG's Prosecutions before Board, 1971	EPA Surveillance Cases, 1972	AG's Prosecutions before Board, 1972
Air pollution control	72	12	285	79
Water pollution control	35	7	182	56
Land pollution control	27	11	153	66
Public water supplies	0	0	25	6
Total	133	30	645	207

Source: Illinois Environmental Protection Agency, August, 1972.

increasing (see Table 1.3), which indicates new waste sources coming under
the review and control of the state agency.

EPA's role in drafting standards has become more significant over the
last two years. After recommending few standards its first year, EPA
drafted the air quality implementation plans, had a considerable say in the
final water effluent standards, and assisted the IIEQ in drafting noise and solid
waste standards. EPA is also developing new regulations for public water
supplies.

Monitoring and surveillance have increased both for purposes of enforcement and to improve data for program operations (see Table 1.4). The U.S.
Environmental Protection Agency cited Illinois as having the best statewide
system in the Midwest for testing waterways for pollution. In 1972 EPA had
658 sampling stations that would take a projected 7,896 water quality samples.
The next state, Michigan, has about 250 monitoring stations.[27] Over
100,000 additional samples of public water supplies will also be taken in
1972.

TABLE 1.3

Permits Issued by Illinois EPA
(fiscal years)

	1971	1972
Air pollution control (construction of facilities; operations require permits as of December, 1972)	561	1,122
Water pollution control (construction and operation of facilities; mines)	916	1,214
Public water supplies (construction and operation of facilities)	1,178	1,354
Solid waste (construction and operation of disposal facilities)	37	105
Total	2,692	3,795

Source: Illinois Environmental Protection Agency.

CONCLUSIONS

Illinois' three new environmental organizations have substantially stepped-up regulatory activity in that state. The focus has been on setting environmental standards—the research, drafting and approval of some of the strictest and most comprehensive regulations in the country. New permit systems have been established and existing ones streamlined so that most significant waste sources are subject to state permit review. These steps represent a necessary gearing-up to fight pollution and indicate the state is beginning to respond to the public's wishes for environmental protection.

But the crunch has yet to come in Illinois, as in many states, when the new tough antipollution requirements will be strictly enforced and variances regularly denied. While enforcement and surveillance have substantially increased in the last two years, compliance, even with the older and more lenient standards set by previous air and water boards, is still inadequate. Enforcement data do not show that the state has the full determination or the capability to go after significant numbers of private polluters in Chicago, in large industries, or in large municipalities. This is the breakdown on complaints filed by the attorney general before the Pollution Control Board from 1970 through August, 1972:[28]

TABLE 1.4

Illinois EPA Monitoring and Surveillance

	1970	1971	1972
Water quality			
(stations)	363	464	658
(samples)	3,955	4,858	7,896*
Air quality	4 trailer labs; telmetry network hooked up to EPA headquarters; 10 continuous SO_2 monitoring stations; system will expand to monitor all air pollutants regulated by standards by January, 1974		
Land pollution control			
(inspections)	—	7,512	9,027*
Public water supplies			
(samples)	—	74,428	100,189
(inspections for enforcement)	—	746	969
Noise	—	215 investigations for purposes of drafting regulations in 1971-72.	

*Projected.

Source: Illinois Environmental Protection Agency.

383 total complaints filed by the attorney general before the PCB.
  36 of these cited large companies;
  33 of these cited municipalities, mostly small towns: only three involved communities over 50,000 population;
  44 cases involved alleged polluters in Cook County, but a much smaller number were located in the City of Chicago;
  7 complaints involved agriculture-related sources.

While formal complaints are not the only indicators of the strength of a regulatory system, they are the state's strongest tool for enforcing compliance. Voluntary compliance has been ineffective, and state grants to municipalities and tax breaks to industries cover only a part of the costs of pollution abatement. It is still cheaper for a town or company to discharge untreated wastes and pollute than to install pollution-control equipment. A court ordered clean-up or substantial fine, or the very real threat of one, is imperative to enforce compliance, even if it is negotiated compliance.

Of course, the true test of the effectiveness of the three environmental agencies is not these program activity levels—numbers and kinds of regulatory actions, subsidies, planning, and research—but whether these efforts result in the quality of air, water, and land desired by the people of Illinois. It was beyond the scope of this study to determine actual changes in environmental conditions that are attributable to actions of the three state agencies.*

While environment changes caused by the new organizations are not measured here, the short-run Illinois experience demonstrates some political and administrative effects of its unique institutional system.

Three Agencies with Functional Specialities

The considerable pollution control activity in Illinois is partly a result of having three full-time organizations instead of one. Three organizations produce more action, but, more importantly, each unit has a clear-cut function and specific antipollution program mission, which allows it to pursue its goal unconstrained by other objectives and jobs. The clearer the mission, the less time and attention an organization must give to setting priorities among several competing jobs, organizing internally to handle varied work, and, generally, trying to perform many duties at once.

The strengthened regulatory roles of the PCB and EPA show that the state's own reorganization objective of increasing administrative activity through functional specialization, particularly in the regulatory field, is beginning to be met.

The Illinois Institute for Environmental Quality has already shown some benefits from the separation of planning and research from operations. More planning and research has resulted than under the pre-1970 system, even though the research products have a short-range perspective designed to meet the immediate needs of the other two environmental agencies, and particularly the PCB.

---

*Illinois' EPA has reported improvements in air quality for one or two parameters in each of four urban areas. Chicago's metropolitan air quality region had a reduction in 1971 of nearly 14 percent in average particulate concentrations. East St. Louis' regional average for suspended particulates was reduced nearly 27 percent. Chicago's average sulfur dioxide concentrations decreased 40 percent in one year. However, there are several reasons why these data cannot serve as performance measurements for EPA or other state agencies, even for their air quality programs. First, only two types of air pollutants were measured and other significant parameters were not monitored. Furthermore, the data are urban averages and do not represent air quality in particular areas, making human exposure rates impossible to calculate. Finally, and most importantly, the improvements are not necessarily the result of EPA or other state agency actions. In fact, in announcing the sizable reduction in Chicago's sulfur dioxide levels, EPA said the change "is due largely to fuel sulfur limits *imposed by local ordinances.*" (Emphasis added.) (Press release from EPA dated June 28, 1972.)

The three agencies provide Illinois citizens with more access to the state's environmental decision-making than existed prior to 1970. Now, if a citizen does not get satisfaction from one agency, he can appeal to two others. However, the public must be sufficiently informed to understand the functional distinction among the agencies. Public accountability of program leaders tends to be reduced when three instead of one are involved.

The interdependence of the three organizations, without a formal coordinating mechanism, has created the main problems in the Illinois system. First, competition was created among several agencies, restricting the interagency cooperation required for effective environmental policies. Competition can be generated easily when several agencies operate in the same popular policy field, such as the environment; but this condition cannot realistically coexist with interdependency. Second, even when competition is eliminated, as it eventually was in Illinois, some institution or mechanism is needed to coordinate the agencies systematically and do planning for all three, allocating work loads when responsibilities overlap. This is missing in Illinois, although ad hoc cooperation among officials compensates to a degreee. Third, it is more difficult for the public to identify the state official responsible for particular program decisions and to hold him accountable when several leaders are involved.

Where competition occurred, it proved counterproductive rather than healthy. Director Klassen said standards-drafting and planning should be done by the IIEQ, which had the funds for those purposes, but IIEQ and PCB members criticized EPA for not formulating standards. In fact, Klassen was operating as an independent leader, which one should expect in a competitive situation.

As tensions grew among state officials, the interdependency of the pollution control organizations was increasingly demonstrated. The Illinois agency system had been designed so that no single organization had all the tools it needed to regulate pollution, for such concentration of powers was thought to lead to arbitrary state action.

The final resolution of the conflict between competition and interdependency came in a very pragmatic way—competition was eliminated by political agreement.

The conclusion to be drawn here is that it is unrealistic to expect truly rival agencies to work closely and effectively together. A governmental structure cannot have both interagency competition and interdependency. A state government that establishes several pollution control agencies should select either a competitive system, in which each organization has all the powers it needs to perform independently, or the interdependent system of agencies, in which case a mechanism is provided to allocate resources and work loads among participants and do comprehensive policy analyses for all units.

A final note on competition. Organizations and their leaders usually feel uncomfortable with the tensions that result and will seek to eliminate, rather than live with, them. If political conditions are right, as they were in Illinois, a competitive system can and most likely will be undercut by political agreement.

Illinois' tri-agency system was designed by lawyers to meet legal objectives—the separation of the conflicting legal jobs of prosecution and adjudication. While this was accomplished, it resulted in a lack of comprehensiveness in environmental policies and programs. The only organization with a formal overview is the budget bureau where the same budget examiner handles funds for all three agencies, as well as for the Conservation Department. While no organizational system is "people proof," the heavy reliance on personal compatibility of the three agency leaders to make the system work makes the Illinois system overly "people sensitive."

In such a situation the power of the governor to appoint all three agency directors is vital. The Illinois governor appoints the PCB chairman who serves at his pleasure, while the EPA and IIEQ directors serve a term. Although these terms are short—two and three years respectively—a new governor could conceivably have to wait three years to make the IIEQ compatible with the other organizations and two years for similar EPA cooperation. A better approach would be to make the appointees to the three top positions all serve at the governor's pleasure.

A further improvement would be to assign the responsibility of planning and evaluation for the three antipollution organizations to some state institution that has a broad overview of all state programs. The most effective environmental strategies require a mix of functions—standards setting, enforcement, research, planning, monitoring, and issuing of permits and grants. Such integrated action is difficult enough to orchestrate when all jobs are done by one agency, but it becomes much tougher with multiple organizations. Also, pollution controls need to be tied to conservation and other natural resource management agencies. The job could be the Institute for Environmental Quality, or a strong state planning office that is tied to the program budgeting system, if one is established in Illinois. Or the responsibilities of the present budget officer could be expanded and he be given adequate staff and fund to carry out comprehensive environmental planning. These plans could then be tied to the budgeting system for implementation purposes. All three of these organizations would have a perspective broader than just antipollution and could tie pollution controls to other state activities, such as natural resource conservation and development.

A further useful tool would be a requirement for environmental impact statements by state agencies.

Organizational Physics

Illinois' experience in setting up three agencies at one time—two of which were completely new and the third an agency created by reorganization of existing programs—provides a lesson in organizational physics, or how to get government moving. EPA had to undergo a transition period of about two years, which slowed down programs, while the PCB and IIEQ could begin immediately with a burst of activity. It should be noted, however, that EPA's transition difficulties were far less severe than those in other states where reorganizations affected many more types of programs moved into "super-agencies," and less than those of Washington's Department of Ecology, where programs similar to those in Illinois were radically restructured along completely functional lines.

Watching a completely new organization and a reorganized one show that it is more difficult to change an established organization, such as EPA, than to launch a completely new one. When a new policy direction is sought, such as increased pollution regulation, it always takes more political and administrative energy to halt an organization, turn it around, and start it moving on another policy route. Shifting the administrative locale and implementing a new internal structure means a reorganization for an existing agency, which creates confusion and tension among personnel and is more difficult than establishing a fresh administrative structure. Instilling new policies in old agencies requires redirecting existing staff or replacing them, which takes time and can demoralize the remaining personnel. To be sure, however, existing staff who wish a policy change can be given new vigor by such moves. In Illinois a policy change required a new director and almost completely new top management.

New agencies with completely new staffs also initially have a more intense sense of program mission than do established agencies. Particularly, environmental government agencies such as the Illinois PCB and IIEQ have spirit and vigor when they are new, since they are established with a great deal of public fanfare and are bathed, at least initially, in the public spotlight and have considerable legislative and popular support. All this attention instills a high degree of motivation in the new staff and attracts environmental activists to leadership positions. Governors, such as Ogilvie, who initiate such environmental reorganizations as a clean-up move are likely to go on to appoint such activists to key positions. Unfortunately, the vigor attendant at the inception of a new agency tends to diminish with the years and often, when the honeymoon is over, subsequent appointees are lesser advocates.

Full-Time Board to Set Antipollution Policy and Adjudicate Disputes

The fact that the PCB works full time, has its own staff and funds, and must be "technically qualified" has had these results: it produces more work more quickly than the former Illinois antipollution boards; its products and decisions are based on a greater understanding of pollution problems; and its members have all become environmental advocates, to some degree, rather than strictly speaking for special interests.

Consequently the PCB's environmental standards and regulations are tougher than those of former boards. In its role as administrative court, the "judges" have been more knowledgeable about and committed to pollution abatement than the judges of the regular courts. Penalties to date tend to be stiffer and decisions handed down more quickly. The Illinois record, at least in the short run, seems to refute the theory offered by some legal scholars that specialized courts tend to acquire an "insiders perspective," becoming overly sympathetic to the abatement problems of polluters and become lax in enforcing the law.

There is an important qualification to this, however. The present climate of public opinion in Illinois and particularly in Chicago supports a tough pollution-control posture. Should this climate change, or a new governor be elected who is less supportive of pollution control, then new appointments might be more lenient on polluters. The PCB's character can change very quickly because terms are staggered and run for only three years.

The conclusion is that an adjudicative board whose members serve three-year appointments are more immediately responsive to public opinion and state politics than regular courts. This is good for environmental clean-up as long as the public supports this objective, but could have the reverse effect if environment became unpopular. This is a necessary risk if government organization is to be responsive to changing public demands. The Illinois PCB seems to be striking a balance between fully accountable policy-makers, who serve at a governor's pleasure and can be removed at any time, and boards that serve long terms and are insulated from the winds of political change and the public. Since it is full time and a separate organization from the EPA, the Illinois PCB does not appear to the public to be making decisions for the EPA. Thus, a full-time PCB is less likely to reduce the EPA's public accountability than a part-time body would be.

If the current PCB's advocacy approach has resulted in stiffer penalties and standards, this proenvironment stance has also somewhat compromised the PCB's credibility as a fair review body. Polluters do not believe they can secure a fair ruling from the PCB and particularly its chairman. While environmentalists had no faith in the "unbiasedness" of previous polluter-oriented boards, these earlier boards did not settle disputes.

The judgmental function would be more credible if it were not mixed in the same board with environmental standards-setting, which has encouraged an advocacy role. In the future, if the IIEQ, EPA, and private citizens propose more regulations, the PCB may assume a more adjudicative posture toward standards-setting. The PCB had increasingly moved toward the position that final standards adopted by it should reflect the official record established in public hearings and not be supplemented by its own research and opinions. This will not solve all problems, for as standards-setting becomes more adjudicative, and decisions are made entirely on testimony in a public record, the state policy-making may favor polluters. All interests within the state are not fully and equally represented at public hearings. While expert witnesses can make a detailed technical record for polluters' interests, the conservationists and environmental activists must rely on volunteer witnesses and private donations. The usual result is that the public record becomes stacked in favor of the polluters. EPA and the IIEQ will provide the main technical contribution to the record, but these agencies' views must reflect all interests in the state and will not be as protectionist as private environmental interests. Thus, it would not be appropriate for standards-setting to become a purely adjudicative process.

There is a possibility that the PCB's two jobs of standards-setting and adjudication may conflict in another way—it may be tougher in adjudicating alleged violations of its own standards. But it is still too early to tell, since there have been few enforcement cases, and most of these relate to the rules established by the previous air and water pollution control boards.

Role of the Private Citizen

The Illinois citizen has considerably more opportunity to participate in his state's environmental decision-making than he had prior to 1970. Government processes and files are more open to public scrutiny, and the private citizen has more power to initiate state action. There are more points of access to government through three organizations. If access is greater, it is formal and not simple, requiring the services of attorneys, scientists, and engineers, to make a valid legal record.

The authority for citizens to bring suit against polluters has resulted in no rash of formal complaints, despite industries' fears. In fact, PCB members, as well as others, have charged that environmentally concerned citizens have failed to take full advantage of their new powers. This failure results because citizen groups lack the funds and experts needed to participate. This could be remedied if Illinois were to fund a legal staff specifically to aid private citizens in actions to protect the environment.

Despite these limits, citizens are learning about government decisions *before* they are made, attending more state meetings, articulating their views, and have more control over the outcome of decisions than before 1970. All these factors contribute to making the environmental structure of Illinois government more responsive to all the affected individuals of the state and broadening the base on which public environmental decisions are made.

NOTES

1. Illinois Environmental Protection Act of 1970. House Bill 3788, approved June 29, 1970, effective July 1, 1970. 76th Illinois General Assembly. Ill. Rev. Stat. Ch. 111½ secs. 1001-51 (1970).
2. Richard B. Ogilvie, Governor of Illinois, "Special Message on the Environment," April 23, 1970, p. 2.
3. *Ibid.*, p. 2.
4. Colman McCarthy, "Pollution Control Through Lawsuits," *Washington Post*, January 20, 1970, Editorial page.
5. Sec. 5(a), Environmental Protection Act, House Bill 3788.
6. Remarks of Richard B. Ogilvie to the National Association of Attorneys General, St. Charles, Illinois, June 29, 1970, p. 4.
7. House Bill 785, 1971 session of the Illinois General Assembly.

8. PCB Newsletter No. 20, April 19, 1971, p. 20.

9. David P. Currie, "Illinois Pollution Control Board, Second Report," June 28, 1971, p. 2.

10. PCB Newsletter No. 19, April 12, 1971.

11. PCB Newsletter No. 37, December 5, 1972, p. 2.

12. PCB Newsletter No. 17, March 8, 1971. See also "Pollution Control Board Regulations Compared to Federal Standards," memorandum dated May 20, 1971 to the Illinois House Appropriations Subcommittee No. 3.

13. Sec. 31 (a), Ill. Rev. Stat. sec. 1031 (a), provides:

> If such investigation discloses that a violation may exist, the Agency shall issue and serve upon the person complained against a written notice, together with a formal complaint, which shall specify the provision of this law or the rule or regulation under which such person is said to be in violation, and a statement of the manner in, and the extent to which such person is said to violate this law or such rule or regulation and shall require the person so complained against to answer the charges of such formal complaint at a hearing before the Board at a time not less than 21 days after the date of notice, except as provided in Section 34 of this Act. A copy of such notice and complaint shall also be sent to any person who has complained to the Agency respecting the respondent within the six months preceding the date of the complaint, and to any person in the county in which the offending activity occurred who has requested notice of enforcement proceedings. 21 days notice of such hearings shall also be published in a newspaper of general circulation in such county. The respondent may file a written answer, and at such hearing the rules prescribed in Sections 32 and 33 of this Act shall apply. In the case of actual or threatened acts outside Illinois contributing to environmental damage in Illinois, the extra-territorial service-of-process provisions of sections 16 and 17 of the Civil Practice Act shall apply.

14. Pollution Control Board, Press Release of August 14, 1972.

15. Sec. 32, Ill. Rev. Stat. sec. 1032.

16. PCB Newsletter No. 20, April 19, 1971, State of Illinois Environmental Protection Agency, Summary Fines Assessed by Pollution Control Board, July 1970-October 31, 1972.

17. PCB Case Nos. 70-7, 12, 13, 14.

18. Data supplied by the Illinois Environmental Protection Agency.

19. PCB Case No. 71-11, affecting the GAF Corporation.

20. David P. Currie, "Illinois Pollution Control Board, Second Report," June 28, 1971, p. 11.

21. House Bill 1116, 1971 session of the Illinois General Assembly, introduced at the PCB's request.

22. See Institute for Environmental Quality "Project List," June 1, 1971.

23. Remarks of William L. Blaser to Chicago Association of Commerce and Industry, November 11, 1971, p. 5.

24. Interview with William L. Blaser, August 15, 1972.

25. Remarks of William L. Blaser to Illinois Municipal League, Peoria, October 17, 1971, p. 11.

26. Letter from William L. Blaser to Elizabeth Haskell, August 30, 1972.

27. *Chicago Tribune*, August 12, 1972.

28. Data Supplied by the Illinois Environmental Protection Agency, August, 1972.

CHAPTER 2

INTRODUCTION

In 1967 Minnesota created its Pollution Control Agency (PCA) to act as the state's sole regulator of water, air, and solid waste pollution. The reorganization act[1] shifted the existing water pollution control program, which had been administered by the Interagency Water Pollution Control Commission under the Health Department's leadership, and added a newly created state authority to study air pollution and solid waste disposal problems. In 1969 the PCA was given the go-ahead by the state legislature to regulate air and solid waste pollutants,[2] and its water pollution control powers were expanded.[3] Noise pollution control was added to the PCA's responsibilities by legislation in 1971,[4] but pesticides and radiation control are shared with the Agriculture and Health Departments, respectively. The current organization, functions, and budget of the PCA are outlined in Chart 2.1.

The PCA was entirely a legislative creation. The purpose of reorganization was to create a highly visible, strong advocate for environmental clean-up. In 1967, the legislature felt the state was entering a new phase of pollution control, and the time was ripe for this move. The Health Department was considered an inappropriate locus for the tough regulatory approach to pollution that seemed to be called for. A new organization, with a new leader and new focus was needed to promote this mission.

From the beginning, the PCA was conceived of as a regulatory agency. It was not meant to be *the* environmental agency in state government, but rather the advocate of pollution control among other state agencies promoting other public goals. Minnesota has two other agencies with environmental tasks: the

CHART 2.1

Minnesota PCA Organization, Main Functions, and Budget, 1972

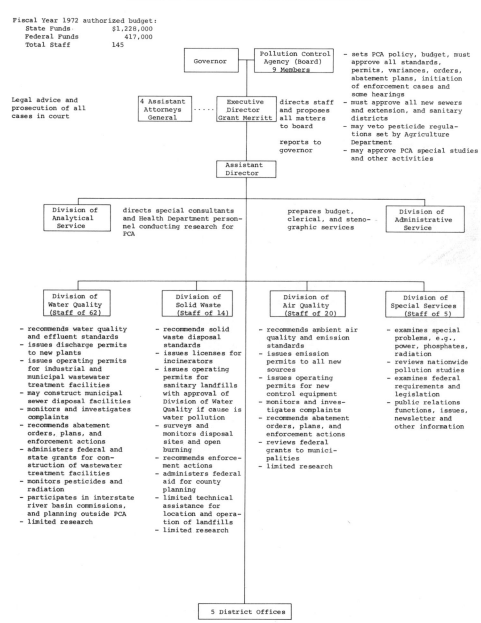

Fiscal Year 1972 authorized budget:
State Funds $1,228,000
Federal Funds   417,000
Total Staff   145

```
                                    ┌─────────────┐  ┌──────────────────┐
                                    │  Governor   │  │ Pollution Control│   - sets PCA policy, budget, must
                                    └─────────────┘  │  Agency (Board)  │     approve all standards,
                                                     │   9 Members      │     permits, variances, orders,
                                                     └──────────────────┘     abatement plans, initiation
                                                                              of enforcement cases and
                                                                              some hearings
Legal advice and        ┌─────────────┐   ┌──────────────┐  directs staff  - must approve all new sewers
prosecution of all      │ 4 Assistant │···│  Executive   │  and proposes     and extension, and sanitary
cases in court          │  Attorneys  │   │   Director   │  all matters      districts
                        │   General   │   │ Grant Merritt│  to board       - may veto pesticide regula-
                        └─────────────┘   └──────────────┘                   tions set by Agriculture
                                                            reports to        Department
                                                            governor        - may approve PCA special studies
                                          ┌──────────────┐                   and other activities
                                          │  Assistant   │
                                          │  Director    │
                                          └──────────────┘
```

| Division of Analytical Service | directs special consultants and Health Department personnel conducting research for PCA | prepares budget, clerical, and stenographic services | Division of Administrative Service |

Division of Water Quality (Staff of 62)

- recommends water quality and effluent standards
- issues discharge permits to new plants
- issues operating permits for industrial and municipal wastewater treatment facilities
- may construct municipal sewer disposal facilities
- monitors and investigates complaints
- recommends abatement orders, plans, and enforcement actions
- administers federal and state grants for construction of wastewater treatment facilities
- monitors pesticides and radiation
- participates in interstate river basin commissions, and planning outside PCA
- limited research

Division of Solid Waste (Staff of 14)

- recommends solid waste disposal standards
- issues licenses for incinerators
- issues operating permits for sanitary landfills with approval of Division of Water Quality if cause is water pollution
- surveys and monitors disposal sites and open burning
- recommends enforcement actions
- administers federal aid for county planning
- limited technical assistance for location and operation of landfills
- limited research

Division of Air Quality (Staff of 20)

- recommends ambient air quality and emission standards
- issues emission permits to all new sources
- issues operating permits for new control equipment
- monitors and investigates complaints
- recommends abatement orders, plans, and enforcement actions
- reviews federal grants to municipalities
- limited research

Division of Special Services (Staff of 5)

- examines special problems, e.g., power, phosphates, radiation
- reviews nationwide pollution studies
- examines federal requirements and legislation
- public relations functions, issues, newsletter and other information

```
                                  ┌──────────────────────┐
                                  │  5 District Offices   │
                                  └──────────────────────┘
```

Conservation Department, renamed the Department of Natural Resources (DNR) in 1970, which carries out traditional resource management and conservation programs; and the State Planning Agency (SPA) created in 1965,[5] which does broad environmental planning. It was reasoned that if a system of special mission advocacy agencies were maintained, open debate, public access, and political choice would be maximized.

The PCA's staff is led by a strong director, appointed by the governor with the advice and consent of the Senate, and serving at the governor's pleasure. However, the real power to make regulatory decisions is located in a part-time, citizen policy board. The Pollution Control Board acts as a quasi-legislative body, making all the significant regulatory decisions—approving pollution control standards, permits, abatement orders, compliance plans, variances, and enforcement actions. There are now nine members, appointed by the governor and approved by the Senate, and they serve overlapping four-year terms.

Over the years, the Pollution Control Board has used all the powers granted to it. However, it has not been able to take a broad, balanced position on pollution control issues, because individual members speak on behalf of the special interests they were appointed to represent. Overall, the board has been conservative, sometimes restraining the PCA's aggressiveness against certain polluters, and has served to limit the agency's public responsiveness and direct accountability.

Despite this, the PCA got off to a running start in 1967. It promulgated a very inclusive set of water, air, and solid waste regulations and tackled some large polluters in court. It has acted as a strong and vigorous public spokesman for environmental clean-up, and its current director is widely supported by environmentalists. Although critics complain that some of its actions are too strict, its supporters believe that the objective in creating a small, single-purpose agency has been vindicated.

The reorganization debate, however, still rages in Minnesota. Some persons hope that the PCA will be merged with the Department of Natural Resources to advance administrative efficiency and improve natural resource planning and management. Also, because none of Minnesota's three environmental agencies has a sufficiently broad outlook to draft comprehensive environmental strategies, a five-member interagency Environmental Quality Control was set up in 1972 in the governor's office to act as environmental arbitrator and coordinator.

THE REORGANIZATION PROCESS

Minnesota has a long history of creating small, new agencies like the PCA to promote single-purpose, discrete missions. Despite the administrative complexity, fragmentation, and overlap that may occur, the state's inclination is to support a system composed of many strong and competing government agencies, each concerned with its own limited problems and specified goals. Public administration experts have called this an "advocacy" system. Competition between single missions is intended, indeed institutionalized, to increase the public representation of each goal or interest and to highlight political choices.

Theorists contend that conflicts and trade-offs among single public goals should be freely aired to public view and debate. They should be solved through the political rather than administrative process—by the governor and other elected officials or through an open interagency process rather than within one administrative house. Under an advocacy system, individual public goals are more clearly articulated and more strongly competitive. A system of checks and balances is built within the executive branch of government, and equity of access of public decision-making is more readily assured. When seemingly related programs are consolidated into one executive department, there is a greater likelihood that all differences of opinion will be resolved internally. This limits the political process and the public's access. Over the long run, if programs do intermingle as a result of consolidation, there is a high probability that eventually their unique and valuable differences will be lost.

Minnesota also has a long history of an active and strong state legislature, and a history of weak governors. The state legislature has a reputation for competence and integrity and, although it meets only every other year, for energy. State legislators typically remain in office for many years. The state legislature has always maintained an active overview of executive branch affairs. As students of Minnesota government have noted, the legislature not only takes a major responsibility for policy and program initiation, it also involves itself intimately and forcefully in executive agencies' activities to the point of legislating, in detail, the programs to be implemented, their timetables, and exact budgetary worth.

For example, until recently the legislature held strict reins of control over the DNR, even setting hunting seasons each year. If an executive agency varies from its prescribed course, specific legislation may be drafted to bring it back on track. If the legislature wishes a special study undertaken, directives may be issued for this and special legislative funds may be used. Agency directors, and the governor, sometimes see this interference as fractious and inappropriate. However, the legislature has had some success in creating a broad overview capacity and arming itself with research staff and data. An example of this is the Minnesota Resources Commission, a joint legislative body that studies broad environmental and resource matters. California has a similar legislative body for the environment. Minnesota's legislature has also initiated a number of executive reorganizations. In 1965 it created the State Planning Agency, and it set up the Pollution Control Agency in 1967.

An Advocacy Agency

The idea for a new pollution control regulatory agency was first conceived in the early 1960s by the then acknowledged Republican leader of the State

45

Senate, Gordon Rosenmeier. Before creating the new agency, however, Rosenmeier felt it strategic first to consolidate and strengthen the state's statutory authority for pollution control, particularly state power over local units of government. At that time the state's only antipollution program was for water. This was in the hands of a seven-member interagency Water Pollution Control Commission, which had been nearly dormant for some time. The Water Pollution Control Commission was chaired by a member of the State Board of Health, and included the directors of the Conservation and Agriculture Department, the State Livestock Sanitary Board, and three members from the public at large. It was basically an ex-officio body, carrying out its business on an informal and ad hoc basis. Meeting only occasionally, the commission relied entirely on the Health Department's staff and technical services to do the real work. Its main function was to issue permits to municipalities and industries for sewage treatment plants, water supply systems, and wastewater discharges. However, it had no real enforcement powers and its inadequacies were generally recognized. The Health Department itself had the authority to regulate drinking water purity.

The authority of the Water Pollution Control Commission was gradually widened in a series of heated battles between the legislature and sanitary officials of the Twin Cities (Minneapolis-St. Paul) and surrounding suburban areas. In 1963, the legislature ordered the commission to adopt water use classifications and water quality standards for interstate and intrastate waters. Still, however, there were no law suits and little controversy surrounding most of the commission's activities. Many persons regarded this as a sign that the commission was only a rubber stamp for the interests of industry, agriculture, and municipalities. Furthermore, its domination by the Health Department implied a very limited focus for the pollution control work. As it has been written: "Major deficiencies were associated with the ex-officio character of the commission and the ascent on the health aspects of water pollution at the expense of broader regulatory responsibilities."[6]

The bill creating the PCA was first drafted in the legislature, by Senator Gordon Rosenmeier, in 1964. This bill passed the Senate and an amended version passed the House a year later, but subsequently died in the Senate because of Senator Rosenmeier's strong opposition to a House amendment giving the Minneapolis-St. Paul sanitary district a position on the PCA's governing board. Rosenmeier rewrote the reorganization bill, which then passed both houses. But this version was vetoed by the then Republican governor, who felt that a clear separation of functions between the PCA and the Health Department had not been made and that the PCA would remain too dependent on that department for staff and services. The PCA bill was reworked by a private consultant to Rosenmeier and the Minnesota Resources Commission. It passed the legislature in 1967 with almost no dissent. Outgoing Democratic Governor Karl Rolvaag had promised to sign it, and incoming Republican Governor Harold LeVander did so. The 1967 act also authorized the new PCA to study and recommend to the legislature standards for air pollution and solid waste disposal. Two years later the legislature gave the PCA power to enact these standards. That same year the legislature expanded the PCA's water quality permit-granting authority, and gave it the power to create sanitary districts on petition and the authority to require municipalities to construct or alter their sewer disposal and treatment facilities.

The rationale behind the PCA was not complex. The legislature felt that the state was about to enter into a new era of strong pollution control. A brand new, full-time organization with antipollution expertise and regulatory emphasis was needed to lead the attack on across-the-board pollution problems. This organization would have greater visibility to the public and legislature, be run by a new leader, and could signal the state's commitment to tougher pollution regulation. The state had outgrown the institutional arrangement for water pollution control—policy-making by a committee and administration by the Health Department. Rosenmeier reasoned that pollution control should be a separate and distinct governmental goal, since it related to such a wide variety of public and private programs, beyond merely health concerns. The Health Department, which focused primarily on municipal and not industrial pollution, was not the proper locus for an expanded regulatory effort. If antipollution programs remained in the Health Department, it might appear as if the issues were being intentionally buried. In short, pollution control needed its own institutional spokesman.

Minnesota was also influenced in 1967 by the federal government. The Federal Water Pollution Control Administration, it was noted, had recently been transferred from the Department of Health, Education and Welfare to the Department of the Interior. In that location it was supposed to be concerned with the economic, resource, recreational, and aesthetic effects of water pollution, not just its public health aspects. It was argued that this federal agency's sizable new grants for water treatment facility construction might gravitate toward those states with a similar orientation, demonstrated through a new special agency.

Two alternatives to a separate PCA were given some, although very limited, consideration outside the legislature. The first consideration was to combine the state's water management programs, such as neighboring Wisconsin had done in 1966 and Washington State had attempted.* However, the legislative proponents of the pollution control reorganization felt that water, per se, was no longer a separate task of government. Minnesota, land of many lakes, has never had any shortage of water, and quantity was not a crucial issue. The real issues concerning water were what people put into it—or water quality—and how they used it—for recreational and other purposes. A separate agency for water therefore did not fit the state's environmental objectives. Also, a separate water agency might still leave unsettled the problem of where to put the new air pollution and solid waste control programs. Water, air, and solid waste control programs, it was argued, belonged together since these pollutants interacted in the environment.

---

*See Chapter 3 (Washington) and Chapter 4 (Wisconsin).

A second option was to combine pollution control programs with the Department of Natural Resources, then called the Conservation Department, which carried out traditional conservation programs for fish, wildlife, forest, mineral, and water management. However, in marked contrast to reorganization thinking in Wisconsin in 1967, the disadvantages of this merger were thought to far outweigh any potential benefits. While there were important connections between pollution control and resource management work, and the thought of a single agency concerned with the environment was attractive to some, many persons felt it was more valuable to preserve the unique differences between them than to merge them into one overall program.

There were, it was pointed out, large and important dissimilarities between pollution control and conservation efforts that should be maintained to ensure that all private individuals in the state were represented in the state program. The DNR tended to be management- rather than regulatory-oriented. It had a rural rather than urban orientation and constituency, and had little interest or understanding of industrial and municipal pollution problems. The DNR itself was a strong advocate of very strict standards to protect fish, wildlife, and land areas, and tended to be very one-sided in its support for these. Any pollution control agency, it was felt, would have to be more realistic and balanced in its approach to standards-setting. Some people felt that the DNR's quasi-developmental and promotional resource activities—such as mining regulation and assistance, park developments, and the granting of water use permits—might compromise tough antipollution work.

Thus while Wisconsin in 1967 sought to consolidate similar programs in order to increase their relationship, Minnesota decided to keep them separate so as to maintain their unique differences. While Wisconsin hoped to maximize administrative efficiencies by setting up a consolidated environmental super-department that would resolve program conflicts internally, Minnesota placed higher value on retaining a system of political advocacy that perhaps created increased administrative problems. It worried that, over time, pollution control and conservation programs might intermingle more and more and the lines between them eventually dissolve. Since department personnel might tend to feel that all conflicts and trade-offs between their programs would be resolved internally by one director, they might feel less and less inclined to voice their views. Gradually, the unique values and differences between pollution control and conservation work might be undermined and lost. The public would hear and see less about resource decisions, and the range of political choice and debate would diminish.

Other reasons for not placing the antipollution unit in the Department of Natural Resources were that the large size of that department might dominate the new antipollution effort. Furthermore, many persons felt that the DNR was lacking in the professionalism and prestige necessary to pollution control regulation at this critical time. Some persons also pointed out that the DNR was composed of widely different, autonomous parts, operating quite independently of one another, each with its own constituency base. Since the divisions were not linked by a departmentalwide planning effort, these persons saw little value in simply adding pollution control programs.

To create a new special mission agency for pollution control was not considered a departure from good administrative principles. It was considered the natural and best way to attack a new problem. The PCA might have its disagreements with the DNR or the two-year-old State Planning Agency, but these conflicts or trade-offs would occur in any event. And, it was argued, they should be debated publicly and resolved by the governor or through some open interagency process, rather than by one administrative official not directly accountable to the voters.

The legislative drafters of the reorganization bill felt that the PCA's initial functional emphasis here should be on regulation. The PCA's enabling statute specifically describes the agency's mission as protecting the state's water, land, and air resources from pollution. There is not much to suggest that the PCA is, or should become, a broader environmental policy-making, planning, or research body. Its task is to *control* harmful physical-chemical pollutants, not *manage* environmental resources. The 1967 reorganization statute stated that the PCA may draw up comprehensive plans for air pollution and land use control as part of its recommendations.[7] The 1969 legislature did require the PCA to draw up a plan for its pollution abatement activities every two years, but this is mainly to be a statement of intended actions.[8]

Although most state legislators felt that creation of the PCA was a good step, the reorganization bill did not receive wide popular support in 1967. The general public, it has been explained, did not really understand or take interest in the new pollution control effort. As in most states, health officials and medical interest groups opposed the PCA, since they would lose control over some antipollution programs. However, the State Board of Health was at a low ebb of prestige and the legislature was not impressed by these arguments. Some of the strongest opposition came from some municipal officials who opposed the role carved out for the state in some sewer issues and permit granting. Some members of the University of Minnesota did not strongly support the reorganization, since they preferred a merger of the PCA with the DNR. Support for the reorganization did come from the press, some environmental interest groups, and several industries who said they preferred to deal with one organization that hopefully would generate more systematic and less random pollution regulations.

The Board's Role

Minnesota, like its neighboring state, Wisconsin, has long operated under the "weak governor" concept of government whereby executive agencies are governed by part-time, citizen policy boards whose members serve appointive terms and are not directly responsible to the governor. Like Wisconsin, Minnesota in recent years has attempted to abandon this system as an outmoded limitation on the responsiveness of executive agencies to elected officials, namely the governor. However, because pollution regulation was considered such a uniquely controversial and emotional subject even in 1967, the legislature designed two bodies to handle it.

The PCA's director and staff were to perform only the highly technical functions of formulating antipollution standards and monitoring harmful pollutants. The staff director was to be directly responsible to the governor who appointed him. The real regulatory decisions, however, were to be made by a policy board. In the reorganization, this board is actually termed the "Pollution Control Agency" and often is referred to as the "Agency".[9] It has the quasi-legislative functions of setting pollution control standards, initiating enforcement cases, and forming all departmental policies and rules.

Thus, the policy leadership for the PCA is group leadership, not a single director. Gordon Rosenmeier, who conceived this strategy, realized that a part-time citizen board might dilute the strong advocacy position of the agency. However, he felt it was needed as a check against the arbitrary power of any one director or governor. The board was supposed to act as the highest decision-making body for the PCA's affairs. Not directly responsible to the governor, it also was to have no ties or debts to, or interest in, the governmental bureaucracy. In the sense that it is to be a separate state organization for policy-making, the board is more like Illinois' Pollution Control Board than Wisconsin's Natural Resources Board.

It was hoped that the board's, or agency's, membership could be limited to five persons so that a cumbersome decision-making process might be minimized. However, the 1967 statute provided for seven members, appointed by the governor, with Senate confirmation, for staggered four-year terms.[10] By statute, no member can be a state official or employee, including membership on other state boards. No more than two members can be municipal officials or officials of other governmental subdivisions, and no member can be a sewer district official. A 1969 amendment expanded this membership to nine, specifying that one member must be "knowledgeable in the field of agriculture."[11] This addition resulted from agriculture's heated battle with the PCA over certain water quality standards.

In Support of Advocacy

Minnesota's advocacy system, with a series of environmental agencies with their own special missions, has required an array of interagency arrangements in order to ensure coordination. This system includes not only equipment, personnel, and data sharing, but also—and in sharp contrast to a state such as New York—elaborate provisions for formal interagency comment, approval, sign-off, and veto. For example, the PCA along with the Health Department may exercise a veto power over all pesticides regulations proposed by the Agriculture Department. New legislation in 1969 authorized both agencies to veto flood plain and lakeshore zoning regulations that were to be developed mainly by the Department of Natural Resources, with the help of the other two.[12] Coordinating organizations were also established. In 1965 the legislature created the State Planning Agency in part to undertake and coordinate resource and environmental planning. In 1967 the legislature sought to expand the role of the existing Water Resources Board, composed of private citizens, to act as a hearing board to settle conflicts between agencies on water questions and to listen to appeals from agency decisions.[13] However, this board was never strong or prestigious enough to act as a conflict-resolution body.

The PCA and the Health Department have some overlapping authority for water quality, and the exact breakdown has never been clearly articulated. The two are to advise each other on water pollution control standards, with the Health Department having the authority to set drinking water standards. They are to offer advice to each other on a variety of permits, although the Health Department actually sets regulations for sewer constructions. While the PCA gives grants and permits for the construction of wastewater treatment facilities, the Health Department offers technical assistance and trains and certifies operators for these. The PCA is located in the same building as the Health Department.

The legislature's commitment to a system of many single-purpose, advocacy agencies is demonstrated by the fact that the PCA initially was very small. In 1967 it had a budget of $263,000 and a staff of 35. Its first director appointed by Republican Governor LeVander, was John Badalich, a civil engineer. Badalich had formerly been the city engineer and member of the sanitary commission of South St. Paul. Some persons felt this disqualified him as director, since that city's clean-up efforts had hitherto been inadequate. Badalich was succeeded by Grant Merritt, who was appointed by incoming Democratic Governor Wendell Anderson in 1971. Merritt is a young lawyer who was formerly a member of the state's best organized and most active environmental interest group, the Minnesota Environmental Control Citizens' Association (MECCA). He represents a new trend in environmental leaders who are legally oriented rather than representative of a scientific or engineering discipline.

CURRENT ORGANIZATION AND ACTIVITIES

Since the reorganization, the PCA has operated in a relatively unemcumbered, straightforward manner, even though the board has proven to be very powerful as a decision-maker. The PCA's organization remains relatively small and noncomplex. It currently consists of three operating divisions in water, air, and solid waste control, two units for administrative and outside work contracts, and, as of 1971, a Special Services Division. The water pollution control effort dominates the agency's activities and has over two-thirds of the professional staff, mainly sanitary engineers who were transferred from the Health Department.

Regulatory Actions

Since the reorganization, the PCA has vigorously pursued its specific mission of pollution regulation. A wide array of standards were set in its first two and a half years. Departmental spokesmen state that a strategy of setting

51

very strict antipollution standards was deliberately pursued, with the idea that variances could be granted later to a particular industry, municipality, or individual if the board deemed compliance would cause undue hardship or was impractical under the circumstances. As in most states, variances may extend the time period for compliance or lessen or otherwise alter the conditions necessary for compliance, with the burden of proof on the "polluter." Since standards are admittedly very tough, the number of variances offered in the future is a critical issue in Minnesota.

By 1969 the PCA had a full set of interstate and intrastate water quality standards, varying according to different water uses.[14] Effluent standards for discharges into all waters limited heat discharges, phosphorous content, and a long list of chemicals and metals (excluding mercury). Secondary treatment or its equivalent was required as a minimum for all industrial and municipal wastes. These regulations also covered the storage of liquids and liquid wastes, including oil, for which permits are issued by the PCA. The PCA argues that it was so far ahead of the federal requirements for interstate water standards that, when separate federal public hearings were held, these were merely duplicative. The final deadline for compliance with this first set of water quality standards was July, 1972. Agriculture feedlot regulations were set in 1971, and the PCA is now updating and issuing new water quality standards.

The PCA has strong authority relating to sewers, which includes the certification of all sewage disposal systems, sewer extensions, and sanitary districts on petition. It is also one of the few state pollution control agencies that has the authority to construct, upgrade, or order the construction of a municipal wastewater disposal system if the municipality has not previously complied with its requirements to abate pollution. In such cases, the construction cost would be assessed back to the municipality.

By mid-1969 the PCA had promulgated statewide ambient air quality and emission standards for six pollutants—sulfur oxides, hydrogen sulfides, oxidants, dustfall, suspended particulates, and a soiling index.[15] Regulations also covered all particulate matter from industrial processes and fuel-burning equipment, odors from animal processing plants and the storage of gaseous wastes, and visible emissions from vehicles. The final deadline for compliance with this first set of standards was July, 1971. Open burning was banned in 1970, and the agency has now proposed a new set of air quality standards in response to federal requirements.

By the end of 1968, the PCA had investigated and classified all the state's solid waste disposal sites.[16] Adopting a strong statewide regulation in January, 1970, the PCA required all counties to have in operation a complete system of sanitary landfills by July, 1972. The location and construction of all landfill sites is strictly controlled to prevent underground water pollution. For example, sanitary landfills must be at least one mile away from municipal wells or municipal water intake facilities, and solid wastes must be compacted as densely as practicable. In addition to regulations prohibiting open burning and unsanitary disposal sites, regulations govern existing and new incinerators, and permits are required for composting (the controlled biological decomposition of certain solid wastes).

The PCA, along with the Agriculture Department, set pesticides standards in early 1970, banning all but seven major types of pesticides. The agency actively monitors radiation emissions from all sources under the state, and this effort will increase under a recent agreement with the federal Atomic Energy Commission (AEC). The PCA was given power in the 1971 legislative session to begin a noise control program. The PCA exercises some authority over power plant siting through its wastewater discharge permits and, under its 1972 air quality implementation plan, requires public hearings for all new power plants. If the proposed plant violates ambient air standards at the site proposed, a permit will be denied.

The PCA has a history of attacking large polluters in the state in an effort to enforce its regulations, and these frequently have involved the agency in long legal battles in court. Two cases highly popular among environmentalists have achieved both statewide and national notoriety, and deserve special mention. Both the PCA's current and previous directors have spent a large portion of their time on them, and they have been regarded by many as significant test cases. The oldest and most widely known case is the state's battle to set radiation standards higher than the federal Atomic Energy Commission's for Northern States Power Company's new nuclear power-generating facility at Monticello.[17] The PCA has claimed that the federal government has inappropriately preempted from the states the authority to set radiation standards, and that the AEC's standards are not strict enough. The case was decided against the PCA in the State Supreme Court in 1970 and after the case was heard by the U.S. Circuit Court of Appeals in St. Louis, it was also turned down in the U.S. Supreme Court by a vote of 7-2. Aside from California's successful effort in the late 1960s to set statewide automotive emission standards higher than the federal government's, Minnesota was the first state to undertake a challenge of the federal government's preemptive standard-setting authority.

Another highly popular battle is the PCA's effort to prohibit Reserve Mining Company at Silver Bay from dumping taconite tailings in Lake Superior, which it has done for some time at the rate of 67,000 tons per day. The PCA tried to prohibit Reserve's taconite dumping in late 1969, but the company resisted in state district court and won on the grounds that the PCA had not proven that Reserve Mining was polluting the lake. In mid-1972, the PCA was appealing that decision to the Minnesota Supreme Court. A Federal-State Lake Superior Enforcement Conference began meeting in May, 1969 and completed its work in April, 1971, concluding that the tailings had a harmful effect on the ecology of the lake by reducing organisms necessary to support fish life.[18] The PCA and the conference endorsed a resolution that Reserve Mining Company draw up plans to dispose of its wastes on land, at a cost it is believed the company can easily absorb. Reserve Mining protests that this is too expensive a method and that it would be forced to close down. Instead, it offered to pipe the taconite tailings directly to the lake bottom. Many persons worry that both these alternatives are harmful. The federal government found the second one unacceptable, and in the spring of 1972 the Justice Department filed suit in federal court requesting an order to "abate the pollution."[19]

With most standards set, the PCA's real phase of enforcement will begin in 1973, when most standards must be met and pollution abatement orders begin to come due. In 1972 the PCA spent much of its time studying compliance plans offered by industries and municipalities, reviewing permit and variance requests, and enforcing existing prohibitions. Maximum fines on polluters are set by statute and are only nominal. A bill offered in the 1971 legislative session to raise these up to $10,000 per day failed to pass. Nor does the PCA have any "cease and desist" emergency powers, as do many other states. This would allow the agency's director to call a temporary halt to any practice, without a prior public hearing, that it considered immediately dangerous to the public health and welfare.

The PCA is, however, among a number of state departments housing assistant attorneys general for the environment. Four assistant attorneys general are currently located in the PCA to perform on-the-spot legal analysis and pursue cases in court, with one acting as the agency's general counsel. Close proximity allows these lawyers to become more intimately involved in pollution cases and gain scientific and engineering expertise. This subsequently reduces the time necessary for the court enforcement process and increases the probability of legal success. As in most states, the attorney general's office has the statutory responsibility of actually prosecuting pollution cases in court. However, the past and current attorneys general in Minnesota are on a decidedly friendly basis with the PCA, and have been willing to allow it to handle many of its cases initially. This contrasts sharply with states such as Illinois, Wisconsin, and New York, whose elected attorneys general are highly political figures and have preferred to make all decisions regarding legal pollution abatement.

Thus far the PCA has made little effort to establish any formal relationship between its water, air, and solid waste programs. With the exception of procedures for the water pollution control division to comment on the sanitary landfill sites approved by the solid waste division, the PCA's three divisions operate quite independently of one another. Grant Merritt argues that his staff is so small that the opportunity for informal communication is large, and he sees no immediate need for formally linking these efforts. The staff also present separate reports to the board on water, air, and solid waste issues, and the board, in turn, deals with them separately.

Nonregulatory Programs

The PCA is a good example of an agency that concentrates on one function—regulation—to the exclusion of most all others. Aside from some necessary and limited program planning, the PCA has done little in-house planning or research. When the need arises, it hires special consultants for specific tasks, and may even house them temporarily in the agency. For example, legislation in 1969 required the PCA to complete a pollution-related land use study, and this was contracted out to a private consultant firm in California.[20] In 1971 the staff tried to engage a consulting firm, National Biocentric Inc., to undertake a study of Reserve Mining Company's financial and employment situation. The board, however, vetoed this move. Much of the scientific and medical research in support of the PCA's activities has been carried out on a contract basis by Health Department personnel in their own laboratories, paid for from the PCA's budget. The PCA also relies on the Conservation Department for some biological research and water data.

The agency has recently set up a new Special Services Division, which is designed to study special pollution problems not handled by the other three operating divisions—for example, radiation, recycling questions, phosphates, power generation, and eutrophication. It is meant to be entirely practical, to handle current agency needs. While it will not undertake scientific research or do long-range planning, it will attempt to become more familiar with work being done elsewhere on these special problems. The division will also attempt to provide some research overview on the entire pollution control field. For example, it will review some economic research being done in the country on standard levels, effluent charges, and other issues. Thus far, the new division has acquired considerable expertise on federal legislation that has proved valuable in informing the PCA on the new federal requirements and the status of important bills. Finally, it will perform public relations activities, a function the current PCA director feels has been neglected.

Until legislation in 1971 authorized a state bonding program, Minnesota did not contribute to federal and local funds for the construction of wastewater treatment facilities. The PCA has always administered these federal funds and now will administer state funds as well. However, technical assistance to localities on treatment works is performed largely by the Health Department. Until recently, the PCA also has had no field staff and its monitoring capability was decidedly weak. Because of this, Merritt explains that his staff has always worked with a critical lack of economic data, and therefore has always acted on a completely reactive basis to such issues as variance requests. What the agency needs, he says, is more precise information. The PCA is attempting to improve its data and monitoring capability, and will set up a predictive monitoring system for Lake Superior and other state waters. Its air pollution monitoring has been concentrated around the seven-county metropolitan area around the Twin Cities, but will expand to other areas. The PCA currently is setting up five regional offices, with a small staff in each.

The Board as Final Decision-Maker

The PCA has had two strong directors and the current 1973 one, Grant Merritt, is particularly so. However, the nine-member Pollution Control Board has always had the final decision-making power and used it. The board not only approves all of the pollution control standards and regulations proposed by the

PCA director, but it also controls most other remaining daily program decisions. It approves all pollution abatement orders issued to industries and municipalities and approves all abatement or compliance plans subsequently submitted. It grants or denies all operating and discharge permits, including permits for sewer extensions. It approves requests for public hearings on permits from industries or municipalities. It grants or denies all variances and time extensions. It must approve all formal enforcement actions against polluters initiated by the agency, and must approve all agency appeals to court decisions.

The board is also intimately involved in the PCA's nonpolicy affairs. For example, it approves all requests from the director for funds to contract out for special research. It takes positions on pollution control bills and measures being discussed in the state legislature, and requests that the PCA director or staff member represent the board's opinion in legislative hearings. For example, a vigorously debated bill to guarantee citizen class-action suits against polluters in the 1971 legislative session not only gave citizens that right to sue alleged polluters for violation of PCA's standards, rules, and regulations, but also shifted the burden of proof to the defendant and allowed citizens to sue according to both the letter and the spirit of existing pollution control law. The board protested these latter provisions, and directed Merritt to reflect this opinion in the legislature. The board also keeps close tabs on the progress of important pollution cases, such as the Reserve Mining case, and requires monthly agency reports. This kind of detailed involvement in agency affairs is in sharp contrast to Wisconsin's Natural Resources Board, which considers pollution abatement orders, permits, variances, and other activities as purely administrative matters to be left to the expertise of the DNR's staff.

Required to meet once a month, board meetings now often go on for days and special meetings are often held. All nine members are usually in attendance, even though financial compensation is minimal. Most issues are thoroughly and often heatedly discussed by the members, and rare is the instance when the board only rubber-stamps the PCA's proposals—for example, it often does this for small sewer extensions, but never for other kinds of operating permits for larger companies. The PCA director and his staff prepare most of the agenda, which the board approves, and they are on hand to present reports and recommendations. However, only since late 1971 has Merritt himself begun to lobby before the board for his opinions. Previously, the staff considered their role to be that of expert technical advisor, presenting all the options and some preferences to the board. They did not believe they should actively lobby for or against most measures before the board. Although more often than not Merritt and his staff now strongly present their own views, Merritt still believes that he should not often attempt to round up support among individual members between the regular meetings. He may canvass individual members by telephone between meetings—for example, on whether to initiate an enforcement action—but this is in the interest of speedily gaining approval or denial.

Board meetings are well attended by interest groups, individuals, and the press. A number of interest groups are always present—for example, MECCA, the League of Women Voters, a few other smaller antipollution groups, municipal groups, and the Minnesota Association of Commerce and Industry (MACI). Representatives of industrial firms are present in force when a particular decision affecting them is on the agenda. Recently, lawyers from Northern States Power Company have attended most every meeting. In general, interest groups tend to focus as much attention on the board as on the PCA itself. Their views are not only forcibly expressed at meetings, but they spend much time calling on individual members in the interim. Minutes of board meetings are written up, printed, and available at the PCA's office. The environmental newsmen of the several newspapers in the Twin Cities, and frequently others, cover all of the board meetings. Frequently, newsmen of the major television networks are present. The board probably receives as much publicity as the PCA itself.

Although the board members are generally regarded as high-quality appointees, there is no doubt that a majority of them have been more conservative than either of the PCA's two directors and the staff, and that some of them are not only sympathetic to but also directly connected with industry. On individual issues where they feel they may be personally affected by a decision, members may leave the room during voting. In 1972, membership included a farmer (required by the 1969 amendment), a doctor associated with the Mayo Clinic, a member of a large paper company (Northwest Paper, Inc.), a former bank vice-president, a retired army engineer, a lawyer, a political science professor, an employee of 3M Company, and a woman environmentalist active in the League of Women Voters and other groups. The last two members were appointed in February, 1972, the woman having been earlier denied appointment by the Senate. Out of these nine, only three or four vote more or less consistently in favor of tough antipollution measures. Prior to 1972, there were only two or three votes that could be counted on. Although on the average the PCA's director probably gains approval on over 70 percent of the matters he puts before the board, most of the "defeats" are in the important areas of permits, variances, and orders. The board has generally approved most of the standards recommended by the PCA, although in 1970 odor standards were diluted to protect agricultural interests.

A Troika in Environmental Quality

Two other agencies besides the PCA work on environmental quality. The Department of Natural Resources (formerly called the Conservation Department) carries out traditional programs for water development and use, fish and wildlife, forests, minerals, and parks and recreation. The State Planning Agency (SPA), created by the 1965 Planning Act, does some long-range, comprehensive environmental planning as well as planning for other social and economic purposes. The SPA is meant to "relate, coordinate, and harmonize planning being carried on by the various agencies in the state."[21] Its mission is to stimulate and assist the specialized planning efforts of each agency and assume direct leadership of some planning projects that involved a number of agencies. It is charged with comprehensive planning that links or coordinates the "fractionalized" planning of individual agencies. However, "state planning must go beyond simply building a comprehensive state plan from a mosaic of individual functional or agency plans." It should "be a creative force in the executive branch by exploring alternative means of accomplishing the overall goals of the State."[22] The governor is head of the State Planning Agency, and in 1966 he designated it as the locus for comprehensive water and related land resource planning.

The SPA is currently undertaking a land use planning study that is regarded by many resource economists as very innovative. By aerial photography, the agency is carrying out an inventory and computerized land classification, region by region. This includes a computerization of the ownership, water, minerals and other characteristics. The staff do not intend, in the short-run, to write a comprehensive statewide plan. Rather, they hope to be able to do what is labeled "selective zoning," whereby a limited number of valuable and endangered land areas are recommended for certain limited uses or nonuses.[23] For example, some areas contain valuable wetlands or a natural flood plain that should be preserved; others are ideal sites for recreational facilities and farming; others are distinctly poor locations for sanitary landfills or highways. If these areas are threatened by another use—for example, the location of a new industry—the SPA hopes to be able to suggest an alternative geographical site for that industry. The agency does not have any zoning authority, so its recommendation will not be binding on other state agencies of the private sector. Another planning study involves an inventory of all state-managed parks, recreation, historical, scientific, and other land sites to determine their best future use.

Although the PCA, DNR, and SPA form a seemingly logical troika for environmental affairs, they have rarely related in the past. Each tends to perform its own highly specialized role, and the interface is only occasional. The directors of the PCA and DNR have stated that they rarely meet with each other. Although both are new, young, and aggressive advocates of their programs, their contact tends to be limited to formal meetings of the governor's new interagency environmental council created in 1972, occasional exchange of technical information among their staff, and some quarrels. Bob Herbst, director of the DNR, has stated that the PCA could benefit from a greater reliance on the biological and other scientific data generated by his staff and his department's vast field operations. However, for the time being the two agencies operate in relative isolation. Their constituencies, likewise, rarely intermingle. The conservation constituency consists of sportsmen and recreation clubs, wilderness groups, forest owners, professional biologists, and others. The pollution control constituency is generally much younger, urban-oriented, and more activist.

Both agencies also seem to be too busy to bother with the State Planning Agency, and the SPA has no way to compel their attention. They tend to regard it as an ivory-tower operation that does not meet the immediate needs and time frame of their work. However, neither the PCA nor DNR does any planning of its own. It is only recently that the legislature gave the DNR funds, along with an explicit directive, to initiate departmentwide planning. In 1971, Governor Anderson also suggested in a special message on the environment to the legislature that the DNR begin a planning effort.[24]

A fourth nonexecutive member of Minnesota's environmental club is the state legislature. In fact, the legislature is one of the first members through its joint committee, the Minnesota Resource Commission (MRC). Originally called the Minnesota Outdoor Recreation Resources Commission, the MRC was created under an omnibus natural resources and recreation act of 1963.[25] Its mission was to make recommendations to the legislature, the governor, counties, and municipalities on a long-range program for developing and protecting natural and recreational resources. It had a small staff and its own funds, from a "penny a pack extra" tax on cigarettes. Because some legislators thought it had become too powerful, a 1967 amendment limited the MRC's role to a legislative service committee, while at the same time broadening its focus.[26] Over the years, the MRC has become increasingly involved in environmental issues, and in 1971 its role was formally extended to all environmental quality matters. The MRC cannot legally act as a substantive legislative committee in the reporting out of bills, but many proposals are assigned to it for study, and it regularly presents proposals and special staff studies to the entire legislature. Most of its recommendations have been adopted. The MRC has always had a strong planning orientation and has funded many recreational, land-use, and pollution studies in the State Planning Agency, DNR,[27] PCA, and the private sector.

EVALUATION

Advantages of an Advocacy Agency

Minnesota demonstrates several advantages of limiting a merger to antipollution programs, rather than including traditional conservation work in a larger environmental superdepartment. A major advantage is that a smaller new state agency can begin work more quickly and vigorously. An initially small, single-purpose organization can focus all of its attention, from the beginning, on effective pollution regulation. Any reorganization creates substantial administrative confusion and political difficulties, but these effects will be minimized if the reorganization occurs within a limited and defined area, such as pollution control. The new agency thereby deals from the outset with only a small number of highly related programs. The new perspective that the reorganization seeks to implement—control of physical-chemical contaminants in the environment—can be easily understood by the staff, the governor, the legislature, and the public.

PCA's first director concentrated most of his energy on setting pollution control standards, and the second director has worked to upgrade and vigorously enforce these. They did not have to go through a long and arduous process of housing, integrating, and balancing a whole range of environmental programs such as fish, forests, and parks. Tough antipollution work was not hindered or publicly embarrassed by potentially biasing programs within the agency such as the development of water and minerals. They did not have to settle internal conflicts between the pollution control staff and, for example, other personnel for fish and wildlife who might lobby for pristinely pure waters. There was no bitterness or harassment from conservationists, who in Minnesota would have opposed a merger of their department with pollution control programs.

When the PCA was set up in 1967, its staff and budget were almost inoperably small, most of its personnel were sanitary engineers who had worked on water pollution in the Health Department, and the air and solid waste control programs were new. The antipollution effort, in general, enjoyed no statewide recognition or popularity. Yet two years later the PCA had gained statewide support and recognition, and its regulatory powers had been substantially increased by the legislature. By the end of 1969, the PCA had promulgated a set of statewide standards for water quality and effluents, and ambient air quality and emissions, and in January, 1970, laid down a statewide requirement for sanitary landfill to dispose of solid wastes. In this, the PCA was ahead of Wisconsin, which had earlier reorganized water pollution control programs and created an environmental superdepartment in 1967. The PCA's standards are regarded as being very tough by state environmentalists and others. By 1970 the PCA had taken on some major polluters in court and became one of the first states to adopt pesticides, odor, and feedlot regulations, and actively began radiation monitoring. Its budget and staff levels have also steadily increased. If the PCA's past record is any indication, and depending on the decisions of the board, it will probably continue to act vigorously as it enters its real enforcement phase in late 1972 and 1973.

PCA's second director, Grant Merritt, is widely regarded in the state as a very strong public advocate for tough environmental clean-up measures, and even a zealot by many conservative legislators and some of the business community. He had gained a substantial reputation, before taking office in 1971, through his legal efforts to prohibit Reserve Mining Company from dumping taconite tailings into Lake Superior. A vigorous spokesman for the PCA, he speaks widely throughout the state and spends a large portion of his time lobbying in the legislature for popular environmental issues and increased authority for his agency. For example, in 1971 he fought for a strong citizen class-action bill, a statewide moratorium on the construction of nuclear power plants, tough regulation of boat waste disposal, and authority for the PCA to regulate noise. A believer in tough enforcement of laws in the courts, he has worked arduously on the Northern States Power radiation and Reserve Mining taconite cases, and has tackled other big polluters such as Northwest Paper and the Twin Cities. He enjoys a sizable and relatively favorable press. Environmental interest groups find him easily accessible, and he is highly popular among them. Merritt is beginning to receive nationwide attention as the leader of a strong, successful pollution regulatory agency, and as a defender of state rights in pollution control. He speaks frequently at regional and national conferences, and has lobbied vigorously in Washington against the federal government's increasing preemption of the states' role in pollution standards-setting.

Paramount in the rationale to keep the PCA separate from the Department of Natural Resources was the belief that conflicts and trade-offs between the program objectives and means of these two agencies were significant enough to be advocated publicly. Political choice and public access to governmental decision-making would thereby be maximized, and the unique differences between the two would be preserved. Although disputes between the PCA and DNR have not been widespread, such conflicts have been publicly aired and duly recorded in the press, as hoped for by proponents of Minnesota's advocacy administrative system. For example, the PCA's interest in tough thermal pollution control has led it to advocate a closed water cycle for cooling and high water use for Northern States Power Company's new plant at Prairie Island, while the DNR has opposed this in its concern for water supply. Since the PCA offers a water discharge permit and the DNR must grant a water use permit, both agencies will have had their say. The PCA believes that the DNR's flood plain zoning provisions are weak, and that the department still has a penchant for dam building over waste treatment as a pollution control technique. On the other hand, the DNR's fish and wildlife personnel have publicly advocated very strict water quality standards to protect habitats, which in some cases the PCA considers unrealistic in economic terms. The two departments have had different opinions on some other state agency programs such as power plant siting and certain land uses.

Minnesota's PCA demonstrates that a small, single-purpose advocacy agency can unite its constituency better than a larger department can. Unlike most states, Minnesota has a strong and united antipollution interest group, which can effectively lobby with the PCA, governor, and legislature on all pollution issues. This group, the Minnesota Environmental Control Citizens Association (MECCA), was formed in 1968 to prod the PCA on one particular sewer issue. Since then it has grown in size and now represents a fairly good cross-section of citizens in the state. MECCA's membership overlaps with other more newly formed and specialized environmental interest groups, and it carries out a strong, consistent, and well-publicized lobbying effort.

There are two chief criticisms of the PCA offered in Minnesota and outside the state, both of which relate to its single-purpose, advocacy mission. First, the PCA is criticized by some industrial and municipal groups for being too tough, which may mean that the agency's pollution clean-up measures are taking hold. The PCA, they complain, takes a far too narrow view of things. Its posture is definitely antiindustry and antidevelopment, its constituency is too radical, and it has become just another special-interest lobby. It is said that the agency's standards are so strict that they not only make compliance difficult, but also are wasteful and may drive industry out of the state or bankrupt some

61

municipalities. For example, the PCA's requirements are such that they may necessitate tertiary wastewater treatment facilities in even some of the smallest communities in the northern and western parts of the state. The PCA's standards against the mining industry and power plants have caused these companies to threaten shutdown or location elsewhere.

The second criticism is more relevant in this analysis, but is somewhat linked in that it claims that the PCA's focus is a too narrow regulatory one. Some scientists and public administration experts worry that the PCA does not have the capability or even the mandate to do broad environmental planning and research, and does not do much inhouse planning and research related to its own regulatory programs. It is too small and thus cannot easily develop an adequate data-gathering and field-monitoring capability. The DNR cannot act as a broad environmental department either, and the State Planning Agency, however good its work, suffers from the ailments of many such state planning bodies—it has no operational responsibilities, no implementation power, often operates in a vacuum, and is usually ignored by line agencies.

Who Is To Be the Environmental Arbitrator?

The existence of this troika of executive agencies—PCA, DNR, and SPA—with important environmental protection programs leaves several important environmental functions unperformed. Since the PCA was created, this has been the topic of much debate, many studies sponsored by the executive and legislative branches, as well as in the private and academic worlds, and proposed legislative amendments. Since each agency focuses on one or two main problem areas, no one has a large enough jurisdictional claim to being *the* environmental agency. This creates several vacuums. First, who should solve conflicts among the environmental troika? Secondly, how should environmental work be co-ordinated, and how can it be assured that all environmental work proceeds according to some comprehensive environmental policy so that issues that cross agency jurisdictions are not ignored? And third, how should environmental protection interests be instilled in other state agencies that have a resource development orientation? In other words, it is understood that a system of many single mission advocacy agencies can go only so far. Then someone must step in to turn narrowly based advocacy into coordinated action.

Is it the governor who can be held most directly accountable to the electorate; consequently, he should make the major policy decisions within the executive branch that involve trading one basic public goal for another. However, there have been several competing recommendations on who should participate in the governor's decision-making for the environment.

One bill, opposed by the PCA and defeated by the 1971 legislature, would have created a large interagency board with the governor as chairman, advised by a citizens' council,[28] Opposition to this structure was based largely on the experience of the seven-member interagency environmental cabinet set up by

Governor LeVander in the spring of 1969 to act as a coordinative and advisory unit to him on environmental matters crossing agency lines. Consisting of those departmental directors whose work most directly—adversely or favorably—affected the environment, this cabinet had proven to be a cumbersome and almost completely ineffective unit. Since each department head concentrated on his own special programs, the only topics discussed were those on which some consensus could be reached or those that did not adversely affect any one department. Thus key issues were avoided. Attendance was irregular and the interagency cabinet was incapable of reacting to an issue that was not an immediate crisis.

Minnesota's Citizen League and the League of Women Voters argue that one highly professionally trained person should be brought on the governor's staff to act as an "environmental czar," making all arbitration decisions.[29] The Citizen League argues that committee arrangements are too inefficient. It also does not favor a formal citizens' council for these tasks, since such councils may have the effect, over time, of reducing informal citizen activities and access. The Minnesota Association of Commerce and Industry has supported a three-member citizen board with one or more members representing the business community. Another proposal, drafted by the legislative staff, created a five-man citizen board in the governor's office, which might have acted nearly full time.[30]

Following the recommendations of the PCA and DNR directors, in the spring of 1972 Governor Anderson created by executive order a five-member Environmental Quality Council (EQC) in his office. This council consists of the director of the State Planning Agency as chairman, the PCA director, the DNR director, the Highway Department director, and the governor's existing environmental liaison person. It has recently hired a full-time executive secretary, with considerable environmental expertise, and eventually will have a small staff. The EQC is advised by a 24-member citizen committee representing a wide array of private interests.

The EQC's mission is to set up guidelines for evaluation and to review and make recommendations on the environmental impact of all state agencies' proposed projects. The governor will exercise veto power over any state project considered to have an adverse environmental effect. The EQC will also consider private sector activities, over which the governor will have recommendation authority only. For example, Northern States Power Company has recently agreed to submit power plant siting decisions to the EQC for review.

The rationale behind the Environmental Quality Council's membership is that only departmental directors have the prestige and competence to make broad recommendations affecting more than one state agency, and they can help implement decisions through their department's programs. A "pro-environmental" and small membership was also sought. However, since the EQC was unilaterally created by a Democratic governor, it is highly likely that the Republican-dominated state legislature will wish to formalize and perhaps change its membership and will statutorily require the submission of environmental impact statements from state agencies to it.

Some persons in Minnesota still hope that the PCA can be combined with the DNR in an environmental superdepartment to reduce program fragmentation and promote administrative efficiency. For example, this merger has been considered and rejected by two gubernatorial task forces since 1968. This consolidation is currently favored by the University of Minnesota's Water Resources Center to allow more comprehensive water and related land resource planning and improved water management.[3 1]

As the PCA's director states, the merger of his agency with the DNR is an ever-present option. For the time being, however, the objections to it have won out, and these are practical and political. Both PCA and DNR directors oppose a merger on the grounds that, on balance, their programs are only slightly related and the problems of integrating them would be immense. Both believe they stand a better chance of increased budgetary support if not co-located. And the PCA director, particularly, feels that the visibility of his programs in their own agency is important to their success. Finally, both argue that they can be better advocates of their missions if separated and they place high value on this role.

The Board Decreases Public Responsiveness

The governor's power to appoint the PCA's director clearly helps make the agency responsive to him and, consequently, to the public. For example, popular concern with environmental protection was high in 1971 when the incoming governor appointed Grant Merritt. The PCA's image under Merritt has almost totally changed from that under its former director. Environmental interest groups ranging from radical to more conventional welcome the agency's new and easy accessibility and its tough-minded posture.

However, it is clear that the nine-member Pollution Control Board is the PCA's final decision-maker, making all the important regulatory decisions and many others besides. In theory, part-time policy boards are supposed to lead to more effective policy-making by acting as a higher, more deliberative body, removed from the bureaucracy, that can take a long-range view of matters and represent the interests of the public at large. Composed of private citizens, they are meant to broaden the base of decision-making by providing input from all walks of life and an overview of agency activities. Boards are meant to serve as a check on the power of any one governor or his departmental director, and the members' overlapping terms are supposed to provide continuity of leadership. Board membership is supposed to be balanced and should increase citizens' direct representation in, and access to, governmental decision-making.

Yet, Minnesota's Pollution Control Board serves almost none of these purposes. Perhaps the major disadvantage is the fact that the board does serve as a buffer between the PCA and the governor, thus decreasing its direct public accountability and responsiveness. The state's chief elected official by no means has effective control over the PCA, because no one governor can easily appoint a majority of board members. Gubernatorial appointees are, in fact, frequently voted down by the state Senate, and the board's overall composition and leanings can be altered only over an extended time period.

Secondly, the board does not take a broad, balanced view—the most obvious disadvantage and chief complaint being that its membership is biased in behalf of some special interests and, as a whole, more conservative than the PCA itself. Effective policy-making that serves all the affected public cannot result from a biased and lopsided base. The theory states that boards are meant to produce judgments reflecting a compromise and balancing of the various interests of its members. However, the Pollution Control Board's decisions typically represent not a broad consensus, but rather the intrusion of special interests. This voting style is particularly clear on some issues. While the board has a fairly good record of approving the pollution control standards recommended to it, it has handed down almost an equal number of wins and defeats on what may be even more critical issues, particularly in the future—the granting of permits and variances, approving of abatement orders and plans, and initiation of enforcement procedures.

The board's decision-making style has two major effects. First, it dilutes the PCA director's authority, advocacy role, and tough stance against polluters. If the board's membership were more balanced, a more consistently firm position might be taken—e.g., less variances would be granted, more permits denied. Secondly, this style often results in inconsistent and unpredictable decisions—a tough action against one firm, a weaker posture in another case. The PCA and board do not present a united front, there is no consistent leadership, and resulting actions are sometimes confusing. Even industrial spokesmen have increasingly complained about this lack of consistency, charging that the PCA sometimes seems to go back and forth on specific standard levels, permits, and orders.

The board's deliberations undoubtedly slow down the process of environmental decision-making. This process is long anyway, since public hearings accompany most major actions. But the board adds another layer of decision-making that is repetitous and slow. For example, deliberations on pollution control standards may continue for six months or more, and even decisions on individual permits and variances may take months.

In spite of its slowness, the board cannot be said to add a great deal that is new to a policy-making discussion. Although several of its members have had professional competence in pollution matters, most have little technical expertise since they are chosen to reflect a variety of interests. Also, in spite of its power, the board is still mainly reactive to the agency. Instead of taking a board viewpoint, the board discusses mainly what the PCA director puts before it. For example, on only a handful of occasions, one in 1971, has the board attempted to persuade the agency to do some planning.[32] Nor does the board encourage significant consideration of pollution interrelationships. Water, air, and solid waste problems are discussed separately. In addressing this issue, however, the PCA's current director does cite several major advantages of the board. First, some board members have been extremely helpful to him on an individual basis. Second, the fact of having to go before the board on most matters often induces him and his staff to do their homework better. In several instances the board has acted as an effective sounding board for some of his ideas and has asked him to take a plan back for further study. However, it is highly likely that this would occur anyway, without the board.

The PCA's current (1973) director cites another practical advantage of the board's existence, that may, however, decrease the PCA's direct public accountability and responsiveness. Merritt has stated that the board may take some immediate heat off the PCA by acting as a buffer between him and the public in two ways. First, much public attention as well as criticism is focused on the board. Thus, the agency probably has to deal with a lower level of criticism and may spend less time visiting with interest groups. This saves the director some time and energy. Second, since interest groups are aware of the board's power and conservative orientation, they probably place less constant demands on the agency. Merritt argues that without the board he might continually be forced to respond to every pollution problem the public declared a "crisis," regardless of its real significance. Without the board he might also be forced to undertake a larger number of court cases, which are costly, time-consuming, and not always realistic. Thus the board sometimes serves as an umbrella for the agency to proceed with its own work with its own priorities and time schedule.

The only benefit of the board's existence may be for citizen access and publicity. Board meetings are always controversial and well-attended by the public and the press. Interest groups frequently testify vigorously and take notes back to their members. They also call board members between meetings to lobby for or against an issue. Minnesota, like its neighbor, Wisconsin, has a long history of creating part-time, citizen-composed policy boards to serve as a check against the power of any one governor or agency director, and many citizens are used to dealing with them. When questioned about the Minnesota Pollution Control Board, several environmental interest groups supported it. Despite the conservative nature of the board, they argued, without it they would be denied a significant access point to real decision-making. No matter how open the agency director may be to their complaints, it makes things easier if there are nine additional people to talk to. The League of Women Voters stated that they wouldn't really know what to do without the board. If disbanded, there would have to be something similar to take its place. Merritt also argues that the board's existence provides a "democratic" public forum.

However, the question here is access to what kinds of persons, with what authority? It seems more likely that the decreased public accountability of the PCA, along with decreased gubernatorial control, more than offsets any gains in citizen access. If one man could be held accountable for all decisions, the system as a whole would be more responsive and effective.

NOTES

1. Minnesota, Laws of 1967, Chapter 882, approved May 25, 1967.
2. Minnesota, Laws of 1969, Chapter 116.

3. Minnesota, Laws of 1969, Chapter 115 (Water Pollution Control Act of 1969).

4. Minnesota, Laws of 1971, Section 116.07.

5. Minnesota, Laws of 1965, Statutes 1971, Sections 4.10-4.17.

6. William C. Walton and David L. Hills, *Water and Related Land Resources State Administration, Legislative Process and Policies in Minnesota, 1970* (Minneapolis: University of Minnesota, Water Resources Research Center, WRRC Bulletin 27).

7. Minnesota, Laws of 1967, Chapter 882, Section 9 (3 and 4).

8. Minnesota, Laws of 1969, Chapter 116, Section 10.

9. Minnesota, Laws of 1967, Chapter 882, Section 2.

10. Minnesota, Laws of 1967, Chapter 882, Section 2 (3).

11. Minnesota, Laws of 1969, Chapter 116, Section 2.

12. Minnesota, Laws of 1969, Statutes 1971, Sections 105.485, 394.25, and 396.03.

13. Minnesota, Laws of 1955, Statutes 1971, Sections 105.71 to 105.79.

14. *Minnesota Administrative Rules and Regulations*, Rules, Regulations, Classifications and Water Standards, Minn. Reg. WPC 1-32, adopted January, April, and subsequent months in 1969.

15. *Minnesota Administrative Rules and Regulations*, Air Pollution Control Rules, Regulations, and Air Quality Standards, Minn. Reg. APC 1-15, adopted May, 1969.

16. *Minnesota Administrative Rules and Regulations*, Solid Waste Disposal Regulations, Minn. Reg. SW 1-11, adopted January, 1970.

17. See, for example, Minutes of the Pollution Control Agency monthly meetings, June, 1969 through March, 1972; speeches by PCA directors John Badalich and Grant Merritt, on file at the PCA, 717 Delaware St. S.E., Minneapolis, Minn.; and David Zwick and Marcy Benstock *Water Wasteland: The Nader Report* (New York: Grossman Publishers, 1971).

18. *Transcript of Proceedings of the Conference, In the matter of Pollution of Lake Superior and its Tributary Basin-Minnesota-Wisconsin-Michigan*, Volumes 1 and 2, August, 1970. See also statement by the PCA, July 9, 1971, and speeches by Grant Merritt, 1971, on file at the PCA, Minneapolis.

19. *Time Magazine*, March 13, 1972, p. 44.

20. Planning Research Corporation, *Pollution Control through Land Use Management*, 2 vols (Prepared for the Minnesota Pollution Control Agency) (Los Angeles, 1970).

21. Walton and Hills, *op. cit.*, p. 186.

22. *Ibid.*

23. The final report has not yet been completed. See *Alternate Programs and Projects for Managing Minnesota's Water and Related Land Resources through the Year 2020*, January, 1971, and *Minnesota Water and Related Land Resources*, June, 1970, Water Resources Coordinating Committee, State Planning Agency, 550 Cedar Street, St. Paul, Minn. See also John R. Borchert and Donald O. Carroll, *Minnesota Land Use and Settlement, 1985* (Prepared for the State Planning Agency, 1970).

24. Governor Wendell R. Anderson, "Restoring and Preserving Minnesota's Environment," Special Message to the 67th Session of the Legislature for Minnesota, April 1, 1971.

25. Minnesota, Laws of 1963, Chapter 790.

26. Minnesota, Laws of 1967, Chapter 86.

27. For example, see *Planning in Minnesota*, prepared by F. Robert Edman for the Minnesota Outdoor Recreation Resources Committee, 1967, and *MRC mid-Decade Review* (St. Paul and Minneapolis: Minnesota Resources Commission, 1969).

28. Bill introduced to the Minnesota House of Representatives, April 13, 1971, H.F. No. 2405, by Representatives Dunn, Norton, Becklin, Munger, and Knutson.

29. "Needed: Better Ways of Making Environmental Choices," The Citizen League of Minneapolis-St. Paul, Committee on the Environment, April, 1971, p. 5.

30. "1969-1970 Report of the House Subcommittee on Water Resources and Pollution, and River Flooding and Drainage," (St. Paul: Minnesota House Research Department, 1970).

31. Walton and Hills, *op. cit.*, p. 41-44.

32. Minutes of the Pollution Control Agency, May 10, 1971 on file at the PCA, Minneapolis.

3

INTRODUCTION

Washington's Department of Ecology (DOE) was created in 1970 to administer the state's previously separated programs for water pollution control, water resources management, air pollution control, and solid waste management.[1]

As tribute to the new department's prestige and image as a broad environmental department, the legislature assigned several new programs to DOE in 1971, including shoreline management,[2] litter control,[3] and review of state environmental impact statements.[4] However, very limited funds were provided to conduct these new activities.

About half of DOE's staff and funds are devoted to the older, more extensive state programs of water quality and quantity. Much of the air pollution regulatory authority is delegated to autonomous regional agencies, and the state's solid waste management effort is mostly planning, financial aid, and an advertising campaign against litter. The new shorelines program is potentially significant authority for the new department; environmental impact review is less important.

While the first goal of Washington's environmental reorganization was to strengthen pollution control and water management through program consolidation, the second goal, and an equal one for Governor Daniel Evans, who initiated the move, was to eliminate the boards that made policy for air and water pollution control. These boards, made up of private citizens and state departmental directors, were appointed by the governor for a term to represent various special interest groups. They met occasionally and made key state decisions. Since terms were staggered, some board members were appointed by previous governors and unresponsive to wishes of a new chief executive. Evans' legislative supporters were successful in abolishing the air and water boards and shifting most of their policy-making powers to the director of DOE, who is appointed by the governor and serves at his pleasure.

But Washington is a populist state and both environmentalists and businessmen feared that this concentration of power in the governor and his appointee might produce arbitrary decisions that would be "politically motivated." Consequently, both groups lobbied successfully in 1970 for the creation of two new types of environmental boards to check the new department's power. The first, the Ecological Commission[5] —a seven-member group of private citizens appointed for staggered terms by the governor—was created to advise the director of DOE. The law requires that labor, industry, and agriculture be represented on the commission, and while the remaining members are not statutorily specified, they also have been selected to represent different points of view. Theoretically, the commission can veto departmental standards but the law is vague, perhaps intentionally, on this point. In fact, the commission is purely advisory and its operations can be heavily influenced by the director who supplies all its funds and staff, much of its information on issues, and most agenda items.

The second organization created to oversee the DOE is the quasi-judicial Pollution Control Hearings Board.[6] This three-member panel is also appointed by the governor to hear appeals from decisions of the DOE and the regional air pollution control agencies. It tries to resolve as many appeals as possible through prehearing conferences, but if reconciliation fails, the board conducts formal or informal hearings and enters orders disposing of the appeals. DOE or the appealing party can then appeal the board's decision to the state's courts. A majority of the cases to date— mostly appeals from regional air quality agencies—has been concluded before the board and never reached court.

Another key issue in Washington's reorganization is the internal structure adopted by the agency that is unique among stage environmental organizations—one based exclusively along functional lines. (See Chart 3.4 for the DOE's structure as of September, 1972.) Initially, DOE completely eliminated administrative, budgetary, and job distinctions based on air pollution, water pollution, water resources, and solid waste management and replaced them by categories of "planning, standards, operations, technical assistance, etc." for all programs. The objective was to integrate the newly combined programs to give a total "environmental" approach. However, coping with this new structure has consumed much of the department's attention during its first years of operation and actual functional integration is still limited. Difficulties of accountability for programs within the department and participation in the state's program budgeting system have required a partial return to a program organizational concept for budgetary and time-accounting purposes.

REORGANIZATION PROCESS

The major impetus for creation of the Department of Ecology came from Republican Governor Daniel Evans, who, since he took office in 1964, had sought to streamline and consolidate state agencies in order to increase his control over the executive branch and realign programs to meet new social needs. In Washington, as across the country, 1970 was "the year of the environment." Public enthusiasm and interest in pollution control programs were high, making that year a logical one for environmental restructuring.

The Governor's Reorganization Efforts

The process leading to the environmental reorganization began in 1968 when Governor Evans appointed a Task Force on Executive Reorganization, which recommended the creation of several new state departments, including a cabinet-level department of environmental quality to administer water and air pollution control and solid waste management programs.[7] The task force expressed the need for streamlining the executive branch this way:

State government today faces a crisis. Every year, the role played by government in our lives becomes more important. Relations between the chief executive and those who work with him continually grow more complex. An expanding federal bureaucracy increasingly impinges on areas once thought the primary responsibility of the state. Governmental machinery that functioned well enough in a simpler time is no more adequate to cope with today's complex problems than an abacus in the age of the computer.[8]

A chief aim of each reorganization recommended by the task force was to strengthen the governor's control over executive agencies. The group felt that the governor had been denied an effective policy and managerial role because of the proliferation of agencies and part-time, policy-making boards.

At that time, there were three main public units for pollution control work:

1. *Water Pollution Control Commission,*[9] which set and enforced water quality standards for all surface and ground waters of the state. The commission was composed of the directors of the Departments of Water Resources, Fisheries, Game, Health, and Agriculture. The commission had its own staff that carried out water quality monitoring, enforcement, water surveys, issuance of industrial waste discharge permits, approval of design criteria for new disposal facilities, and approval of state and federal grants for the construction of municipal wastewater treatment facilities. Other divisions carried out program planning and administrative functions.

71

2. *Air Pollution Control Board,*[10] composed of nine citizen members serving part time, who by statute included representatives of the Health Department (chairman), the Agriculture Department, the University of Washington or Washington State University, labor, a city, a county, two representatives of industry, and one representative of the "public at large." The board's major role was to establish and then oversee regional air pollution control authorities, which were responsible for air quality standards and enforcement in their areas. The board's staff work was done by the Health Department. The state set standards and enforced them only in areas where no regional authority existed, and for four sources of air pollution considered to be of statewide significance.

3. *Health Department, Division of Solid Waste Management,* administered the solid waste management activities, which were enacted in 1969,[11] and which were intended to be administered by a "department of environmental quality" when it was created. The new program was to be supervised by a seven-member Solid Waste Advisory Committee.

Legislation to consolidate these three programs was introduced in 1969, but failed, in part, because of lack of strong backing from conservationists. Then, in January, 1970 the state's Office of Program Planning and Fiscal Management (OPPFM), a new agency that conducts planning and budgeting work, recommended creation of a cabinet-level state department for pollution control.[12] OPPFM pointed out, as the governor's task force has done previously, that fragmentation of policy-making authority was hindering effective integrated pollution control and waste recycling.

By 1970 the environment had become a commanding political issue, creating bipartisan support for a new department, although the Democratic version of the enabling legislation[13] differed on the three key organizational issues from the Republican governor's bill.[14] These key issues were: (1) which environmental programs to combine, (2) should there be a policy-making board or commission, and (3) should a special adjudicative board be created.

The Environmental Programs Combined

The Democrats proposed a consolidated Department of Pollution Control to administer water pollution, air pollution, and solid waste controls. This alternative was supported by the Labor Council, the Association of Washington Business, and the Washington Environmental Council (WEC), a coalition of conservationists and environmentalists that actively lobbies in Olympia.

The Republican version called for a Department of Environmental Quality, to include water pollution control, air pollution control, solid waste management, and water resources management. Water resources was included, in part to ease out that program's existing director and in part to satisfy the conservationists of the state who for ten years had been urging for a consolidation of water quality and quantity programs.

72

As early as 1959, a 17-member study group called the Water Resources Advisory Committee recommended combining the functions of water quality from the Water Pollution Control Commission and Health Department with the regulation of water use by industry and agriculture from the Department of Conservation. The group argued that water quantity and quality were inseparable issues, particularly since most economical dam sites had been developed in the state and the only added sources of water would have to be produced by recycling existing supplies. This, of course, required water quality management. These analysts evidently did not fear that the development orientation of the water resource program would dominate or bias the water pollution regulatory effort, perhaps because the water resource program was weak.

In 1967 a Water Resource Department was created,[15] taking water resource planning and management functions out of the Conservation Department, which was then abolished.[16] The new department was run by a director who was appointed by the governor and advised by a Water Resources Advisory Council, composed of the heads of the Departments of Water Resources (chairman), Health, Fisheries, and Game, Director of the Water Pollution Control Commission, and six private citizens representing the "public."

However, the new Water Resources Department continued to administer the water management program in the resource development spirit that is contained in its 55-year-old statutes. These were primarily the activities of adjudicating water rights claims and processing applications for water rights and flood control permits. Even in these tasks the department was estimated in 1970 to be some 20 years behind in adjudication programs, and high-level state officials feared some streams were overappropriated.

In Washington, as in many Western states, water rights are considered a property right, unlike discharging wastes to a waterway, which is considered a regulated privilege. Like staking out the old homestead, the first to claim a water right has an absolute right to it in perpetuity, once he perfects the claim.

Furthermore, the legislature had assigned the Water Resources Department the task of drafting a state water plan, but this work was never completed. These facts led many state legislators and executive officials to wish new program leadership for the water management activity.

Even the irrigating farmers of eastern Washington, the principal constituency of the department, did not oppose the transfer of water resources to DOE, because they, too, agreed that a streamlining of the program was needed.

Although many interest groups initially preferred the Democratic version of programs to combine, the Republicans finally garnered the support to secure the governor's version in the legislative conference committee that drafted the final text of the law.

Chart 3.1 summarizes the environmental programs not assigned to DOE, including some anti-pollution activities, conservation and natural resource management work.

Unlike states such as Wisconsin and New York, there was no major effort in Washington to create an environmental superdepartment, combining

CHART 3.1

Environmental Programs Not Assigned
to Washington's Department of Ecology

Program	Department or Agency
Pesticides	Agriculture Social and Health Services
Drinking water quality	Social and Health Services
Radiation	Social and Health Services New Thermal Power Plant Site Evaluation
Noise abatement	No noise control law existed, but the problem was mentioned as possible concern of Ecology Department
Thermal power plant siting (fossil-fueled and nuclear)	New Thermal Power Plant Site Evaluation Council Commerce and Economic Development
Forests	Natural Resources
Parks	Parks and Recreation
Wildlife	Game
Fish	Game and Fisheries
Campgrounds	Parks and Recreation Natural Resources Fisheries Game
Land use planning	Natural Resources Commerce and Economic Development
General land use controls	Natural Resources on public lands and local governments on other land
Industrial facilities siting	Commerce and Economic Development, Local governments
Mines (including strip mining control)	Natural Resources
Landscaping of public lands	Highways Parks and Recreation
Billboard control	Highways
Certification of shellfish beds	Social and Health Services

pollution controls and water management with other conservation and resource management activities. In Washington these other programs are administered by several departments, each with their own traditions, directors, boards, and strong political constituencies. By contrast New York and Wisconsin's conservation programs had been combined in one conservation department prior to reorganization. The other resource departments in Washington include the Game, Fisheries, Parks and Recreation, and Natural Resources Departments. This last department[17] is a resource management and development agency with jurisdiction over public lands and directed by the Commissioner of Public Lands, Bert Cole, an elected official who is a Democrat.

While water resource management had long been regarded as highly compatible with water quality control, quite a different attitude prevailed with respect to natural resource use programs such as forests, parks, fisheries, and minerals, particularly among conservationists. The DNR resource development activities, particularly, are seen to conflict directly with the environmental enhancement goals of the DOE.

The Washington State Constitution and its federal Enabling Act requires the DNR to administer the 3 million acres of land deeded to the state "for the benefit of the common schools"—meaning state revenues. Some of this is agricultural land, but most is forest land. The department not only manages forests as a crop, but with the added requirement of producing income for schools. Some environmentalists worried that, as a consequence, a too close working relationship had developed between the DNR and the private timber and logging concerns. Likewise, the DNR regulates mining on state lands, which also is developed in part to produce income for schools.

No matter how much the DNR might be motivated by environmental goals, its development-oriented activities were, inherently, seen as potentially biasing to tough pollution regulation if housed within the same environmental department.

Abolishing Policy Boards

The second key reorganization issue was whether policy for the new department was to be made by a board or by the departmental director. A major reorganization goal of the governor was to shift policy-making powers from part-time appointive boards to the DOE director, whom he would appoint, and who would serve at his pleasure. The governor recommended abolishing the air and water pollution boards and creating a new board composed of departmental directors and private citizens, but with only advisory powers.

It is the tradition of Washington state government to set up boards and commissions composed of private citizens selected to represent various special interests to make policy for many departments. These groups are seen as a necessary check on the powers of the chief executive, who, it is feared, might take arbitrary and "political" actions if given too much power. Members are appointed for staggered terms, some by a previous governor, and do not necessarily respond to the wishes of the current chief executive, who is supposed to be the present choice of the public.

While these bodies are meant to bring varied views and broad citizen participation to state pollution control policy-making, they turned out, as was the case in most states, to be bastions of the regulated interests, which reduce public participation in state programs and dilute regulatory controls. Boards reduced the accountability of state decision-makers to the public, for their members could not be recalled for the quality of their decisions, but only for "cause."

The Democratic version of the 1970 legislation called for the traditional style policy-making Pollution Control Board, with seven members to be appointed by the governor. This leadership alternative had been supported in 1969 by the governor's own Task Force on Executive Reorganization. In addition, this position was supported by the environmental, labor, and business groups alike. Each group feared arbitrary and politically motivated actions of a strong departmental director that might be contrary to their own interests.

However, this leadership question was a "gut issue" with the governor, and he ultimately prevailed to a major extent in the final legislation. The act called for a single director appointed by the governor, but to pacify environmental and industry groups, provision was made for a seven-member, part-time Ecological Commission to advise the director, with limited veto powers over environmental regulations. (See Section on "The Ecological Commission" p. 92 ff.)

The Adjudicative Board

The same unusual alliance of industrialists, environmentalists, and labor that supported a policy commission was successful in securing a second organization designed to check the power of the DOE. A quasi-judicial board to hear appeals from departmental decisions and regional air quality agencies was included in bills passed by both the Democratically controlled Senate and the Republican House. Authority to hold hearings on violations of departmental rules, permits, licenses, and standards had previously belonged to the boards and commissions along with policy powers, but proponents of the new appeals board felt this quasi-judicial task conflicted with the department's responsibility of setting standards and prosecuting violators. This appeals power was the only one that previous boards held that was not transferred to DOE.

The Washington Environmental Council favored a board to whom they could appeal decisions of a weak director who might, for instance, grant more waste discharge permits than they thought appropriate for environmental quality. This group also felt the director could be tougher if he were not also an arbitrator, since he then could function unfettered as an advocate for the environment. WEC also favored strong investigatory powers, including subpoena powers for fact-gathering purposes.

The Association of Washington Business and various industrial groups supported the board, but for opposite reasons. They hoped such a board would safeguard their own interests against a potentially biased and too tough departmental director. They saw the body as adding another layer in the pollution enforcement process.

Opponents of such a board, including the governor, pointed out that the Administrative Procedures Act of the state would apply to the new department, assuring appeal to the courts for those who objected to departmental decisions. Further, since an appeals board would not eliminate court appeal, they feared a real potential for slowing down the antipollution enforcement process. However, blocking such a board was not a key issue for the governor, and since both environmentalists and industry supported it, he eventually withdrew his opposition.

Thermal Power Plant Site Evaluation Council

The legislature also created in 1970 a Thermal Power Plant Site Evaluation Council,[18] an interagency body designed to consolidate into one process and one permit all the state's regulatory requirements relating to power plant sites and associated transmission lines. Governor Evans had already established the group by executive order in 1969, based on the recommendations of the governor's Advisory Council on Nuclear Energy and Radiation (established in 1950) and the legislature's Interim Joint Committee on Nuclear Energy (set up in 1967), but in 1970 he sought legislative endorsement.

The council is only advisory to the governor, who actually issues the permit and may accept or reject the council's advice. It consists of the directors of those 12 state agencies responsible for resources and the environment, including the DOE. Other departmental members are Fisheries, Game, Parks and Recreation, Social and Health Services, Commerce and Economic Development, Natural Resources, Civil Defense, Agriculture, Interagency Committee for Outdoor Recreation, Utilities and Transportation Commission, Office of Program Planning and Fiscal Management, Planning and Community Affairs Agency, and a temporary member appointed by the legislative authority in the county in which each proposed site is to be located.

The motive for creating the siting council was to establish a procedure whereby the state could speak with a single voice to the federal Atomic Energy Commission, local governments, other states, the power industry, and individuals. Also, it was intended to reduce red tape and conflicting state requirements on applicants. While industry supported creation of the council, primarily because it would eliminate necessity for dealing with several different agencies for certification of a particular site, some governmental agencies worried about the dilution of their decision-making power. Some environmentalists also feared that the "one-stop" approach might mean that conservation interests would be outnumbered by development-oriented departments, and thus their influence would be less than under the many separate permits system.

The siting council's authority is limited to thermal power plants (fossil fuel and nuclear), and is further limited in terms of the size of the proposed installations. It has no authority to consider proposed hydroelectric projects, pumped storage facilities, or the like and no authority to examine nuclear waste disposal facilities. A minimum of two public hearings must be held on each permit application, and both the governor's actions and rules adopted by the council are subject to judicial review in the courts, although not the Pollution Control Hearings Board. While the permit supersedes all other state permits, it is not clear who is supposed to conduct surveillance and enforce permit requirements—the council or individual state departments. The council is not authorized to undertake a comprehensive policy and planning approach to energy issues, e.g., considering such factors as demand for power and alternate power sources. Rather, it reacts on a case-by-case basis to each siting application it receives. It also is not involved in the site selection process, but rather reviews the sites selected by the applicant.

One of the most innovative features of the law requires that a legal representative be appointed to represent environmental interests in each case the council considers.[19] This environmental advocate participates as a party to the processes of review and selection.

This council had only reviewed and approved one application by 1973. It was an uncontroversial site approved for a nuclear facility at Hanford, the site of other nuclear energy operations.[20]

DOE'S ACTIVITIES AND FUNCTIONS

The Department of Ecology came into existence in July, 1970, and Governor Evans appointed John Biggs as director. Biggs, a career state employee with 37 years in Washington government, worked his way up the ranks of the Game Department to become its director in 1951 and from there went to the DOE. He is regarded as a seasoned state administrator, nonpartisan, and politically savvy. More of a traditional conservationist than an environmental activist, he has built a strong constituency among the sportsmen and fishermen of the state and has a record of opposing various public works projects, such as dams and dredging, harmful to fish and game.

Biggs' style is to be very open and direct with all interest groups and private citizens. But in seeking compliance with regulations he prefers to negotiate with polluters and work out agreements privately, avoiding open confrontation either in the courts or the press. He is more apt to invite company officials into his office for a private negotiating session than to levy a fine, issue a regulatory order in the early stages of proceedings, or go to court.

Contrary to the strategy in Illinois, Biggs sees problems with having negotiations take place in public proceedings such as administrative hearings with statements "on the record," feeling that this polarizes parties and does not secure added environmental control. Biggs does not see penalties and court action as a key deterrent to potential polluters or as a means of strengthening the hand of the state in negotiations, but rather as a sign of failure of administrative bargaining sessions.[21] This is the older strategy of pollution program administration that prevailed in state and federal programs until the late 1960s and continues in most states today. This strategy is also shared by Biggs' top staff, all of whom were transferred with the DOE's programs in 1970. Biggs sees the close control of the state's permit systems as his strongest enforcement tool.[22]

The new department that Biggs took over in 1970 devotes about half its staff and funds to water protection. The water resources and water pollution control programs have 115 out of 253 of the current staff. Water program funds are about $3 million annually out of the $6.7 million for the whole DOE (construction grants are excluded from these figures). The DOE's new program for shoreline management can also have significant impact on the state's water resources. In contrast, the DOE's air pollution control and solid waste management programs lag far behind its water programs in terms of regulatory and other authority, staff time, and funds.

Water Pollution Control

Water pollution control program elements are to:

1. *Set water quality standards for interstate and intrastate waters.* The interstate standards were set in December, 1967 to meet federal requirements[23] and the intrastate standards were approved in 1970,[24] just prior to creation of DOE. Since 1970, DOE has established a standard for dissolved nitrogen[25] in response to massive fishkills caused by nitrogen supersaturation from spilling water over hydroelectric dams on the Snake and Columbia rivers. By March, 1973, dissolved nitrogen is not to exceed 110 percent of saturation at the point of collection regardless of the quality of the surrounding waters.

2. *Make grants to help fund municipal wastewater treatment plant construction.* Funds come from a $25-million clean water bond issue approved in 1968. DOE also approves local government applications for federal construction funds. In the 1969-71 biennium, DOE made grants totaling $12. million, of which $4. million was bond money and the remainder general state funds. Authorized funds for 1971-73 total $21.4 million, the unexpended funds from the bond issue. DOE also approves local government applications for federal construction grants. A bond issue approved on the 1972 election ballot authorizes $225 million for wastewater and solid waste management facilities. Another $75 million was okayed for water supply and $40 million for recreation (not a DOE responsibility).

3. *Approve permits required for discharge of waste to state surface or ground waters.* Permit authority includes review of design criteria, issuance of

temporary permits if necessary, and approval of a permit valid for five years. Current industrial permits total 1,241.[26] Municipal permit requirements did not take effect until July, 1972,[27] but 487 municipalities and sewer districts are expected to apply for permits. DOE may grant to municipalities the power to issue waste discharge permits, but has not done so to date.

4. *Authorize and approve pollution control and abatement plans for drainage basins.* DOE has designated 62 drainage basins and issued planning guidelines to localities who must draft plans and submit them to the department for approval following public hearings.[28] After July, 1974, federal and state construction funds may go only to municipalities that have adopted such a plan. No project will receive state funds unless it qualifies for federal money. The plans will coordinate all major discharges and encourage regional treatment. Since passage of the law in 1967[29] until July, 1972, DOE has adopted only one comprehensive plan comprising two basins. Localities are in various stages of preparation of 40 other basin plans.

5. *Administer Pollution Disclosure Act of 1971.*[30] This act requires all major commercial and industrial dischargers into water and air to monitor and file annual reports with DOE on discharges, nature of enterprise, and process materials. The act requires that discharges shall be afforded all known, available, and reasonable treatment regardless of the quality of the receiving water and regardless of the standards for the waters.

6. *Certify water or air pollution abatement facilities for industry*[31] prior to installation to entitle the industry to tax relief, which may be a deduction or exemption from sales or use tax or a credit of 2 percent cumulatively per year of the total costs of the facility for the life of the certificate.

7. *Administer oil pollution control law.* This 1969 law[32] is by far the toughest regulatory law administered by DOE. Approved in the furor created by massive spills such as Santa Barbara's, the act outlaws the discharge of oil into waters of the state from any ship or any facility located offshore or onshore "regardless of the cause of the entry or faculty of the person having control over the oil."[33] Thus, strict liability is established for damages to private or public persons or property. Civil penalties of up to $20,000 a day are authorized, while the limit for other water pollution violations amounts to only $100 a day. The polluter is also liable for clean-up costs. Enforcement of this act is being increased and nine monitors of oil transfer operations were hired by August, 1972.

8. *Monitor at 75 permanent water sampling stations and test* about 18,000 to 20,000 samples a year.

9. *Enforce the Water Pollution Control Act.* Enforcement and penalty provisions include authority for civil penalties, regulatory orders, and damage claims. Civil penalty provisions authorize the DOE director to issue written notice to a polluter assessing a penalty based on a formula of $100 a day for each violation and $100 a day for each day thereafter or $20,000 for an oil spill. The recipient of the notice has 15 days to respond and if none is made, the director may request the attorney general to bring an action in superior court to recover the penalty.

Regulatory orders are issued to notify any person violating or about to violate the Water Pollution Control Act. These orders give the recipient 30 days to file a report outlining corrective measures. If any person having an economic or noneconomic interest feels aggrieved by the order, that person is entitled to a hearing before the Pollution Control Hearings Board if an appeal is filed within 30 days of the order. In addition, the state attorney general may bring an action to recover damages necessary to restock waters of any injured or destroyed aquatic life, wildlife, or vegetation and to restore the water quality.

Emergency hearings can be called by the director within 24 hours.

Civil penalties have been the most common enforcement device. However, the fines are low (except for oil pollution) because of statutory ceilings and because DOE sets some fines low and mitigates or drops others it initially levied. Even these have been mostly uncollected because they are waived by the department or in the extended appeal process. Table 3.1 shows the amounts of fines collected from violators of the Water Pollution Control Act. Typical of fines paid are the $200 fine against the ITT Rayonier paper mill at Port Angeles for violating a waste discharge permit condition, and a $100 fine against Weyerhaeuser Timber Company in Longview for discharging untreated wastes into the Columbia River. Most of the collected fines since 1970 have been about $100-$250, while a few have been in the $5,000 range—including two oil pollution fines—one for $15,000 against the United Transportation Company for an oil spill in Anacortes and another for $20,000 against Pan Alaska Fisheries, Inc. for the "Mercator" oil spill.

In the first six months of 1972, two maximum fines of $20,000 were imposed for a June 4, 1972 oil spill at the Atlantic Richfield Refinery at

TABLE 3.1

Civil Penalties Collected for Water Pollution Violations in Washington

YEAR	$ Collected	Number of Cases	Average Amount Collected Per Case
1970	$35,025	51	$687
1971	$22,000	41	$537
1972 (Jan-July)	$ 8,530	21	$406

Sources: 1971–1971 Annual Report of Natural Resources and Recreation Agencies, State of Washington, December, 1971, p. S-5; 1972–*Ibid*; 1973–DOE press releases dated April 14 and August 21, 1972.

Cherry Point, a facility twice approved for state and federal permits by DOE. These two oil pollution fines in 1972 also remain unresolved, pending outcome of appeals.

One observer reported that only 5 percent of imposed water pollution fines had been collected for the year ending July, 1972.[34] Commenting on this record of collecting fines, Director Biggs called the record "awful."[35] For instance, over one-half of the fines assessed for oil pollution from July, 1970 to July, 1972 were dropped or reduced. These actions were taken on the oil pollution fines:[36]

$ 13,000   fines in seven cases that DOE decided after imposing that it did not have sufficient evidence to litigate, i.e., dropped.

$ 28,000   the amount that DOE reduced fines it had initially imposed on 11 polluters.

$ 8,600   amount of fines dropped because parties agreed to take some corrective action.

$ 46,500   amount in 11 cases where alleged polluters appealed to the department, asking for a reduction of the fine. DOE will not reduce them and will appeal to the hearings board.

$ 14,500   amount collected on 23 cases without litigation.

$ 25,250   amount of fines referred to the attorney general for collection in the superior court.

$136,000* Total fines assessed by DOE against oil polluters.

Because of the public's opposition to uncollected and low fines, DOE in late 1972 adopted a policy of imposing maximum fines in most instances and opposing any suspensions or mitigations.

DOE estimates that all industries and municipalities are in compliance with DOE water quality standards schedules. There are no water variances issued, but DOE has approved changes in schedules for installation of facilities. In one instance the DOE granted a one-year waiver of pollution control requirements on the Weyerhaeuser pulp mill in Everett after the company announced it would close in 1973 because of costly pollution controls. The real question is whether schedules are tight enough. For instance, the Scott pulp mill at Everett has been granted a final compliance deadline of 1978 for installation of wastewater treatment devices estimated to cost $52 million. The federal Environmental Protection Agency and many environmentalists want to move up the deadline that was established by DOE's predecessor. But Biggs said if the federal government chooses to sue Scott to speed up the project, it also will have to take on the state, which will stand with the company.[37]

---

*Figures rounded.

Water Resources Management

The water resource management program is the oldest that DOE administers, dating to 1917 when the state surface water code was enacted. The program[38] is to:

1. *Allocate surface and ground water rights; issue permits for water withdrawal or diversion.* DOE decisions on water rights matters can be appealed to the Pollution Control Hearings Board and 21 cases were appealed from July 1, 1970 through June 30, 1972.

2. *Register water rights claims.* The water rights claims registration act of 1969[39] required claimants to register with DOE by June 30, 1974 all claims to divert or withdraw proposed waters that have not benefited by permit or certificates issued by DOE or one of its predecessor agencies. The department estimates that some 100,000 to 300,000 such claims may exist. Between July 1, 1969, when the act became effective, and July, 1972 the department received 20,996 claims and registered 15,162 of them. The remainder were returned for revision. Impetus for passage of this act was in part due to Congressional debate of the diversion of Pacific Northwest waters to the Southwest and the resulting ten-year moratorium that was declared for study of such diversion. Also the state needed to investigate and adjudicate the extensive unrecorded claims. The registration law purports to extinguish all rights not registered by the 1974 deadline, which some DOE officials admit may violate Washington's constitution.

3. *Set standards for water-well drillers and issue permits to drillers.*

4. *Certify and issue permits for weather modification.*

5. *Administer reclamation project loans.*

6. *Give flood control grants.*

7. *Set minimum flow and water withdrawal standards.*

8. *Test ground water supply and quality by a series of test wells.* Five of these were drilled in eastern Washington in the past two years.

9. *Issue of reservoir permits and minimum design criteria for storage dams.*

10. *Regulate hydroelectric projects.*

11. *Issue flood control permits* to construct, operate, and maintain works on banks in and over a channel, or over and across the flood plain or flood way in established flood control areas.

12. *Conduct dam safety inspections and review and approve engineering plans and specifications for dam construction.*

13. *Develop guidelines for control of storm water runoff.*

14. *Prepare the state water plan.* The Water Resources Act of 1971[40] mandated, for a second time, the drafting of a state water plan. The department is developing the state water plan now to meet the mid-1975 deadline.

15. *Conduct geologic, hydrologic, and meterological studies.*

Air Pollution Control

Washington State's approach to air pollution control is to decentralize most authority to autonomous regions. The Clean Air Act of 1967[41] created a state air pollution control board[42] and authorized it to establish regional air pollution control authorities, in which contiguous counties would join. Nine of these authorities have been established, covering 26 of the state's 39 counties and 93 percent of the population.

Each regional authority has its own board of directors representing the counties and major cities involved and one member at large. They set their own standards, which must be at least as stringent as state and federal minimum standards. The regions approve variances, which can allow deviations from standards for periods of time not limited by statute; require approval of a notice of construction for any new contaminant source; monitor; and initiate all penalties and enforcement actions against violators of their standards and permits.

The remaining DOE role, then, consists of four types of activities:

1. *Set minimum standards* that apply statewide for ambient air quality and emissions. Surveillance and enforcement of these standards is left to regional agencies. Chart 3.2 lists those standards DOE has adopted or amended. Some standards were first adopted in response to the federal Environmental Protection Agency requirement for states to adopt air quality implementation plans. Others were modified to conform with federal formats.

2. *Coordinate activities of regional agencies* and offer technical and financial assistance. DOE helps prepare some grant applications and in the six federal air quality regions the state has developed it is responsible for the air quality implementation plans. All local agencies must submit a quarterly report including all enforcement actions and significant activities to DOE. Funding of regional agencies is approximately one-fifth by local governments in a region, one-fifth by the state, and three-fifths by the federal Environmental Protection Agency. DOE may take over from a regional agency that does not perform adequately, but has not yet found it necessary to do so.

3. *Regulate "special sources"* DOE considers to be of statewide significance. DOE has the power to preempt from regional authorities all jurisdiction over key sources. This was done, prior to DOE's creation, for automotive air pollution (which is now exclusively regulated by the federal government) and the state's seven kraft and nine sulfite-type pulp mills and seven aluminum plants. DOE has preempted no new sources. For these industrial "special sources" DOE sets emission standards, grants variances, conducts surveillance and monitoring, and is the only agency to levy penalties and initiate enforcement actions against them. While there is no air emission permit system, DOE reviews notices of construction for new contaminant sources. This division of responsibility and the state and air quality regions can result in such situations as, for example, power boilers within kraft mills in Seattle, Everett, Tacoma, and Port Angeles coming under control of the Puget Sound Air Pollution Control Agency, while the mills' remaining air emissions are under state authority. Unlike states such as Illinois and New York, where there are state programs *and* local programs in major cities regulating the same air pollution sources, in Washington it is *either* a state program *or* a regional program, but *not both* for the same source in one area.

84

4. *Administer all aspects of the program for that 7 percent of the population that does not reside within a regional agency's jurisdiction.*

DOE enforcement provisions require regulated sources to submit a proposed schedule for their own compliance, which is reviewed by the director. A regulatory order establishing a compliance schedule is then issued. An oral hearing may be requested prior to the order. If the compliance schedule is violated, a notice of violation is issued. The next step is a meeting with the polluter and a request by DOE that he provide "assurance of discontinuance." Failure to comply at this point can result in a civil penalty of a fine up to $250 daily for each day of discharge. DOE can obtain a restraining order or injunction from Superior Court after the notice of violation is issued. There are provisions for faster procedures during emergencies.

DOE orders may be appealed to the Pollution Control Board. No appeals have been made from DOE air pollution control decisions for the year ending June 20, 1972, but 84 appeals have been made on civil penalties imposed by regional authorities—most by the Puget Sound Agency.

As in many states, the air pollution control agency for a large urban area—the Puget Sound Air Pollution Control Agency (PSAPCA) in Washington's case—has a larger program than the state agency. In 1971, PSAPCA had a staff of 50 compared to DOE's 32 in air pollution and the regional agency had a large budget. DOE's director would like to see the state gradually assume statewide responsibility for comprehensive air pollution control with emphasis on major sources of pollution.[43] Some prominent legislators feel even more strongly that the system of local regions should be phased out in favor of state control and this view was the subject of serious discussions by legislative leaders in the 1972 session.

Solid Waste Management

The state's solid waste management program consists of technical and financial aid to local governments in planning, implementation, training, and enforcement. As a follow-up to the 1969 act [44] the legislature appropriated $669,000 to fund local planning between July 1, 1970 and June 30, 1973. Of the 39 counties, 38 will finish their plans by July, 1973, providing a compliance schedule for converting all land disposal sites to sanitary landfills, a state-established minimum. Implementation of these programs is carried out by local governments where the health department is responsible for issuing disposal site permits which are then reviewed by the Department of Ecology. Enforcement is by both the local health department and the DOE regional staff.

The department has different guidelines for preparation of 20-year solid waste management plans. Counties and cities draft these plans initially and submit them to DOE for review and approval. County plans must include agreements with cities and implementation schedules, together with permit

CHART 3.2

Air Pollution Standards Adopted or Amended by DOE

Standard	Action Taken/Date	Citation
Minimum emission standards that apply statewide for other than "special sources"	Adopted, Jan. 1972	Chapter 18-04 WAC*
Sulfur oxides (minimum ambient air quality standard, statewide)	Amended, Jan. 1972 (originally adopted Apr. 1970, before DOE's creation)	Chapter 18-56 WAC
Emergency episode plan for air pollution control during health emergencies	Adopted, Jan. 1972 pursuant to 1971 law (Chapter 194, Laws of 1971 Extraordinary Session)	Chapter 18-08 WAC
Open burning regulations, minimum standards and a requirement for permits for commercial and agricultural open burning; DOE standards and permits apply unless a local agency has a permit system	Adopted, Jan. 1972	Chapter 18-12 WAC
Suspended particulates (minimum air quality standards, statewide)	Amended, Jan. 1972. (originally adopted in 1970 before DOE's creation)	Chapter 18-40 WAC
Particle fallout (minimum air quality standards, state-wide)	Amended, Jan. 1972 (originally adopted in 1970, before DOE's creation)	Chapter 18-44 WAC
Burning of field and turf grasses grown for seed. (permit required from DOE)	Adopted, Jan. 1972	Chapter 18-16 WAC
Photochemical oxidants, hydrocarbons, nitrogen dioxide (minimum ambient air quality standards)	Adopted, Jan. 1972	Chapter 18-46 WAC
Fluoride (minimum ambient air quality standards)	Amended, effective Feb. 1971	Chapter 18-48 WAC
Carbon monoxide (minimum ambient air quality standards)	Amended, Jan. 1972, (originally adopted in 1969)	Chapter 18-32 WAC
Kraft pulping mills—emission standards (one of 4 sources exclusively regulated by the state) some compliance by July, 1972, all by July, 1975	Amended, effective March, 1971 (original standards set 1969)	Chapter 18-36 WAC
Sulfite pulping mills—emission standards (one of the 4 sources regulated exclusively by the state) compliance due July 1, 1974	Adopted, Jan. 1972	Chapter 18-38 WAC

*WAC = Washington Administrative Code.

systems and a list of participating disposal sites and facilities. Primary work to date has focused on residential and commercial waste, while federal funding has recently been extended for hazardous and industrial waste.

A new solid waste control activity was authorized by the Model Litter Control Act of 1971.[45] An industry-supported measure, designed to counter efforts for a deposit on disposable containers, the Model Litter Control Act is primarily an advertising-educational campaign, seeking through posters, clean-up drives, and standardized waste receptacle placement to improve the look of things. Authorized penalties are $10 for littering or the requirement to pick up trash on the scene. The program is to be financed by a tax based on gross proceeds of the sale of litter-producing products. As this fund has not been allocated by the legislature, administration of the act has been financed by the Industry Committee for Quality Environment.

The 1972-approved bond issue for waste control can be used for grants to localities to fund solid waste management as well as sewage treatment.

Shoreline Management

One of the most significant new types of authorizations for DOE is the Shoreline Management Act of 1971.[46] This is the first major Washington State effort to integrate land use with water quality and water resources planning. This will incorporate decisions of where, whether, and how to develop real estate, preserve natural systems, locate industries, dispose of waste, and the possible uses of the waters and associated shorelines.

The act provides for management of all water and shorelines of streams with a mean annual flow greater than 20 cubic feet per second; lakes larger than 2 acres, marine water areas; and land extending landward 200 feet from the ordinary high-water mark or associated wetlands. DOE has established guidelines for local governments to develop master plans for development and protection of these areas. DOE must approve the plans.

Guidelines required the adoption by localities of comprehensive inventories of their shorelines by November, 1972.[47] Substantial developments must have a permit from the local government. This includes any development over $1,000 or which materially interferes with the normal public use of the water or shorelines. Variances and conditional use permits are permitted, but only with DOE approval. Final decisions on permit problems rest with the Shorelines Appeals Board, named in March, 1972. This board includes the three members of the Pollution Control Hearings Board, one representative of the Association of Washington Business, one representative of the County Commissioners, and the State Land Commissioner. Board decisions may be appealed to court. From June 1, 1971, when the act took effect, until August, 1972, DOE reviewed 629 shoreline permits, and just over 4 percent had been appealed to the board, but none decided.

Under the act, the attorney general can bring an action for damages or injunctive relief undependently of DOE.

The 1971 Shoreline Management Act was on the 1972 ballot as Initiative 43B along with an alternate Initiative 43. The alternative measure was considered stronger, because more developments and water areas would be regulated—and by the state directly rather than mostly local and county governments. About 55 percent of the voters indicated they wanted shoreline controls, and an overwhelming 75 percent of these chose the weaker Shoreline Management Act version.

DOE's FUNCTIONAL STRUCTURE

The DOE's top management has spent a substantial amount of time designing and implementing an internal organization structure based on functions instead of programs. The DOE has undergone the most radical change in the structuring of its programs of any of the new environmental agencies studied in this book. The program distinctions between air pollution control, water pollution control, water resources management, and solid waste management were initially completely eliminated and replaced by a structure based on functions: planning, standards, operations, technical assistance, laboratory services, comprehensive investigations, etc.

This structure was devised primarily by a consultant to the department, the Stanford Research Institute (SRI), funded by a grant from the Ford Foundation. The goal was to develop a model organizational structure that could aid other states in setting up new environmental agencies. DOE adopted most of SRI's recommendations for internal organization.[48] The department's structure in September, 1972 is shown in Chart 3.3.

The goal of the functional structure is to integrate the four programs into one whole unit, rather than administer the same programs side by side with a common umbrella of executive management. This, it was hoped, would reduce the possibility that one set of pollution control policies could be turned into another environmental ailment. The aim is to look at the total environment instead of attacking each problem piecemeal. Organizational objectives were to provide: (1) the minimum number of layers of authority vertically, (2) clear lines of authority and assignments of responsibility, (3) appropriate expertise in the right places, (4) efficiency, (5) flexibility, and (6) emphasis on planning and new program development.

The director, his deputy, and the executive assistant and assistant directors constitute a management team. This arrangement has the advantage of utilizing the best executive leadership of the previous agencies consolidated in the department, but it has been criticized as being top-heavy. Present-oriented operational and technical service functions are separated from future-oriented planning and program development functions. In the public services branch, the function of environmental monitoring and measurement is separated from the function of investigations and enforcement.

CHART 3.3

Department of Ecology Organization Chart
(September, 1972)

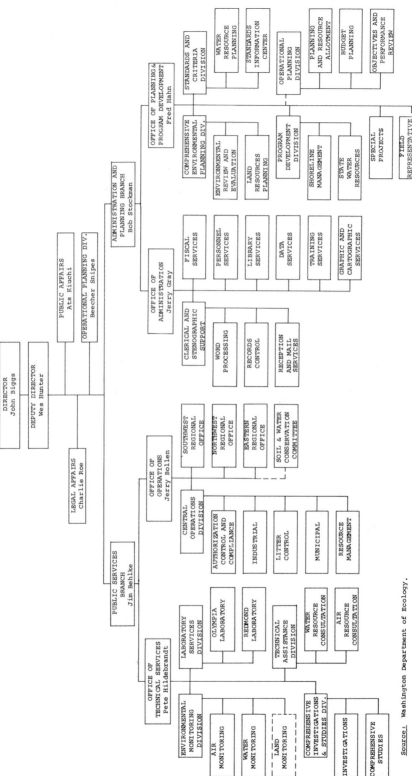

Source: Washington Department of Ecology.

The SRI scheme required new job assignments for nearly all of the existing supervisory staff and many of the technical staff. Under Washington's Civil Service Act, therefore, many personnel were retested for new assignments. This not only created confusion, but much time that was needed for environmental work had to be spent on administrative tasks. These internal bureaucratic problems still continue, but to a lesser degree. For example, the structure assumes that the department is staffed by and will be able to hire "ecologists" —professionals, trained in more than one environmental problem. Unfortunately, current staff and most education and training are geared to specific programs, such as air pollution, rather than functions, such as planning or enforcement for *all* environmental problems.

Another limit to functional integration is that DOE's authority differs for each major program. The size of the staff, funding levels, histories, age, political constituences, and strategies of each program also differ. Air pollution control has a regional focus and solid waste management and shorelines control a local one. While water quality and water resources programs apply statewide, water resources activities have been centered in eastern Washington servicing irrigating farmers, while water pollution problems are greatest in the urbanized western part of the state. Water use has been a development effort and water quality a policing activity.

The SRI structure called for an unrealistic increase in staff generally—nearly twice the staff as the previous agencies combined—and in planning, in particular. However, the same year that the "environment" boomed in Washington, the economy began to slump, and thus the department has been denied the increase in staff and budget needed to implement functional integration.

The complicated internal structure has created a number of everyday operational difficulties for the DOE. For example, it has made more difficult the department's dealings with regional air pollution control authorities and sewer districts around the state since these single-purpose units must deal with several DOE officials instead of just one.

The director himself has no one person within the department to hold responsible for action on one pollution problem that involves all aspects of a program (planning, operations, etc.). Internal evaluation of major program areas thus becomes extremely complex. Various personnel, whose work is highly fractionalized, must communicate continually with their numerous functional counterparts working in the same program area. Specific work assignments and divisions are as yet sometimes unclear, and some duplication of effort or slippage on a particular problem can go unnoticed.

The department initially maintained no internal accounting of staff and dollars devoted to each major program area, such as water pollution control. Departmental leaders were frustrated in efforts to determine where each program stood. Also integrating DOE's budget into the state's program budgeting system proved very difficult.

Although the DOE director is deeply committed to the functional structure, he has recognized these problems and realigned the system so that it is several steps back toward a program concept. For instance, budgets and time-accounting of personnel are now maintained on a program basis.

The agency gives two examples of successful major program consolidation resulting from the functional structure.[49] The industrial section within operations has total agency responsibility for air, water, and solid waste management programs over the kraft and sulfite paper mills and the aluminum plants within the state. The single unit administers permits, variances, enforcement, development and adoption of regulations, tax credits, and all other associated activities. This group, which has become the agency focal point for industrial environmental controls, can consider the total impact of each upon the land, air, and water resources.

The agency has also successfully integrated some program units within the regional offices. Strong decentralization of operational programs has taken place, and permit functions, such as water rights, waste discharge permits, flood control permits, and review of shoreline permits, are administered in the regions. Personnel from all agency programs have been combined into a single regional staff with many individuals working in all facets of the agency activity. For instance, water resource staff now may additionally investigate complaints of violations of water and air quality laws.

Yet, complete functional integration, if it occurs, is a long way off in Washington's DOE. To date no integrated water/air/land plans have been drafted, nor have standards or many other products of the agency been meshed. New staff hired are called "environmentalists," but in fact many perform single jobs as before, such as monitoring oil pollution. Existing staff may have had their job descriptions changed, but many still perform specific single-mission tasks. Even in the most related program areas—water resources and water pollution control—only slight sharing of expertise and data occurs.

DOE BUDGET CRUNCH

The birth and infancy of the new Washington environmental agency has been affected by a state governmentwide budget crunch. Although the 1971 legislature showed confidence in DOE by assigning it ten new laws to administer, it refused adequate funds to existing programs and appropriated money for only three of the ten new programs.* The Department of Ecology suffered

---

*Of the ten new programs assigned to the DOE, the three funded totaled $800,000: $100,000 for clean-up of minor oil spills under the coastal protection act, which comes from a revolving fund account funded by 1¢ a gallon tax from each marine use refund claim; $200,000 for development of the water plan; and $500,000 for the Shoreline Management Act, which includes funds to help local governments, but which Biggs estimates will not even cover the departmental operating costs of $531,000.

The DOE estimates it will cost "more than $2.2 million to administer the seven unfunded acts for the next two years." The largest single cost would be for the administra-

along with all other state departments in a year when a budget that countenanced "no growth" in state bureaucracy was the aim of the legislators. But DOE also suffered from an "economic backlash" against environmental funding in particular.

In 1971, when DOE's 1971-73 biennial budget was up for approval, the economy of the state had plummeted. Unemployment was up as much as 9 percent statewide and 17 percent in the Seattle metropolitan area. Much unemployment was blamed on environmental actions, such as the demise of the SST and the delay of the Trans-Alaska pipeline. Weyerhaeuser announced it would close its sulfite paper mill in Everett in 1973 because of pollution control requirements. (The plant utilized an older manufacturing process and had been marginally efficient for some time.) These events and others helped produce an economic backlash to the DOE budget proposal. The original request from the governor was $10.9 million for the biennium for DOE, less than the operating budget for DOE's predecessor agencies for the previous biennium. The legislature eventually reduced the appropriation to $10.07 million.

Subsequent modest funding for newly enacted laws and for grants for river basin planning brought the basic operating budget for fiscal year 1971-73 to $12.8 million in state funds. Another $1.9 million is provided in federal program grants and $0.2 million through the federal Emergency Employment Act for a total two-year operating figure of $14.9 million. This is a $1-million increase from DOE predecessor agencies. DOE staff as of July 1, 1971 was 192 and was authorized to increase to 255 by June 30, 1973. See Table 3.2 for the sources of DOE funds and Table 3.3 for expenditures and staff levels for DOE programs.

THE ECOLOGICAL COMMISSION

The Ecological Commission, in practice, has proven to be just as the governor and his supporters had hoped: a purely advisory body, despite its vague statutory power to veto DOE standards.

The governor appointed all seven members. After the original appointments expire, succeeding members will serve staggered four-year terms, and

---

tion and enforcement of the Model Litter Control Act, expected to cost $1.6 million. However, this act has its own fund provided by taxes of litterable objects and fines. The six other laws will require a total $621,600 in the two-year period and have no such fund: $85,982 to review the 200 environmental impact statements from the highway department expected in two years and to oversee highway contractors; $225,395 for setting well drilling standards and conducting field investigations; $99,976 to administer the Pollution Disclosure Act; $120,246 to administer the state's Environmental Policy Act; $22,445 to issue permits to abate forest fire hazards and otherwise improve forest lands; and $67,550 for emergency control actions to reduce air pollution emissions in times of crisis.

TABLE 3.2

Sources of Funds of DOE and Predecessor Agencies, 1969-75

State Funds	DOE Predecessor Agencies 1969-71 Biennium	DOE 1971- 73 Biennium	DOE 1973- 75 Biennium[a]
General fund		$10,513,010	$14,176,751
Reclamation		536,618	499,980
Basic data		170,000	170,000
Litter control		617,771	1,715,869
Coastal protection		100,000	100,000
Jobs now		631,635	
Contingent funds		234,453	
Total state operating funds	$12,906,928[b]	$12,803,487	$16,662,600
Federal funds	$ 788,299[c]	$ 1,891,321	$ 2,012,798
Total basic operating funds	$13,695,227[d]	$14,694,808[d]	$18,675,398[d]
State construction grants	$12,500,000[e]	$20,075,629	-- [f]
Grand total Departmental funding	$26,195,227	$34,770,437	$18,675,398

[a]Funds requested by DOE from state budget office, September, 1972.

[b]Breakdown of source of state funds not available for DOE's predecessor agencies. This figure is only an estimate of their actual expenditures.

[c]Excludes federal grants for construction of local wastewater treatment facilities.

[d]The annual budget is calculated by dividing the biennial budget in half, although expenditures in the second year usually are higher than in the first.

[e]This figure includes $4.3 million in state bond issue money and the remainder in general state funds. This is for bond sales purposes only. The general fund is reimbursed from bond sales made when favorable interest rates can be obtained.

[f]The bond issue approved for water supply and waste treatment, totaling $300 million, was approved on the November ballot, after this budget was prepared. Presumably some of these funds will be granted to localities for construction purposes in the 1973-75 biennium.

Sources: Chart III, DOE Program Budget 1971-73 Biennium, October, 1972; Chart IV, DOE Program Budget 1973-75 Biennium, September, 1972 submission; and DOE officials.

they are removable only for "cause." The governor also appoints the chairman, who in 1973 is Dr. Arpad Masley, a Bremerton surgeon and sportsman.* By statute the membership includes one representative each from organized labor, business, and the agricultural community, and four persons to represent the

*The first chairman was Gordon Tongue.

TABLE 3.3

DOE Expenditures and Staff by Program, 1971-73 and 1973-75

Program	1971-73 Biennium[a] Estimated Program Expenditure	1973-75 Biennium Expenditures Requested from State Budget Office	1971-73 Biennium Man-years	1973-75 Biennium Man-years Requested
Water quality	$ 1,999,167	$ 2,345,968	120.7	137.4
Water resources management	3,762,660	4,611,759	108.1	147.8
Air pollution control	1,530,281	2,314,155	65.6	88
Solid waste and litter control	1,290,356	2,104,049	50.3	81.5
Other:	811,457	1,441,645	51.7	82.8
Shoreline management				
Environmental review				
Flood control				
Soil and water conservation				
Administration	3,154,652	3,999,171	86.3	93.6
Federal emergency employment act aid	234,453	–	27.7	–
"Jobs now" grant	631,635	–	–	–
State grant and loan assistance to localities	21,355,776	1,858,652[b]	0	0
Total	$34,770,437	$18,675,359	510.4	631.1

[a]Washington state government operates on a biennial budget system. To determine annual budget and staff size divide dollars and man-years in half, although typically the second funding year is higher than the first.

[b]The bond issue approved for water supply and waste treatment, totaling $300 million, was approved on the November ballot, after this budget was prepared. Presumably some of these funds will be granted to localities for construction purposes in the 1973-75 biennium.

Source: Chart III, DOE Program Budget 1971-73 Biennium, October, 1972; Chart IV, DOE Program Budget 1973-75 Biennium, September, 1972 submission.

"public at large."* No member may serve more than two consecutive terms. None of the members selected are viewed as hostile to environmental objectives, and the majority could be labeled strong environmental proponents.

In the legislative compromise between a purely advisory board and a policy-making unit, the commission was given, theoretically, limited control over pollution control standards. The DOE's director is required to submit in writing to each member of the commission "all rules and regulations, other

---

*Other members serving as of August, 1971 are Harold W. Heacock, Walter Williams, John McGregor, Gordon Orians, Ann Widditsch, and Charles Stewart Sargent.

than for procedural matters, proposed by him for adoption in accordance with the procedures of (the Washington Administrative Procedures Act)." The statute reads:

Unless, within thirty days of such notification, five of the members of the Commission notify the director in writing of their disapproval of such rules and regulations and their reasons therefor, such rules and regulations shall be adopted by the director in accordance with the procedures of (the Administrative Procedures Act).[50]

The statute does not indicate what happens if five members of the commission do indicate their disapproval. Presumably this is a veto power, but the commission has not used it, and the present organization, whose members are all appointed by Governor Evans, is not likely to use it as long as the DOE director stays on good terms with the members. A better test of this power of the body will come under a new governor and a new director who may have views that differ from commission members.

The director appoints a secretary for the commission and provides such other assistance, staff, and facilities as may be necessary to fulfill its duties. The commission does not initiate investigations without DOE approval, which must supply the necessary funds. Each commission member individually submits in writing his views on requested matters to the director within the time he specifies. These are not necessarily made public or even circulated to other commission members unless the director chooses to do so.

By majority decision the commission may agree to consider any matter pertinent to the purposes for which the Department of Ecology was created, but as a practical matter the commission's agenda is often set by DOE's director. However, the current Director Biggs is open to agenda items that members suggest.

Biggs set out immediately to establish a good working relationship with the advisory Ecological Commission. He had been accustomed to dealing with citizen commissions from his years of service under a policy-making Game Commission. Furthermore, Biggs was new to the pollution control business and was seeking real guidance and public support from the commission. He seeks member views frequently, more than required by law. However, Biggs made it clear early and in no uncertain terms that he would run the department and that the commission should not meddle in program administration. They were to be purely advisory.

During the first several months of its existence, the commission met monthly, commented on proposed regulations, controversial issues, and the new organizational structure of DOE. It holds public meetings, less often now, around the state on environmental issues and local problems. Matters on which it has received reports include tax exemptions and credits for installation of pollution control facilities by industry, minimum flow regulations, allocations of financial aid to counties and cities for solid waste disposal facilities, regulations for handling public complaints, procedures for its own advice and guidance to the department, and advisability of increasing the height of Ross Dam on the Skagit River. On this last, highly controversial issue, commission members split: three in favor, three opposed, with one abstention. The make-up of the commission makes unanimity rare, but should a strong, united stand be publicly stated on some matter other than regulations, it would be politically difficult, although legally possible, for DOE's director to take opposing action.

Commission members also receive requests for action on environmental matters from private citizens, which they refer to DOE for disposition.

THE POLLUTION CONTROL HEARINGS BOARD

The three-member Pollution Control Hearings Board has been an active mediator of disputes between regulated parties and the DOE, and particularly the regional air pollution control agencies.

The board must have at least one lawyer member and no more than two members may be from the same political party. After the first members serve varied terms, all members are selected by the governor to serve six-year terms. They cannot be removed except for "inefficiency, malfeasance, or misfeasance." The members select one of their number to be chairman and establish their own rules and regulations of practice.

Hearings may be either formal or informal, and either party may require proceedings to be formal. All appellants have 30 days after a decision to appeal. Decisions made in informal hearings are appealable to the State Superior Court (lower courts) where a trial de novo is held. Appeals then go directly to the State Supreme Court. Decisions made in formal hearings, however, are appealable first to Washington's intermediate Court of Appeals, where no new trial is held, and then to the State Supreme Court. Any party may appeal a decision of the board. Formal hearing proceedings are subject to the rules of the Washington Administrative Practices Act, which adopts, among other things, the clearly erroneous, arbitrary, and capricious tests.[51]

Table 3.4 indicates the number and type of appeals to the board through mid-1972. Most of these have been from civil penalties imposed by regional air pollution control authorities, particularly the Puget Sound Air Pollution Control Agency. All appeals have been lodged by regulated parties. Although environmentalists also have the power to appeal decisions they consider weak, none have chosen to do so. It is not clear whether the absence of environmental appeals means citizens are completely satisfied with state regulation or just unaware of this power and underfunded to initiate such action.

In the first ten-month period, 29 cases reached final disposition, 9 were dismissed, 4 withdrawn, 4 achieved a compromise settlement, and 12 went the full route of contention in public hearings. In the 12 fully contested cases, the Hearings Board found for the respondent 8 times and for the appellant 4 times.

96

TABLE 3.4

Appeals to the Pollution Control Hearing Board,
September, 1970-June 30, 1972

Subject of Appeal	Sept., 1970 to June 30, 1971	July 1, 1971 to June 30, 1972	Total Appeals
Water pollution control	8	4	12
Water rights	21	0	21
Air pollution control	24	84	108
Tax credits	0	1	1
Total	53	89	142

Source: DOE, August, 1972.

The style adopted by the board has been to act as mediator, relying heavily on the use of informal, prehearing conferences to get parties to agree. If no agreement is reached, the board then holds hearings and issues its order. The board's credibility and, indeed, its principal power as a mediator comes from the clearly unbiased character of the chairman, a retired chief justice of the Washington State Supreme Court, Matthew Hill of Olympia.* Board members would like to expand their environmental jurisdiction, but this is not the current mood of the legislature which has set up other appeals bodies for other environmental programs.

There has been little controversy surrounding most of the appeals to the Hearings Board. In the most controversial case to date, the board appears to have resolved a long-standing battle between the Puget Sound Air Pollution Control Agency and the American Smelting and Refining Company in Tacoma by gaining concessions from both sides while upholding the thrust but not the dates of the agency's compliance schedule.

Most cases have been settled by the Hearings Board with only two cases appealed to the State Superior Court as of September, 1972. Neither of these had been heard in court. Thus, the Hearings Board seems to be meeting its statutory purpose of providing for a "more expeditious and efficient disposition of appeals . . ." and reducing the load on the state's courts. However, more

---

*Other board members are James T. Sherhy, retired executive vice president of ITT Rayonier, and Walt Woodward, a semiretired public affairs and conservation newspaper columnist.

record will be required to tell whether this small number of cases appealed to the courts means that regulated parties feel they are gently treated by the board or whether they feel that appeals would be worthless after the board's expert record had been established. If the former is true, stronger enforcement might be secured in the courts, without the board, even if it took longer. If the latter is true, the board may strengthen the regulatory hand of the agencies by securing compliance through credible mediation that might not have been secured in a traditional adversary proceeding. Board members feel that their success lies in resolving disputes without further appeal, as well as in providing a continuity of decision that the many court jurisdictions throughout the state cannot possibly give.

EVALUATION

Effects of Program Consolidation in a New Department

Creation of the Department of Ecology has given the state's pollution control and water management work added status in state government and increased visibility and popularity with the legislature and the general public. The department provides a focus for support of these programs, as well as opposition, as demonstrated by the 1971-73 budget crisis.

Industries and local governments that are regulated by the state for more than one type of waste or water use find that doing business with the state has been streamlined.

Although the DOE began as primarily a pollution control agency, it has moved by increments to a broader environmental mission and has established itself as *the* environmental agency among those several Washington departments that could claim some of that role. Director Biggs sees himself as the spokesman for environmental issues that range beyond the statutory concerns of DOE and has helped to create an image for the department as having a broad ecological mission despite the fact that half his staff and operating funds and most legal power are in the water programs. He has played a key role in getting the legislature to assign new types of authorities to this department, such as litter control, shoreline management, and review of state environmental impact statements. The governor supports this broader role for DOE. This is understandable, in part, because the main agency rival to be *the* environmental department is the Department of Natural Resources, directed by the elected Democratic Public Lands Commissioner.

The establishment of an environmental protection department such as DOE that is popular with the legislators has helped to create an incentive for the legislature to pass new laws in this field, knowing that there is a department to administer them. The new department has also been active in proposing such measures.

The linking of pollution controls in one agency also creates an incentive to make currently dissimilar programs more alike by eventually granting statewide authority to DOE for air pollution control and assigning regulatory authority such as standards and state permits for solid waste management. Similar programming would simplify public administration in DOE, particularly because of its functional structuring, and allow the experience of regulating one form of pollution to improve regulation of others. While there was discussion in the 1972 legislative session of giving some of the regional air control agencies' powers to DOE (an assignment that Director Biggs would like to see), nothing came of it. The effort was supported in part by some industrialists in the Puget Sound area who felt that the regional agency was too "zealous" in its air pollution controls and that they would fare better under state regulation. Consequently, dismantling regional authorities and assigning their powers to DOE may not necessarily strengthen pollution control policy, at least in the Puget Sound urban corridor.

However, if the DOE is to be the lead state government agency for pollution control, it should be assigned the administration of all programs in this field now located in other state agencies in Olympia. These are the drinking water quality program from the Department of Social and Health Services and the regulation of pesticides pollution, now run by the Agriculture and Health departments. New antipollution laws, if enacted, such as for noise abatement, should also be assigned to the DOE, which will then be able to take a compatible approach to all waste and water resource management.

Although the 1970 reorganization was initially intended to consolidate pollution controls, the placement of water resources management in the new DOE, which occurred in the legislative process, has proved a good one. In fact, this program has perhaps been the one that has benefited most by placement in DOE. New program leadership, new directives from the legislature, and association with conservation-oriented pollution abatement programs has somewhat moderated the previous development orientation of the water management work, streamlined its procedures, and improved its public image. The program is moving toward a rationalization of the water rights allocation process and water resources planning.

Despite the water use program's traditional emphasis on resource development—such as reclamation and hydroelectric power generation—this exploitation bias has not compromised Washington's water quality regulatory effort. In part, this results from the previous weakness of the water management program in the Water Resources Department. Also, the era of dam building in Washington has mostly passed as most economic water-development sites have been utilized already. By contrast, water pollution control is becoming a growingly important public issue.

Additionally, DOE has a very real potential to develop comprehensive water policies and programs by administering both water quality and quantity efforts, as well as regulation of shoreline areas. With a large percentage of staff and dollars devoted to water quality and quantity efforts, DOE can develop a strong and integrated approach to river basin and sewage treatment planning.

99

Integrated permit systems can be used as a way to carry out the plans. . Monitoring services and facilities can be usefully shared. To some degree, staff and water data are now shared and if such integration, which has just begun, is carried out in all respects and on a regular basis, improved water policy assessment and cost-savings can be realized in the future.

However, DOE is now seriously undermanned and underfunded to carry out effectively such program integration techniques as mathematical modeling, comprehensive resource planning, and improved monitoring. DOE's regulatory, financial, and technical assistance functions also suffer from lack of funds. While the popularity of DOE and environmental issues in the state resulted in ten new environmental laws for DOE in 1971, prevailing economic troubles kept legislators from adequately funding either these new efforts or existing programs. The legislature left completely unfunded the litter control program (while it has its own fund from a tax on litterable objects, the legislature must approve spending from the fund), review of environmental impact statements from the highway department, administration of the state's Environmental Policy Act, permits to control forest hazards, the Pollution Disclosure Act, setting of well drilling standards, and the emergency control of air pollution.

DOE's modest $1 million increase in funds for 1971 through 1973 will scarcely cover the built-in added costs of inflation and automatic salary raises and certainly is insufficient to administer the new programs and hire the 63 new staff members who have been authorized.

Prospects do not look much brighter for the 1973-75 budget. Economic conditions are not much improved, and both Governor Evans, in his successful reelection campaign, and his Democratic opponent promised "no growth" in state government.

Washington may be an example of where the public is ahead of its elected officials on matters of spending for environmental protection. The approval of $340 million for environmental bond issues on the November, 1972 ballot, along with approval of the shorelines protection program, shows the voters are willing to commit funds and regulatory controls to protect their resources.

In some states, such as New York and Illinois, the creation of a highly visible department, combining pollution controls under new program leadership, has resulted in tougher regulatory standards backed up by higher fines, faster enforcement procedures, and an active litigation program. This has not been the case in Washington, however, where the DOE director is reluctant to levy fines and regulatory orders and initiate court action.

Fines are low by statute (except for oil pollution) and, until late 1972, by administrative policy. Most water pollution fines since 1970 were about $100 to $250 each. Oil pollution fines were higher—the statutory limit is $20,000 per violation—but over one-half of the $136,000 total fines imposed by DOE between 1970 and 1972 were dropped. DOE's stated position now, as a result of public pressure, is to levy maximum fines and not reduce them. Fines often go uncollected because of failure to litigate and because of the extended appeals process that includes the Pollution Control Hearings Board as well as the courts.

In Washington, as Director Biggs has said, penalties and court action are not key deterrents to other potential polluters, nor do they strengthen the hand of the state in negotiations with the party in question. However, the assistant attorney general says "the most effective tool for enforcing the [Water Pollution Control] Act has been the civil penalty provisions."[52] Both are probably right. While the civil penalties may be the best Washington has, they do not seem adequate to deter pollution. Of those fined, 21 percent are repeaters,[53] although the assistant attorney general refers to this number as "relatively small."[54]

Negotiations with industries and local officials are not likely to produce effective regulation unless they are backed up by the credible threat of court-required clean-up or plant closure. In Washington these are not credible deterrents because fines are low and the department is reluctant to take parties to court, even after negotiations have been in process for some time. While Director Biggs says he relies on permits as the chief enforcement device, permits cannot be separated from penalties, regulatory orders, and court action required to enforce permit conditions.

However, if fines and regulatory orders were imposed in more instances, and DOE had an increased willingness to take the offender to court after reasonable time for negotiations had elapsed, enforcement might be faster and abatement requirements higher. This is not to say a lawsuit should be the department's first step, but the willingness to take this step, after initial negotiations have stalemated, needs to be more apparent. However, it may well be that Washingtonians, or at least their elected political officials, do not want faster environmental law enforcement. The political climate created by economic conditions does not support strict regulatory controls if these high fines and tough legal actions that require faster abatement schedules mean—or appear to mean—job cutbacks and plant closures. Some of the multimillion-dollar companies in Washington, which employ hundreds or thousands of workers, have threatened to do just that, blaming environmental controls for a variety of other economic problems.

In the balancing of environmental against economic objectives, Washingtonians seem to lean more toward economic objectives than Illinoisans, for example, producing less political support for fast environmental clean-up.

Consequently, Biggs' middle ground position—not pushing industries and municipalities too fast and hard on abatement schedules—may suit most Washingtonians. To be sure, environmental activists want him to move faster; regulated parties want him to move slower. But on the matter of regulation, as on environmental spending, the voters may also be ahead of their elected and appointive officials if the public's pressure to forego the uncollected and low fines policy is any indication. A reporter summed up Biggs' reputation quite aptly: "Legislators are satisfied with the department's progress. And environmentalists, who worked for the organization of the department, have not been outraged by any of Biggs' actions."[55]

On balance, the DOE's experience with a functional internal organizational structure seems to demonstrate that adopting such a structure at the start of a new environmental agency may be counterproductive, or at least unnecessarily difficult and time-consuming. The DOE's top leadership has been extremely committed to the functionalization effort and has spent an inordinate amount of time getting the organization set up, working with it, and revising it. This was valuable administrative energy spent on organizational problems that could better have been spent on the substantive problems of pollution regulation, water management, and developing the several newly enacted laws.

Setting up a new agency by reorganizing existing ones is confusing in all cases. But a functional internal structuring that calls for a total staff shake-up and job reclassifications makes confusion, proves to be much more protracted, and requires more leadership attention than continuing, at least initially, with the traditional program-oriented structure.

The purpose of the functional structure—to integrate programs and create a truly "environmental" program, rather than separate subunits—has not yet been achieved in Washington. There are only limited examples of real uniting of programs functionally. Many people continue in their previous single mission tasks, but they now report to different bureau directors. Functional integration has been difficult, not only because of civil service requirements, but because staff have single-mission training, and programs have differing legal components, data requirements, geographical focus, objectives, constituencies, and regulated parties. Also, a structure that required a major increase in staff, in general, and planners, in particular, was unrealistic in 1970 when the departmental budget outlook was bleak.

It is not clear that all DOE's program units, such as solid waste management, shoreline regulation, and water use management, can ever be fully integrated functionally. Water resources management and water quality control have the greatest potential for effective meshing, since the functions of these two programs most nearly match and program missions and staff expertise are highly related. Both do standards-setting, water quality and quantity monitoring, water research and planning, and permits are issued for water uses and water discharges. Data on surface and ground water flows, stream inventories, seasonal variation, and biological and chemical content are critical to both programs. Thus, while the origin and orientation of the two programs have differed marketly in the past, increasing demands on a limited water supply may make a more unified approach to water quality and quantity more logical. In any event, it is too soon to expect broad environmental policies and programming, since this is a new approach to information and management. The best that can be said is that the functional structure provides an incentive for such an approach and perhaps "environmentalists" will be attracted to work for the department and a broad environmental perspective will result in the long run.

But, should true functional integration occur, one problem remains. Perhaps the most serious problem is that functionalizing reduces public understanding of DOE's work and so limits the accountability and responsiveness of the staff to the director, and of the department itself to the governor, the legislature, and the public. Problems occur in the real world as air pollution, water pollution, or solid waste and litter. The environment is air, water, land, and living resources. It is in these terms that people look for governmental solutions. DOE distinctions of standards-setting, monitoring, planning, and operations are frequently meaningless to those outside the department. Accountability has been difficult even for the director to establish among his staff and has required him to make some shifts back toward a program approach. The structure that creates confusion for the DOE staff and leaders creates almost total noncomprehension for the public and other state officials. A person looking at the DOE's organization chart has no idea whom to call when an oil spill occurs, or for an air pollution or open burning violation. The structure fails to communicate the interests and objectives of DOE. No one person can be held accountable for the whole air pollution effort, for example. Formal program evaluation, which is very important for effective policies and administration, is discouraged by the system. Confusion and diffused responsibility allow buck-passing within the organization.

Thus, while the rhetoric surrounding the original DOE design was to increase public participation in environmental protection—by getting the programs to the people—in fact, the structure's effect is to reduce public and legislative understanding and participation in DOE programs, and to reduce the accountability and responsiveness of public officials.

In conclusion, a functional structure might be easier to implement and more likely to produce an "environmental" approach to programs at some later point in the department's life. Then, functions and program foci will more likely match, environmentalists may staff the department, there may be more scientific and engineering information to show ways to interrelate air, water, and solid waste pollution, shorelines, and water management. After several years of operations a department will have solidified its political bases of support and overcome the bureaucratic hassles of initial establishment.

But, because it is so difficult today to implement, functionalization takes an unnecessary amount of valuable environmental leadership time. A program-oriented structure is less likely to slow down pollution controls and resource management in the early life of an environmental agency. Also, the more traditional staff designations are more clearly understood to the legislature and the public, at least at this point in history. But the program-oriented operational divisions should be accompanied from the agency's start by a strong capability in the office of the director for integrated policy analysis, planning, and coordination of various program divisions. This would be a group of analysts who would seek to devise new "environmental" policies, affecting DOE programs, while day-to-day operations are carried out on a well-understood basis.

103

A Comprehensive Environmental Unit in the Governor's Office

Each state government, including Washington, needs a capability to take a truly comprehensive approach to its environment, an organization that can conduct comprehensive planning and evaluate all state work that affects its air, water, land, living, and nonrenewable resources. Pollution needs to be effectively regulated at its point of discharge, but it is just a symptom of a more basic misuse of natural resources.

Washington needs such a unit within the executive branch to examine the effects of one state policy on another—to develop integrated multiagency policies for energy, cycling of resources, land use management, and other issues that when properly approached may prevent much pollution and other of today's environmental ailments.

The Department of Ecology should not be expected to carry out this job. Its main mission is to regulate pollution and shoreline development and manage water use. Comprehensive planning requires trading-off environmental, economic, and other state goals, and to do this would compromise DOE's important advocacy role toward its own programs. Other departments have responsibilities for other pieces of the environment—the Departments of Parks and Recreation, Game, Fisheries, Agriculture, Natural Resources, and the Thermal Power Plant Site Evaluation Council. These departments are not likely to implement plans drafted for them by DOE, an equal, sister agency.

The executive office of the governor is the logical administrative location for planning, policy analysis, and program evaluation affecting all relevant state agencies. Here environmental work in several agencies can be coordinated and linked to the resource development departments, such as the Highway Department and the Commerce and Economic Development Department. This organization, whether it be the planning office, a unit in the budget office, or a new group, should report directly to the governor, who can then make and be held responsible for the basic policy choices and trade-offs among varying state objectives that are involved in such comprehensive environmental planning. Here, the comprehensive environmental plans could then be incorporated into the program budgeting system as a device to implement the plans.

Washington's governor will be limited, however, in his ability to plan policies and implement programs in several departments that have policy-making commissions or boards, appointed for a specified term, or in the case of the DNR, a separately elected official from the opposing party. These boards and commissions intervene and can prevent the governor's directives from being carried out.

Elimination of Policy Boards and Creation of the Ecological Commission

Washington's 1970 environmental reorganization successfully eliminated two of these intervening policy-making commissions—those for air and water pollution control. Almost all powers of these part-time commissions were assigned to the director of the DOE, resulting in improved efficiency and the public accountability of environmental programs.

The governor's control over environmental policies has increased through his direct appointment of DOE's director and full executive control of the department's budget and staff. With increased control comes increased accountability to the voters, for a governor cannot disclaim responsibility for decisions made by a policy commission. Nor can the reverse happen, as is so often the case, where the governor is unfairly held responsible by the voters at election time for state environmental actions over which he had little or no control. Meanwhile, commissioners who actually made those decisions are insulated from the electoral process because they are appointed for a specified term and removable only for malfeasance, not the quality of their policies.

Director Biggs can perform as a stronger public advocate for his environmental programs and can make faster, firmer, and more consistent decisions since the elimination of the policy boards, whose membership was intentionally composed of opposing interests. This was demonstrated by the vote on the controversial Ross Dam matter by the Ecological Commission—which is the advisory replacement for the previous boards. After extensive deliberations, the commission, also composed of representatives of regulated and environmental interests, was stalemated—three voting for the proposal, three against, and one abstention. Whereas the commission could make no decision, Biggs came out firmly against the development.

Diversity is the inherent nature of government commissions, and while a group of widely varying opinions is useful for advisory purposes, it slows down, confuses, and dilutes effective environmental departmental leadership when it has policy powers. The performance of the Ecological Commission has shown both some of these advantages and some disadvantages of a purely advisory environmental citizen-commission.

The commission has served as a useful sounding board for Director Biggs, transmitting DOE positions to the public and serving as a way to sample public opinion on forthcoming matters.

The many public meetings around the state, with citizens invited to testify, have publicized environmental matters in general, and DOE concerns in particular, raising the visibility and public understanding of environmental issues. These meetings have provided a forum for communication of citizen views to DOE that otherwise would be missing. Commission members themselves represent different points of view—labor, industry, agriculture, and various conservation and environmental positions. Biggs reports that the commission members, who write their individual views on matters considered, have provided him with technical and political insights on major issues.

But, since the commission is purely advisory, there is no requirement that the director follow its advice. Only if members are united and vocal would the director find it difficult to deviate from their recommendations.

Thus, while citizen awareness and access is increased by the advisory commission, it is increased to a body that does not have real powers. While Biggs made it clear to members from the start that they had no authority, this powerlessness is not always clear to the public. For instance, commission members receive letters from citizens asking that they take actions beyond their powers. This creates a risk that the citizen panel can become a buffer between the DOE's director and the general public. The commission could serve to deflect public attention and expression of views away from the director who is the real decision-maker to the commission, which has visibility but no real authority.

The commission is not an independent advisory group, because it relies on the DOE for all funds and staff and the director provides most of its agenda items. Thus, the DOE director could either make the commission impotent or a tool for his own publicity purposes. He could refer controversial items to the panel, thus stalling the making of unpleasant or controversial decisions. This can also confuse the public as to the real location of decision-making.

All current commission members are quick to point out that John Biggs has not performed in this way. He seeks a wide variety of opinions on issues and is open and direct with all interest groups. He has been receptive to adding agenda items of interest to commission members and consults them more than is required by the law. Biggs also has a reputation for squarely facing controversial matters and making decisions himself, without stalling or diverting them to the commission.

However, the institutional structure is such that another director, or another governor, who is less sympathetic to environmental protection, might dominate the commission or use it for his own purposes.

These problems could be averted and the commission could have a more effective role as an independent advisory body if it had its own funds and staff. On its own initiative the commission should be able to initiate investigations, write and publish reports, and otherwise review and comment on state environmental issues. Such independence would eliminate the potential of domination by another less sympathetic DOE director and improve the quality of advice the members can give the director.

NOTES

1. Revised Code of Washington (hereafter referred to as R.C.W.) 43.21A (Supp. 1971).

2. R.C.W. Chapter 90.58 (Supp. 1971).

3. Chapter 70.93, 1971 Extraordinary Session c. 307.

4. Chapter 109, 1971 1st Ex. Session.

5. R.C.W. 43.21A.190 (Supp. 1971).

6. R.C.W. 43.21B.230 (Supp. 1971).

7. Task Force on Executive Reorganization (Brewster C. Denny, Chairman), *Report to Governor Daniel J. Evans*, November 29, 1968.

8. *Ibid.*, p. 1.

9. R.C.W. 90.48.021.

10. R.C.W. 70.94.300.

11. R.C.W. 70.95.

12. Office of Program Planning and Fiscal Management, State Planning Division, *Environmental Quality . . . A Program for Washington*, January, 1970.

13. Senate Bill 1, 41st Leg., 2d Ex. Sess. (1970).

14. House Bill 47, 41st Leg., 2d Ex. Sess. (1970); and Senate Bill 47, 41st Leg., 2d Ex. Sess. (1970).

15. R.C.W. 43.27A.030.

16. The Conservation Department's only other program, forests management, was transferred to the Department of Natural Resources.

17. R.C.W. 43.30.

18. R.C.W. 80.50.

19. R.C.W. 80.50.080.

20. Certification for the Hanford Nuclear Power Plant No. 2; an application by Washington Public Power Supply System for a 1,100-megawatt nuclear power plant.

21. Letter from John Biggs to Elizabeth Haskell, December 27, 1972. On file with the author.

22. *Ibid.*

23. Washington Administrative Code (hereafter referred to as WAC), Chapter 372-12 (1969) WAC, AMD by DE 72-9 (April, 1972).

24. Washington Administrative Code, Chapter 372-64 (1970) WAC, AMD by DE 72-11 (April, 1972).

25. WAC, Chapters 372-12 and 372-64, amended May 24, 1972.

26. WAC, 372-24, Authority approved in 1955.

27. Chapter 140, Laws 1972, 2nd Extraordinary Session.

28. Washington Department of Ecology, *Sewage Drainage Basin and Urban Area Planning Guide for Water Pollution Control and Abatement*, March 31, 1970, Second Edition, September 1, 1970.

29. R.C.W. 90.48.270 (Supp. 1971).

30. R.C.W. 90.52.040 (Supp. 1971).

31. R.C.W. 90.50 (Supp. 1971).

32. R.C.W. 90.48.300-910 (Supp. 1971).

33. R.C.W. 90.48.320 (Supp. 1971).

34. Dick Young, article in the *Seattle Post Intelligencer*, July 26, 1972, p. A-1.

35. *Ibid.*

36. Memo from Wes Hunter, Deputy Director, DOE, to Elizabeth Haskell, August 18, 1972. On file with the author.

37. *Seattle Times Magazine*, February 27, 1972, p. 10.

38. WAC, Chapter 508-12 and 508-60.

39. R.C.W. 90.14.

40. R.C.W. 90.54.

41. R.C.W. 70.94, as amended by 1972, 2nd Ex. Session.

42. The Board's powers were transferred to the new Department of Ecology in 1970 by R.C.W. 43.12A.060.

43. Letter from John Biggs to Elizabeth Haskell, December 27, 1972. On file with the author.

44. R.C.W. 70.95.

45. Chapter 70.93, 1971 Ex. Sess. C. 307.

46. R.C.W. Chapter 90.58 (Supp. 1971).

47. Department of Ecology, *Final Proposed Guidelines, Shoreline Management Act. of 1971*, January 26, 1972.

48. Stanford Research Institute, Project No. 8859 (Howard Vollmer, David Ackerman, and Richard A. Schmidt), *Development of an Organizational Design for the State of Washington Department of Ecology*, Submitted to Department, November, 1970.

49. Letter from John Biggs to Elizabeth Haskell, December 27, 1972. On file with the author.

50. R.C.W. Chapter 43.21A.190.

51. R.C.W. Chapter 43.21B.180, 190 (Supp. 1971).

52. Robert Jensen, Assistant Attorney General, *Report Prepared for American Bar Association, Relating to the Laws of the State of Washington Pertaining to Water Pollution,* June 27, 1972, p. 6.

53. *Ibid.*

54. *Ibid.*

55. *Seattle Times Magazine*, February 27, 1972, p. 10.

4

WISCONSIN'S DEPARTMENT
OF NATURAL RESOURCES

INTRODUCTION

An acknowledged leader in conservation work, Wisconsin was one of the first states to undertake a major environmental reorganization. Program realignment was accomplished by a two-step process, illustrated in Chart 4.1. In 1966, the state consolidated water quality and water quantity regulatory programs in a new Division of Water Resources within the existing Department of Resource Development.[1] A year later this unit was merged with the entire Conservation Department in an environmental superdepartment called the Department of

CHART 4.1

Two-Step Wisconsin Environmental Reorganization

Before Reorganization	*1966*	*1967*
1. Interagency Committee on Water Pollution (industrial water pollution control)	1. New Division of Water Resources, in the Department of Resource Development	1. Department of Natural Resources (DNR)
2. State Health Department's program for municipal water pollution control		
3. Water Power Section of the Public Service Commission (water use permits)		
4. Conservation Department (fish, wildlife, forests, parks, recreation, tourism)	2. Conservation Department	

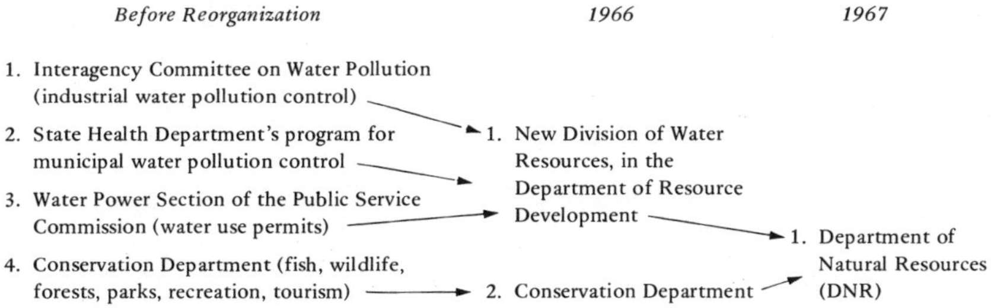

Natural Resources (DNR).[2] At this second stage, the state's first programs for air pollution and solid waste regulation were enacted and assigned to the DNR.[3] The DNR is thus responsible for water use and water, air, and solid waste pollution control programs along with fish and wildlife, forests, parks, and recreation management. However, it does not have sole responsibility for pesticides and radiation control. The DNR's current organization, functions, and budget are described in Chart 4.2.

The major purpose of the first reorganization was to create a strong, consolidated water pollution control effort, and this first move has had the strongest impact on the state's antipollution policies and programs. Wisconsin is a state that is highly conscious of its public administrative systems and the logic for the second move, the creation of the DNR in 1967, was largely that it would make administrative processes more efficient. The reorganization's focus was as much on "good government" principles in general as on better environmental protection per se.

In theory, the 1967 reorganization was to create one highly related, smoothly running environmental unit. However, close integration of the DNR's pollution control and conservation programs has not occurred. Although formal and informal communication between them is increasing and, following a field reorganization, conservation personnel will be used for pollution monitoring, the DNR is not a place where the "total ecology" is considered in joint policy-making, planning, and administration. Further, in a department where traditional conservation programs compete with pollution control programs for staff time, attention, and public support, the latter effort often loses out in the competition. The reorganization created an aftermath of political hostility, and the fledgling pollution control effort has not become a strong, highly visible public advocate and has not been able to build the base of political support it vitally needs. For these reasons, recent recommendations from several sources in Wisconsin have called for separation of the pollution control effort from conservation programs in the DNR.

The DNR is supposed to be governed by a seven-member, part-time citizen policy board called the Natural Resources Board, whose members are appointed by the governor and approved by the Senate for overlapping six-year terms. The board has the authority to approve all the DNR's policies and standards, and it also appoints the DNR's secretary. However, in practice, the board has not turned out to be the locus of real decision-making for the department. The DNR's secretary makes most decisions and the board merely ratifies them. Overall, the board has served to weaken the public responsiveness of the DNR, since its secretary is not directly accountable to the governor and because to citizens it often appears that the board, not the secretary, is the decision-maker. Thus the secretary is protected from public scrutiny.

A TWO–STAGED REORGANIZATION

Compared to the environmental reorganizations in most other states, Wisconsin's two-staged realignment was a highly deliberative, political, and

CHART 4.2

DNR Organization, Main Functions, and Budget, 1972

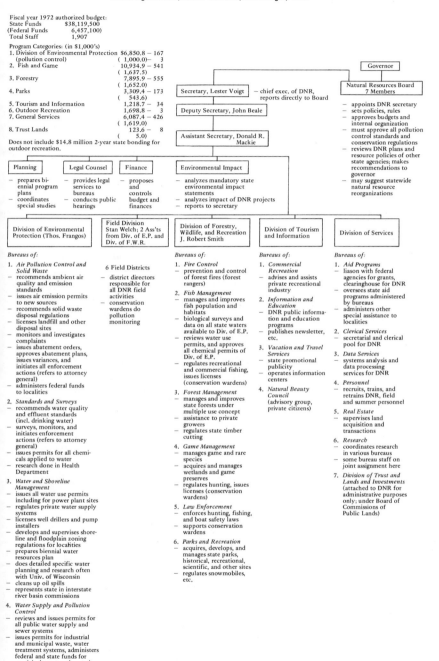

Fiscal year 1972 authorized budget:
State Funds $38,119,500
(Federal Funds 6,457,100)
Total Staff 1,907

Program Categories: (in $1,000's)
1. Division of Environmental Protection $6,850.8 — 167
   (pollution control) (1,000.0)— 3
2. Fish and Game 10,934.9 — 541
   (1,637.5)
3. Forestry 7,895.9 — 555
   (1,652.0)
4. Parks 3,309.4 — 173
   (543.6)
5. Tourism and Information 1,218.7 — 34
6. Outdoor Recreation 1,698.8 — 3
7. General Services 6,087.4 — 426
   (1,619.0)
8. Trust Lands 123.6 — 8
   (5.0)
Does not include $14.8 million 2-year state bonding for
outdoor recreation.

Governor

Natural Resources Board
7 Members

Secretary, Lester Voigt — chief exec. of DNR,
reports directly to Board

Deputy Secretary, John Beale

Assistant Secretary, Donald R.
Mackie

- appoints DNR secretary
- sets policies, rules
- approves budgets and
  internal organization
- must approve all pollution
  control standards and
  conservation regulations
- reviews DNR plans and
  resource policies of other
  state agencies; makes
  recommendations to
  governor
- may suggest statewide
  natural resource
  reorganizations

Planning
- prepares bi-
  ennial program
  plans
- coordinates
  special studies

Legal Counsel
- provides legal
  services to
  bureaus
- conducts public
  hearings

Finance
- proposes
  and
  controls
  budget and
  finances

Environmental Impact
- analyzes mandatory state
  environmental impact
  statements
- analyzes impact of DNR projects
- reports to secretary

| Division of Environmental Protection (Thos. Frangos) | Field Division Stan Welch; 2 Ass'ts from Div. of E.P. and Div. of F.W.R. | Division of Forestry, Wildlife, and Recreation J. Robert Smith | Division of Tourism and Information | Division of Services |

Bureaus of:

1. *Air Pollution Control and Solid Waste*
   - recommends ambient air quality and emission standards
   - issues air emission permits to new sources
   - recommends solid waste disposal regulations
   - licenses landfill and other disposal sites
   - monitors and investigates complaints
   - issues abatement orders, approves abatement plans, issues variances, and initiates all enforcement actions (refers to attorney general)
   - administers federal funds to localities
2. *Standards and Surveys*
   - recommends water quality and effluent standards (incl. drinking water)
   - surveys, monitors, and initiates enforcement actions (refers to attorney general)
   - issues permits for all chemicals applied to water
   - research done in Health Department
3. *Water and Shoreline Management*
   - issues all water use permits including for power plant sites
   - regulates private water supply systems
   - licenses well drillers and pump installers
   - develops and supervises shore-line and floodplain zoning regulations for localities
   - prepares biennial water resources plan
   - does detailed specific water planning and research often with Univ. of Wisconsin
   - cleans up oil spills
   - represents state in interstate river basin commissions
4. *Water Supply and Pollution Control*
   - reviews and issues permits for all public water supply and sewer systems
   - issues permits for industrial and municipal waste, water treatment systems, administers federal and state funds for municipal construction, trains and certifies operators

6 Field Districts
- district directors responsible for all DNR field activities
- conservation wardens do pollution monitoring

Bureaus of:

1. *Fire Control*
   - prevention and control of forest fires (forest rangers)
2. *Fish Management*
   - manages and improves fish population and habitats
   - biological surveys and data on all state waters available to Div. of E.P.
   - reviews water use permits, and approves all chemical permits of Div. of E.P.
   - regulates recreational and commercial fishing, issues licenses (conservation wardens)
3. *Forest Management*
   - manages and improves state forests under multiple use concept
   - assistance to private growers
   - regulates state timber cutting
4. *Game Management*
   - manages game and rare species
   - acquires and manages wetlands and game preserves
   - regulates hunting, issues licenses (conservation wardens)
5. *Law Enforcement*
   - enforces hunting, fishing, and boat safety laws
   - supports conservation wardens
6. *Parks and Recreation*
   - acquires, develops, and manages state parks, historical, recreational, scientific, and other sites
   - regulates snowmobiles, etc.

Bureaus of:

1. *Commercial Recreation*
   - advises and assists private recreational industry
2. *Information and Education*
   - DNR public information and education programs
   - publishes newsletter, etc.
3. *Vacation and Travel Services*
   - state promotional publicity
   - operates information centers
4. *Natural Beauty Council*
   (advisory group, private citizens)

Bureaus of:

1. *Aid Programs*
   - liason with federal agencies for grants, clearinghouse for DNR
   - oversees state aid programs administered by bureaus
   - administers other special assistance to localities
2. *Clerical Services*
   - secretarial and clerical pool for DNR
3. *Data Services*
   - systems analysis and data processing services for DNR
4. *Personnel*
   - recruits, trains, and retrains DNR, field and summer personnel
5. *Real Estate*
   - supervises land acquisition and transactions
6. *Research*
   - coordinates research in various bureaus
   - some bureau staff on joint assignment here
7. *Division of Trust and Lands and Investments* (attached to DNR for administrative purposes only; under Board of Commissions of Public Lands)

open-ended process in which the executive and legislative branches, special interest groups, and management experts took an active part. Both the 1966 and 1967 reorganizations were preceded by studies of special administrative task forces set up by Republican Governor Warren Knowles, composed of state officials, legislators, outside experts, and private interest groups.

In each case there was a lengthy discussion of the pros and cons attached to a long list of alternative organizational and leadership arrangements. The task forces huddled for months, first behind closed doors and then in public hearings, arguing why certain programs should be merged and how they should be directed. The administrative rationale for each alternative was clearly articulated and thoroughly debated. In fact, the creation of the DNR in 1967 seemed to have more to do with well-laid-out principles of administrative efficiency and management reform than with actually strengthening the state's environmental effort. In each reorganization, questions of institutional design were quickly translated into political terms, and Republicans and Democrats rallied behind their preferred options. Partisan activity was intense in the legislature, interest groups actively participated in the heated debates, and compromises were necessary to pass both final reorganization bills.

Because of its strong public administration flavor and political intensity, Wisconsin's two-staged environmental reorganization process represents an interesting and well-documented study of public institutional change. It also reflects the state's traditional and long-standing interest in the administrative conduct of public affairs. Wisconsin is a state in which public and private citizens have always displayed a high level of concern for proper governmental relationships, including the insurance of adequate administrative and private checks and balances. There is a populist tradition that seeks to insure an appropriate level of competition and citizen participation in public policy-making. This is predicated on suspicion of strong centralized governmental power.

For example, Wisconsin is one of a number of states that has traditionally operated under the "weak governor" style of government, whereby the power of the chief executive is limited by the existence of part-time, citizen policy boards that have a major role in the governance of executive agencies. These policy boards are meant to serve the negative role of checking the power of single agency directors and the governors who appoint them. It is feared that one person may be too apt to make hasty decisions, or decisions based on a limited viewpoint, special interest, or single-purpose constituency. By a contrast, committee leadership is expected to incorporate several points of view and result in more balanced, deliberative, and realistic (even if slower) judgments. Thus the seven-member Natural Resources Board was set up to govern the DNR. In addition, the DNR and its constituent bureaus are advised by at least a dozen other citizen-composed, part-time committees.

Wisconsin has also subjected its executive agencies to close evaluation. As a "good government" state, conformity to principles of efficient management and responsible government are often as important in evaluation as what an agency has actually accomplished. The University of Wisconsin, constitutionally described as a state agency, has been a strong participant in this process. For example, soon after the DNR was set up, the university's Water Resources Research Center initiated a river basin management study,[4] one portion of which concluded that the DNR's superdepartment structure limited its capacity to consider and carry out innovative work that was responsive to a wide range of public interests and opinions. This portion recommended a return to the previous organizational arrangement whereby environmental work was carried out among many, sometimes competing, agencies.[5]

The 1966 Reorganization of Water Regulatory Programs

The main focus of Wisconsin's first environmental reorganization was a stiffening of the state's water pollution regulatory effort by linking water quality and water quantity programs in a new Water Resources Division within the existing Department of Resource Development. Governed by a seven-man board, this new division pulled together two separate threads of the water quality effort: (1) industrial waste control, which had been administered by the interagency Committee on Water Pollution consisting of one representative from the Conservation Commission and the Public Service Commission, the state sanitary engineer, and two persons from the State Board of Health; and (2) municipal sewage and public water supply (including drinking water) from the State Board of Health. The Health Department, which had staffed both these programs, lost all jurisdiction in 1966, except for regulation of septic tanks and plumbing. In an innovative move, the two major water quality efforts were combined with the water use regulatory program of the Public Service Commission, which issued permits to industrial and agricultural water users. Water quality and quantity were said to be integrally related in the environment and required integrated program administration.

The consolidation of the water pollution control effort was both politically and administratively inspired. It has been written of its political genesis:

> During the summer of 1965, it became apparent that the Republican Administration was going to seek changes in the water regulatory set-up. The specific impetus for the change is unclear, although it would appear that certain political leaders decided that more rigorous pollution control could be good politics. Once the move for change was underway, leaders of both parties made efforts to capture the credit for their particular party. A long series of legislative and executive studies, hearings, and maneuvering resulted in the Water Resources Act of 1966.[6]

Republican Governor Warren Knowles also felt that reorganization was urgently needed on effective management grounds, and in this he was supported by the Department of Administration and the University of Wisconsin.

Expressing dissatisfaction with the many scattered agencies regulating water, he was frustrated in his inability to pinpoint responsibility and hold one agency accountable for failures or successes. It was even difficult to determine how much the state was spending on water pollution control efforts. Fragmented programs made planning and a coordinated approach almost impossible. There was no focus for public interest, support, or criticism, and it was difficult to recruit new professional staff. It was observed that the institutional structure for water quality was so complex that whatever accomplishments had been made "evolved in spite of the structure and not because of it."[7] In response to this fragmented institutional network of water programs, and by the time Governor Knowles set up an 18-man Committee on Water Resources to study the problem in the fall of 1935, some 36 Senate and Assembly bills were pending to change the state's water pollution control efforts.

Three key issues were hotly contested throughout the reorganization process: (1) what water programs to consolidate, (2) where to place the new integrated activity—in an existing agency or a new one, and (3) who would lead the operation—a single powerful director or a board of some type.

After six months of work, the governor's Committee on Water Resources recommended creation of a new Water Quality Commission.[8] This was to be a three-man body, serving full time, that would be responsible for the two, then separate, programs for industrial and municipal water pollution control. The committee reasoned that these programs belonged together since both regulated liquid wastes and river clean-ups involved both kinds of wastes. A new independent unit would increase the stature of the state's water pollution control program and give it added political visibility, resulting in a new focus for added funds and public support. This was a particularly important objective in 1966, since the pollution control effort did not then enjoy wide popular recognition or support.

Another aim was to reduce the influence at the Health Department, which had provided 85 percent of the employees working in the field of water quality and which had a reputation for leniency when it came to dealing with polluters on a legal basis. Further, as one task-force member stated, "the problem of pollution, which involves so many interests, cannot be solved by placing it under any agency with only one interest" such as the Health Department.[9] One leading state Senator argued: "People want something and they don't want to talk to a division head within the State Board of Health. They want to talk to a department head or a commissioner of an agency."[10] Health officials on the governor's committee strongly opposed the removal of water pollution control responsibility from their purview. As they argued; "One cannot separate public health and water; . . . the highest priority of water is for drinking."[11]

The governor's Committee on Water Resources strongly considered merging water quantity along with water quality programs. However, transfer of the Public Service Commission's water use permit authority was rejected by only one vote on the grounds that this program was more related to the commission's development-related mission than to pollution control. Another major alternative was to combine all water management and water pollution control programs into a new Department of Water Resources, which would mean some additional program transfers from the Conservation Department. Although it was agreed that this consolidation was administratively efficient and should take place sometime in the near future, it was rejected on two counts. One was political—it was feared that the more extensive reorganization would not pass in the coming legislative session, and the water regulatory reorganization was a top priority. The second objection to broad-scale reorganization was administrative. It was argued that "drastic reorganization" into a large department might overwhelm or set back the pollution control effort as it was just getting its feet on the ground.[12]

The governor's committee debated four leadership alternatives for its proposed Water Resources Commission: "(1) a director (appointed by the governor and serving at his pleasure) with an advisory board; (2) a director appointed by a policy board; (3) a three-man full-time commission with an advisory board; and (4) a large part-time commission with an advisory board,"[13] such as the existing Committee on Water Pollution. The third choice was selected as a middle-ground position. It was feared that a single director might be too dictatorial, biased, or limited, and a full-time body could concentrate greater expertise and energy on its work than a part-time one. The rejection of the single leader principle at this time aptly reflects the state's traditional preference for the "weak governor" style of government.

The Republican Senate passed the governor's committee's reorganization bill virtually intact, although support was initially lukewarm and a plethora of modifications were soon offered. As expected, the bill was bitterly opposed by the chairman of the State Board of Health and various health interest groups. The reaction of conservationists and groups such as the League of Women Voters and League of Wisconsin Municipalities was mixed since the former feared a subsequent reorganization including the Conservation Department and the latter were more inclined to that alternative. Two large paper companies— the industry responsible for most of the state's water pollution—supported the reorganization since they felt it would result in more rational and consistent policy.

The Democratic-controlled Assembly promptly rejected the Senate version and adopted one of its own that differed on all three major reorganization issues. Charging that the Republicans were "soft on industry," the Assembly bill transferred the Public Service Commission's water use permit authority along with the other water quality programs. The regulation of water quantity, it was argued, should not be dominated by the economic development interests and orientation of the Public Service Commission. And since water quantity and quality considerations could not be separated in a river or lake, how could they be efficiently separated in state programming? The Assembly also added important new state authority to set criteria governing local flood plain zoning and lakeshore zoning.[14] Wisconsin was the first state to enact this kind of land use zoning.

On the locational issue, the Democratic Assembly argued that a new state agency was not needed and thus recommended a new Division of Water

Resources within an existing department, the Department of Resource Development. Since this department happened to be the state's principal economic development planning organization, the Republicans had the opportunity to counter with the charge that the Democrats were "selling out to industry." Despite the fact that a Republican governor was in office, the Democratic Assembly also recommended a "strong governor" approach on the leadership question by calling for a single director for the new water unit, to be chosen by and directly responsible to the governor. And, despite the fact that this might mean new powers for a Republican governor, Republican legislators promptly predicted that a single director would become a "water czar."

A Conference Committee set up to resolve the difference between the Assembly and Senate versions resulted in the creation of a Division of Water Resources in the *reconstituted* Department of Resource Development. That department's principal economic promotional activities, such as developmental planning, were removed to reduce its "resource exploitation" flavor and provide a more palatable home for the water pollution control package. Water use regulation was included in the transfers along with industrial and municipal water quality regulation. In a compromise on the leadership question, the new Division was to be led by a 7-member part-time policy board, and advised by a 17-member interagency and legislative Natural Resource Committee.

The Creation of the DNR in 1967

Seeds for further reorganization, however, were planted at this time. As another compromise, the 1966 reorganization act stated that the new Division of Water Resources was to be an interim arrangement only and should be merged into a larger resource superdepartment as soon as possible.[15] And before the fledgling Water Resources Division could get its feet on the ground, it was consolidated along with new air and solid waste pollution control responsibility and the entire Conservation Department into the present structure—the DNR.

This second reorganization occurred within the context of statewide governmental reorganization, prompted by analysis of a special reorganization task force set up by Governor Knowles in early 1966. This group was known as the Kellett Commission for its chairman, and some of its members had served on and influenced the earlier reorganization task force. The Kellett Commission's primary aim was to reduce the 91 existing state executive and regulatory agencies to a more manageable number. Programs were to be rearranged to match current social issues, and the state's executive structure streamlined to make it more accountable to the governor and the legislature. In this way, state government was expected to become more responsible to the voters through their elected officials.

With a theme of overall governmental reform along principles of good management, administrative efficiency, and increased political responsiveness, the Kellett Commission operated under these administrative and political precepts:

a. The governor should be provided with the administrative facilities and authority to carry out the functions of his office efficiently and effectively. . . .

b. The administrative agencies which comprise the executive branch should be consolidated into a reasonable number of departments to be consistent with executive capacity to administer effectively at all levels. . . .

c. The integration into departments of agencies in the executive branch should be on a functional basis, so that programs can be co-ordinated. . . .

d. Each agency in the executive branch . . . should be integrated into one of the departments of the executive branch as closely as the conflicting goals of administrative integration and responsiveness to the legislature will permit. . . .

e. Structural reorganization should be a continuing process through careful executive and legislative appraisal of the placement of proposed new programs and the coordination of existing programs in response to changing emphasis or public demands.[16]

One of the major administrative reforms sought by the Kellett Commission was the elimination of old-style policy boards and their replacement with single departmental directors. In debating whether "to continue the weak governor concept by having directors responsible to and appointed by a policy board, or whether to have a single director elected or appointed by the governor,"[17] the Kellett Commission chose the single-director principle. Single directors could be held directly accountable to the public through its chief elected official, the governor, whereas policy boards were insulated from direct control. Single directors could also more efficiently manage departmental affairs than policy boards, which were cumbersome, slow, and lacking in technical expertise.

In support of its objective to reduce the overall number of executive departments, the Kellett Commission argued that broad decisions involving a trade-off or compromise between two or more program objectives are best "reached within the administrative structure—in collaboration rather than conflict."[18] The political "adversary process," whereby many small advocacy agencies with similar yet competing programs constantly did public battle against one another, should be abandoned in favor of an internal administrative decision-making process.

The Kellett Commission developed four principles for reorganizing the state's natural resource programs. These were:

1. Response to popular control. (The leadership of a resource agency should be elected or appointed so they would be

117

responsive to the public will. The present agencies are now insulated from the public.)

    2. Facilitate communication between the governor and citizens. (This would suggest a smaller number of agencies.)

    3. Assure effective and efficient control of programs.

    4. Effort to consolidate state government as a whole and integrate agencies on a functional basis.[19]

The commission's logic for creation of an environmental superdepartment was that conservation and pollution control were similar resource management programs, and that policy, planning, and administrative benefits would accrue from their co-location. Various resources such as water, land, and wildlife interacted in an ecological system in the natural environment, and there was a need to consider the total ecology in policy-making and program design. Consolidation would also allow all resource management decisions to be regarded as primarily administrative ones and to be made in the rational atmosphere of one executive department rather than by an "adversary process," whereby conflicts between agencies were suddenly politicized and thrashed out in a public context.

    Other reorganization aims were to line the pollution control and conservation interest group constituencies in order to build a strong alliance in support of the new pollution control effort and, through a dramatic reorganization, underscore the state's commitment to stronger environmental protection.

    Despite its preference for a single director, the Kellett Commission was forced to recommend a policy board to govern the new DNR in order to neutralize the anticipated opposition of conservationists and some state legislators to the single leadership approach. The seven-member Natural Resources Board that was created has broad responsibilities, including the authority to approve all the DNR's policies, standards and regulations, and budgets. However, its most influential power has proven to be that of appointing the DNR's secretary. After the work of the Kellett Commission was completed in 1967, the DNR remained one of only three major Wisconsin departments that still had a secretary selected by and serving at the pleasure of a policy board. The other two are the Agriculture Department and the Department of Health and Social Services.

    The Kellett Commission's proposal for an environmental superdepartment did not receive wide popular support when it reached the legislature in the spring of 1967. The public's interest in pollution problems was only starting to bud, and to heighten this the *Milwaukee Journal* published a series of colorful Sunday articles on pollution problems throughout the state. Industry, including the pulp and paper companies, did not lobby against the reorganization bill. They reportedly believed it preferable to deal with one, hopefully systematic, antipollution agency rather than a series of agencies that might be more likely to generate conflicting and politically motivated pollution standards.

    The most significant opposition to the DNR came from the Conservation Department and conservation interest groups. Conservationists were vigorously opposed to any merger, and, publicly, the reason given was that they feared that conservation would become too political an issue if merged with pollution control—i.e., that it might be adversely affected by association with a program that was increasingly popular and that involved constant contact with industry and other "black hats." Conservationists felt that natural resource programs were well-established and smoothly running, and "that it would be a mistake to put the fish management agency in the same department with the water pollution control agency."[20] The opposition of the Conservation Congress, a statewide federation of fish, game, and sportsmen's clubs, was so strong that it called upon its affiliate groups to organize rallies and marches around the state capitol.

The most critical issue at stake, however, was who would control the DNR. The seven-man Conservation Commission, which had governed the Conservation Department, worried that it might not have a majority on the new Natural Resources Board, and thereby would lose control over conservation programs. To overcome this opposition, an important legislative compromise was reached specifying that the DNR's seven-member Natural Resources Board should initially consist of four incumbent members of the Conservation Commission, and only three from the former Department of Resource Development. A further stipulation was added that at least three members of the board must always be from the northern portion of the state—the recreation-rich area.

The Department of Natural Resources, along with most of the other Kellett Commission reorganization proposals, passed the legislature in mid-July, 1967, over the continued opposition of the Conservation Commission and conservation interest groups. One reason passage was reportedly fairly prompt was that the legislature was annoyed with the special-interest lobbying of the conservationists and the so-called redshirts who were demonstrating around the Capitol. The battle, however, did not end here. Having attained a majority control over the Natural Resources Board, the conservationists then tried to get their man appointed secretary of the DNR. Since a legislative compromise specified that the DNR was not to begin operations as a combined unit until July, 1968, the vigorously fought battle for the leadership of the new department was carried out over a year's time. In the end, the conservation members on the board won out. Lester Voigt, who was the former Conservation Commissioner and also a member of the former interagency Water Pollution Commission, was appointed secretary. He, in turn, appointed his two principal deputies from the Conservation Department's forestry division.

CURRENT ORGANIZATION AND ACTIVITIES

The most significant organizational facts about the DNR's current operations are the lack of any substantial integration of its conservation and pollution control components, the dominance of the conservation effort and dependent status for pollution control, and the failure of the Natural Resources Board to affect departmental decision-making.

119

Despite the fact that the DNR was predicated on the rationale that administrative efficiency and planning benefits would result from a merger of pollution control and conservation programs, close integration of these programs after five years has not occurred. Wisconsin has taken a number of useful steps in this direction. However, these are a far cry from a structure that easily permits consideration of the "total ecology," and the DNR is not organized on the premise that it should. In fact, in the early stages some persons despaired of any integration, since the conservation and pollution control programs seemed so different. Basically, one was viewed as a manager and the other a regulator, each with separate daily tasks. Instead of joining hands with pollution control, the conservation constituency has also remained opposed to integration. Thus it was felt that forced integration might even have negative effects.

Until mid-1971, the DNR's internal organization reflected the fact that no real integration of the department's two main components was immediately intended or hoped for. Initially, there were five main divisions, representing the components as they were prior to reorganization. The Division of Environmental Protection is responsible for all pollution control programs, and is headed by Thomas Frangos, an engineer and lawyer recruited from outside the state. Three divisions constituted the former Department of Conservation and, since there initially was no one person in charge of all three, each division head reported directly to the secretary. He was to resolve all conflicts between the pollution control and conservation components, as well as to coordinate various aspects of conservation work. Under the secretary were located staff bureaus for planning and legal services. A fifth division, the Division of Services, was added in 1968 to perform research, engineering, financial, data, and other administrative services for the entire department.

In 1971 the DNR combined the three conservation divisions into one Division of Forestry, Wildlife, and Recreation, with supposedly equal status to the Division of Environmental Protection (see Chart 4.2). The DNR also set up a new Field Division and created six coterminous districts for pollution control and conservation. In structure, this field reorganization is similar to New York's Department of Environmental Conservation. The main stated purpose in Wisconsin is to decentralize and coordinate administrative processes for the pollution control and conservation components. A newly appointed district director in each region is in charge of both programs and reports directly to the Field Division director in Madison. The DNR's field reorganization occurred within the context of a statewide regionalization effort under incoming Democratic Governor Patrick Lucey, presented to the legislature as an economy measure.

However, the DNR does not intend any integration of conservation and pollution control programs in the field, at least in the near future. Although there will be a main headquarters in each district, some conservation units will maintain subregional offices. Although they will report to the same district director, the conservation and pollution control staff will report to separate program directors and will do mainly their own work. Conservation wardens are being retrained to do pollution monitoring and data gathering in the field.

In general, the DNR's pollution control and conservation divisions have continued to operate relatively autonomously. Wisconsin's DNR, however, has made more short-term gains in integration than New York's environment superdepartment, where intradepartmental communication and formal relationships are less well developed. The DNR has slowly developed a system of formal intradepartmental coordination, comment, and sign-off, and such procedures are clearly outlined in administrative handbooks. The formal contact, particularly between the water pollution control and fish management personnel, has thereby increased. For example, the Fish Bureau is required to comment on the Division of Environmental Protection's water use permits and must approve all permits for chemical applications to water. This bureau also supplies much of the essential data for the water pollution control effort, e.g., on water levels, flows, depth, biological content, temperature, etc. Informal departmentwide communication at the bureau level between the pollution control and conservation personnel is also gradually increasing. In the field, conservation wardens already have been helpful in gathering information and enforcing so-called one-shot polluters. However, the division heads in Madison talk very infrequently and usually meet only at the monthly staff meetings.

Unlike New York, by late 1972 the DNR had not yet initiated an across-the-board, joint planning effort for the whole department, and Secretary Voigt feels it will be several years before the DNR attempts this. Responsibility for water resource planning is statutorily assigned to the Division of Environmental Protection. The Bureau of Planning under the secretary only does program planning, and this is done separately for each division. A research unit in the Division of Services has made some attempt to coordinate individual research projects, but so far this is mainly to avoid duplication and to insure that results are available for everyone's use. Some persons in the Division of Environmental Protection and the Conservation Division have joint assignments in this research unit. Each division uses some of the central engineering, data, financial, and other services of the Division of Services. Each division, however, does its own legal work, relying on the central Legal Bureau mainly for technical input and legal advice.

Secretary Voigt has always acted as a strong secretary. He has kept to himself the solving of the competition and conflict between his pollution control and conservation components. Issues are usually handled on an ad hoc basis as problems arise and are resolved privately, in his own office. To date, these differences have not been that large. However, the DNR has experienced more differences than New York's environmental superdepartment, in part because it has existed longer and because it contains recreation and tourism programs. There is constant competition for DNR funds and new staff, and there are a large number of continuing jurisdictional disputes. For example, the Fish and Wildlife Bureaus would like to have a stronger say in water pollution control standards and water use permits, since their programs demand especially pure water. The Division of Environmental Protection would like to control all pesticides, including their use by the Fish and Forestry Bureaus.

Outright conflicts between program objectives have been less frequent. They have occurred, for example, when the conservation bureaus have opposed the issuance of dam building permits by the Division of Environmental Protection, and the latter has opposed forest burning and some methods of fire control. On occasion the water pollution control personnel have sided with the fish management staff against several proposed park developments, lakeshore constructions, artificial lakes, and tourist promotion.

In 1971, the secretary gave formal recognition to the existence of internal differences by setting up a new staff unit to help him resolve these—the Environmental Impact Bureau. The major responsibility of this new unit is to analyze and submit formal recommendations to the secretary on the environmental impact of other state agencies' proposed projects, in response to federal requirements under the National Environmental Policy Act of 1969. In 1971, Wisconsin became one of a handful of states to pass a law requiring the mandatory submission of environmental impact statements from each state agency on all their proposed projects,[21] and the new unit will also set up guidelines, evaluate, and make recommendations on these. However, reporting directly to the secretary, it will also review and submit a written evaluation of intradepartmental conflicts and trade-offs.

Conservation Programs Dominate

In competition for leadership attention and support, the DNR's conservation component dominates the pollution control effort. Basically, this stems from the fact that the secretary and his top management staff are all from the former Conservation Department and naturally have some greater interest and expertise in these programs. The secretary does not regard himself as a pollution control advocate, but rather as a resource program manager. He rarely uses the public forum to lobby for pollution control programs, rarely speaks to pollution control interest groups, and almost never goes before the state legislature in support of them. Whereas the conservation personnel can always find a sympathetic and technically component ear and ready supporter in the secretary and his deputies, Thomas Frangos, head of the Division of Environmental Protection, must stand on his own. Yet, he does not have strong, independent status within the DNR and unencumbered access to the public. In general, all his proposals and recommendations are filtered through the secretary. Even editorial changes are made there. For attention, funds, and the passage of pollution control measures, Frangos is entirely dependent on the secretary.

The conservation staff outnumber the pollution control personnel by more than 10 to 1. The Natural Resources Board is still dominated by persons more interested in conservation and resource issues than in pollution control. By early 1972, there were still only one or two acknowledged environmentalists on the board and little expertise in pollution control. The board spends

122

approximately three-fourths of its time on conservation matters. The DNR's field reorganization will probably further dilute the Division of Environmental Protection's position of independence in the DNR. Although the new Field Division director has two assistants, one representing pollution control and the other conservation, the director himself was formerly the head of the Division of Forestry and Recreation. Five out of the six new district directors in the field are from the conservation side. Directors were chosen on the basis of which problem, conservation or pollution, seemed most important in each region, and the Milwaukee region is the only one whose director was chosen from the Division of Environmental Protection. Since all field staff will ultimately be under the control of the district directors and the new director of the Field Division in Madison, Frangos will lose direct control over all his field staff, remaining in charge of his Madison staff only.

The dominance of conservation programs may also stem from the fact that historically these programs have been popular, strong, and independent. The conservation ethic in Wisconsin is well-established. These programs are regarded by the citizenry as some of the state's most valuable, and the conservation constituency is large, entrenched, and prospering. Each of the conservation units—fish and game, forestry, recreation, and wilderness—has its own special interest groups, and each is advised by a separate citizen council. Statewide associations of interest groups, such as the Conservation Congress mentioned previously, are particularly powerful. Conservation interests are well represented in the state legislature, particularly by legislators from the water and recreation-rich areas of the state. These programs in Wisconsin, as in many states, have traditionally been funded by segregated revenues from fish and game licenses, fines, and other sources, and these funds are separate from general revenues and less subject to legislative and public scrutiny. The conservation effort also specializes in strong public relations. While pollution control information is generally highly technical and sparse, the prolific conservation journals and newspapers are colorful, attractive, and useful to the average citizen.

Secretary Voigt argues that, over the next several years, the concern for pollution control work will gradually increase, catching up to the conservation programs. He explains that in 1971 he devoted an equal share of his time to the Division of Environmental Protection, since these programs seemed to require much more detailed attention than the conservation ones. Whereas the pollution control budget was originally less than 7 percent of the DNR's budget for conservation programs, in 1972 it was over 20 percent. However, some of this difference is made up by federal funds for the construction of wastewater treatment facilities. The secretary has also stated that he is able to divert some of the conservation budget, mainly from segregated revenues and trust funds, to the pollution control side. Although he does not see himself as an environmental advocate, he did step up the compliance timetable for one set of water standards proposed by the Division of Environmental Protection because he felt the public demand for it. However, this was done over that division's firm protest that this timetable was unrealistic.

123

As in most states, the DNR's conservation programs are quite independent of one another. In Wisconsin, there is also some built-in conflict among them. The Fish and Game Management Bureau pride themselves on a "Mr. Clean" image. They consider their major functions scientific (e.g. biological surveys of waterways), regulatory (e.g., administration of hunting laws), and preservationist. Some of their most prided programs are the "wild rivers" program, wetlands preservation, and protection of rare species and habitats. A majority of the staff are biologists. In contrast, recreation and tourism are more developmental and promotional. Lands are acquired and developed for parks and access roads, concession stands are built, and vacationing and traveling are promoted. The Forest Management Bureau is both protectionist and development-oriented. It develops forests, regulates timber cutting, offers assistance to private forest growers, fights fires, and manages forest recreation areas under the multiple-use concept.

The Division of Environmental Protection

Although its position and importance in the DNR is ambiguous, the Division of Environmental Protection does not lack pollution control authority. It is particularly strong in the number of laws it administers to regulate both water quality and water use, a result of the far-reaching 1966 water regulatory reorganization that combined these programs. Unlike Minnesota, New York, and many other states' environmental reorganizations, an almost clean break was made with the Health Department in 1966, and the Division of Environmental Protection has responsibility for public water supply facilities and drinking water purity. The division has very clear-cut permit authority over the location of power plants and grants permits to all persons wishing to apply any chemical to water. The 1966 reorganization act also gave it authority to develop statewide criteria for flood plain and lakeshore zoning, which local government units must follow in zoning, and charged it with developing a comprehensive water resources plan. With the aid of the University of Wisconsin's Water Resources Center, the Division of Environmental Protection has developed a strong planning orientation and has conducted or funded some sophisticated water treatment studies. For example, there have been studies on the regional location of treatment facilities according to the natural river basin system, solutions to lake eutrophication, automatic water quality monitoring, nitrate removal, and abatement costs.[22] In Wisconsin, however, authority over pesticides remains an interagency function in which the DNR participates and has a veto power. The radiation control program is primarily concerned with medical and industrial uses and is administered by the Department of Health and Social Services.

The Division of Environmental Protection's standards-setting work over five years has been steady, but slower and less complete in comparison to Minnesota's Pollution Control Agency, also set up in 1967. Water pollution control is the oldest, largest, and strongest effort, and the newer programs for air pollution and solid waste management have been slow in getting off the ground. By the end of 1968 the division had issued a set of water quality standards for interstate and intrastate waters, setting minimum standards to protect different uses—public water supply, aquatic life, recreation, industrial, and cooling water.[23] These limited solids, dissolved solids, dissolved oxygen, bacteria, pH range, and temperature. Effluent standards were only adopted gradually thereafter. For example, phosphates were limited in early 1971 and standards for mercury were adopted at the end of that year. Most water pollution abatement orders will come due in 1973, and the division spends much of its time currently riding herd on individual cases.

Air standards for particulate matter were set in 1970, limiting smoke, dusts, open burning, fly ash, and other airborne particles.[24] Industries were given 18 months to comply. However, except for the federally designated Milwaukee Air Region, no standards for gaseous (nonparticulate) emissions were set until 1971, including sulfur oxide and carbon monoxide standards. By mid-1972, emission standards had not yet been completed.

By early 1969 the division had surveyed and classified all solid waste disposal sites and practices and had adopted regulations requiring certification of all sites and practices (including incineration and composting) and detailed regulations limiting the location of sanitary landfills.[25] However, by mid-1972 no deadline date had been set for compliance. Stringent pesticides standards were set in 1970, which outlawed all but six major pesticides.

Although the Division of Environmental Protection will begin to enter its most demanding enforcement phase in 1973, many observers feel that the division may be criticized for its lack of enforcement activities so far. There have been only a few cases against large polluters, including the pulp and paper industry. The division is criticized for granting too many variances and time extensions to the industries and municipalities, and some pollution control interest groups charge that the division is too closely associated with industry, especially the pulp and paper companies through their Technical Advisory Association. The division has referred a relatively small number of enforcement cases to the attorney general for prosecution, and thus far seems instead to prefer to negotiate technical and engineering solutions with polluters rather than taking legal action against them.

The Division of Environmental Protection has made no attempt to integrate its water quality and water quantity programs. Despite the rhetoric accompanying the 1966 water reorganization, the division's permit systems for wastewater discharge and water use remain in two bureaus. Frangos explains that this is logical since water quantity considerations come first in the permit-granting process, and it is the water use permit that will usually decide whether or not an industry or power plant can proceed with its construction plans. The water discharge permit is considered a more highly technical one, and at the time when industries apply for the initial water use permit, their full engineering plans are incomplete. Thus they cannot provide the necessary information on which to base the granting or denying of a water discharge permit.

Similarly, the division has made no formal effort to integrate its water, air, and solid waste programs. Several years ago, consideration was given to organizing these programs on a functional basis—i.e., separate divisions for pollution research, standards-setting, monitoring, enforcement, financial and technical assistance—thus dissolving the traditional lines drawn between water, air, and solid waste efforts. However, Frangos considered this approach too complicated, since the staff was accustomed to dealing in the established categories for water, air, and solid waste. He suggests that a functional approach might be more feasible if the division were larger, since the large size would allow for the necessary duplication and overlap that would occur immediately following a functional reorganization.

The Division of Environmental Protection is staffed mainly by sanitary engineers, most of whom were transferred from the Health Department by the 1966 reorganization. Like most of the DNR, many are older civil servants. Frangos has stated that the pollution control effort is badly in need of new middle-management staff, a broader scientific expertise, and lawyers. Although the division had early established pollution control field offices, unlike Minnesota's PCA, its pollution monitoring work requires a vast increase in experienced staff.

The Role of the Natural Resources Board

The Natural Resources Board has not proved to be an active, aggressive, or deliberative body, but rather a rubber stamp of department decisions. Its most influential deed has been to appoint the DNR's secretary. Since the board chose a very strong secretary who preferred to make as many decisions as possible, its other powers have been limited. Board members see their role as basically a broad policy-making group. They do not see themselves as the primary decision-making power over the department, and do not feel they should be intimately involved in every detail of the department. In early 1972, the Natural Resources Board consisted of a banker, two lawyers, a marine architect, one person in real estate, one person with an agricultural firm, and the director of the University's Water Resources Center (who served on both reorganization task forces). The current chairman is regarded as the secretary's close associate.

As a policy-making body, the board issues or approves broad statements and objectives governing the DNR's operating procedures. An example of a policy set by the board is that public hearings should be required for pollution permits and orders, the proliferation of sewer treatment plants in small communities should be avoided, and that the DNR should take a certain stance vis-á-vis the federal government. These policies are all written, codified, printed, and distributed. The board also approves the department's biennial budget, internal organization, and whatever long-range plans it might generate. For pollution control, the board limits its role to approving standards recommended by the secretary. So far, all of these except for pesticides were approved with little modification, although the debate on some was lengthy. For conservation programs, for which there is considerably more expertise, the board frequently gets involved in what are more purely administrative rather than policy matters. For example, the board approves the dates and times of hunting seasons, the wildlife included, the contracts, bids, and final authorization of all land acquisitions over $200,000.

The board has evolved as basically a reactive body to the secretary. The board meets only once a month, often for less than a day. Instead of initiating issues, it usually briefly discusses those raised by the department, gains consensus, and then signs off on the secretary's recommendations. Board members are mailed written material from the DNR's staff on each proposal prior to the meetings, but this is often highly detailed and difficult to wade through. As a matter of conviction, most members agree that the real expertise lies within the department, and they take for granted the merit and validity of its proposals. As a matter of preference, they avoid controversy at their meetings. Often departmental proposals are approved in-between the board's monthly meetings, when the secretary canvasses members by phone to gain agreement. Much of the board's actual work is done at dinner the night before the monthly meeting. Also, much of the work is done not by the full body, but by two- or three-man special committees.

Board members do not seek to add to their specific authorities or broaden their influence. In fact, some would like to leave the more routine matters for conservation programs to the DNR's staff. The other change they would like is to be better informed as to departmental activities, controversial activities, new research ideas, and failures. Several times in 1971 they have been caught off-guard. For example, the board took considerable public criticism following two land scandals involving several DNR employees in 1971. In one case, an employee allegedly received a kickback from a land sale to the DNR. In the other, an employee was charged with being cognizant of the fact the DNR was seeking to purchase a piece of land, bought it himself, and then sold it to the department at an increased price.

Since little of real controversy is discussed, board meetings are not a focus of interest group activity. The most vigorous lobbying is done instead at public hearings. More often than not board meetings are attended only by a few individuals interested in a particular decision, although on some conservation issues, such as hunting seasons, a larger number will turn out. Individuals and groups must have the approval of the board to be present and testify. The board holds many executive sessions that are closed to the public.

EVALUATION

In many ways, Wisconsin has been considered a leader among states in environmental management. It has always had a strong resource preservation ethic. It was the first state to undertake an environmental reorganization in 1966, and the first state to form an environmental superdepartment. The DNR is significant in the number of specific regulatory authorities it locates in one place, particularly for water. Its decision to combine water quality and quantity programs was especially innovative in 1966, and its flood plain and lakeshore zoning requirements enacted at the same time have served as a model for other states. With the help of the University of Wisconsin, the DNR had undertaken some complicated river basin and other planning before there were federal requirements for it. Since 1967, the DNR has made slow but steady progress in pollution standards-setting. Although there is little evidence of strong enforcement through the courts thus far, the DNR's record can only be fully evaluated in the next few years as standards and abatement order deadlines come due. The DNR was also one of the first state environmental departments to ban several major pesticides, including DDT. It has enjoyed an increasingly large budget and staff.

Disadvantages for Pollution Control in a Superdepartment

The DNR, however, is an excellent example of the paucity of benefits, and even some negative effects, of an environmental superdepartment. One of the most obvious outcomes of a large department combining similar yet competing environmental programs, each with its own objectives, style, and political base, is that one program will dominate. In the case of Wisconsin, the conservation effort dominates the pollution control work. The negative impact on the pollution control effort pertains mostly to the subjective, political atmosphere in which it works. The aggressiveness, image, visibility, and, consequently, the political support of the pollution control effort have clearly been undercut by its location in the DNR. This, in turn, has probably slowed down its actual output.

First, there may have been a large opportunity cost paid by the early merger. Pollution control programs were merged in 1967 with the Conservation Department at a time when the consolidated water regulatory unit was a fledgling institution and before air and solid waste programs had yet begun. Since then, the Division of Environmental Protection has had to compete with the conservation programs for the attention and interest of the DNR's secretary and his principal deputies. It does not act independently within the DNR, since most of what is written or recommended must be cleared with the secretary, whether it is to be sent to the board or not. The Natural Resources Board also cannot be regarded as a friend in court, because its membership is more interested in conservation than pollution control affairs. Thus from the beginning, the Division of Environmental Protection has had to take a second-place position in the DNR and to fight battles for independence, support, and jurisdiction that have cost time and energy and also probably have weakened morale.

Importantly, in the years when the pollution control movement badly needed a state governmental spokesman and institutional rallying point, there was none. If Wisconsin had had a governmental environmental advocate, the amorphous but general public interest in pollution control might have been solidified and focused and a base of political support built. In fact, even now there is no one environmental interest group with which the department has contact and to which it responds on a regular basis. Thomas Frangos is not in the position to lobby publicly on behalf of the Division of Environmental Protection, as the secretary can, and he does not receive much publicity. But Secretary Voigt does not see his role as an environmental advocate. He does very little public speaking, rarely has contact with antipollution interest groups, and does not appear personally to lobby in the legislature. He also has rarely sought to widen the DNR's influence over other state agencies on environmental matters. He believes the DNR's main interest group contact should be confined to its many formal citizen advisory councils. Unlike conservation interest groups for hunting and fishing, forestry, wilderness, and the like, pollution control groups thus remain badly fragmented.

The DNR illustrates that one program element can be confused with another in the public eye when both are administered in the same superdepartment. In this case, the image of the pollution control effort may have been hurt by public criticism of conservation. Much of the public views the DNR as a vast, complex bureaucracy. Many citizens either fail to distinguish between the DNR's two components, or, being more familiar with the conservation programs, ignore or misunderstand the pollution control work. Recently, the conservation efforts have come under severe public criticism. As a result of the two alleged land scandals involving conservation employees, the legislature started an investigation of the DNR's activities in the fall of 1971. The DNR's use of state condemnation powers to acquire land for park developments has also alienated some who have lost their land or are threatened by the loss. Several environmental groups also criticize the development-oriented nature of the DNR's recreation activities. They believe the pollution control effort is tainted by administrative association with the bureaus that develop wilderness areas, regulate motorboating, snowmobiles and land rovers, create artificial lakes, regulate timber cutting, and promote tourism.

Observers also suggest that the image of the DNR and its pollution control work has suffered from the bitter controversy surrounding the merger of this program with the Conservation Department. Conservationists did not initially complain, as they did in New York, that their programs were being overwhelmed by the new antipollution effort. However, they have increasingly voiced the fear that this will happen as the pollution control program gains some momentum, popularity, press, and interest group attention. In general, there is a lingering sense of bitterness and malaise in both camps, and from the outset the DNR has had a history of being publicly attacked and criticized. Because of this, the DNR seems to be increasingly taking on a defensive manner, and the department is not always easily open to evaluation or accessible to interest groups.

129

A good example of the aura of criticism surrounding the DNR is the fact that no official connected with it is above reproach. Recently two members of the Natural Resources Board, once believed in the environmental camp, have been "exposed" by radical environmentalists—one for his connection with a law firm whose clients include several large paper companies, and the other, director of the University's Water Resource Center, for accepting funds for research from a paper company.

Recently, more criticism has focused specifically on the Division of Environmental Protection. Some of the technical processes of pollution control seem difficult to understand compared to conservation activities, and the division's constant contact with industry is questioned. Whereas the stand of the fish and wildlife personnel in favor of tough water quality standards and wilderness preservation and against dam construction leads them to be regarded as "white hats," the Division of Environmental Protection sometimes wears the "black hat." Conservationists complain that the pollution control effort is too political a process. This distinction is supported by Frangos, who argues the need to better define his role in the DNR. He sees the division as the broad regulator of pollution and admits he must balance ecological against economic and other considerations. He sees the conservation units, in contrast, as resource managers *and* ecological advocates, representing only one among many interests that must be taken into account in pollution regulation.

A major criticism of the Division of Environmental Protection comes from environmental groups and the press who complain that it constantly is dragging its feet on enforcement. The Republican attorney general, Robert Warren, has frequently directed the division to speed up its compliance timetables and bring more enforcement cases to court. When Democratic Governor Patrick Lucey took office in 1971, he directed his staff to draw up a complete list of pollution control orders issued by the division and to keep track of its enforcement score card. The attorney general, with an eye on the gubernatorial seat, is hinting that he will use his "public intervenor" powers more frequently and broadly. This authority, set forth in the 1967 reorganization act, permits the attorney general to intervene in or appeal to all proceedings or rulings for water polluters who appear to be violating public rights law.[26]

Lack of Integration Benefits

The failure of the Division of Environmental Protection to become a successful and energetic public advocate for tough pollution control might have been offset by the benefits of integration of this effort with conservation. Presumably, integration might lead to improved environmental policy-making, more effective management of problems, and efficient administration. This was argued in 1967 by the designers of the superdepartment who believed that pollution, fish, forests, and recreation were intimately related. If the secretary had taken on the role of environmental arbitrator, balancing and integrating each program, the presence of separate departmental advocates and bases of political support might have been less desirable.

However, so far there have not been any sizable integration benefits from Wisconsin's environmental superdepartment. A first step has been taken in that there are some formal provisions for intradepartmental comment and sign-off. There is also increasing informal communication, expertise, and information sharing. The consolidation of conservation and pollution control field units under six common district directors may be regarded as a second step, although for the time being this is viewed as a cost efficiency rather than an integrative move. Wisconsin has stopped here, however. The DNR's secretary does not spend much time attempting to plan the integration of his two main components. If he is an arbitrator between them it is only for the purposes of internal conflict resolution, and this is done on an entirely ad hoc basis as competition arises. It is interesting that several departmental spokesmen, including Thomas Frangos, consider the personnel and equipment sharing that may result from the field reorganization to be *the* principal benefit of an environmental superdepartment so far, rather than planning or policy-making improvements. Use of conservation field staff for pollution control monitoring is seen as particularly helpful to that effort since it lacks adequate field personnel.

Advocacy and Accessibility versus Economic Efficiency

Because the pollution control program has not developed into a strong, highly visible, and innovative effort, recent recommendations from several sources have called for its separation from the DNR. This was first suggested in 1970 by members of the University of Wisconsin's Water Resource Research Center, the State Administration Department, and was also considered by incoming Governor Lucey. The former argue that a separate pollution control effort could operate in a much more innovative, independent, and aggressive manner. They advocate a return to the old "adversary" system, whereby separate pollution control, conservation, and other state agencies can publicly argue out their own viewpoints. In 1972, this reorganization proposal gained substantial support in the state legislature, particularly among conservationists. Some persons predict that a reseparation of pollution control and conservation programs will take place in 1973.

The recommendation for a return to a governmental system of many single-purpose, competing advocacy agencies highlights another negative effect of an environmental superdepartment. In such a superdepartment, competition or conflicts between its component parts tend to be resolved internally, as with the DNR. Only recently have differences between the DNR's antipollution and conservation units come into public view, mainly by accident. Secretary Voigt has stated that his role is to solve such conflicts internally, within his administrative house. However, some slippage has occurred at public hearings, when

DNR staff have suddenly found themselves publicly taking different sides on an issue. For example, at a public hearing in 1971, the pollution control and fish personnel lined up against the recreation bureau opposing the creation of an artificial lake in northern Wisconsin. The pollution control staff worried about dredging and siltation, while the fish and wildlife bureau argued that this would harm trout fishing.

Public administration and political scientists argue that the choice here may be between optimizing economic efficiency or individual accessibility and participation in government. Resource economists have argued that it is efficient to combine all resource programs in one superdepartment, such as the DNR. It is efficient in the sense that similar jobs can be integrated, such as administration, legal services, and pollution and conservation monitoring. Some facilities can also be shared and also less time must be spent on interagency coordination. It is efficient because separate components can benefit from the skills, expertise, and data of one another. Examination of each component's objectives and program means will permit the elimination of potential conflicts. Some problems can then be nipped in the bud—for example, the use of harmful pesticides by forestry and fish management personnel and the issuance of a water use permit to an industry whose discharges cannot be absorbed easily in the water. Eventually, planning and programs may be merged. Finally, a superdepartment may provide an administrative umbrella for the component units to proceed with their tasks on a systematic basis, with as little politics involved as possible.

On the other hand, many political scientists and others would argue that when pollution control programs are combined in one overall department with conservation activities, in an attempt to optimize economic efficiencies, political choice and accessibility may be compromised.[27] This position holds that governmental decisions that involve trade-offs of different values of society— such as resource development for economic purposes versus pollution control for health and aesthetic aims—should be made in such a way as to maximize private citizens' understanding of the issues and their participation in the basic decision-making. However, when one natural resource department considers, or trades off, conservation objectives against pollution control in a joint process, all important choices will be made internally and are less likely to be articulated. Further, private citizens will have less ability to participate in that decision-making, through their elected representatives or interest groups, than if the two programs were in separate departments. It is believed that if one department speaks just for pollution control and another agency speaks just for conservation the degree of public debate on the resources issue will increase.

Such persons would argue that program efficiencies will have to be sacrificed in order to implement democratic control, which is not always an efficient system in the short run. To close the circuit, however, it may be that active public participation in governmental decisions, and equal access by all groups, will improve decision-making by bringing to it a real-world and innovative focus. It will also increase the likelihood that governments serve the public interest. Thus, in the long run, programs will be more relevant to actual resource problems and their basic efficiency will thereby be increased.

The Natural Resources Board illustrates well how policy boards may serve to limit the public responsiveness and direct accountability of executive agencies. The board acts, as the theory goes, as an effective buffer between the governor and the DNR. Because the board appoints the DNR's secretary, the secretary is accountable to it and not to the state's chief elected official. The governor is thereby denied one of the most important ingredients of executive power—the power to hire and fire departmental directors as he chooses. Nor can the governor easily gain control over a majority of board members. Since the members are appointed by the governor, subject to Senate confirmation, for overlapping six-year terms, no one governor can appoint more than two or so members except under unusual circumstances, such as the early resignation of a member. One of the major objectives of the Kellett Commission's 1967 reorganization proposals was to consolidate and streamline executive agencies to make them more responsive to the control of elected officials, and thereby the public. However, this objective was clearly compromised by provision for the Natural Resources Board. Granted, all pollution control and most natural resource programs are located in one place, and the current governor finds it easier than his predecessors to evaluate successes or failures than if these programs were scattered. However, the DNR is not directly accountable to him.

The situation in Wisconsin also demonstrates that policy boards do not necessarily serve as an adequate negative check against the "arbitrary" power of a single departmental director. The DNR secretary's authority is very large, in practice. In fact, it is the authority of the board to appoint the secretary, and its choice of the man, that more than anything else may have influenced the DNR's course of activity.

Because the Natural Resources Board does not make the major departmental decisions, and because the inclination of its citizen members is to avoid controversy at meetings, the board cannot be considered a means of increasing the public's direct access to governmental decision-making. In fact, board meetings are not well-attended by citizens, and many of its decisions are made behind closed doors. Still, however, the general public *believes* that the board has some real power over the DNR, and it is sometimes the board, not the DNR's secretary, that is held responsible in the public eye for particular departmental decisions. Wisconsin is a state that has typically relied on policy boards and the public has grown used to them. The fact that the board is often perceived as the final decision-maker is aptly illustrated by the fact that in 1971 there was a barrage of interest-group criticism against the existence of policy boards.[28] Thus one of the most negative effects of the board is this. The board's existence, in the fact of a strong secretary, may serve to hide from public view the real locus of decision-making and thus to diminish rather than increase the public's access. To some extent the board serves as an umbrella, attracting public attention to itself and deflecting public scrutiny away from the DNR.

The Natural Resources Board is an old-style device for committee leadership that no longer serves the purposes for which it was intended. As most policy boards, it is a part-time body required to meet only monthly. Its citizen members cannot concentrate sufficient time, energy, or interest on departmental affairs to affect real decision-making. In fact, only two or three of its current members have any professional or technical expertise in environmental programs. Hence, the board tends to take the secretary's and staff's word for things, and to act mainly as a rubber stamp for decisions already taken within the DNR. While it does not add much that is new to the discussion of environmental problems and solutions, its deliberations and the staff preparation for them sometimes cost valuable time. Since it is difficult for any policy board to achieve a membership that equally balances one special interest off against another, its membership will typically be imbalanced. The Natural Resources Board is biased not so much because its members represent industry or other polluters, but because its membership is lopsided in favor of conservation programs. This exacerbates some of the problems for the pollution control effort.

NOTES

1. Wisconsin, Laws of 1965, Chapter 614 (adopted 1966 and effective July 1, 1966). (This act is also known as the Water Resources Act of 1966.)

2. Wisconsin, Laws of 1967, Chapter 75, Section 25 (adopted 1967 and effective August 1, 1967).

3. Wisconsin, Laws of 1967, Chapter 83 (adopted in 1967).

4. University of Wisconsin, Water Resources Center, *Institutional Design for Water Quality Management: A Case Study of the Wisconsin River*, DWRR c-1228, 9 volumes (Madison: Water Resources Center, 1970 and 1971).

5. David C. Ranney, *An Analysis of Alternative Institutional Patterns for Managing Water Quality on a Regional System Basis*, in Water Resources Center, *op. cit.*, Volume IX, Section K.

6. *Ibid.*, p. 19.

7. State Senator Robert Warren, unpublished Minutes of a Meeting of the Governor's Committee on Water Resources, December 9, 1965.

8. Governor's Committee on Water Resources, "Recommendations of the Governor's Committee on Water Resources," April 25, 1966 (unpublished).

9. State Senator Robert Warren, unpublished Minutes of a Meeting of the Governor's Committee on Water Resources, February 10, 1966.

10. *Ibid.*

11. Members of the State Board of Health, *Ibid.*

12. Unpublished Minutes of a Meeting of the Governor's Committee on Water Resources, February 10 and March 3, 1966.

13. Gerald Rohlich, unpublished Minutes of a Meeting of the Governor's Committee on Water Resources, February 10, 1966.

14. Wisconsin, Laws of 1965, Chapter 614, Sections 22 and 31.

15. Wisconsin, Laws of 1965, Chapter 614, Section 2.

16. Wisconsin, Laws of 1967, Chapter 75, Section 1, Article 2 (a-e).

17. Kellett Commission, cited in the unpublished Minutes of a Meeting of the Governor's Committee on Water Resources, January 28, 1966.

18. Freeman Holner, "Management Coordination—Prerequisite to Rational Budgeting," from the National Association of State Budget Officers Institute, *State Budgeting for Natural Resources Programs* (Chicago: National Association of State Budget Officers, 1968) p. 15.

19. Kellett Commission, *op. cit.*

20. Holner, *op. cit.*, p.15.

21. Wisconsin, Laws of 1971, Chapters 273 and 274.

22. See, for example, University of Wisconsin, Water Resources Center, *Interagency Water Resources Research and Data Collection Program, 1968 and 1970* (Madison: Water Resources Center, 1968 and 1970).

23. Wisconsin, "Interstate and Intrastate Water Quality Standards" (Madison: Department of Natural Resources, interstate standards effective June 1, 1967 and intrastate standards effective September 1, 1968).

24. Wisconsin, "Air Pollution Control Rules" (Madison: Department of Natural Resources, effective July 1, 1970).

25. Wisconsin, "Solid Waste Disposal Standards" (Madison: Department of Natural Resources, adopted March, 1969).

26. Wisconsin, Laws of 1967, Chapter 75, Section 25, Article 9.

27. See, for example, Jerald Hage and Michael Aiken, *Social Change in Complex Organizations* (New York: Random House, 1970); "Program Change and Organizational Properties: A Comparative Analysis," *American Journal of Sociology*, Vol. 72 (1967), pp. 503-19; "Organization Interdependence and Intra-Organizational Structure," *American Sociological Review*, December, 1968, pp. 912-30; James Q. Wilson, "Innovation in Organizations; Notes Toward a Theory," in James D. Thompson, *Approaches to Organization Design* (Pittsburgh: Pittsburgh University Press, 1966); Lawrence Mohr, "Determinants of Innovation in Organizations," *American Political Science Review*, March, 1969, pp. 111-26; and Victor A. Thompson, "Bureaucracy and Innovation," *Administrative Science Quarterly*, June, 1965, pp. 1-20.

28. See, for example, John Wyngaard's editorial column, *Wisconsin State Journal*, June 30, 1971.

5

NEW YORK'S DEPARTMENT
OF ENVIRONMENTAL CONSERVATION

INTRODUCTION

New York's Department of Environmental Conservation (EnCon) was signed into law on Earth Day, April 22, 1970, and began operations shortly thereafter.[1] The Department of Environmental Conservation is an environmental superdepartment that houses pollution control programs along with many conservation and resource management activities. Its pollution control jurisdiction is broad, including water and air pollution, solid waste management, pesticides, radiation, and, in 1971, noise control.[2] These functions were inherited from three departments with shared responsibilities—Health, Conservation, and Agriculture and Markets—and three interagency policy-making councils—the Air Pollution and Pesticides Control Councils and the Water Resources Commission. However, Health Department staff had done most of the actual pollution control work. The entire Conservation Department was also transferred to EnCon intact, with the exception of its Parks Division and motorboat regulation. Thus EnCon is in charge of water use, forests, and fish and wildlife management, aspects of oil and gas regulation, and marine resources. The 1970 act also authorized land use planning powers for the new department. Chart 5.1 shows EnCon's current organization, functions, and budget.

Entirely a gubernatorial product, the major emphasis of the reorganization was on pollution control. Tougher pollution regulation was needed and this required an integration of pollution control programs and a new institutional focus and public spokesman. The Health Department was considered an inappropriate locus for stronger regulatory efforts. However, the exact reason why pollution control was combined with almost the entire Conservation Department was never fully articulated. Unlike the case of Wisconsin's environmental superdepartment, there was little public administration rationale supporting the merger and it is unclear to what extent integrated policy, planning, and administrative benefits were anticipated.

The Department of Environmental Conservation is led by a strong single director, appointed by the governor with Senate confirmation. EnCon's commissioner is thus directly accountable to the governor and serves at his pleasure. EnCon is advised by an originally 15- and now 16-member State Environmental Board, chaired by the EnCon commissioner and composed of eight other departmental and seven citizen members.[3] The board's major statutory power over the department is its authority to approve all pollution control standards and regulations proposed by the commissioner. Choosing to interpret this function and the term "standard" narrowly, EnCon's commissioner has not submitted all proposed regulations to the board. However, as more standards are set and submitted, the board has proved to be a cumbersome and slow decision-making body, and it has been difficult to gain consensus among its members. Some members represent state agencies or private activities that cause pollution.

The new department began with a sense of momentum and openness to it. The commissioner has spent most of his time on pollution control matters, emphasizing particularly regulatory work. Although all EnCon's regulatory work has not been fast-paced, some innovative programs have been launched and the department has sought to widen its environmental authority over other state agencies and the private sector. Recently, the department has come under attack from some environmental interest groups for inadequate pollution monitoring and enforcement. Some persons also feel that the commissioner is dominated by and too dependent on Governor Rockefeller, and this demonstrates the vulnerability of a single departmental leader directly responsive to the governor.

There have been few benefits from the merger of pollution control and conservation programs in EnCon thus far, and perhaps some opportunity cost for pollution control. Making sense out of the environmental superdepartment has absorbed valuable administrative time and energy that might have been devoted solely to pollution control. While both components have competed for the commissioner's attention, staff time, and public support, there reportedly is very little new communication between antipollution and conservation personnel in Albany, and no integrated policy and planning work. No integration of pollution control and conservation interest groups has occurred, and some conservationists oppose EnCon on the grounds that their programs are being neglected in favor of pollution control. However, like Wisconsin's environmental superdepartment, some short-run administrative efficiency gains are anticipated from the use of conservation field personnel for pollution monitoring. Even more than that state, New York's EnCon hopes that substantial field integration will take place in the future.

Fiscal Year 1972 appropriated budget:
  State Funds $38,150,530
  Federal Funds   4,780,000
  Total Staff   2,182

Program Categories (in $1,000's)
1. Environmental Quality   - $3,508.4 -331
   (pollution control)   (2,862.0)
2. Fish and Wildlife   -   6,176.0 -427
                                (920.0)
3. Lands and Forests   -   10,360.0 -661
                                (723.0)
4. Marine and Mining   -   658.6 - 41
                                (215.0)
5. Resource Management
   Service   2,254.5 -172
6. General Services (incl.
   conservation officers)   13,671.5 -550
                                (60.0)
7. Environmental
   Facilities Corp.   1,521.5 -

- chief executive of | Commissioner
  EnCon responsible | Henry Diamon
  for all decisions |
  and management |
  except if require |
  board approval |

- issues cease and | First Deputy
  desist orders to | Commissioner
  polluters prior to | James Bigann
  public hearings | Ron Pederson

Administration   Communication and Education

- prepares and implements   - public relations; newspaper,
  budgets and financial   Conservationist magazine;
  responsibilities   public information releases
- liaison with federal   - assistance to local and regional
  agencies for grants   conservation councils
- personnel

Environmental Quality
Deputy Commissioner, Dwight Metzler

Pure Waters Division - Staff of 186   Air Resources Division - Staff of 90

- sets water quality and effluent   - sets ambient air quality and emissior
  standards (may require board approval)   standards (may require board approva)
- issues water discharge permits to   - issues emission permits to new
  new plants   sources, and operating permits for
- issues permits for construction of   new control equipment
  industrial and municipal wastewater   - monitors and investigates complaints
  treatment facilities   - conducts public hearings
- monitors and investigates complaints   - issues abatement orders and approves
- conducts public hearings   abatement plans, initiates enforce-
- issues abatement orders and approves   ment cases (except New York City)
  abatement plans, initiates enforce-   - some research (relies on Health
  ment cases   Department)
- administers federal state grants for
  construction of wastewater treatment
  facilities (Pure Water Program), and   Division of Quality Services -
  provides technical assistance for   Staff of 55
  local construction and operation
- river basin planning for location of   - sets pesticide standards (may require
  treatment facilities   board approval); monitors pesticides
- some research (also in Health   and initiates enforcement cases
  Department)   - monitors open burning, incinerators,
                                             and all solid waste disposal sites
                                             (no statewide general regulatory
                                             authority yet)
                                           - regional solid waste management
                                             planning and planning grants to
                                             localities
                                           - research on recycling
                                           - monitors radiation emissions from al)
                                             sources
                                           - sets standards for noise control
                                             (classified as an air pollutant)

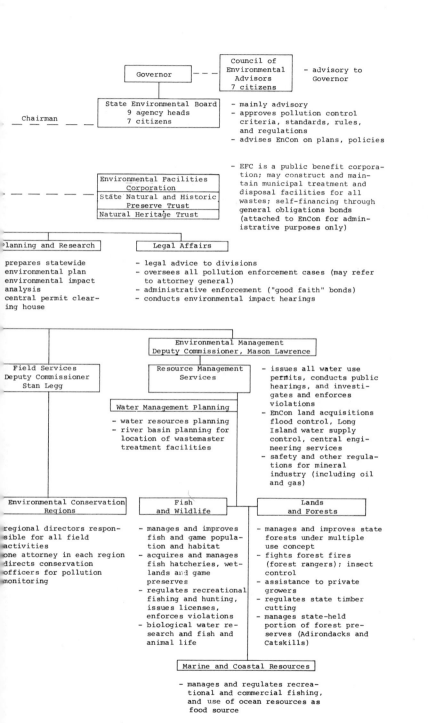

| Governor | Council of Environmental Advisors 7 citizens | – advisory to Governor |

Chairman — — — — | State Environmental Board 9 agency heads 7 citizens |
- mainly advisory
- approves pollution control criteria, standards, rules, and regulations
- advises EnCon on plans, policies

| Environmental Facilities Corporation |
| State Natural and Historic Preserve Trust |
| Natural Heritage Trust |

- EFC is a public benefit corporation; may construct and maintain municipal treatment and disposal facilities for all wastes; self-financing through general obligations bonds (attached to EnCon for administrative purposes only)

Planning and Research

prepares statewide environmental plan
environmental impact analysis
central permit clearing house

Legal Affairs

- legal advice to divisions
- oversees all pollution enforcement cases (may refer to attorney general)
- administrative enforcement ("good faith" bonds)
- conducts environmental impact hearings

Environmental Management
Deputy Commissioner, Mason Lawrence

Field Services
Deputy Commissioner
Stan Legg

Resource Management Services

Water Management Planning

- water resources planning
- river basin planning for location of wastemaster treatment facilities

- issues all water use permits, conducts public hearings, and investigates and enforces violations
- EnCon land acquisitions flood control, Long Island water supply control, central engineering services
- safety and other regulations for mineral industry (including oil and gas)

Environmental Conservation Regions

regional directors responsible for all field activities
one attorney in each region
directs conservation officers for pollution monitoring

Fish and Wildlife

- manages and improves fish and game population and habitat
- acquires and manages fish hatcheries, wetlands and game preserves
- regulates recreational fishing and hunting, issues licenses, enforces violations
- biological water research and fish and animal life

Lands and Forests

- manages and improves state forests under multiple use concept
- fights forest fires (forest rangers); insect control
- assistance to private growers
- regulates state timber cutting
- manages state-held portion of forest preserves (Adirondacks and Catskills)

Marine and Coastal Resources

- manages and regulates recreational and commercial fishing, and use of ocean resources as food source

New York has traditionally operated under a "strong governor" system of government, whereby the governor plays a powerful and direct role in the activities of executive agencies. Unlike many other states, his power is rarely diluted by citizen boards and commissions responsible for departmental policy-making. The creation of the Department of Environmental Conservation in 1970 aptly reflects this administrative system. Whereas the reorganization in Minnesota was a legislative product, and in Wisconsin the result of a special administrative task force study involving private citizens and state officials, New York's was almost entirely the product of Governor Rockefeller. It was here that the idea for consolidating environmental programs in a new department was first conceived—reportedly in 1967. The governor's office decided what programs to combine and what functions to give the new department, drafted the bill, and devised timing and legislative strategy. By late 1968 the commissioners of the Departments of Health and Conservation were brought into the discussions, and their ideas incorporated into the final proposals. However, Governor Rockefeller made all the final decisions and eliminated in private some remaining opposition from these affected commissioners. Thus, dissension within the executive branch did not rise to the level of public debate, and by the time the reorganization bill creating EnCon reached the state legislature, most state officials were publicly in agreement with the governor.

Unlike the Minnesota's legislature, New York's went along with the governor's reorganization proposal in the spring of 1970. Some Democrats in the Republican-controlled Senate and Assembly protested that the bill did not go far enough in regulating pollution. However, only minor revisions were made, and in less than a fortnight the bill passed in the Senate by a unanimous vote and in the Assembly by a vote of 127-19.

A stronger, more visible pollution regulatory effort was the primary stated goal of the 1970 environmental reorganization, although both pollution control and conservation programs were combined in the new Department of Environmental Conservation. The rationale for consolidating antipollution programs in a new organizational location is one used by many states. Pollution control was considered a popular, important, distinct, and long-term concern that warranted a separate department that could guarantee the state's continuing commitment to clean-up. A new departmental director could become a significant spokesman and advocate for tough pollution control among state departments, in the legislature, and with the public, and the new department could serve as a rallying point, solidifying the public's interest and support of environmental quality programs. The reorganization would bring to the pollution control effort the vigor, prestige, popularity, and leadership it now required.

It was also agreed that pollution sources, problems, and control techniques were intimately interrelated, and that a single institution should be created to permit a more comprehensive policy and program outlook and streamlined administrative process. Prior to reorganization, the Health Department carried the lion's share of pollution control responsibility, but policy-making was fragmented among several organizations. Three interagency committees with two-thirds overlapping members actually had responsibility for policy-making—the Air Pollution and Pesticides Boards and the Water Resources Commission. While the first two were chaired and staffed by the Health Department, the Water Resources Commission was chaired and staffed by the Conservation Department. However, both the Health and Conservation Departments administered different aspects of the water pollution abatement effort, and pesticides work was shared by the Departments of Health and Agriculture and Markets.

Unlike states such as Wisconsin, New York did not express concern that severe budgetary and coordination problems resulted from this organizational fragmentation of pollution control programs. The governor's office felt that the governor's strong role in executive agency affairs had minimized some interagency problems, so this was not stated as a major reorganization motive. Nor did New York's reorganization strategists admit that the previous handling of pollution problems had existed on a too informal or ad hoc basis, such as was stated in Minnesota. Unlike the earlier reorganizations in Minnesota and Wisconsin, New York's realignment in 1970 shifted relatively well-established pollution control programs, particularly for water. For example, the state's popular Pure Waters Program for the construction of wastewater treatment facilities was supported by a $1-billion state bond issue approved by the voters in 1965. Pollution control programs had been consolidated in one division within the Health Department for several years. Although somewhat autonomous from the rest of that department, they received strong support from the health commissioner.

While antipollution work had gotten off to a good start in the Health Department, some of the governor's staff worried that that department was too large and carried out too many other important missions for pollution control to receive the increased attention it deserved in the future. Further, it was felt that its orientation should be predominantly the delivery of health services and individual health problems. The presence of a separate pollution control division there might distract its attention away from these programs. Also, pollution had resource, economic, and aesthetic effects as well as health effects, which, it was argued, the Health Department had no expertise to examine. Likewise, the Health Department was not a regulatory outfit. Its staff, which in the pollution field were mainly sanitary engineers, traditionally preferred technical engineering to tough legal solutions. It was hoped that a new organization might reorient programs toward regulation and attract a new legal staff.

Why Create an Environmental Superdepartment?

The exact rationale of why the pollution control effort was consolidated along with conservation programs in EnCon is a question that may be debated for some time to come. While the major objective of the reorganization was to strengthen pollution regulation, spokesmen for the governor explain that the option of a new pollution control organization *separate* from the Conservation Department was never strongly or actively considered within the governor's office. One reason for combining pollution control and conservation programs in a new department was a very practical one. The state constitutional limit of 20 separate executive departments at any one time would have made a separate new pollution control department impossible—although conceivably a new department could have been located in the Executive Department as the Division of Parks, formerly within the Conservation Department, subsequently was.[4]

While the New York reorganization was not promoted by public administration rationale, there were those who did address themselves at the time to some of the apparent administrative logic of combining pollution control and conservation programs in an environmental superdepartment. For example, some officials argued that it was impossible to think about water pollution without thinking about fish, since fish and wildlife depended on water quality. Other spokesmen for the reorganization pointed out that the regulation of water quantity directly affected pollution concentrations. Further, some resource management programs might cause pollution (e.g., forest burning and pesticides use) while others might limit pollution (e.g., oil and gas regulation). Still others noted the common ties between the Health and Conservation Departments on environmental matters. Their directors and staff served on the same interagency councils and shared research and data, particularly for water. For example, under the Conservation Department's leadership, the interagency Water Resources Commission classified streams and issued water use permits, while the Health Department set water pollution control standards according to these classifications and issued water discharge permits. Both departments conducted research on thermal pollution, pesticides, and fish life. Because of this overlap, a few officials worried that the state's manpower and monetary expenditures were not being maximized.

Just as the consolidation and transfer of pollution control programs was seen as a way to increase their programmatic and political strength, for some within the governor's office the transfer of the Conservation Department to the new EnCon was seen as a means of lessening its narrow clientele-oriented behavior. It was felt that attention should be refocused on overall resource problems, rather than on the special interests of fish and game clubs, forest producers, and so forth. Since the Conservation Department's various divisions were traditionally quite autonomous within it, the reorganization might be a way to unite these divisions under a new leader and new focus.

The parks and recreation program, however, was excluded from transfer to the Department of Environmental Conservation because of its strong and independent constituency in the state legislature and conservation community. Traditionally the Parks Division had been the most autonomous within the Conservation Department and also had the largest staff and budget. It had a strong clientele and legislative base of its own, and the state's regional recreation officials were especially strong politically. Many persons felt that parks and recreation was a major mission of New York State government representing one way to use the environment, thus further justifying a separate organizational location. Since the Parks Division commanded an embarrassingly large share of the Conservation Department's budget each fiscal year and acted virtually independently anyway, some Conservation Department officials were not reluctant to see this component omitted from the new environmental department. Some legislative opposition was anticipated if this division were included in the EnCon package, and others worried that, by its sheer size, parks and recreation work might overwhelm the new department's other environmental efforts. Thus the Parks Division was transferred to the executive department to be made a separate department as soon as the constitutional limit will permit. Included in the transfer to EnCon, however, was responsibility for management of the state's constitutionally "forever wild" forest preserves, part of which are in the Adirondack and Catskill parks.

Whatever the logic behind the combined Department of Environmental Conservation, it was never clearly articulated before or during the reorganization process. The governor's early decision was to support a superdepartment, and the alternative of a separate pollution control agency was briefly studied in only one place—the state's central management and budget office. Some members of a small task force set up there to work on the reorganization felt that a separate pollution control agency was the most workable option. In their opinion, the pollution control and conservation efforts had more dissimilar than similar programs and personnel.

Broad Authority and Strong Leadership

1970 became the politically logical year to create a new Department of Environmental Conservation. As one state official put it, "The Governor did not wish to have any political, with a small 'p,' difficulties in getting the reorganization through the legislature." By that year virtually very few could oppose the reorganization, because most everyone agreed on the importance of pollution problems. The legislature and governor were motivated in 1970, which in addition to being the "year of the environment" was also the "year of elections." Governor Rockefeller announced his intentions for the new department in a special message to the legislature in March[5] and signed into law the bill creating EnCon on Earth Day, April 22. The new department began operations July 1, 1970.

The reorganization act creating EnCon gives very broad authority to the new department, compared to the highly specific assignments given in many other states. Some language is deliberately loose in order to give the department flexibility as well as to minimize legislative opposition. The only specific language is that which transfers programs to EnCon—all the pollution control functions of the Health Department (except the regulation of drinking water and public water supply systems), the pesticides functions of the Department

143

of Agriculture and Markets, and the entire Conservation Department (except its Parks and Motorboats Divisions). It abolishes the interagency Air Pollution, Pesticides, Water Resource, and Natural Beauty Councils and sets up a new 15-member Environmental Board composed of state department directors and citizens. The reorganization act then very broadly outlines overall goals for the new department and carves out its environmental jurisdiction.[6] Some environmental problems were assigned to EnCon for which no specific state authority existed and it was anticipated that EnCon would seek additional legislative authority in these areas. They include solid waste regulation, noise control, and land use planning. The reorganization act also required EnCon to draw up an environmental plan by September, 1971. This plan is meant to cover all natural resources of the state and to guide the activities of all New York agencies, and the private sector, that affect the environment.[7]

There was virtually no debate on whether department policy leadership should be provided by a board or a single director, selected by and accountable to the governor. The latter route was selected, in keeping with New York's "strong governor" style of public administration. The EnCon director is appointed by the governor, with Senate confirmation, and serves at the pleasure of the chief executive. Governor Rockefeller appointed Henry Diamond, who was an acknowledged advocate of traditional conservation activities and was also a close and long-time associate of the Rockefeller family.*

New York has traditionally rejected citizen boards or commissions appointed for a term to set policies for executive agencies. Such bodies act as a buffer between a departmental director and the governor and reduce the governor's influence over state programs. Instead, in New York, departmental directors are usually hand-picked by the governor and then given complete control over departmental operations, with accountability to the governor being direct and swift. In this way the governor keeps interagency debates to a minimum and out of the public eye. Policy boards are seen as diluting agency accountability to the governor and through him to the public, since more than one person makes policy and they cannot be removed until their terms have expired. This also adds another layer of decision-making between the governor and a departmental director. There are only two departments in New York, the Departments of Education and Social Services, governed by such a citizen policy board.

The State Environmental Board attached to EnCon was not meant to represent a compromise to this single director principle, since its powers are mainly advisory, and some spokesmen say that it was created mainly for political expediency. At the last minute, the drafters of the bill provided for the board in order to forestall legislative criticism that EnCon required some higher authority to review and check its standards—setting actions on a continuing basis, as did the three policy-making boards prior to reorganization. In particular, it was feared that some legislators might protest the absence

---

*For example, Diamond had worked with Laurence Rockefeller on the Federal Citizen's Advisory Board on Recreation and Natural Beauty.

of industrial representation in such an important area as pollution standards.

So that the board has a broadly based membership, it was given an interagency and citizen composition. Initially, it had 15 members including the commissioner of the Department of Environmental Conservation as chairman, and 8 other departmental heads: Health (as vice-chairman), Agriculture and Markets, Commerce, Transportation, Labor, the Office of Parks and Recreation, the Office for Local Government, and the Public Service Commission. Its six citizen members are appointed by the governor and approved by the Senate for staggered six-year terms. They must be technically qualified and by statute must include representatives of conservation, industry, and other disciplines relating to the environment. A 1971 amendment to the 1970 reorganization act increased the board's membership to 16 by adding, as did Minnesota, one private citizen representing agriculture interests. The board's designers also saw some potential value to its interagency composition as a means of eliciting broader support for environmental programs within state government.

The State Environmental Board has limited powers. Its role is to assist the commissioner in reviewing the policies, plans, and programs of other state agencies affecting the environment, and to serve as a working forum for the exchange of ideas and information relating to environmental quality. Its most important statutory function is that of approving "each environmental standard, criterion, and rule and regulation" proposed by the commissioner.[8] However, this responsibility is limited in several ways, as a practical matter. First, all such proposals are automatically approved if the board does not vote on them within 60 days, and ten members must be present to vote on standards. Secondly, Commissioner Diamond has some freedom to choose what he submits to the board for approval, depending on what he interprets to be an "environmental standard." Finally, the reorganization act transfers to the EnCon commissioner, not the board, all the powers of the four interagency councils abolished by the act.[9] Thus, some persons claim that the board's legitimate role in approving standards and regulations may be disputed. The commissioner was also given unilateral "summary" powers—i.e., the authority to order an immediate cease and desist, prior to public hearings, to any practice considered extremely hazardous to the public health and welfare and to natural resources.[10]

The reorganization act also created a seven-member citizen Council of Environmental Advisors to advise the governor on environmental policy for the state.[11] Its purview ranges across all public and private matters affecting the environment, and, among its tasks, it is to develop guidelines for assessing the interrelationship between environmental quality, economic development, and other state programs and to recommend new legislation and policies. The council may hold public and private hearings and subpoena witnesses. However, it has no jurisdiction over and only limited contact with EnCon. So far it has met infrequently and been largely inactive.

The only organized opposition to the creation of the Department of Environmental Conservation came from some conservation interest groups who objected to "their department" being merged with pollution control. The principal opponent was the Conservation Council, a statewide federation of fish and game, hunting, boating, and other sportsmen's clubs that is affiliated with the National Wildlife Federation. The Conservation Council testified before the legislature and wrote letters to legislators and to the press opposing the reorganization on the grounds that more time was needed to study a radical reorganization that affected very dissimilar programs. The underlying rationale reportedly was that the council's influence over state conservation programs might be considerably weakened if the Conservation Department were merged into a large superdepartment. Furthermore, conservation programs might be dominated in this new location by the increasingly popular pollution control effort. The Conservation Council publicly criticized officials of the Conservation Department who supported the reorganization, and today many of this group continue to oppose EnCon for these reasons. In contrast, there was little public opposition to EnCon from health officials and interest groups, allegedly because the health commissioner publicly supported the reorganization and was able to subdue any private outcry.

CURRENT ORGANIZATION AND ACTIVITIES

Two facts are significant in EnCon's current organization and activities. First, the commissioner has had to spend an inordinate amount of time and energy on establishing the day-to-day administrative relationship between pollution control and conservation programs. In other words, he inherited a combination of programs for which there had been little verbal or analytical justification, and then had to make sense of the mix after the fact. Second, the department emphasizes pollution control work. While Diamond has been associated in the past with traditional conservation interests such as natural beauty and wilderness activities, as head of the EnCon he has become more of a pollution control advocate, emphasizing these programs and particularly their regulatory aspect.

Efforts to Integrate Pollution Control and Conservation Work

EnCon is organized in basically two major components: the Environmental Quality Section, representing all pollution control work, and the Environmental Management Section, composed of conservation programs. This set-up was initially agreed to be the most practical by the commissioner and a special six-member task force from the Organization and Management Unit of the state's Budget Division. In mid-1970 this task force had debated several alternative ways of organizing the new department in hopes of inspiring some integration of its component parts at the outset. One alternative was to

146

organize mainly along *functional* lines—e.g., planning, research, management, standards-setting, monitoring, enforcement—and another was to organize along *media* lines—e.g., air, land, and water resources. Both of these options would have merged select portions of the pollution control and conservation work so as to break down gradually rigid administrative jurisdictions and established constituency power relationships.

However, most persons agreed that these two options were for the time being politically infeasible, intellectually complex, and would place unreasonable demands on existing staff. At a time when the department was just being launched, conservation and antipollution staff would suddenly be asked to relate to each other on a daily basis in new ways, on new problems. Yet they would still have to deal with their old programs and constituencies. While unnecessary duplication, frustration, and confusion would occur, the benefits were highly problematical.

Given these complexities, the third alternative was chosen, a two-sided organization that left the staff and work alignments basically as they were prior to reorganization (see Chart 5.1). Two deputy commissioners for Environmental Quality and Environmental Management were to aid the commissioner in resolving intradepartmental conflicts and trade-offs. They are the same persons who had governed the pollution control and conservation work in their previous locations. Staff functions such as legal services, planning, and administration were centralized to serve both sides of EnCon. It was felt, even then, that future integration would be extremely difficult to achieve. Pollution control was still health-oriented and intended to be a regulatory activity, while conservation was resource and management-oriented. The one was staffed by sanitary engineers with an urban focus, and the other with biologists with mainly a rural focus. Program integration in Albany, it was thought, would be forced, artificial, and perhaps counterproductive.

After two years, the two components—Environmental Quality and Environmental Management— remain mostly separate and distinct. In fact, departmental spokesman report that there has been only slight new informal communication between them, at least in Albany. The two deputy commissioners continue to think mainly about their own programs and have not sought any integration. Most of the staff under the commissioner have not served as an integrative force, since they have either been detailed to special pollution control assignments or have served each component separately. By all accounts, the major formal contact between the two sides in Albany before 1972 was at infrequent staff meetings, as reluctant participants in a departmentwide planning task force in 1971, and at occasional public hearings.

EnCon has not yet gone as far as Wisconsin's environmental superdepartment in developing formal, routinized mechanisms for intradepartmental review and comment. However, one new integrative mechanism developed in 1972 is a permit-clearing effort, which is carried out by the central planning staff. These persons have developed a list of approximately 20 permits requiring intradepartmental review and circulate some permits issued by one EnCon division to another division for comment. Pollution control standards are also circulated throughout the entire department for review and comment. However, these mechanisms do not carry veto power.

Some EnCon officials once thought that an environmental superdepartment might bring the pollution control and conservation interest groups together by providing an integrated institutional focus. However, some conservationists remain bitter over the reorganization because they feel their programs are being neglected in favor of pollution abatement work. In general, the two groups have exhibited marked differences in background, style, and orientation. The focus of the conservationists is rural, their interest scientific or recreational, their temperment conservative, and they have typically operated through traditional political channels. In contrast, the pollution control constituency is urban based, the interest is in tough legal actions, and the political methods and temperment more radical.

During EnCon's first year, the commissioner and his staff spent substantial time considering ways to deal with the inherited program mix. For example, they discussed at length the feasibility of moving several small programs from the Environmental Management to the Environmental Quality section on the grounds that they were related to pollution control. Candidates for transfer were the water resource planning program, pesticides use by the forestry unit, and pesticides monitoring and research from fish and wildlife. There was also some debate on the advisability of merging the two permit programs for water use and wastewater discharge administered by the water management and pollution control staff, respectively. Since any one industry had to have both permits to operate, and since both were related to pollution levels, it was thought that combining them would simplify matters for the applicant and lead to more effective departmental control. Most of these transfers were discarded because of internal opposition, except that the Environmental Quality section's river basin water treatment planning work has been subsequently transferred to Environmental Management. The issue of merging permits will be considered again in the future, although some EnCon officials view this as an unrealistic move given the different time phases of the two sets.

EnCon officials now believe that if integrated work can ever be accomplished, it will occur only over time and first in the field. Thus in a move similar to Wisconsin's DNR, EnCon set up nine administrative field regions in the summer of 1971, providing a common management structure and similar boundaries for pollution control, forests, fish, wildlife, and other programs. Hitherto, the conservation programs alone had over a dozen separate administrative regions, and there were a total of 149 offices throughout the state. Nine new regional directors are henceforth in charge of all EnCon's field forces, reporting directly to the new deputy commissioner for Field Services in Albany. All but two of the nine have been chosen from within EnCon, with four representing conservation programs. EnCon officials state that these choices were based on available talent.

While the pollution control and conservation programs will not actually be merged in the field, they will be responsible to one regional director and it is anticipated that they will increasingly share personnel, services, expertise, and

148

equipment.[12] For example, local conservation officers (i.e., wardens) are being used for pollution monitoring and data gathering. Conservation officers have been retrained to perform such functions as water and air sampling, pesticides monitoring, inspection of solid waste disposal sites, and investigation of open burning and other complaints. Unlike Wisconsin, conservation officers are grouped under a newly hired attorney in each region and carry out these pollution control tasks as directed (see Chart 5.2). They do not, however, have the authority to initiate prosecution of pollution cases on their own, as they can do for violators of hunting, fishing, and other conservation laws. Another example of personnel sharing is that a small environmental impact analysis unit has been set up in each region, drawing on both pollution control and conservation staff. It analyzes the environmental effects of private developments and other agency programs.

CHART 5.2

EnCon Field Organization, 1972

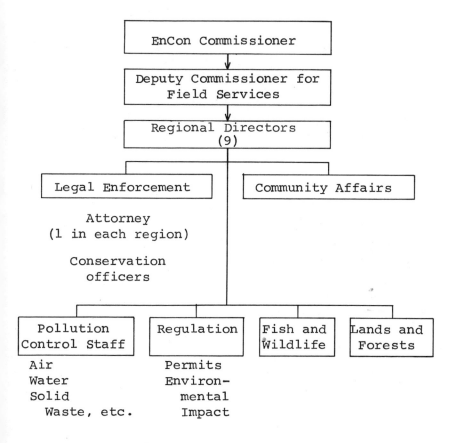

This ongoing regionalization effort represents EnCon's most significant internal organizational change thus far and was preceded by substantial study. Its major stated purpose is to provide a more effective channel for the delivery of services and, eventually, integration. It is hoped that more effective operations will result from the sharing of staff, services, and equipment. The commissioner has stated that these management and cost efficiency gains may be the major benefit of an environmental superdepartment, in the short run, particularly for the smaller and less well-established pollution control effort.

Perhaps more than Wisconsin, New York plans for increased integrated work in the field over time. Eventually, the deputy commissioners for Environmental Quality and Environmental Management in Albany will carry out only long-range functions such as programs planning and research, with the field staff doing all the daily operational work under the direction of the deputy commissioner for Field Services. However, since decentralization and integration involves a substantial loss of power for some persons and retraining and shifting of roles for others, departmental officials feel it will be several years before the new lines of command can be implemented, and even after that it is uncertain how much integrated field work will occur. If possible, some spokesmen would like to see some field integration on a functional basis.

EnCon has not devoted much attention to integrated policy resource planning as a means of linking the pollution control and conservation work, and the commissioner has shown little interest in planning. Despite the state legislature's original requirement that EnCon submit a statewide comprehensive environmental plan by September, 1971, by early 1971 the total central planning office had only a few persons who were from the Conservation Department and who worked on a decidedly ad hoc basis. Several more were added in mid-1971 from the Planning Service Office of the Executive Department, following statewide budget cuts. After getting a one-year reprieve from the legislature for submission of the plan,[13] work began on it in mid-1971. The first six months were spent defining the plan and drafting a rather complicated outline. A departmentwide task force participated in this process.

EnCon subsequently received another ten-month delay from the state legislature, and it now hopes that the environmental plan will be completed on the revised schedule date of July 1, 1973. The environmental plan will be a detailed statement of preferred objectives and recommended actions for each of EnCon's major programs. With the exception of water resources, which is considered as one program category, each of the programs will be evaluated and discussed separately in the plan. Since there has been little effort to establish priorities between them, the plan cannot be considered an attempt to integrate EnCon's components. The environmental plan will also include a brief and broad statement on several areas that are statutorily within EnCon's broad mandate to consider in planning. These include the visual environment, energy production and transmission, and land use.[14] Since these are only brief statements meant to be guides to further EnCon work, the plan will not immediately influence other state agencies or the private sector. Departmental spokesmen describe the plan as a physical resource document, which does not explicitly trade-off environmental efforts against social, economic, and other state objectives.

Emphasis on Pollution Regulation

Most observers agree that the commissioner and his staff have emphasized pollution control programs during EnCon's first two years. The commissioner speaks widely throughout the state on pollution control and actively lobbies in the state legislature for pollution control bills. Most attention devoted to internal operations has focused on pollution control, and most of the commissioner's new staff were hired for these programs. This emphasis responds in part to the public's priority demand in New York for pollution abatement, with the exception of those portions of upstate New York where traditional conservation programs are most popular. Nonetheless, the department's antipollution emphasis has led from the outset to the sometimes hostile complaint from some conservationists that their programs were being neglected.

Most observers also agree that the functional emphasis in pollution control has been on regulation. The commissioner's major interest has been in improving the regulatory process, and most of the movement and innovation has been here. One of EnCon's first internal studies following the reorganization was an evaluation of pollution enforcement procedures.[15] Many of the newly hired staff are lawyers, and the staff unit with which the commissioner has dealt most directly and consistently has been Legal Affairs. This staff unit has been responsible for many of the department's new programs. Originally only a few persons, its staff is now about ten. A major purpose of the regionalization effort is to decentralize and coordinate monitoring and enforcement activities under a newly hired lawyer in each of the nine regions.

Despite the emphasis on tougher pollution control, EnCon's progress in formal standards-setting and court enforcement has not been fast-paced. As of July, 1972, EnCon had promulgated only a half-dozen new standards, mostly for air pollutants, and had upgraded a few others. Initially, some standards were not submitted to the State Environmental Board for approval, such as pesticides. However, as EnCon's standards-setting activity increased in the latter part of 1971 and Commissioner Diamond increasingly felt pressure from some board members to use the board more often, he has more frequently submitted proposed standards to it for review. In only one instance before 1972, for the upgrading of sulfur oxide standards, has the board actually weakened the proposals of the commissioner.

In its first year and a half of operations, EnCon referred almost 100 pollution cases to the attorney general for prosecution in court, but only a half-dozen of these were resolved in favor of the department. Consequently, four cases were referred for prosecution between January, 1972 and September, 1972. Over 100 pollution abatement orders were issued through September, 1972. Before 1972, the majority of these were for water pollution, but in

151

the first nine months of 1972, 76 abatement orders were issued for air pollution, 75 for water pollution, and 32 for solid waste disposal practices. A total of $5.5 million in penalties was assessed prior to September, 1972. Between July, 1971 and July, 1972, almost 300 permits were issued to municipalities and industries to operate waste treatment works and discharge into state waterways. Only 20 permits were denied, but the number of variances is also very small. Existing air contamination sources were not required to have certificates to operate until June, 1972. For these, the number of permits issued almost equals the number denied, with few variances granted. Between July, 1971 and July, 1972, 66 open dumps were closed. However, EnCon has lacked an adequate field monitoring capability, and has recently been criticized by environmental interest groups for not sending out field staff to monitor, investigate complaints, and promptly enforce standards and orders.

EnCon's largest and best established pollution control program is for water in the Pure Waters Division. EnCon inherited a fairly smoothly running water pollution abatement program from the Health Department, along with a set of interstate and some intrastate water quality standards. Much of EnCon's water regulatory work in its first two years has been almost entirely an effort to enforce old abatement orders issued in past years by the Health Department. New statewide stream classifications have been set, and EnCon has upgraded some interstate water quality standards for the New York City metropolitan area. However, as of early 1972, effluent standards had been set only for mercury and thermal pollution. Phosphate limitations were set by the state legislature in the summer of 1971, limiting the phosphorous compound content of household cleansing products to "a trace" by July, 1973.[16] EnCon also set regulations for the storage and handling of bulk commodities, including oil.

EnCon's Air Resources Division, although newer and a much smaller activity, will probably have the greatest regulatory load over the next few years since the department must set more new air emission standards. Prior to the 1970 reorganization, most of the air pollution abatement effort had been in the identification and monitoring of harmful pollutants. Air quality classifications had been completed for the entire state, but only a few ambient air and emission standards had been adopted. Existing regulations limited open burning, dust, odors, the density of smoke discharges, automobile exhaust, crankcase ventilation systems, some incinerators, and the sulfur content of fuel burned in the New York City metropolitan area. EnCon upgraded standards for the sulfur content of fuel in the city, and also sulfur oxide standards, in early 1972. Several new emission standards were set in response to federal requirements, portions of which were higher than recommended federal levels. In June, 1971, the Air Resources Division implemented a new law requiring all companies to inventory their air emissions and, along with the department, agree on a projected ambient air quality rating they must meet. An operating permit is then issued and violations prosecuted. The division has set up a sophisticated continuous air monitoring system in a few parts of the state.

EnCon has delegated to New York City responsibility for enforcing air pollution control standards there. The city's air pollution control staff, at 300, far outnumbers that of EnCon's. Half of the city's total pollution control program is supported by the state. EnCon has gained some increased fines for both air and water polluters from the legislature. Currently, both air and water polluters may be fined up to $2,500 initially and after that up to $500 per day.[17] The 1971 legislature expanded EnCon's authority to regulate fuels and fuel additives for motor vehicles and to require and inspect automobile emission control systems.[18] Noise was also classified as an air contaminant, and EnCon was given the authority to set noise standards.[19]

EnCon's solid waste program, in the Division of Quality Services, is still very new and relatively small. It reviews existing solid waste disposal sites and closes unsanitary facilities. However, as yet there is only limited statewide regulation and few fines for violators, and EnCon will have to seek additional legislation for these. EnCon offers planning and demonstration grants to local and regional units of government. As of July, 1972, almost $1.5 million in solid waste study grants had been contracted. The state may also pay half the cost for preparing construction sites and purchasing equipment for new solid waste disposal facilities in communities. Studies are now being undertaken within the division to evaluate alternative solid waste disposal solutions, and an Office of Recovery, Recycling, and Reuse has been set up to promote planning and the use of industrial, domestic, and municipal wastes, including paper.

EnCon's radiation and pesticides programs, in the Division of Quality Services, are also small. Radiation work has been mainly offsite sampling of radiation contamination in air, water, milk, and plant and animal life. Under an agreement with the federal AEC in the fall of 1971, EnCon is stepping up its onsite radiological monitoring of the state's nuclear power plants and nuclear fuel reprocessing plants. EnCon inherited full responsibility for pesticides regulation, and new regulations were set in 1971. These ban major pesticides such as DDT, Endrin, BHC, and their derivatives, and restrict the use of 60 other pesticides considered toxic. Permits are required for all importation of pesticides into the state. However, until mid-1972, EnCon's enforcement effort was slight.

Several innovative programs in pollution regulation begun in 1971 warrant special mention, since they demonstrate some of EnCon's capability for tough regulation. One innovative step has been taken in internal administration enforcement procedures. In New York, as in most states, the attorney general has the sole power within the executive branch to carry out court proceedings against polluters. However, with the exception of public nuisance authority, the attorney general does not have the power to initiate cases unilaterally. Rather, he is supposed to wait for referral from EnCon. Since the reorganization, EnCon's legal staff has complained about delays in this formal enforcement process. Departmental spokesmen have stated that these delays are the direct result of massive red tape, information, and length of time involved in formal court proceedings. The court process is long and drawn out, usually taking anywhere from eight months to two years and involving constant overview and participation from EnCon. Also, delays may become a matter of political expediency for the attorney general. Although departmental spokesmen say there may be no inherent reluctance on his part to vigorously enforce pollution laws, politics may determine who is to be brought to court and when. For example, after a considerable period of a lack of activity before the 1972 elections, EnCon staff noted an upsurge in enforcement actions, in some instances on cases not referred to the attorney general by EnCon.

In an attempt to enforce on its own without involving the attorney general, EnCon's legal staff developed the "good faith" penalty bond. As of early 1972, New York and Illinois were the only two states relying on this mechanism. As an alternative to immediate court proceedings and fines, an industry, municipality, or individual found violating a water pollution, air pollution, or refuse disposal law may post a good faith bond as a pledge of their intention to comply with an abatement order within a specified time. Compliance may involve construction of a sewage treatment plant or other special facilities. Companies must give monthly or bimonthly reports on their progress. If compliance is not forthcoming by the specified date, the bond is forfeited.

This technique is more or less a gentleman's agreement, and EnCon does not have the ultimate legal power to collect on a forfeited bond. If a polluter balks, the attorney general would have to step in to collect the amount or begin formal court proceedings. However, over a dozen good faith bonds had been posted by the beginning of 1972, amounting to over $1.5 million including one by St. Regis Paper Company. Acceptable as good faith bonds are cash, securities, deposit certificates, or surety bonds. Surety bonds have been most commonly used, and the amounts ranged from $4,000 to $100,000. Two insurance companies have drawn up most of the bonds. Many of the cases have involved companies that had been in violation of the old Health Department orders issued several years ago. These companies may be interested in posting bond even when there is no legal requirement for it, because by this procedure EnCon "forgives" a company's past failure to comply and starts with a clean slate. One interesting provision of the good faith penalty bond is that a company cannot close down rather than invest in the pollution abatement equipment necessary to meet the requirement. The bond is forfeited unless such equipment is installed and standards met. Also, the good faith bond is a means to shift the burden of pollution abatement monitoring on the polluter, since he must keep EnCon informed at every step.

Some of EnCon's legal staff believe that the department, not the attorney general, should prosecute polluters in court. Since this is an extremely unlikely change, they have requested that one or more assistant attorneys general be housed in EnCon so that these persons can become more intimately acquainted with pollution cases and begin to acquire technical expertise. However, this also seems unlikely, at least in the near future, since the attorney general complains that "loaning out" assistant attorneys general to one executive department would prompt requests from other departments. Thus, he would gradually lose control. Finally, the legal staff is pressing for a renewable or "limited life" permit system governing industrial and other plant operations, to be renewed every three to five years. As in most states, the current permit program covers just the installation of new equipment and new plants and provides no continuing check to guarantee that a company is not violating a new order or standards.

In mid-1971, another step was taken to expand EnCon's regulatory power over the private sector. Within a year the legal staff had carried out six environmental impact hearings. These were special hearings for private companies held *before* the issuance of EnCon's required operating permits—e.g., water use and water discharge permits. The purpose was to determine broad environmental effects of a proposed project beyond merely pollution and included aesthetic and other effects. All of the first environmental impact hearings were for private land developers. EnCon cannot enforce its decisions, except on those permits for which it has specific legislative authority. However, the hearings so far have been successful in arousing public concern, attracting publicity, and deterring further action on some developer's part. In one case, Boise Cascade cancelled plans for a proposed recreational home development in Columbia County without going through an environmental impact hearing, and its actions may have been influenced in part by the threat of a hearing.

With the emphasis on regulation, the other functional efforts of the Environmental Quality section have received less support and encouragement from the commissioner and have consequently lagged. For example, little program planning is done in these divisions or in the central planning office. There has been research on eutrophication, thermal pollution, the removal of nitrogen from sewage, recycling, monitoring techniques, and other studies, but EnCon lacks adequate research personnel and relies heavily on the Health Department for scientific and medical data needed to set antipollution standards.

There has also been no significant effort to integrate EnCon's separate water, air, and other pollution control programs. Aside from the fact that, on a case-by-case basis, all pollution control personnel may comment on any proposed standard and some permits, there are no formal mechanisms for insuring that separate standards are consistent, and antipollution personnel have few continuing contacts with one another. EnCon's legal staff, however, is working to make compatible separate standard terms and deadlines, and this information is being computerized.

Conservation Programs

The Environmental Management staff, including conservation officers, currently outnumbers the Environmental Quality staff by almost five to one and has a state budget over five times larger. The five divisions carry out traditional conservation and natural resource programs that are predominantly management-oriented, and operate almost completely autonomously from one another. The two divisions for Fish and Wildlife and Lands and Forests, in particular, have their own strong interest group and legislative constituencies and have separate advisory boards attached to them. Other than some internal reorganization, there has been little change in these programs since the 1970 reorganization. Each division represents a separate and ongoing program with its own administrator, and almost three-quarters of the staff are in the field. Thus, the deputy commissioner for Environmental Management has not been able to exercise strong leadership.

The Environmental Management section's most important pollution-related work is under the new Resources Management Services Division, set up in 1971. This unit is responsible for such diverse activities from the former Conservation Department as land acquisitions, engineer planning, Long Island water supply, flood control, mineral programs, and water use regulation. Water use regulation represents the Environmental Management section's largest single regulatory effort, and is similar to that in other states. Under the Stream Protection Law and other statutes, permits are required for any actions that alter water levels or flows, both surface and underground, affecting municipal and industrial water supply, sewers, drainage and fill, dam construction, irrigation, and flood plain control. Often one company or individual must receive several different types of water use permits before beginning operations, and also before applying for a water discharge permit. Public hearings are required for all water use permits and the 25 staff involved in their issuance participate in more hearings than do the water pollution control personnel. Hearing examiners are chosen from within the division, a practice that has been criticized because biased decisions may result when departmental officials are both adjudicators and advocates and a separate administrative appeal is not available. However, the water use regulatory staff are some of the most experienced and scientifically trained of the entire department, and EnCon officials feel that potentially their expertise can be shared with the water pollution control staff. Since legislation in 1971, fines for violators of water use permits are $500 for the first offense, $2,500 for the second, and $10,000 for the third. EnCon is authorized to require the posting of performance bonds as a condition of granting permits.[20]

The Resources Management Services Division is also responsible for administering the department's laws relating to oil and gas. This program formerly had its own division within the Environmental Management section, but was affected by substantial budget cuts in 1971. The program is responsible for establishing safety and some antipollution rules for some of the mineral industry, leasing state-owned lands for oil and gas exploration, production, and storage, and capping abandoned oil wells. At one time it provided technical assistance to the mineral industry.

A new Division of Water Management Planning is responsible for water resources planning, which formerly also had its own division before being dismantled by budget cuts in 1971. Over 20 staff do water resources planning. Recently, approximately 18 persons were added from the Pure Waters Division in the Environmental Quality section. These personnel do river basin planning for the location of wastewater treatment facilities, which is required by the federal government as a condition for receiving grants to construct such facilities.

Aside from these programs, most of the work of the Environmental Management section is basically management-oriented and in the field. Many of the tasks are entirely different in nature from pollution control, and will always require separate staff to carry them out. For example, the Division of Fish and Wildlife stocks streams and hatcheries, acquires and protects rare species, manages the state's wetlands, and administers hunting and fishing laws. The Division of Lands and Forests plants reforestation areas, builds access roads, and fights forest fires. The Division of Marine and Coastal Resources is responsible for the propagation of ocean fish and shellfish.

The Division of Lands and Forests is also responsible for management of the state's constitutionally "forever wild" forest preserves, part of which are contained within the Adirondack and Catskill parks. One of EnCon's successfully fought legislative battles in 1971 was for the creation of an Adirondack Park Agency to control development on the privately held portions of this park—about 60 percent. Composed of the EnCon commissioner, the director of the Office of Planning Services, and seven members appointed by the governor, the agency is authorized to prepare a land use development plan consistent with environmental quality principles and to review and evaluate all developmental projects in the Adirondacks.

A program to encourage the establishment of local conservation commissions and regional environmental councils is administered by the Communications and Education section under the EnCon commissioner. An idea first started in Massachusetts and now popular in many northeastern states, these local governmental groups are meant to be a coordinating point and citizen access for across-the-board environmental measures, emphasizing land use, natural beauty, recreation, conservation education, and also pollution control. In fiscal year 1972 the program provided $250,000 to reimburse up to 50 percent of the operating expenses of these local and regional commissions, including land use planning.

EnCon's Impact on Other State Agencies

The Department of Environmental Conservation currently has no formal veto power over the programs of other state agencies that affect the environment. An operating principle of the Rockefeller administration has been to avoid public interagency battles, the governor preferring to resolve such conflicts himself. For example, an environmental impact bill in the 1971 legislature required all state agencies to submit statements on the environmental impact of their proposed projects to EnCon, which was given authority to evaluate and veto these. However, the bill did not pass the legislature and it is widely agreed that the governor would not have endorsed it.

However, EnCon has some other powers to influence state agencies short of veto authority. In the past year, Commissioner Diamond has made maximum use of these, and many departmental spokesmen believe these existing authorities may be adequate to influence other state agencies.[2][1] For example, a more than five-year-old Memorandum of Understanding between the Transportation Department and the former Conservation Department is now administered by EnCon. This is a voluntary agreement that all proposed highway construction projects will be submitted to the department for review. Thus far the Transportation Department has been generally cooperative and the agreement is to be updated. The State's Budget Division has also begun to submit to EnCon a list of all proposed state capital construction projects on an informal basis. EnCon replies by way of checking one of three boxes indicating approval, some reservation, and serious reservation. In compliance with the National Environmental Policy Act of 1969, Governor Rockefeller has designated EnCon as the state clearinghouse for all environmental impact statements submitted by state agencies on federal projects. Since many state projects are also federally funded, EnCon has the opportunity to at least review a large number of state projects.

In the spring of 1972, EnCon gained an increased role in power plant siting decisions, one of the major environmental protection issues in New York. A new law establishes a five-man Power Plant Siting Council, with full power to override local zoning restrictions and other local barriers.[2][2] The council consists of the Public Service Commission chairman, the EnCon commissioner, the Health commissioner, the Commerce commissioner, and a fifth member appointed by the governor from the region in which the proposed power plant is to be located. The council's decisions are subject only to review in the courts. This law, although strongly opposed by environmental groups who feel that its membership is too development-oriented, is considered stronger by EnCon than one proposed by Governor Rockefeller in 1970. The earlier bill would have formally given the Public Service Commission full power over site location.

EnCon still shares some water regulatory authority with the Health Department, which retains authority over the construction of public water supply systems, septic tanks and cesspools, and drinking water standards. The Health and EnCon commissioners' emergency powers for water pollution may potentially overlap, since both may order an immediate cease and desist to any pollution practice they consider extremely hazardous to public health.[2][3] The EnCon commissioner's authority also extends to the protection of the public welfare and natural resources.

EVALUATION

Since the creation of the Department of Environmental Conservation in 1970, one of the state's short-term reorganization objectives has been achieved. An aggressive and highly visible public spokesman for environmental clean-up has been created in New York. Commission Diamond has spoken widely throughout the state on needed pollution control measures, lobbied vigorously in the legislature to broaden his jurisdiction, and tried to act as a leader and focal point for the public on environmental issues. As a result, he has generated increased public and political support for pollution control programs, secured some new authority, and staved off budget cuts. The department's newly recruited legal staff has begun a number of innovative environmental regulatory programs that imply effective enforcement of departmental regulations in the future, and EnCon has increasingly sought to influence other state agencies toward environmental protection concerns. The creation of EnCon has generated a renewed sense of momentum and openness to state environmental work. In November, 1972, New York voters approved a substantial bond referendum for EnCon.

Despite its increased concern for pollution regulation, EnCon's regulatory record is not yet strong. Only a half-dozen new pollution control standards had been set by early 1972, and EnCon has not been able to elicit prompt enforcement action from the attorney general. The Department lacks an adequate pollution field monitoring staff and is increasingly criticized by environmental interest groups for inadequate surveillance and enforcement. The commissioner has never used his emergency cease and desist powers to halt pollution. The department has also not yet been successful in longer-range efforts for planning and research. Little program planning and limited research is done, and little effort has been made to institute formal mechanisms for integrating the separate water, air, and other pollution control programs. The statutorily required environmental plan has had a slow beginning.

One problem in New York is the existence of a wide and complicated array of pollution control interest groups, each with varying interests, membership, and focus. Although the commissioner has acted as an aggressive advocate for his programs and is relatively accessible to interest groups, there has been no concerted effort to build a united pollution control constituency among the citizenry. Interest groups remain scattered and divided and most maintain no continual communication with the department. Thus, EnCon lacks a firm base of political support that might strengthen its position vis-à-vis the legislature, governor, and other state agencies. New York's clean air constituency is probably the best organized, composed of health officials and health interest groups and the new urban-based citizen Clean Air Committee. A citizen-sponsored Environmental Planning Lobby set up in 1970 did attempt to inform all environmental groups on important forthcoming legislation, but did not prove effective. It was regrouped in early 1972.

The existence of a single departmental director, appointed by and directly accountable to the governor, does increase the public responsiveness of EnCon, since one person can be held clearly accountable for successes or failures. However, some environmentalists do criticize the EnCon commissioner's responsiveness to the governor as making the department's programs sometimes too geared toward short-term political aims. Also, because EnCon's commissioner governs an environmental superdepartment, and is thus the state's chief spokesman for the environment, he has no bureaucratic allies in dealing with the governor, other state agencies, the legislature, and private interest groups. Thus, EnCon's popularity and support sometimes seem tenuous and easily damaged. This was the case following the commissioner's highly unpopular

159

decision among environmentalists in mid-1971 to issue a certificate of "reasonable assurance" that Consolidated Edison's construction of the proposed power plant on Storm King Mountain would not adversely affect the water quality of the Hudson River. Con Ed's project had been held up for several years on environmental grounds.

Short-Term Disadvantages of a Superdepartment

The benefits of creating an environmental superdepartment in New York seem to be outweighed at this point by some disadvantages. This is because the advantages of EnCon for administering environmental programs are long term and only potential, while the disadvantages are more short term and apply particularly to the pollution control effort.

As yet, no new broad perspective on environmental problems has emerged from EnCon, and since pollution control and conservation programs are administered separately, new communication between them has been limited and no integrated planning is conducted. However, it is possible that the broadly based environmental mission of the new department may, in the long run, provide an incentive for a new "ecological" perspective on resource problems, and EnCon is taking some steps in this direction. Compared to Wisconsin's environmental superdepartment set up in 1967, New York's has less intradepartmental informal communication and fewer formal mechanisms for integrating pollution control and conservation work. Yet, perhaps more than Wisconsin, EnCon hopes for further integration and sharing of personnel and activities in the field. While there have been few gains so far in effective administration within the EnCon's headquarters staff, the department, like Wisconsin's, also expects short-term gains in administrative efficiency from its field reorganization, since some conservation personnel are being retrained and assigned to pollution monitoring tasks. In late 1971, departmental spokesmen stated that this was the major benefit thus far from the environmental superdepartment, because it reduced the need of the smaller and less well-established pollution control divisions for field personnel.

The creation of an environmental superdepartment in New York, as in Wisconsin, has not had positive effects on its interest group constituencies. In fact, the support of conservation interest groups for traditional state programs may have been lessened, since these programs are administered by a department they have always criticized for emphasizing pollution control. This criticism has been extremely hostile, and is a constant factor with which EnCon's commissioner has had to contend. One proposal, subsequently defeated at the Conservation Council's annual fall convention in 1971, called for a separate Fish and Game Commission to govern these programs. Reorganization spokesmen in New York hoped that the new department might bring conservation and pollution control interest groups closer together, although some public administration strategists believe that many special interest groups, with limited goals

160

to articulate, permit increased public advocacy of important trade-off issues. Younger Conservation Council members and groups such as the Sierra Club have shown increasing interest in pollution problems, but this probably was not prompted, and perhaps was slowed, by the environmental reorganization.

The only political gain for EnCon from its combined constituency may have been for EnCon's budget in 1971. When the legislature threatened to cut the conservation budget a good deal more than the governor had done, EnCon's commissioner argued that he would then have to take antipollution funds to use for conservation work. The threat of a cutback in pollution control, along with the effective lobbying of conservationists, was able to avert most cuts so that EnCon's fiscal year 1972 budget was about the same as the year before. Thus the political popularity of pollution control may have been of some help to EnCon's conservation component. This was also true for the 1972 bond issue.

What is paramount in any description of New York's environmental superdepartment is that while the benefits of administering all conservation and pollution control programs together are as yet slight, the time spent trying to make sense of the program mix is large. The commissioner has found that there is more superficial than real resemblance between the conservation and pollution control personnel, their daily activities, outlook, and constituencies. Not surprisingly, he has also found much resistance to any change of operating methods on the part of staff. The commissioner has been forced to spend an inordinate amount of time and energy, perhaps a third of his time in his office, solving jurisdictional disputes between the two components, soothing the ruffled feathers of the Albany staff, pacifying displeased conservation interest groups, and speculating on integrative moves.

For example, the Environmental Management section has lobbied within the department for more water pollution standards—setting authority, water planning, and for control of water quality issues for the interstate river basin commissions on which it represents the department, e.g., the Delaware River Basin Commission. The Environmental Quality section has also fought for more water planning, flood control authority, oil and gas regulation, and intradepartment pesticides control. Some public administration strategists support superdepartments for their ability to resolve these kinds of conflicts. They argue that such internal solution is a way to integrate competitive programs. However, EnCon's commissioner has reacted to such disputes on a completely ad hoc basis, and also has not been helped in this by his two deputy commissioners for Environmental Quality and Environmental Management, who are the chief advocates of the two competitive sections. Every step toward integrative change has been preceded by an enormous amount of internal debate, and most moves then had to be discarded because of the bureaucratic commotion they would create. The commissioner might have had more success in conflict resolution if he had been able to hire two new deputy commissioners for Environmental Quality and Environmental Management.

Locating pollution control programs in an environmental superdepartment cannot be said to have seriously hurt this effort in New York, unlike Wisconsin. However, pollution control might have benefited more by a separate department, and thus the superdepartment represents some short-term opportunity cost to it. At the critical time of reorganization and launching of a new antipollution effort, maximum energy could not be devoted to these programs. Some attention had to be focused on problems arising between the two components, and this has continued. The existence of two sets of programs, each with its own concerns and crises competing for attention, sometimes has made it difficult for the top management to concentrate sufficient time on one problem to solve it thoroughly. The appearance and actions of EnCon are sometimes schizophrenic. The top management staff feel they are constantly moving from one problem to the next, on a completely reactive basis. Thus, in the short run, this may have slowed the pace of pollution control standards-setting and contributed to some delays in monitoring and enforcement and the failure to stimulate internal planning and research. Finally, insufficient energy could be devoted to building a firm base of political support for the department.

New York's environmental superdepartment, like Wisconsin's, illustrates well the dominance one program element may have over another in such a combined structure. It may be difficult to find a leader versatile and interested in both kinds of programs. Perhaps more important, the director may have a predilection for one or another component. In New York, public demand for tougher pollution regulation probably necessitated emphasis on these programs, whereas in Wisconsin the leadership chosen was more interested in conservation programs. Conservation programs do not seem to have been hurt by their association with pollution control in New York's EnCon, and thus the issue of dominance is less significant than in Wisconsin's environmental superdepartment, where the pollution control effort has been hindered. In general, traditional conservation programs are better established, with a historically stronger base of support, than the newer pollution control efforts and thus are better able to operate effectively on their own, even without the continuous support of top administrative time and energy. Conservationists also seem to be more effective lobbyists.

An environmental superdepartment raises another issue for public administration. One supporting rationale for a superdepartment is that the typically subsequent method of internal conflict resolution is more efficient. However, advocates of responsive government argue that open conflict and competition between programs is healthy, and their internal solution limits public understanding of trade-off issues and individual access to governmental decision-making. Within EnCon the commissioner does resolve privately most issues between his two components, and the governor prefers this style in order to minimize public squabbles between agencies. Internal differences within EnCon are not typically aired publicly, since the participants rarely meet in a public forum. In addition to jurisdictional disputes, issues of programatic conflict include the pollution control staff's opposition to conservation activities such as forest burning, use of pesticides to kill carp and the gypsy moth, some water use permits issued for dams, fill, and dredging, and water use on Long Island where cesspools are widely prevalent and water treatment and reuse has lagged. On the other hand, conservation personnel have protested that EnCon's thermal pollution control regulations are too weak, that there are too strict disposal standards for motorboats, that there have been some sewage pipes and discharge pipes in streams and through forests, and there are some open dumps and landfills near wetlands. The two sets of staff have also differed on other state agencies' programs, particularly on various land uses. However, regardless of how these disputes are solved, some EnCon officials do consider them healthy and useful, and also argue that several would not have occurred if the two sets of programs were in separate departments.

Environmental Advocate or Arbitrator

One unresolved issue arising from New York's superdepartmental structure, is what EnCon's environmental role vis-á-vis other state agencies should be. Since EnCon combines pollution control and conservation programs, it has more legitimate claim to being *the* environmental spokesman and regulator for other state agencies than if it were simply a pollution control agency. Also, EnCon has a very broad environmental purview, including the mandate to do land use planning and to construct a statewide environmental plan affecting other state agency programs. However, this does not automatically decide its role.

EnCon must answer the basic question of whether its interagency posture is one of environmental *arbitrator* or *advocate*. An arbitrator who hears arguments from environmentalists and resource developers and adjudicates their disputes might have such powers as vetoing the proposed projects of other state agencies on environmental grounds after reviewing the environmental impact statements submitted to it. As an arbitrator, it would be the final state decision-making authority. However, an arbitrator must be just that—judicious in its decision-making and fairly balancing environmental interests against other state social and economic objectives. In contrast, an advocate is a lobbyist who presents his view for a particular pro-environmental position as strongly as possible to other state agencies, the legislature, and the private sector. He battles for environmental quality interests aggressively and visibly, and by definition has a one-sided view and interests to protect, taking positions uncompromised by other objectives. An advocate should not have veto power, which is an adjudicative function. Thus far, the EnCon commissioner seems to be tending toward the advocacy role, since setting EnCon up as an arbitrator would necessarily limit his ability to act as a vigorous and tough lobbyist for the environment. New York must then face the issue of where to locate the environmental arbitration role, since there is increasing demand and interest in it at the state and federal level, from environmentalists, planners, and other groups.

The statutory role of the 16-member interagency and citizen State Environmental Board in departmental affairs is largely an advisory one, with the exception of its power to approve all standards and regulations proposed by the commissioner. In EnCon's first year, the board members were largely passive and reactive to the commissioner, and it had a neutral influence on the department's activities. Realizing that the board's authority to approve standards may sharply limit his own authority and independence, Commissioner Diamond has chosen to interpret its jurisdiction very narrowly. He argues that the board should not get involved in day-to-day and highly technical regulations, and he has not submitted all pollution control standards to it. Initially, board members did not object to this. Attendance at early meetings was poor, since the eight departmental board members were busy with their own state activities and were not allowed to send their assistants to meetings. In fact, interest in the board's activities by both its agency and citizen members seemed so low that at an early meeting some members discussed its disbandment.

In mid-1971, however, many board members became increasingly interested in strengthening their role in pollution standards-setting. EnCon's standards-setting activity was picking up, and several departmental board members requested that certain matters be discussed at meetings. Since many standards were in response to new federal requirements, board members were also more informed as to possible agendas. Feeling some pressure from board members and knowing that the legality of taking independent departmental action in standards-setting might be challenged, the commissioner has thus begun to send more recommendations to the board for review. More often than not, most proposed standards are submitted to it on a predecision basis as a way to sound out board members. Often they are again submitted for final approval.

If this trend continues, the State Environmental Board is likely to have an increasingly negative impact on EnCon's independence of decision-making, and may slow up and weaken proposed pollution control standards. At least four of the board's agency members represent executive departments whose activities may cause environmental degradation or whose clients or constituencies do— the directors of the Departments of Commerce and Transportation, and the Public Service and Industrial Commissioners. By statute, at least one citizen member must be representative of industry and as such shall be employed by a manufacturer or public utility and another must represent agriculture. Thus there is a strong potential bias against consistently tough environmental actions. Once, thus far, the board actually diluted the EnCon commissioner's recommended standards. This happened in the fall of 1971, when the Public Service Commissioner along with the director of the Commerce Department and other allies fought for lowered sulfur oxide standards in a heated and drawn-out battle. Because it is meant to be a consensus body and because of its diverse and large membership, the board is also extremely slow and cumbersome as a decision-maker, although the 60-day time limit imposed on its deliberations on standards mitigates this somewhat.

There are not many offsetting beneficial factors to the board's existence. The board has not proved to be a mechanism for gaining interagency cooperation or eliciting broader support within government for environmental quality programs, as some persons had hoped. Rather, its members are divided and protective of their own spheres of influence. Although its interagency and citizen members are for the most part highly qualified persons, often with much expertise in environmental matters, the board's deliberations thus far have not been much above the level of argument on particular standard levels. The board does not consider board environmental issues and trade-offs, nor encourage new planning and policy thinking on the environment. Finally, the board is not a point of increased citizen access to public policy-making. Board meetings are always "executive sessions," closed to the public. The only point of possible formal citizen contact with board members is at public hearings for proposed standards, which the board members sometimes attend. Such attendance, however, is not mandatory.

NOTES

1. New York, Laws of 1970, Chapter 140 (signed on April 22, 1970 and effective July 1, 1970). (Also known as the Environmental Conservation Law.)

2. New York, Laws of 1971, Chapter 709 (amending Subd. 3, Section 1267 of the Public Health Law).

3. New York, Laws of 1970, Chapter 140, Article 4, as amended by Laws of 1971, Chapter 277.

4. New York, Laws of 1970, Chapter 140, Article 25.

5. Governor Nelson Rockefeller, "Special Message to the Legislature," March 11, 1970.

6. New York, Laws of 1971, Chapter 140, Article 2, Section 14.

7. *Ibid.*, Section 30.

8. *Ibid.*, Article 4, Section 103 (2).

9. *Ibid.*, Article 3, Section 75-82.

10. *Ibid.*, Article 2, Section 16.

11. *Ibid.*, Article 5.

12. Department of Environmental Conservation, "Regional Organization Study," Volumes I-IV, July, 1971, Field Services Task Force.

13. New York, Laws of 1971, Chapter 592.

14. Department of Environmental Conservation, "Goals for Areas of Environmental Concern," Central Planning Office, September, 1971 (internal departmental study).

15. Breck Arrington and Alexander Grannis, Memorandum to Commissioner Henry Diamond, "Enforcement and Regulation," October 30, 1970 (internal departmental memorandum).

16. New York, Laws of 1971, Chapter 716.

17. New York, Laws of 1971, Chapter 715.

18. New York, Laws of 1971, Chapters 812, 1026, and 1028.

19. New York, Laws of 1971, Chapter 709.

20. New York, Laws of 1971, Chapters 710 and 712.

21. See, for example, *New York State Environment,* monthly newspaper of the Department of Environmental Conservation, September 1, 1971, pp. 4-5.

22. New York, Laws of 1972, Chapter 385.

23. New York, Laws of 1970, Chapter 140, amendments to the Public Health Law, adding Section 16.

PART

II

NEW STATE
STRATEGIES

6

**VERMONT
LAND USE
CONTROL**

TRENDS IN STATE LAND USE CONTROL

State governments are increasingly turning to land use management as a way to prevent pollution and destruction of open spaces and other environmental resources before these problems occur. Expanding industries, new housing developments, expanded transportation systems, and the need for agricultural lands have put new pressures on limited land resources, and are leading several states to take steps to plan for and control the use of their vital land resources. Vermont and Maine are two examples of comprehensive land use control at the state level. Before analyzing Vermont and Maine (see Chapter 7) at length, it will be useful to look at developments in this area across the country.

States have the inherent power to control land use, through their police powers, but the responsibility has traditionally been delegated to local governments, along with much of the land use planning. Land use controls were initially viewed as an exclusive urban problem to be handled by city governments to prevent overcrowding of buildings on land and the separation of incompatible land uses. This local planning and regulation, usually implemented by zoning, has begun to fall into disrepute on many grounds. Zoning has been criticized as racially and economically restrictive and environmentally destructive. Local zoning authorities, it is argued, are too susceptible to political and economic pressures and cannot look beyond their narrow jurisdictional boundaries, although the problems know no such limits.

States are beginning to see themselves as the critical, higher level in this planning and management process. They feel they can take advantage of regional approaches in order to protect natural assets and optimize economies of scale.

A question arises whether land use planning, previously focusing on economic development, will be able to free itself of this traditional perspective.* Or, if it does free itself, will the planning be converted to another single-purpose, environmental protection and thereby make its implementation unlikely? Will the optimum pattern of development depend exclusively on concern for natural systems, or will the land use plan seek to implement multiple social and economic objectives as well? Vermont's land use plan currently being drafted is supposed to do the latter, but how countervailing economic and environmental interests will be meshed is not yet clear. It has become apparent to all levels of government that land use planning becomes a hollow exercise without effective powers to implement the plan. This point was emphasized by Governor John Love of Colorado in his testimony before the U.S. Senate Committee on Interior and Insular Affairs on national land use policy. He said, "Planning without power . . . turns out to be extra expense . . . and bureaucracy, unless it is tied in with the power to act."[1]

States have adopted a variety of tools to implement land use management objectives:

1. use of the state police powers, such as zoning and density controls, implemented by state permits, designed to protect the health and welfare of the state's citizens (see Table 6.1);

2. location of key state facilities, such as highways and airports, and financial incentives for properly located local facilities, through increased funds for communities with desirable placement;

3. purchase of critical land areas for state parks and other state uses;

4. authorization of less-than-fee-simple acquisition, such as easements and covenants;

5. approval of tax incentives for desirable types and location of private development (see Table 6.1).

States are increasingly turning to the first of these—the judicious use of their police powers—to control land use. Some controls previously delegated to local governments are being reasserted at the state level, but only in increments. Even this often proves to be a tough political battle as local officials jealously guard these zoning powers. The usual strategy is to devise a partnership between the state and local governments to control land throughout the state, recognizing and retaining the importance of local zoning in the

---

*A survey of state governments by the Council of State Governments showed that 7 of the 38 respondents had a statewide land use plan in existence. These were Hawaii, Alabama, Delaware, New York, Rhode Island, Puerto Rico, and Guam. Sixteen other respondents indicated they were developing some kind of a state land use plan. However, the survey did not determine whether the land use plans were being utilized, nor was the definition of a land use plan standardized. Therefore, these plans may not necessarily emphasize environmental objectives, but could be the more traditional type of plan for economic development. See Council of State Governments, "The States' Role in Land Resource Management," Lexington, Ky.: January, 1972.

TABLE 6.1

Land Use Control and Incentive Techniques Used by Various States

Column groups — **State Controls** (Statewide: Land Use & Zoning; Large Developments; Unincorporated Areas; Special & Regional Commissions — Selective: Coastal Zones & Wetlands; Drainage Controls, Floodplains; Power Plants & Utility Transmission; New Communities & Land Assemblage; Wilderness Areas; Spring Mining; Solid Waste Disposal; Mobile Home Parks; Scenic Easements) — **State Criteria** (Statewide: Floodplain, Wetlands, or Shoreland & Coastlines — Selective: Exclusionary Zoning Appeals; Open Space Easement; New Communities; Tax on Present Use) — **Tax Incentives** (Tax with Development Restrictions; Inventories) — **Non-Regulatory Activities** (Monitoring Systems; Growth & Development Plans)

State	Land Use & Zoning	Large Developments	Unincorporated Areas	Special & Regional Commissions	Coastal Zones & Wetlands	Drainage Controls, Floodplains	Power Plants & Utility Transmission	New Communities & Land Assemblage	Wilderness Areas	Spring Mining	Solid Waste Disposal	Mobile Home Parks	Scenic Easements	Floodplain, Wetlands, or Shoreland & Coastlines	Exclusionary Zoning Appeals	Open Space Easement	New Communities	Tax on Present Use	Tax with Development Restrictions	Inventories	Monitoring Systems	Growth & Development Plans
Alabama					X																	
Alaska			X																			
Arizona					X																X	
Arkansas										X												
California			X	X	X									X					X	X	X	X
Colorado												X								X		
Connecticut				X	X													X				
Delaware				X							X											
Florida													X	X								
Georgia				X																		
Hawaii	X																	X				
Idaho																						
Illinois										X											X	
Indiana																						
Iowa																						
Kansas																						
Kentucky																			X	X		
Louisiana												X										
Maine	X	X					X			X				X				X				
Maryland				X			X				X								X			
Massachusetts				X	X											X						
Michigan				X																		
Minnesota			X											X							X	
Mississippi																						
Missouri										X												
Montana						X				X												
Nebraska						X																
Nevada																						
New Hampshire																						
New Jersey				X	X																	
New Mexico						X															X	
New York				X			X	X	X										X			X
North Carolina				X																		
North Dakota										X												
Ohio										X												
Oklahoma											X											
Oregon		X		X		X		X				X		X				X				
Pennsylvania						X				X	X						X					
Rhode Island				X																	X	
South Carolina						X																
South Dakota										X												
Tennessee																						
Texas					X																	
Utah																					X	
Vermont	X					X					X			X				X	X			
Virginia										X				X								
Washington							X			X				X				X				
West Virginia										X												
Wisconsin					X	X							X	X								
Wyoming																						

Source: Based on a table presented in "Land Resources, Policies and Programs" by the Pennsylvania State Planning Board, August, 1971, p. 33. Updated with data from "State Control of Land Use in the U.S. Today," a paper presented by Edward A. Williams of Eckbo, Dean, Austin & Williams to the American Institute of Planners Confer-In West, Oct. 24-28, 1971; and "Environmental Quality: Third Annual Report of the U.S. Council on Environmental Quality," Aug. 1972, pp. 183-190.

process. Even in Hawaii, where state controls are the most comprehensive, local zoning bodies regulate urban land use.

The uses of the police powers to control land use range from the most comprehensive controls in Hawaii, Vermont, and Maine to the least state controls through use of selective state criteria as in control of coastal areas in Washington. Some states use more than one of these land management techniques. These are the five categories of controls, based on police powers:

1. *State controls, statewide and comprehensive*—Hawaii[2] is the only state in this category. Here a state Land Use Commission divides the state into four districts: conservation, agricultural, rural, and urban. Local authorities continue to regulate in urban zones, while a state commission regulates the agricultural and rural districts. The state Department of Land and Natural Resources controls the conservation district.

2. *State controls, statewide, over land above a minimum acreage*— Vermont[3] and Maine[4] regulate large industrial, commercial, and residential developments through the use of a permit. In Vermont, anyone (including a state or municipal agency) planning a development over one acre or a subdivision of more than ten units must first have a permit from the state. Or, if there is permanent local zoning, the state's permit is required for developments over ten acres. In Maine, the state controls all industrial and commercial developments including over 20 acres or 60,000 square feet of industrial floor space. This chapter and the following one provide details on these two different state approaches to comprehensive controls.

3. *Selective state controls over endangered environmental areas, or key types of land development*—Many states set regulations over specific geographical areas or troublesome types of development and require developers (often including state and municipal agencies) to secure first a state development permit. Areas and types of development regulated include:

a. *coastal zones* in Rhode Island,[5] Georgia,[6] North Carolina,[7] Oregon (all water areas of the state),[8] Delaware,[9] and Michigan (scenic rivers and Great Lakes shorelands);[10]

b. *wetlands* in New Jersey,[11] Connecticut,[12] Maryland,[13] and Massachusetts;[14]

c. *floodplains* in Michigan,[15] Nebraska,[16] Massachusetts,[17] Wisconsin,[18] and Montana[19] to varying degrees of control;

d. *power plant siting* and transmission lines: Washington[20] requires a state permit from the governor, to be based on the recommendations of the Thermal Power Plant Siting Council. The same problem has been treated in different ways in Wisconsin, California, Maryland, South Carolina, Oregon, Pennsylvania, New York, Vermont, and Illinois;

e. *endangered regions of states* are controlled by the San Fransicso Bay Conservation and Development Commission,[21] the Hackensack Meadowland Development Commission,[22] the Twin Cities Metropolitan Council,[23] New York Adirondack Park Agency,[24] Hudson River Valley and St. Lawrence-Eastern Ontario Commissions;[25]

f. *mobile homes* in Vermont[26] and Delaware;[27]

172

g. *Unorganized areas* in Alaska[28] and Maine.[29]

h. *strip mining areas* are regulated in Washington,[30] North Dakota,[31] West Virginia,[32] and Pennsylvania.[33] Also there are numerous other laws regulating new community development, wilderness areas and scenic rivers.

4. *State criteria, statewide*, to guide local land use control bodies, providing for a state take-over of regulatory responsibilities if localities fail to act adequately. Colorado passed legislation[34] in 1970 providing for the state to specify development standards for local governments to follow throughout the state. A total state land use planning program is required by December 1, 1973, classifying the state into areas of state, regional, and local concern. The state can step in when local governments fail to adopt adequate ordinances and can halt a threatening development. All counties are required to establish planning commissions and adopt subdivision regulation by July 1, 1972, or the state will adopt regulations for the county commissions to enforce.

Oregon enacted a type of statewide zoning[35] in 1969 for areas not covered by local zoning. The state also set broad standards to relate local comprehensive planning to state economic, social, and environmental objectives.

5. *Selective state criteria governing endangered environmental areas, or key types of land development*, for local zoning bodies to follow. The usual technique is for the state to adopt development guidelines for these areas or sources, which local authorities must implement. If local governments fail to act effectively, the state then takes over the job.

a. *Shoreland and floodplains* in Wisconsin,[36] Minnesota,[37] Vermont,[38] Maine,[39] Washington,[40] and California.[41]

b. *Exclusionary zoning* in Massachusetts.[42]

THE VERMONT APPROACH

Vermont is one of the first states to adopt a statewide, comprehensive land use planning and control program for large developments. The Land Use and Development Act—Act No. 250[43] of the 1970 Vermont legislature—requires a statewide land use plan to govern all essential aspects of growth in order to promote environmental objectives, as well as social and economic aims. Act 250 also establishes an institutional structure—an Environmental Board and eight District Commissions—to adopt the plan and issue permits to regulate development. Permits are required for subdivisions of ten or more lots and for commercial and industrial developments over ten acres. If there is no permanent local zoning governing the area, developments over one acre require permits.

At the time Act 250 was passed, there was very little local zoning in Vermont. While the state controlled roadside advertising and set minimum standards for subdivisions, developers were free of significant controls on land use.

173

This lack of effective land use regulation troubled many Vermonters as large-scale vacation home developments sprang up, threatening Vermont's scenic beauty. Environmental side effects of commercial and industrial expansion also worried many residents. One particular large-scale land development in southern Vermont touched off a special public outcry. In 1968, the International Paper Company proposed a recreational and second-home development on 20,000 acres in Windham County in southern Vermont. In response to citizens' concern, the governor appointed a study commission in May, 1969, known as the Governor's Commission on Environmental Control or the Gibb Commission for its chairman, Arthur Gibb.

Immediate development controls at the local level were not possible, for under Vermont law effective regulations must be preceded by the preparation of a comprehensive town plan, which would have taken considerable time. Therefore, in August the commission recommended, as an interim measure, that the Health Department develop subdivision regulations for "slope, ground and surface water quality and water supply and sewer disposal facilities." These emergency regulations were issued in September, under authority provided by a 1965 law.[44] These were ratified by the legislature in 1970, when Act 250 was passed, and are an important supplement to Act 250. In 1970 the regulations controlling subdivisions of three lots or more of ten or less acres were transferred to the Agency of Environmental Conservation.

In its report dated January 9, 1970,[45] the Gibb Commission found that land development by large corporations had become a major activity in the state and posed an immediate threat to the state's environment. Developments at higher elevations were seen as a threat to the water resources of the state due to destruction of holding capacities. Preservation of reasonable amounts of open land was also found to be a desirable goal seriously threatened by unplanned land development. In stating its general conclusion, the commission said:

[The commission] feels that our overall objective should be to insure optimum use of the resources of the state, including land, water, people, and space. We still have more unspoiled resources than do most parts of the Eastern United States. Once destroyed or lost these resources may never be retrieved. Vermont is now enjoying the benefits of a substantial economic development. The function of its government must be to build upon that economic opportunity while making full use of what has been learned from the failures and consequences of unplanned development elsewhere. Facing a period of substantial growth and intense development in the 1970s, we have the opportunity and hence the obligation to utilize the newer understanding of the science of ecology, and the improved knowledge concerning effective government organization, to provide a uniform, comprehensive approach by state government to assure *development without destruction*. A basic goal, therefore, should be the preparation of a comprehensive land use plan for the State of Vermont to be

174

undertaken as soon as practical and completed within the period of one year. . . . We must establish control over any act which has an undue adverse effect on the public health and safety, or the right of people to enjoy an unpolluted environment.[46]

Authority for the preparation of a land use plan recommended by the Governor's Commission was adopted by the 1970 Vermont legislature as Act 250, which created the Environmental Board and District Commissions and gave them authority to control land use. Legislative support was nearly unanimous for the new law, in part because the major economic activities in undeveloped regions—farming, forest products, and electric power—were exempt, except at elevations over 2,500 feet.

Act 250 was not intended as the tool to control *all* land use problems, only large-scale developments and small developments in unzoned communities. Other land-use control measures enacted included shoreland zoning,[47] which requires municipalities to zone all shorelines and empowers the Vermont Water Resources Board to adopt satisfactory ordinances if necessary; mobile home development regulation;[48] and authority for and tax encouragement of the transfer of private property or certain property rights to the state or municipality.[49]

The same legislature in 1970 created the Agency of Environmental Conservation to give stronger and more integrated focus to environmental programs,[50] and approved measures regulating land sale practices,[51] open burning and sanitary landfills,[52] and pesticides.[53] Permits were required for all waste discharges into state waters and an effluent charge was authorized.[54] New authority was established for state review of all alterations in watercourses, currents, or cross sections of any streams.[55]

THE ENVIRONMENTAL BOARD AND DISTRICT COMMISSIONS

Act 250 regulates the large-scale physical growth within the state in order to promote pollution control, aesthetic values, protection of open space, sound economic development, and proper population distribution.

The administering arm of this system is the Environmental Board and eight District Commissions (see Chart 6.1). The board is an independent regulatory group, composed of nine members appointed by the governor. Members serve for four-year terms, with the exception of the chairman who is appointed for a two-year term, but serves at the governor's pleasure. Five appointments expire in each odd-numbered year. Board members are not required to have any particular expertise, are compensated at the rate of $25 per day, and meet about four times a month. Members are chosen to represent various interests, although this is not required by law.

The Environmental Board may appoint one full-time executive officer and other professional and administrative employees. Additionally, the board may

175

CHART 6.1

State of Vermont
Organization of Act 250 Administrative Agencies

Budget FY 1972: $146,000
Staff   FY 1972:   12

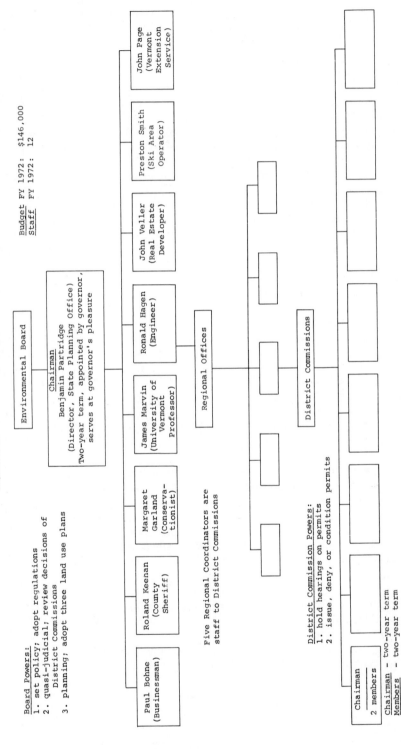

Board Powers:
1. set policy; adopt regulations
2. quasi-judicial; review decisions of
   District Commissions
3. planning; adopt three land use plans

Environmental Board

Chairman
Benjamin Partridge
(Director, State Planning Office)
Two-year term, appointed by governor,
serves at governor's pleasure

Paul Bohne
(Businessman)

Roland Keenan
(County
Sheriff)

Margaret
Garland
(Conserva-
tionist)

James Marvin
(University of
Vermont
Professor)

Ronald Hagen
(Engineer)

John Veller
(Real Estate
Developer)

Preston Smith
(Ski Area
Operator)

John Page
(Vermont
Extension
Service)

Regional Offices

Five Regional Coordinators are
staff to District Commissions

District Commissions

District Commission Powers:
1. hold hearings on permits
2. issue, deny, or condition permits

Chairman
2 members

Chairman - two-year term
Members - two-year term

establish as many regional offices as necessary. Five of these have been established around the state to carry out the business of the eight District Commissions. Kenneth Senecal is the executive officer of the board (1973) and the staff includes five area coordinators, two full-time secretaries, and four half-time secretaries. The board plans to hire three full-time and five half-time field investigators for enforcement purposes.

Funds appropriated to the board for fiscal year 1972 are $146,000, which covers salaries and expenses of the executive officer, coordinators, staff, and per diem expenses of the board and district commission members.

While the board has independent regulatory authority, it is located within the Agency of Environmental Conservation for administrative purposes, as well as for added staff. This agency administers programs for fish, game, parks, forests, recreation, natural resources management, water resources development, water and air pollution control, sewage regulation, and solid waste controls.

The secretary of the agency is appointed by the governor with the advice and consent of the Senate, serving at the governor's pleasure. His salary is fixed between $20,000 and $30,000 a year. The secretary controls the budgets of the units within his agency and possesses all the rule-making and regulatory powers of the component parts.

While the secretary of the overall agency provides policy direction and can have an effect on the budgets and staff of the Environmental Board, board members who are separately appointed by the governor for a term appear to have a substantial degree of autonomy within the parent agency. The exact degree of policy direction that the secretary will provide to the board is an evolving relationship.

Eight District Commissions are established as subagencies of the Environmental Board. The district units carry out the day-to-day responsibilities, holding hearings and issuing Act 250 permits, while the board sets policy and reviews decisions of the commissions in a quasi-judicial manner. The commissions' jurisdictional lines are set forth in the statute and follow county boundaries, some districts representing several counties where population is sparse.

Each District Commission has three members, all appointed by the governor, one of whom the governor selects to be chairman. Members serve staggered four-year terms, and the chairman serves two years. Again, the act requires no special expertise and makes service part time. Compensation is the same as for the board. Chairmanship of an active commission is nearly a full-time job, and other members spend about one day every two weeks at hearings.

PERMITS

Act 250 sets up a permit system for commercial and industrial developments and for subdivisions in order to insure implementation of environmental

177

objectives and land use plans, once these are drafted. All businesses, corporations, individuals, associations, and state and municipal government agencies are required to secure a permit for the following:

1. The "construction of improvement on a tract or tracts of land, owned or controlled by a person, involving more than ten acres of land within a radius of five miles of any point on any involved land, for commercial or industrial purposes";

2. ". . . (T)he construction of improvements for commercial or industrial purposes on more than one acre of land within a municipality which has not adopted permanent zoning and subdivision bylaws";

3. Any housing or multifamily dwellings, condominiums, or trailer parks that involve ten or more units and are owned or controlled by a person within a radius of five miles of any point on any involved land;

4. Construction of improvements on a tract of land involving more than ten acres of land which is to be used for municipal or state purpose;

5. Construction of improvements for commercial, industrial, or residential use above the elevation of 2,500 feet.

Specificially excluded from "developments" are:

1. Construction for farming;

2. Construction for logging below 2,500 feet;

3. Construction for forestry purposes below 2,500 feet;

4. Electric generation or transmission facilities (power plant siting is regulated under a separate statute);

5. Any developments already under way at the time of passage of the act.

Applications for permits are filed with one of the District Commissions. See Chart 6.2 for permit review process. County foresters, employed by the Agency of Environmental Conservation, are designated environmental advisors for purposes of aiding applicants and providing investigative information to the agency. After an application is filed, the environmental advisor advises the applicant about policy and criteria established by the Environmental Board and about other state and local permits required.[56] Information may be required on condition of slopes, waterways, soils, wetlands, flood plains, natural growth and ground cover, land contours, water availability, air pollution, sewage disposal and water pollution effects, roads, aesthetic conditions, adjacent land uses, impact on local school districts and on valuable historical or natural areas. Applicant must show the estimated total costs of the development, describe his financing arrangements, and indicate the physical characteristics of the proposed development.

The permit applicant is required to give notice of his filing to any municipality where the land is located, any municipal or regional planning commission affected, any adjacent Vermont municipality, or municipal or regional planning commission if the land is located upon a boundary. He must also post a notice in the town clerk's office and publish notice in a local newspaper of general circulation not more than seven days after the District Commission has received the application.

CHART 6.2

Act 250 Permit Applications Review in Vermont State Government

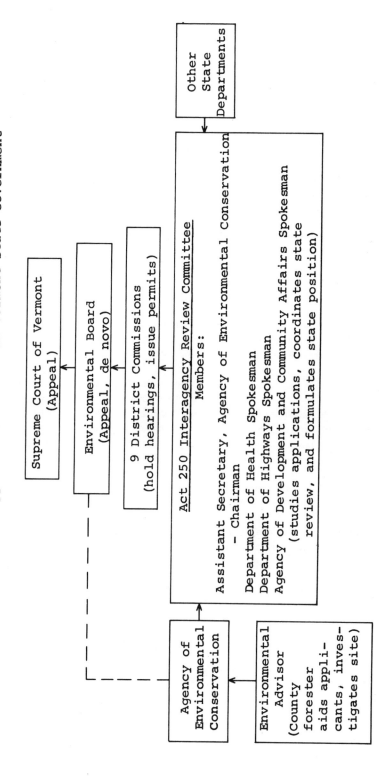

Copies of the permit application are sent to the Agency of Environmental Conservation and the environmental advisor, who visits and inspects the site if he has not already done so. Reports of his inspection are submitted to the agency. The agency formulates its overall position on the application and in conjunction with other state agencies files a statement with the District Commission, affected communities, and parties to the proceedings. The agency has the same status as any other party before the commission.

The agency's review and that of other relevant departments is coordinated by the Act 250 Interagency Review Committee, chaired by Schuyler Jackson, assistant secretary of the agency. This committee, which meets biweekly, includes the Department of Health, Department of Highways, and the Agency of Development and Community Affairs. The committee determines which state offices can be useful in evaluating the application and requests those reviews. While state review to date has been largely related to environmental impact, the governor recently directed that future investigations will include matters of concern to localities, such as impact on roads, schools, and local economy. These evaluations will assist local authorities in forming their own position on permits in their areas. After the district has received the position paper from the Interagency Committee, it determines hearing necessity and dates. As a matter of policy, hearings are now held on all applications. The law does not make a hearing mandatory but does entitle interested parties to request one. Parties to a hearing are the municipality, local and regional planning commissions, any state agency, any person receiving notice, or an adjoining property owner. If no hearing is requested or ordered, the commission must act within 60 days from the filing date or the application is automatically approved with no appeal. Usually four or five witnesses testify on each application. These witnesses and the state's report provide all technical information on which the commission makes its decision. To date, the District Commissions do not conduct their own investigation, but rather act as a purely adjudicative body, deciding solely on the technical record.

Before granting a permit, the commission must find that the application is consistent with specific criteria—not limited to compliance with any land use plan that exists. These are that the project:

(1) Will not result in undue water or air pollution. In making this determination it shall at least consider: the elevation of land above sea level; and in relation to the flood plains, the nature of soils and subsoils and their ability to adequately support waste disposal; the slope of the land and its effect on effluents; the availability of streams for disposal of effluents; and the applicable health and water resources department regulations;

(2) Does have sufficient water available for the reasonably foreseeable needs of the subdivision or development;

(3) Will not cause an unreasonable burden on an existing water supply, if one is to be utilized;

(4) Will not cause unreasonable soil erosion or reduction in the capacity of the land to hold water so that a dangerous or unhealthy condition may result;

(5) Will not cause unreasonable highway congestion or unsafe conditions with respect to use of the highways existing or proposed;

(6) Will not cause an unreasonable burden on the ability of a municipality to provide educational services;

(7) Will not place an unreasonable burden on the ability of the local governments to provide municipal or governmental services;

(8) Will not have an undue adverse effect on the scenic or natural beauty of the area, aesthetics, historic sites or rare and irreplaceable natural areas;

(9) Is in conformance with a duly adopted development plan, land use plan or land capability plan.[57]

No application may be denied solely on the basis of criterias (5), (6), and (7). Permits are for a period of time specified by the District Commission, after which a renewal application must be filed.

The commission may deny an application, approve it, or approve it with conditions. To date, the commissions have broadly used their powers to impose conditions. Many conditions have been attached to subdivisions and other developments to protect scenic, historic, and aesthetic resources, wetlands, and other natural areas. Other conditions are similar to traditional zoning requirements, such as adequate parking, proper plumbing and electrical systems. Conditions have limited the use of pesticides and protected against soil erosion. The Environmental Board is authorized to set standards to guide District Commission review of permits, but to date has only set detailed standards for power transmission lines.

A District Commission's permit decision can be appealed to the Environmental Board, where. interested parties must be notified and a de novo hearing held on all issues, whether raised in the initial hearing or not. Parties who may appeal were limited by the act to the applicant, a state agency, the regional or municipal planning commission, and the affected municipality. However, the Supreme Court of Vermont has now ruled that adjacent property owners have the right to appeal District Commission decisions, since the board's proceeding is de novo.

The District Commissions have been tougher on proposed developers than the Environmental Board in requiring environmental protections. Since the board hearing is the last review of the facts surrounding an application, and decisions are reviewed by the Supreme Court of Vermont, the board has felt it should follow court-like procedures. District Commission proceedings are more like administrative public hearings, with more generalities permitted. The board requires a stronger showing of the need for environmental controls before it will require them, and invokes stricter rules of evidence.

A party to the appeal can further appeal board decisions to the Supreme Court of Vermont. Here, however, no new issues may be raised. Findings of fact by the board are conclusive when the record generally supports them. Only one supreme court decision has been handed down, on the issue of the right of adjacent property owners to appeal.

As of June 1, 1972, 812 applications had been filed for Act 250 permits. Of those, 718 were for developments and 94 for subdivisions. Of those filed, 682 have been acted upon. Only 27 applications were denied, mostly for deficiencies such as inability to dispose of sewage adequately. Other denials were attributable to poor planning or application preparation, which could be or has been remedied by modifying the project or more engineering analysis.[58] Withdrawn applications numbered 18 and the remainder were approved, about 80 percent of them with conditions attached.[59]

Most permits are processed in about 30 days, although a few have required several months.

As of June 1, 1972, 25 District Commission decisions had been appealed. Of these, 15 had been decided, 9 were pending, and 1 withdrawn.

THE THREE PLANS

The board is directed to adopt three plans to manage the state's land resources and guide growth: (1) an Interim Land Capability Plan, describing current land uses and capabilities; (2) a Capability and Development Plan, setting forth state goals for development; and (3) a Land Use Plan translating these goals into a detailed land use designation for the future. The State Planning Office has identified four purposes for these plans:

—provide criteria for issuing development and subdivision permits under Act 250,
—guide state agency actions,
—guide regional agencies and local governments in land use planning and control,
—inform private enterprise of public goals and policies, to facilitate their activities.[60]

Interim Land Capability Plan

The first plan adopted was the Interim Land Capability Plan, which describes "in broad categories the capability of the land for development and use based on ecological considerations. . . ."[61] The state planning office defined this requirement to include:[62] geology, surficial and underlying topography; hydrology, surface and flood plains; historic sites; scenic vistas; settlement patterns and urbanization; land transfers; soil characteristics; agricultural lands; forest types and coverage; alpine and mountain habitat; unique natural

182

areas; significant land holdings; population distribution; other graphic information about the land and its capability.

The Interim Plan was completed largely by a consultant in mid-1971. It is an inventory of present uses of the land and of available natural resources and a statement of land use ideals. The plan summarizes the factors that ought to be taken into account in regulating development, but does not make specific recommendations for land use. The Interim Plan offers these development principles:

1. development would be logically related to established settlements;

2. development would not occur in those places where environmental damage or damage to sites of historical or educational significance would most likely exceed gains from development;

3. protection of the environment and increases in efficiency can be achieved by conforming with known environmental limitations;

4. ideally, development would not displace important nonurban uses relying upon basic characteristics of the land.[63]

Only in a few instances were these principles translated into usable, specific environmental controls, such as opposition to septic tanks when ground waters are likely to become polluted.

While permit applications are supposed to conform to this and all other plans, the legal standing of the Interim Plan has not been settled. The assistant secretary of the Agency of Environmental Conservation, Schuyler Jackson, and the first executive director of the Environmental Board, Robert Babcock, Jr., have said that they do not believe that any permit could be *legally* denied because it varied from the Interim Plan.[64] However, it is a moot point, since the Interim Plan was completely ignored in issuing permits and the plan lapsed on July 1, 1972. It is only significant because the act says future plans are not to deviate from this first one.

Capability and Development Plan

The act calls for a Capability and Development Plan (C & D Plan) that is consistent with the Interim Land Capability Plan, which shall be made with the general purpose of

> guiding and accomplishing a coordinated, efficient and economic development of the state, which will, in accordance with present and future needs and resources, best promote the health, safety, order, convenience, prosperity and welfare of the inhabitants, as well as efficiency and economy in the process of development, including but not limited to, such distribution of population and the uses of the land for urbanization, trade, industry, habitation, recreation, agriculture, forestry and other uses as will tend to create conditions favorable to transportation, health, safety, civic activities and

educational and cultural opportunities, reduce the wastes of financial and human resources which result from either excessive congestion or excessive scattering of population and tend toward an efficient and economic utilization of drainage, sanitary and other facilities and resources and the conservation and production of the supply of food, water and minerals. In addition, the plan may accomplish the purposes set forth in section *4302 of Title 24—1969, No. 250* (adj. Sess.), 19, eff. April 4, 1970.[65]

A basic statement of goals and policies governing the future development of Vermont, this plan was originally set for completion by July 1, 1972, but will not be completed until some time in 1973. The C & D Plan and the Land Use Plan to accompany it will be concerned with three types of policies, as defined by the State Planning Office.[66] These policies are:

1. *Public authority and policy* (consideration of national and state legal structures, programs, and policies regarding tax systems, public expenditures, and forms of police power execution).

2. *Appropriate use of land* (identifying areas that are renewable if properly managed, or nonrenewable if used at all; areas of optimum use by type for forestry, agriculture, recreation, urban settlement, preservation, and public service corridors; comparing optimum use to dominant economic demands by category and to competing economic and other demands by category).

3. *Population growth and optimum settlement pattern* (trends concerning population growth and distribution, projected according to the following optional patterns: permit existing urbanized areas to expand into currently nonurbanized areas; draw boundaries around currently urbanized areas, and/or intensify existing urban area densities, locate new sites outside existing urbanized areas for future dense settlement; and limit absolute population growth in the state through economic and other policies).

Land Use Plan

Due at the same time as the C & D Plan, the Land Use Plan will consist of a map and statements that indicate the general land use implication of the policies set out in the C & D Plan. The plans are to be carried out by state action and "further implemented at the local level by authorized land use controls such as subdivision regulation and zoning."[67]

The plans are supposed to address issues such as an ideal number of people for Vermont, where they should live, and what services they should have. They are the vehicle for setting priorities for general development and land use and recommendations on ways the state can implement the land policies, such as taxation, public funding, and regulation.

Prior to the adoption of each of these three plans, the board must hold at least one public hearing in each of the state districts. The Environmental Board must also send each proposed plan to each "municipal and regional planning commission" for comment. The board shall consider these views, but is not required to follow them. When the board finally approves a plan, the document is sent to the governor, who has 30 days in which to approve or disapprove it, in whole or in part. If the governor fails to act, the plan is deemed approved.

Approval by the governor was the final step in the adoption of the Interim Capability Plan. However, after approval by the governor, the Capability and Development Plan and Land Use Plan must be submitted to the general assembly for approval by both the House and Senate.

The statute allows both public and private landowners to petition for variances from adopted land use plans. Applications for such variances will be directed to the appropriate District Commission, which in turn will hold a duly advertised public hearing on the request.

No variance from the final Land Use Plan may be granted unless the petitioner shows that: (1) the land is *needed* for a different use; (2) the land is usable for the proposed use; and (3) conditions and trends of development have so changed since the adoption of the existing classification as to warrant reconsideration. These broad criteria will be more fully developed in regulations not yet adopted by the Environmental Board.

The District Commission for the area affected, guided by the statutory language and by the board's regulations, will act upon petitions for variances. Denial of a variance can be appealed to the Environmental Board, with subsequent judicial review before Vermont's highest appellate court.

PREPARING THE PLANS

Preparation of the statewide plans has been a difficult process, without precedents in other states or Vermont to follow. The planning and permit processes have gone on as completely separate processes, conducted largely by different agencies.

While the board was directed by the act to adopt all three plans, the lead role in their preparation until summer, 1972 had been assumed by the State Planning Office, which is located in the Office of the Governor. The governor himself was active in organizing the planning process. He selected citizen task forces in each of seven designated planning regions. These regions matched the boundaries of the seven District Commissions that had been created at that time, but had different membership. Most task force chairmen were also the heads of the regional planning commissions, administered by the Vermont Agency of Development and Community Affairs. Other task force members included citizens and legislators of various persuasions, and generally these bodies were balanced in their representation of special interests.

The regional task forces were assigned the job of drafting land use objectives and plans for their areas. The contributions these task forces have made have varied greatly on the quality and quantity of data and recommendations. Much of the material they presented to the state is based on the previous regional plans prepared by the regional planning commissions.

In the summer of 1972 the board took over the responsibility for drafting the two final plans. These are to be based on the contributions of the regional task forces, regional planning bodies, local agencies, other state agencies, and the private consultant hired full time to work on the plans.

There has been a major effort to ensure significant citizen participation in the planning process. The Ford Foundation awarded a grant to the Vermont Natural Resources Council, a statewide conservation group, to increase public awareness and participation in Act 250. The principal citizen contribution to the planning process has been at the public meetings held in seven areas around the state. Over 2,000 people attended these meetings to hear about proposed plans for future use of the state's land, as drafted by the task forces. Each person was asked to complete a questionnaire for the purpose of surveying citizen attitudes and wishes, and presumably the board will refer to these in drafting the final plans. However, the general public's contribution to the plans was limited by the failure of the regional task forces to solicit views in the early stages of planning. Like many governmental public hearings, these public meetings were held after the task forces had made key planning decisions. Thus, in some cases the public hearings were pro forma gestures. Nonetheless, the public meetings and publicity surrounding them have served to increase the awareness of the average citizen to land use problems in the state and to the existence of Act 250.

To formulate the two permanent plans, the board has designated four people to outline the document, and once this is approved by the board, the four will write the final plans. This group consists of the chairman of the board (who is also the director of the State Planning Office), an attorney hired by the board, the executive director of the board, and an official of the State Planning Office. The dual appointment of Board Chairman Partridge is a practical, Vermont-type solution to the need to integrate the land use planning conducted by the State Planning Office with the plan's adoption by the Environmental Board.

In June, 1972, a newspaper editorial charged that citizens were confused about the planning process, and that most board members were too.[68] The planners will have to reconcile the differences among state, local, and regional plans and objectives. A second set of policy decisions will have to mesh competing economic, social, and environmental objectives. Just how these decisions will be made, and the exact form the plan will take, was still unclear by August, 1972. In general, the planners tend to see their products as flexible instruments to guide development, which can be changed with new circumstances and perceived needs. They say the plans will not be statewide "zoning," although initially the governor spoke of the plans as zoning. On the other hand, developers and District Commissions think of the plans as "zoning," or detailed statements and regulations covering the whole state. This latter interpretation arises, in part, because the act requires that development permits must conform to the plan. The final two plans will try to carry out the ideals stated in the

186

Interim Plan and in this way meet the statutory requirement that they do not deviate from the first product.

Once the plan is adopted by the board it must go to the governor and the legislature for approval. State officials currently interpret legislative approval to mean "all-or-nothing"; i.e., that the legislature cannot change or veto individual sections of the plan. Indeed, legislators may not wish to decide which individual areas of their district should be free for development or restricted.

While one assumes that the plans are supposed to protect the "public interest," the legislature gave little guidance to the Environmental Board in Act 250 to define this general welfare. The board must make many fundamental policy decisions that will affect most Vermonters. How will the board define "the public interest?" The questionnaires completed by citizens attending earlier hearings, while useful, are not likely to represent more than the select segment of citizens sufficiently concerned about environmental problems to attend meetings. Another way to determine the "public interest" is through pressures from organized special interest groups. However, all interests are not well organized and sufficiently powerful politically to protect their stake in the outcome of state planning decisions.

The larger the contribution of private Vermonters to the final plan, the more likely the plan will represent the public interest. Participation could be either by direct participation at the public hearings that will be held in the winter of 1972-73 or indirectly through their elected representatives—the governor and legislators. To participate meaningfully, citizens will need to review the plans, while they are still in the draft stage, before they become "cast in cement."

While prior consultation between the Environmental Board and legislature is one possible route to such legislative participation, open hearings in that body, with "on the record" votes, are more likely to make legislators responsive to the interests of all their constituents.

IMPLEMENTING THE PLANS

After the legislature approves the C & D Plan and the Land Use Plan, the board will promulgate regulations to implement their provisions. While Act 250 permits must conform to the adopted plan, this is not a sufficient administrative tool to implement fully the land use plans. Many activities are exempt from Act 250 permit requirements—farming, logging, developments initiated before the act was passed, lots over ten acres in size, and developments under a total of ten acres when local zoning exists. For instance, much strip development is exempt under the ten-acre minimum provisions.

The board may need additional statutory authority to require that regional plans and town regulations comply with the plan. This may be more a political necessity than a legal one. State officials may wish the public endorsement of the legislature for such a policy, whether or not they currently have

187

statutory authority from Act 250 to require such compliance. While Act 250 says that the state land use plan must conform to "duly adopted" regional or local plans, "duly adopted" could be so narrowly defined as to eliminate the necessity for the state plan to conform to any others.

The plans must be specific and realistic, and yet meet the several objectives of the act to protect the natural environment as well as social and economic needs of the state. The content of the plan, its quality, degree of specificity, and powers for implementation are the key to comprehensive and coherent state guidance of Vermont's growth. Without the plans as a set of long range objectives, Act 250 permits and other state permits will continue to be issued on a case-by-case basis.

As a rule, developments that have sought Act 250 permits have not been reviewed in terms of long-range goals or regional objectives. The notable exception to this rule is that developments in ski areas have been required to present a long-range growth plan to the District Commission at the permit hearings. This requirement resulted from the urging of the U.S. Forest Service and the Vermont Agency of Environmental Conservation.

The more general linking of permits to comprehensive land use goals must await the adoption of the state land use plans.

Effect of Act 250 Permits

The main benefit of Act 250 permit implementation to date has been to enforce other existing, but previously unenforced, state and local environmental controls.

Approximately 34 other state environmental regulations and 4 or 5 types of town regulations have been on the books, but compliance has been poor for lack of vigorous state and local enforcement. Now, the District Commissions require that an applicant secure other necessary permits from state and local governments as evidence that environmental protections required by Act 250 are met. As enforcement of these other laws increases, developers complain of red tape, which they sometimes erroneously attribute solely to Act 250.

Act 250 has been successful in protecting the natural environment from the major hazards of large-scale developments that have come to the attention of the District Commissions and the Environmental Board. Most review of applications has focused on the impacts to the natural environment—air, water, land, and wildlife. Few applications have been considered in connection with the other requirements of the Act—that the development not place undue social and economic burdens on the local community, such as congestion to schools or highways. Most proposed developments have not been sufficiently large in proportion to the community to warrant such examination. However, one pending application goes directly to this issue. An application for a huge condominium development in Stowe has been approved by the District Commission and is pending an appeal before the board. The issue here is whether the community can absorb the rapid growth proposed.

While conditions attached to permits have been generally protective of the environment, many developers are not applying for permits, and enforcement of Act 250 has been weak. Most large developers comply because local residents are highly aware of their actions, but some state officials believe that a great many minor developments covered by the act have not been approved.

The board has no enforcement personnel of its own, rather the Agency of Environmental Conservation surveillance staff investigates violations of Act 250 along with other laws within the agency's jurisdiction. The agency plans to hire three full-time and five part-time employees in the near future to inspect for violations of various acts, which should step up Act 250 enforcement. Act 250 subdivision permit requirements are now enforced by a requirement that every sale of land in the state of Vermont must be accompanied by a certification signed under oath by the seller, "that the conveyance of the real property and any development thereof by the seller is in compliance with or exempt from the provisions of (Act 250)." A copy of the certificate is sent to the Agency of Environmental Conservation. No town clerk shall record or receive for recording any deed to which has not been affixed . . . a certificate in the form prescribed by the Environmental Board. . . . A town clerk who violates this section shall be fined $50.00 for the first offense, and $100 for each subsequent offense.

A lesser effect of the permit system has been the establishment of some new land use principles, particularly relating to aesthetics, that can guide future state decisions. These include provisions for landscaping, protection of scenic highways, and proper location of power transmission lines. The only matter on which the board has adopted specific standards is power lines. It is not clear whether board standards or commission precedents will be incorporated into the land use plans, because the permit and planning processes have been conducted separately.

The development principles established through permit cases include:

1. Protection of scenic highway corridors. The Chittenden District Commission denied an application of Mobile Oil Company to build a service station near one exit of a state highway.[69] This denial was based in part on a quasi-official state recreational plan, published in 1967, that called for the protection of one-half-mile scenic corridors along interstate and certain other Vermont highways.

2. Special landscaping requirements and scenic screening on construction in the scenic highway zones. The applicant was ultimately denied permission to expand a mobile home park in the area around the interstate highway and the case was appealed to the Vermont Supreme Court.[70]

3. Denial of permission to drain and dredge a beaver pond—Ryder Pond—to make a recreation lake for homesites.[71] In this case, a district commission denied the permit and the applicant appealed to the Environmental Board. However, the developer withdrew his appeal to the board when he determined that the project would be a poor investment anyway.

4. Single access policy to state roads to prevent strip developments and their resulting aesthetic and safety problems. In November, 1971, the State Highway Board adopted a policy that provides that, in general, a property owner may obtain only one point of access to the public way. Also, the developer must bear the costs of installation of traffic control facilities such as traffic control signals. This policy was subsequently endorsed by the Environmental Board and is being applied in the evaluation of "250" applications.

A problem of administering the Vermont law has been the lack of good technical data available for District Commissions' decision-making. The Agency of Environmental Conservation's position paper is usually the most detailed technical statement presented to the District Commission on an application, and consequently it has been very influential in the final decision. However, the agency does not always cover in sufficient detail all the factors a commission must consider, and to date the District Commissions have not personally investigated proposed developments. For example, it has been difficult to project likely effects of smaller developments. The commissions rely on the testimony presented at hearings, and then, in an adjudicative manner, decide the permit application on the record presented by others. This is also the procedure followed by the board. When District Commissions were initially established, they were instructed to behave as juries, but these bodies may now be moving toward a more aggressive posture, investigating applications for themselves. To do this properly, they will need additional staff and funds.

The present use of the adversary proceeding as the sole tool to review applications puts great importance on local expertise. The regional planning commissions are legal parties to a hearing on a permit, but their comments have been very general. The local planning commission is also a party when one exists. Local officials and private citizens are taking an increasing interest in these proceedings, but the quality of their technical contribution is variable. People from the larger towns and from areas already affected by rapid, uncontrolled development—the southern sections—more strongly support the state law, participate more fully in hearings, and make a better technical presentation.

The regionalized administrative structure of District Commissions and regional task forces for planning encourages local differences. While regional variations in resources and social needs have been recognized by this system, as intended by the act, the degree of environmental protection required of permitees has also varied considerably. In the undeveloped areas to the north, where towns are small, planning weak or nonexistent, and the public less aware of development problems, the controls may not be adequate to carry out the intent of Act 250. It is in just these less developed areas that pressures for rapid and uncontrolled growth are now the greatest.

Act 250 does not supplant the need for local zoning. In fact, the act has incentives to encourage local government action. Incentives are provided in three ways: the application of the law to developments of over ten acres in zoned towns and over one acre in unzoned communities; town plans have the force of law because a District Commission may not issue a permit unless the

190

project complies with local plans; and local officials are made parties to the state permit proceeding. At best, the success of these incentives for independent local action has been slight. Very few towns have subdivision regulations or zoning ordinances that would limit the state review to over ten-acre developments.

In some communities these provisions have had a reverse effect from the law's intent. Local officials, particularly in smaller communities, are *less* inclined to adopt local controls now, because they feel the state can handle the job. In some cases local officials participate in the state's 250 program in lieu of developing their own zoning regulations. To help local and regional officials who have few investigatory and planning capabilities develop a position on pending 250 permits, the state agencies will now investigate local effects of pending permit applications as an advisory service. Ironically, in this way the active participation in the state program of local officials and the public which is a highly desirable condition, may serve to limit community-based zoning action.

THE PUBLIC REACTION

One significant benefit of Act 250 has been to increase the awareness of the average citizen to land use and other environmental problems. The act's implementation has been widely covered in the press. Private citizen groups have launched vigorous public information programs. Citizen participation in the state program has been active and constructive, and the public's support for environmental protection in general has been strengthened.

NOTES

1. John A. Love, Remarks to the Committee on Interior and Insular Affairs, U.S. Senate, 91st Cong., 2nd sess. "National Land Use Policy" (Washington, D.C.: U.S. Government Printing Office, 1970).
2. Hawaii Land Use Law; Rev. Stat. Ch. 205, 1968.
3. Vermont Land Use and Development Act; Act 250 (H. 417), 1970.
4. Maine Site Location Law; Ch. 571 (H.P. 1958 - L.D. 1834), 1970.
5. Rhode Island Session Bill H 2440 Substitute "A" as amended, 1971.
6. Georgia, Act 1322, 1970.
7. North Carolina Statutes Act 21, Chapter 143, Part 7.
8. Oregon S.B. 224, Chapter 754, 1971.
9. Coastal Zone Act, Delaware Code, Chapter 70.
10. Land Use Programs for Michigan—Interim Report to Governor Milliken's Special Commission on Land Use, August 26, 1971. p. 6.
11. New Jersey Stats. Ann. 13: 9A1 through 9A-10.

12. Connecticut Statutes, Sections 22-7h to 70.

13. Maryland, Chapter 241, 1970.

14. Massachusetts Coastal Wetlands Act of 1965, 130 Mass. General Laws Ann. Mass. Inland Wetlands Act of 1968, 131 Mass. General Laws Ann.

15. Land Use Programs for Michigan—Interim Report to Governor Milliken's Special Commission on Land Use, August 26, 1971. p. 6.

16. Letter from Nebraska Office of Planning, July 26, 1971.

17. Massachusetts Hatch Act of 1965, 131 Mass. General Law₃ Ann.

18. Wisconsin Senate Bill 81, 1971.

19. Montana Session Laws 1971, Chapter No. 393, H.B. No. 265.

20. Thermal Power Plants—Site Locations Law; R.C.W. 80.50.

21. McAteer-Petris Act, California Gov't Code, Sections 66600-652—1969 (West Supp. 1971).

22. New Jersey Stats. Ann. C13: 17-1 et. seq.

23. Minnesota Stat. Ann. Ch. 473B (Supp. 1971).

24. Laws of New York, Ch. 140, 1970.

25. New York State—Establishing Hudson River Valley Commission and St. Lawrence Ontario Commission. Executive Law SS 736.

26. Act 291 (H. 433), 1970.

27. H. Con. Res. 43, 1970.

28. A.S. SS .07.05.040.

29. Maine Land Use Regulation Commission; Ch. 494, P.L., July 1969.

30. S.B. 139, 1970.

31. Ch. 38-14, 1969.

32. West Virginia Code 20 SS SS 2, 8-11, 14-17, 30.

33. Act of April 27, 1966, Bituminous Mine Subsidence and Land Conservation Act, State of Pennsylvania; Act of July 19, 1965, Act 117; authorized Commonwealth to acquire, reclaim, use, or dispose of certain mining lands.

34. Colorado Land Use Act Ch. 106, Col. Rev. Stat. 1963 as amended by Art. 4 as amended in 1971.

35. Oregon Zoning Law; Ch. 324, Laws of 1969.

36. Wisconsin Shoreland Zoning Law; Wis. Stat. Ann. Ch. 59.971, 144.26 (Supp. 1970).

37. Minnesota Stats. Ann. SS SS 104.01-104.07.

38. Act 281 (H. 309), 1970.

39. Maine Revised Statutes, Ch. 424, Mandatory Zoning and Subdivision Control.

40. The Washington law and an initiative were before the voters, November, 1972, for final adoption and the law was approved.

41. Chapters 761, 974, and 1308, 1970.

42. Massachusetts Zoning Appeals Act; 40B Mass. Gen. Laws Ann. Sect. 20-23.

43. Act 250 of the Vermont General Assembly, 1970 Adjourned Session, 10 V.S.A. Chapter 151 (Hereafter refered to as Act 250).

44. 18 V.S.A. Chapter 23, Vermont Health Regulations, Chapter 5, Sanitary Engineering, Subdivisions.

45. *Governor's Commission on Environmental Control, Interim Report*, (Arthur Gibb, Chairman), January 9, 1970.

46. *Ibid*., p. 1.

47. Act No. 281 (H. 309).

48. Act No. 291 (H. 433).

49. Act No. 229 (S. 18).

50. Act No. 246 (S. 263).

51. Act No. 278 (H. 250).

52. Act No. 287 (H. 399).

53. Act No. 273 (H. 10).

54. Act No. 252 (S. 165).

55. Act No. 281 (H. 309).

56. The following is a partial list of the state permits in addition to the Act 250 permits required for various environmental and related objectives:

—Agency of Development and Community Affairs: for outdoor advertising.

—Agency of Environmental Conservation: for brush burning; sawmills; anyone who uses state forests and park land, such as for logging; any direct or indirect discharge into the waters of Vermont; dams; stream alterations; lake and bed alterations; well drilling; subdivisions of three or more lots of ten acres or less; mobile home parks; public buildings; sanitary landfills; emissions into the atmosphere; travel trailer and tending area.

—Department of Agriculture: licensing of slaughterhouses and other meat -handling establishments; licenses for milk dealers and pesticide control.

—Department of Education: for construction of buildings or improvements in school districts.

—Department of Health: for public water systems; food and lodging, bakeries, children's camps; nursing homes, hospitals, and homes for the aged.

—Department of Highways: for any construction in the highway right-of-way; any change in topography affecting highway drainage; zoning permit for development of land within 500 feet of the intersection or exit ramp providing access to any limited access highway; to operate a junkyard or automobile graveyard.

—Department of Labor and Industry: any "complex structure" for electrical purposes.

—Department of Public Safety: for fire alarm system installers and lightening rod installers; letter of approval for all public buildings; to ensure facilities for the handicapped in public buildings.

—Public Service Board: Certifies for construction of electric generation facilities or transmission lines over 48 KV; for construction or remodelling of any dam related to hydroelectric power; organization of any new public utility corporation; for the operation of any public utility business by a person, partnership, or unincorporated association.

—Vermont Aeronautics Board: letter of approval for all airports or private landing strips and navigational facilities.

57. Act 250, Sec. 12.

58. Agency of Environmental Conservation, "A Guide to Land Use and Development: Vermont's Environmental Programs," August 1, 1972.

59. Environmental Board, Agency of Environmental Conservation, "Statistics on Act 250," July, 1971, p. 1.

60. Vermont State Planning Office, "Preparation and Implementation of Plans Under Act 250," July, 1971. p. 1.

61. Act 250, Sec. 18.

62. Vermont State Planning Office, "Preparation and Implementation of Plans Under Act 250," p. 2.

63. Vermont State Planning Office, "Vermont Interim Land Capability Plan," June, 1971, p. 3-5.

64. As reported in Fred Bosselman and David Callies, "The Quiet Revolution in Land Use Control," a report prepared for the Council on Environmental Quality, January, 1972, p. 74.

65. Act 250, Sec. 19.

66. Vermont State Planning Office, "Preparation and Implementation of Plans Under Act 250," pp. 7-8.

67. Act 250, Sec. 20.

68. *Rutland Herald*, June 24, 1972.

69. Application No. 300008.

70. Application No. 300013, Ward A. Fuller.

71. Application No. 700001, Haynes Bros. Inc.

7

MAINE
LAND USE
CONTROL

Tourists and the oil industry are threatening the serenity and natural loveliness of the Maine landscape and the state is moving forcefully to protect it.

Maine's Site Location Act[1] passed in 1970 regulates major industrial and commercial developments through permits issued by a Board of Environmental Protection, which also administers the state's other environmental control. Development conditions can be attached to the permit or the site denied altogether. The Site Location Law is the main part of a package of laws that give Maine one of the most comprehensive state land use management systems in the country. Other parts include three other land use laws—controlling shorelands,[2] wetlands,[3] and undeveloped or "unorganized" regions[4] —and anti-pollution laws relating to air, water, solid waste, and mining.

MAINE'S LAND USE PROBLEM

At first, it may seem odd that this New England state, known for its reverence of unfettered property rights, is now one of the most advanced states in land regulation. But Maine also has a sense of place—a timelessness and loveliness unchanged in a changing world, and a most precious commodity on the American scene: undeveloped scenic land.

A recent economic analysis of Maine concludes that the demand for land, for recreational and industrial use, is the "most significant economic development in Maine in over one hundred years, since the development in the 1860s of mechanical processes for converting low grade wood pulp to paper."[5] Since the great era of textile and paper-making factories, Maine, even more than the rest of Northern New England, has gradually fallen behind in development, and has remained a place where a sense of privacy and reserve grew, and where a love of open country and a hard life were the lot of most residents. The best-educated young people had to travel south to earn a good living. Because of this economic situation, Maine has an abundance of land that, by American standards, is pure and unspoiled and very much in demand.

Seventy million Americans now live within a 24-hour drive of Maine, and many of those 70 million wish to flee the urban scene and can afford to do so. Maine has the combination of water and predictable snow that guarantees success in the second-home market. The advance guard of the second-home owners, the summer tourist, pours up into Maine regularly and brings home to Mainers the interest of outsiders in their state. These annual migrations, still uncharted or uncounted but clearly enormous, make the year-round residents very much aware of the affluence of the visitors and the mounting costs of land.

A second and most intense pressure upon the land is currently generated by oil companies seeking terminal and refinery facilities to accommodate the deep-draft supercargo tankers now being built. The only natural harbors on the East Coast deep enough to receive these ships are in Maine. Thus, the exquisite Maine coast, long the symbol of the state and its principal lure to visitors, is doubly threatened by uncontrolled land use.

By 1969 these factors, plus the national ecology boom, combined in Maine to create a strong awareness of the vulnerability of the state. There is almost no zoning in Maine; few of the tranquil coastal towns are willing even to face the necessity for establishing land use guidelines. (In mid-1972 less than 15 percent of the coastal communities had any zoning or land use laws; over 400 of 497 organized towns had no planning organizations.[6]) Unwilling to act locally but fearing exploitation, citizens turned to the state for help. A crisis was sparked in the early part of the 1970 special legislative session when four proposals were made for deepwater ports and oil refineries along the scenic Maine coast.[7] In this political climate the state legislature overwhelmingly voted approval of an extraordinary land use control tool—the Site Selection Act. Exemptions from the law may have accounted for the lack of opposition to the bill. Residential developers and realtors convinced the legislature to delete a provision that would have explicitly covered "residential" developments.[8] (Subsequently, however, the term "commercial" developments covered by the law has been construed to include large residential developments.) Also, a "grandfather" clause excluded any development in existence or licensed on January 1, 1970. Developments by public agencies were also excluded (although they are now covered). The act was aimed specifically at large industrial facilities, and state powers over these developments are significant.

The extensive powers to control industrial and commercial development in this act were assigned to the Maine Environmental Improvement Commission (EIC), the air and water pollution control body, thus consolidating the state's regulatory powers affecting development. Through hard work, skillful handling of problems, and constant and growing public support, the EIC, which in 1972 became the Board of Environmental Protection, has become a powerful force in Maine, and is clearly influencing the pattern of growth.

SITE LOCATION ACT

The Site Location Act requires the board to "control the location of . . . developments substantially affecting local environment in order to insure that such developments will be located in a manner which will have a minimal adverse impact on the natural environment of their surroundings."[9] Aimed at large-scale projects, the specific targets of the law are

> any state, municipal, quasi-municipal, educational, charitable, commercial or industrial development, including subdivisions, but excluding state highways and state aid highways, which require a license from the Commission, or which occupies a land or water area in excess of 20 acres, or which contemplates drilling for or excavating natural resources, on land or under water, excluding borrow pits for sand, fill or gravel, regulated by the State Highway Commission and pits of less than 5 acres, or which occupies on a single parcel a structure or structures in excess of a ground area of 60,000 square feet.[10]

Any project coming under this definition would require a special permit under the Site Location Act. This permit is in addition to any others the board issues under other laws, for instance for wastewater discharges or dredging.

Before issuing the permit, the board must conclude the project is adequate by these four specific criteria listed in the law:

1. Financial capacity. The developer has the financial capacity and technical ability to meet state air and water pollution control standards, has made adequate provision for solid waste disposal, the control of offensive odors, and securing and maintenance of sufficient and healthful water supply.

2. Traffic movement. The developer has made adequate provision for traffic movement of all types out of or into the development area.

3. No adverse effect on natural environment. The developer has made adequate provision for fitting the development harmoniously into the existing natural environment and will not adversely affect existing uses, scenic character, or natural resources in the municipality or in neighboring municipalities.

4. Soil types. The proposed development will be built on soil types that are suitable to the nature of the undertaking.

Permits are not issued in accordance with any comprehensive land use plan to indicate where industrial and commercial sites would be most suitable. Rather, the developer selects his own site and the board may then condition his use of that site, or deny it altogether if likely environmental damage is serious. Consequently, the board reacts to private initiative, rather than taking positive, initiating action on land use.

Judicial Review

The law provides that any developer has 30 days from a board order to appeal a decision to the Supreme Judicial Court of Maine, with review limited to the record of the hearing and the order of the board. The court will then decide whether or not the commission acted within the scope of its authority and on the basis of substantial evidence. On February 9, 1973, the Maine Supreme Court ruled the Site Location Act constitutional. In a unanimous decision, the court ruled that Lakesites, Inc. cannot subdivide 92 acres into lots until it receives the Commission's approval, which is declared a valid exercise of the state's police power.

HISTORY, COMPOSITION, AND POWERS OF THE BEP

The Board of Environmental Protection (BEP) is the successor to an agency originally established in the mid-1940s as the Sanitary Water Board, then an advisory and informational bureau. In the mid-1950s it gained enforcement power over water pollution, but apathy on the part of the appointed commissioners and the public kept their powers insignificant. Then, in 1969, control over air pollution was added, and the agency formally became the Environmental Improvement Commission. This change coincided with a drastic change in public attitudes toward control of development and pollution, and a simultaneous change in the attitude of politicians toward the ecology issue. Governor Kenneth Curtis appointed outspoken environmental supporters to the commission, and these new commissioners felt that they had been given real tools for protection of the land and an important responsibility. More legal support from the office of the state attorney general became available. With the passage in 1970 of the Site Location Act and shorelands regulation in 1971, the commission became the state's defense against exploitative development. In 1972 the commission was renamed the Board of Environmental Protection, and some state responsibilities for solid wastes, dredging, and wetlands were transferred to it.

BEP is an independent board composed of ten private citizens, appointed by the governor with the approval of his Executive Council.* Two members represent each of these interests: manufacturing, conservation, municipalities,

---

*The governor recommends appointments, which may be rejected by the Executive Council. The council may be controlled by the political party opposing the governor.

198

the general public, and air pollution experts. The commissioners are appointed to three-year terms and receive $25 a day for their services at meetings or hearings, plus travel expense. (See Chart 7.1 for the organization of Maine's land use control agencies.)

The authority for holding hearings, previously limited to members, may be delegated to any qualified employee or representative of the board.

In addition to the land use control powers provided by the Site Location Act, the board's other responsibilities are to:

1. recommend new water quality standards and stream classifications to the legislature,

2. approve plans for new municipal systems of drainage, sewage disposal or sewage treatment,

3. establish and maintain standards for the operation of municipal waste treatment plants,

4. provide technical assistance to towns and industries regarding waste control, and supervise waste treatment plant construction programs,

5. establish ambient air standards and emission standards for action by the legislature,

6. register sources of air contamination,

7. grant variances from water and air quality standards,

8. experiment and research on waste disposal,

9. enforce regulations under its jurisdiction,

10. certify to the Corps of Engineers all cases where navigable waters are affected by development activities,

11. approve and supervise mining activity, formerly supervised by the Maine Mining Commission,

12. establish policy for wetlands and approve development altering the wetlands, formerly the responsibility of the Wetlands Control Board,

13. approve all dredging permits,

14. supervise all state action under the Solid Waste Disposal Act.[11] (Items 12-14 were transferred to the board as of July 1, 1972.)

Thus, the board's powers are complementary and range from land use controls to water development regulation to pollution controls.

The board sets policy for the Department of Environmental Protection, which performs day-to-day administrative functions, and the commissioner of the department is the chairman of the board. On board matters he votes only in case of a tie. A full-time appointee of the governor, the commissioner is a cabinet-level officer with an annual salary of $23,500.

The department staff is organized into three bureaus: Land, Air, and Water Quality, and two support divisions of technical and administrative services. The staff prepares recommendations for licenses and Site Location permits and submits these to the board for action. Staff hiring is the responsibility of the commissioner. Although not directly involved in hiring, the board does participate in preparation of the biennial budget, and thus has power to effect staff distribution and emphasis. Board members have been effective lobbyists in securing legislative approval for the budget.

CHART 7.1

Organization of Maine's Land Use Control Administrative Agencies

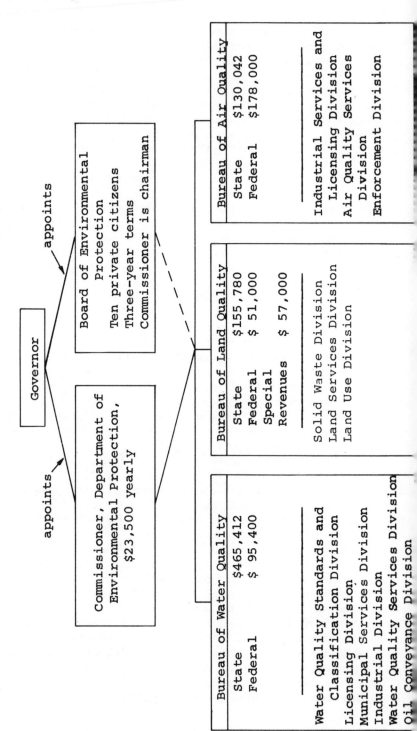

Governor

appoints ← → appoints

Commissioner, Department of
Environmental Protection,
$23,500 yearly

Board of Environmental
Protection
Ten private citizens
Three-year terms
Commissioner is chairman

Bureau of Water Quality

State $465,412
Federal $ 95,400

Water Quality Standards and
  Classification Division
Licensing Division
Municipal Services Division
Industrial Division
Water Quality Services Division
Oil Conveyance Division

Bureau of Land Quality

State $155,780
Federal $ 51,000
Special
Revenues $ 57,000

Solid Waste Division
Land Services Division
Land Use Division

Bureau of Air Quality

State $130,042
Federal $178,000

Industrial Services and
  Licensing Division
Air Quality Services
  Division
Enforcement Division

The departmental staff has now grown to approximately 50 full-time professionals, currently supplemented by additional persons on federal grants under the Emergency Employment Act. This professional staff includes persons with experience in oil, economics, chemistry, biology, engineering, planning, and fresh and salt water ecology. The agency receives over $1 million from the state and federal governments. All available disciplines can be used to examine any one permit application.

THE PERMIT SYSTEM IN OPERATION

The board's permit power over development is its key authority. Any person (corporate or otherwise) intending to construct or operate a development that may "substantially affect local environment" shall, before commencing construction or operation, notify the commission in writing of his interest and the nature and location of the work. The original legislation allowed only 14 days within which the location had to be approved or a hearing scheduled. If no action was taken in this period, the application was automatically approved. Many critics of the legislation felt that the 14-day period was impossibly short for any type of in-depth review, and that this would inevitably lead to the rash granting of permits. Fourteen days was also the period of time allowed to hold a hearing if one was requested after denial of a permit, and the period following a hearing within which a decision was mandatory.

In actual practice, the time problem was circumvented by a series of bureaucratic devices. Initially, the board requested waivers from all applicants and tried to comply with the 14-day requirement only if an applicant would not sign. This worked, but was obviously an interim solution, and after some consultation with the state attorney general the board declared that the period of time would not begin to run until "notice" was given, and notice would consist of the submission of a completed application including all advisory opinions and concurring remarks from every state agency, municipality, and planning unit involved in the proposed development. As the permit is a 25-page document of considerable complexity, designed to elicit a vast amount of information, much work had to be done by the developer to reach the "notice" stage. The conferences with state and local officials involved in application preparation invariably alerted and involved the staff and usually the board members themselves, as well as the press and conservation groups in the development area.

In 1972 the law was changed so that the current time intervals for action are 30 rather than 14 days. The department has now assumed responsibility for obtaining all coordinating clearances and recommendations except that of the locality. The applicant must still obtain this.

The staff provides guidance and information during the preparation period, but will not begin processing until the form is completed. The application form itself is divided into four sections: information on the applicant, including his financial and technical resources; information on the site, specifically soil, water, traffic patterns, and other area features; information on the project, designed to elicit the objectives and plans of the developer; and information on the development, listing details of construction.

While public hearings are required if a permit is denied, one can be approved with no hearing. The board interprets this to mean that approval, even with significant conditions, does not require a hearing. But the board holds hearings anyway on major issues and controversial applications.

An additional control device strengthening the hand of the board against the deadline for action has been the issuance of permits "subject to conditions attached." These conditions can be so extensive and specific or difficult to meet as to constitute denial while technically approving development. Standard conditions are: limitation to the project as described, approval of all related licenses and consents, and the submission to the board of any additional information requested. Specific conditions for each project are then appended to the general conditions.

Many of the specific conditions are generated by other state agencies with specific expertise, such as on soil quality from the Department of Agriculture. Thus, the effective staff and strength of the board is greatly expanded and the full resources of the state bureaucracy are brought to bear. Agencies that had been unable in the past to impose conditions on development are now able, through their advisory opinions, to exert a strong influence on private actions. A recent interview study with Maine officials indicated that while some agencies resent the additional work load these opinions represent, they are glad to have a say and so have accepted the responsibility.[12]

The Work Load to Date

The potential coverage of the Site Location Law is extensive because of its requirement for a site permit for any development requiring another BEP license. The BEP issues licenses and permits for: waste discharge, oil conveyance, oil terminals, air emissions, dredging (on any great pond or inland waterway), wetlands alteration (license also requires approval by municipality), mining rehabilitation, waste treatment plant operator certification, minimum lot size (dwelling on any lot less than 20,000 square feet not connecting to sewage system must have a permit), and site location.

In processing permits under Site Location, the BEP has dealt with major-sized projects, which require a permit because they meet the 20-acre or 60,000-square-feet minimum. Additionally, certain smaller projects that would create adverse environmental impact have been reviewed when deemed appropriate, with this decision made on a case-by-case basis.

While the press and the legislature at the time of enactment of Site Location anticipated that most efforts would center on the oil issue (and much time has been spent on it), the bulk of the permit applications have in fact been for housing development. This emphasis should not be surprising in view of the present housing shortage in Maine as in all of North New England, and the extreme pressure for second-home development and recreational areas.

The first systematic survey of work load, covering the initial 15 months of operation (January, 1970 to March, 1971) showed that 83 percent of the total applications (136) were for housing; of the 83 percent, 42 percent were for seasonal housing, 12 percent for mobile units, 8 percent transient lodging, and 22 percent permanent housing. Of the remaining permit requests, 8 percent were for distribution facilities, 5 percent for processing, 2 percent for services, and 2 percent for extraction industries.

Although a phrase specifically including "residential" development was removed from the original bill, the board subsequently defined "commercial" as clearly covering residential developments meeting the 20-acre requirement. Developers who protested that their projects should be exempt were told that the deletion of "residential" was done only because it was a redundant term.

During the first months of operation there were apparently a few builders who ignored the law and built without a permit. This practice seems to have stopped as the board has gained political and legal strength and publicized its hearings and procedures. The law provides the use of the temporary restraining order and/or injunctive relief to stop any such action. The office of the attorney general provides this service.

What About Oil?

If the greatest volume of the work load has affected housing, the most widely publicized permit cases and the most controversial issues have been on oil facilities.

In July, 1970, the board's predecessor, the Environmental Improvement Commission, denied King Resources Company permission to erect an oil terminal on Long Island in Portland Harbor, after a 6-3 vote. This was the first rejection of an industrial proposal made under the act. Eighteen reasons were listed for denying the permit, emphasizing largely the need to preserve the island as a recreational area and the risk of oil spills in this heavily populated and trafficed waterway. King Resources appealed this decision on the basis that the EIC was without jurisdiction as work had begun on the terminal prior to the effective date of the law.

The Maine Supreme Court found with King Resources in this case,[13] interpreting the term "in existence" broadly. There was some opposition to the decision as the court weighted heavily the wartime naval oil operations in the area and public knowledge that a terminal was to be built. The court also drew on a Common Law doctrine emphasizing the importance of commerce. Hence, the case made no contribution toward limiting or further defining the Site Location Act, except to support the grandfather clause.

Next, the Environmental Improvement Commission denied the application of Maine Clean Fuels, Inc.(MCF), to build an oil refinery at Sears Island.[14] Extensive hearings had been held on this application and there was broad media coverage of the hearings and subsequent denial. In August, 1971, MCF appealed to Maine's Supreme Court, concluding it could show, as required, that the "Commission's findings of facts and conclusions are not supported by the facts as reported during the hearings." This case has now been argued but as of August, 1972, no decision had been handed down. Attorneys and board members generally feel that this decision will not likely provide general interpretation of the Site Location Law, as the facts themselves presented during the hearings were quite unusual. For instance, the overlay map of the refinery facility that the developers presented did not match the geography of Sears Island and extended well into the Bay. Additionally, MCF representatives displayed no knowledge of such basic issues as the turning circle needed for supertankers. The developers' financial capability appeared questionable. It is unlikely that the decision will deal with any basic issues when such a profusion of immediate questions can be used to decide the case.

The continuing onslaughts against the Maine coast by oil companies have convinced many Mainers that oil will come sooner or later (it already comes into Maine through Portland Harbor) and others that oil must be kept out at all costs.

In view of the tremendous financial advantage to oil companies in using the existing deepwater harbors in Maine, it is understandable why there continue to be requests for terminal and/or refinery facilities. The hearings held on these requests have been clearly the most dramatic instances of the Site Location Law in action. National media have reported the fiery exchanges between oil company officials, property owners, lobstermen, and local representatives. The oil companies have chosen successive sites up the Maine coast, moving toward the very sparse and depressed eastern tip, away from population and from the affluent coastal areas of Penobscot Bay.

During the 1971-72 special session of the Maine legislature, an interesting proposal developed to "complement" the authority of the state's environmental agency on oil development locations. It was proposed that the state create a "Maine Industrial Port Authority (MIPA)," expecially designed to see that the most benefits would accrue to the state from whatever oil facility would eventually locate there. While the EIC would have retained control over the initial location, the MIPA would have supervised all operations, taken the land itself through eminent domain and then leased it to the oil company, encouraging additional industrial development in the chosen area, and generally acting as the state's direct agent. The power of eminent domain was dropped from the bill during the legislative session, and much opposition was generated by people who felt that such use of the state's powers would in fact benefit the developers rather than the state. The bill was withdrawn in the face of defeat at the last minute, but by the time of its death it had acquired coalition backing of a fascinating nature, including leaders of the conservation movement and industrial lobbyists. The MIPA proposal was supported by John Cole, editor of

Maine Times, Maine's weekly journal on conservation, life in Maine, and the Maine counterculture. *Maine Times* is most influential in Maine intellectual circles and with out-of-state property owners, who generally desire to retain the state's present natural condition, and Coles is an opinion-maker and a strong supporter of the board. It seems likely that there will be recurring attempts by the legislature to grapple directly with the oil problem unless a facility is approved by the board.

EVALUATION

Staff, Budget, and Follow-up

To function effectively, any regulatory agency must have competent, responsible members, a good staff, and the funds to do its job. The recent appointees to the board have included people who are not afraid to speak out as advocates for environmental protection and who act to keep the board in the spotlight, generally responding to the state's concern for its land and waters. These people take their responsibility seriously, give thoughtful review to staff suggestions, and are sensitive to public concern and interest. Although the members have other occupations that require time, they have in most cases managed to participate regularly in meetings and hearings. Despite their other jobs, members have embodied few conflicts of interest with their state work.

Even though during the initial period of administration of the Site Location Act the specific staff consisted of only one professional, the board managed to deal with the application competently. In part this reflected the clever use of the extensive permit system that elicited information from the developer and from other state agencies, in effect broadening the staff effort. In part it reflects the fact that the first Site Location Officer was an experienced and productive worker.

Also, economic development in Maine is slow, and there has not been the tremendous avalanche of applications that might have occurred in a state with a greater range of industrial possibility, or a state actively encouraging heavy industry.

It will be interesting to see if the expanding staff includes some professionals with training in the social sciences in addition to the present technically oriented employees. Since the criteria for weighing permit applications do not include humanistic concerns, the views of the board members themselves have represented whatever importance these disciplines contribute. The present staff has the capability to review applications well.

Inadequate funds will continue to be a problem, but the cabinet-level status of the commissioner should help make him an effective lobbyist for obtaining adequate funding.

Not enough is being done to insure that developments, once approved, actually comply with permit conditions. This is true of most government regulatory programs—state, federal, and local—but is most important when questions of harmonious adjustment are so paramount. Perhaps with the expanding staff of the board, and the continued vigilance of local citizens, steps can be taken here to improve postapproval inspection.

Temporary restraining orders and injunctive relief are available to the board following approval if the development does not conform to the approval specifications, but this will not prevent ecological damage already underway.

Efforts have been made by the board to authorize the issuance of compliance certificates when a project is completed in accordance with its permit. This would both relieve any uncertainty on the part of builders and financiers and give the board an additional method of insuring its directives are carried out. During the 1972 special session of the legislature, one change requested by the board, but not approved, was the prohibition of service by public or private utilities to *any* development not approved by the board. A certificate of compliance would be a more positive and equally effective means to this end.

A newly enacted revision does require that any person securing approval by the board shall maintain the financial capacity and technical ability to meet the state air and water pollution control standards *until he has complied* with such standards.

Planning

The ability of the board to make decisions in the absence of a state comprehensive land use plan is certainly going to be a test of its future effectiveness. Maine communities have traditionally rejected government planning and regulation that threaten the current system of land allotment by uncontrolled private market decision-making. The private property value is extremely strong and planning is perceived as a governmental imposition of values. The coastal communities in the past three years have in many cases abandoned even locally constituted planning and zoning boards.

Since there is almost no land use planning or control at the local level, the State Planning Office and the Regional Planning Authorities have most of the expertise and the power in these areas. The state has chosen to work slowly, generally through the issuance of guidelines, in encouraging towns to face the land use management issue. Many conservationists have urged "coastal zoning," to be drawn directly by the State Planning Office. This has not been initiated and would not be a popular approach in Maine.

The absence of local controls is both a strength and a weakness in implementing the Site Location Act. Since communities are so clearly vulnerable to exploitation, they have accepted the authority of the board as a protective instrument and have supported it. One of the few instances in which forceful opposition to a site location decision occurred was the King Resources case. The city of Portland, which does have a strong planning program, felt that the board was simply interfering in a local matter as the proposed oil terminal was in accord with city zoning regulations.

But since state and local planning is mostly nonexistent, the board must deal with each development application on a case-by-case basis. Obviously, the board can only stop development, not encourage it selectively.

Recent state legislation[15] requires mandatory zoning and subdivision control for land areas, any part of which are within 250 feet of the normal high water mark of any navigable pond, lake, river, or saltwater body. The statute states that should a municipality fail to adopt such controls by June 30, 1973, or if enacted controls are unacceptable to the board and the Maine Land Use Regulation Commission, these bodies shall, following consultation with the State Planning Office, adopt suitable ordinances. The current thinking of the board indicates that increasingly specific guidelines and standards will be issued to towns, rather than the approval by the board of model codes. Assuming that such guidelines will include densities and proposals for locating development, the board can take a strong positive step through this device.

Growth of Authority and Power of the Centralized Body

The board centralizes the state's control over air, water, solid waste, dredging, mining, and site location, is a tremendous asset to the state in seeking to control development effectively, and causes previously competing state agencies to become mutually supportive. All the strengths of licensing and inspecting are focused at one point. It provides a single point of reference that can be used by any environmentalist in opposing a development. The new powers granted the board in 1972 emphasize this point.

The centralized organizational approach is particularly appropriate for a small state where the population is not fractionalized by region, and where high value is placed on protection of the natural resources.

The continuing gains in authority the board has made since 1969 underscore the confidence that the people of Maine, through their legislature, place in it. From an independent board with very little staff of its own and control limited to industrial and commercial developments, the board has grown to a body whose chairman is a member of the governor's cabinet, which has authority to enact any regulations necessary, and which has power over state, municipal, quasi-municipal, educational, and charitable development. The board continues to press for greater power by asking a smaller acreage requirement for site location permits.

In Maine, with its population of less than 1 million, the board personifies a sense of state identity. A considerable influence is exerted on potential development simply through the existence of the board. Power placed in the board by the state indicates such a real commitment to protecting the natural values that developers who clearly disregard these concerns are discouraged by the state as well as solidified public opinion. Board activities receive continued and close coverage by Maine media, and the average citizen knows well who are the key state decision-makers on land use. Accountability of public officials and citizen participation are active forces as a result.

As the board continues to expand its power and towns move toward planning, conflicts will increase. The board appears willing to work with the State Planning Office in developing guidelines and planning aids to help prevent such problems. These guidelines (or something similar) must be prepared wisely and followed if the board is to avoid becoming the arbiter of every small development in Maine. Too great an expansion of power, particularly in the absence of planning framework, could make the board's influence so pervasive as to erode its present support at local levels.

Problems of Depressed Economy versus Natural Environment: The Larger Question

The revised Site Location Act states that "the developer has made adequate provision for fitting the development harmoniously into the existing natural environment and that the development will not adversely affect existing uses, scenic character, or natural resources in the municipality or in neighboring municipalities." This of course is clearly impossible; the board must simply weigh these considerations in making final decisions on permits. No one can "harmoniously" develop an oil refinery or a housing development that does not adversely affect the scenic character of the land or the fishing industry of an area. Were the act to be strictly construed, it would be difficult to develop anything. And yet Maine desperately needs some type of stimulus for its economy. Adequate housing is also badly needed for year-round residents. The board is not empowered by the act to weigh sociological or economic considerations in permit cases, and this could be a serious problem. Some critics have suggested that the environmental bias of the board is necessarily so strong that it will eventually have to be by-passed or reconstituted if controlled, desirable development is to take place. If the board were to rule against development desired by many citizens and legislators, support for the board might wane; and if the current spurt of environmental concern begins to fade, the same problem could arise. While this situation surrounds environmental controls in every state, the potential conflict of the environment and the economy is greater in economically depressed Maine.

A great many people are now moving to Maine to escape urban life and the problems of industrial development. Native Mainers are caught between rising pressure on land and rapidly inflating land value, rising property taxes, and no increase in available income. While the Mainer has a strong attachment to the land, he does not wish to be impoverished so that refugees from the Northeast corridor can live a life of rural purity. These potential conflicts are beginning to be more apparent as the newcomers increase in number. In many areas, the immigrant's idea of appropriate zoning and control represents an elitist taste that those living in the depressed economy can ill afford and do not desire. Mobile homes and housing developments represent something far different to those who can no longer afford to build on their own land than to one newly arrived from New Jersey. Many of the new arrivals have a strong need to protect their rights of private ownership and "No Trespassing" signs are appearing in areas that have traditionally provided public open space in an area where there is in fact almost no publicly owned open space.

The newcomers are the natural constituency of a board with a strong environmental bias; the long-time residents may have more to lose.

But this is speculative, since as of 1973, there seems to be continuing general public confidence in the board. An October, 1971 poll of residents in a river clean-up area showed that 85 percent of those polled favored expanding the powers of the EIC.[16] In a state where there is traditional distaste for government controls, this is a very high figure. The value that Mainers place on their natural resources is so high that thus far they have been proud of the board for strongly protecting these resources.

NOTES

1. 38 Me. Rev. Stat. Ann. SS481-488.
2. 12 Me. Rev. Stat. Ann. SS4811-4814.
3. 12 Me. Rev. Stat. Ann. SS4701 et. seq.
4. 12 Me. Rev. Stat. Ann. SS681-689.
5. *Maine Manifest*, The Allagash Group, Bath, Maine, 1972, page 8.
6. John N. Coles, "Recognizing Maine's Value," *Maine Times*, May 7, 1971, p. 4.
7. John MacDonald, "Oil and the Environment: The View from Maine, *Fortune*, April 1971, p. 84.
8. Interview with Orlando Delogu, as reported in Fred Bosselman and David Callies, "The Quiet Revolution in Land Use Control," Council on Environmental Quality, January 10, 1972, p. 188.
9. 38 Me. Rev. Stat. Ann. SS481.
10. 38 Me. Rev. Stat. Ann. SS482.
11. 42 U. S. C. A. SS3251-3259.
12. Bosselman and Callies, *op. cit.*
13. *King Resources* v. *Environmental Improvement Commission*, 270 A. 2d 863 (Me. 1970).
14. *In the Matter of Maine Clean Fuels, Inc.*, Supreme Judicial Court Law Docket No. 1342.
15. 12 Me. Rev. Stat. Ann. SS4811-4814.
16. Kathy and Gore Flynn, "Q: Who Cares About Maine's Environment? A: The Voters Do," *Maine Times*, October 8, 1971, p. 1.

8

INTRODUCTION

The Maryland Environmental Service (MES),[1] created in 1970, gives the State of Maryland a new function that traditionally has been left exclusively to local governments—the actual construction and operation of solid and liquid waste treatment and disposal facilities. In 1972 MES was also assigned authority to provide water supply services, including water treatment facilities.

MES is a public corporation, administered within the Department of Natural Resources, acting as a wholesaler of environmental protection services to local governments and industries.

The state initiates service in three ways: (1) Primarily, through the implementation of five-year regional plans for solid and liquid wastes and water supply, which set out a division of services between the state and local governments. These plans are drafted by the service and approved by local governments. (2) When a local government or industry requests aid, MES must provide the desired facilities or services. (3) If an industry or municipality violates a compliance order to conform to state water quality standards or regulations governing solid waste disposal, the secretary of Natural Resources or the secretary of Health and Mental Hygiene can direct MES to take over the violator's waste operations and upgrade procedures or construct new facilities to bring the violator into compliance.

Thus, MES is intended to provide an actual management solution to environmental problems, to supplement the state's policies of pollution regulation and subsidies for waste treatment and water supply. But MES is also a potential new enforcement weapon in the state's arsenal to gain compliance with water quality and solid waste objectives.

By giving Maryland this new tool to protect resources, these benefits are expected to result:

1. *Institute regionalization* in planning, construction, and operation of waste control and water supply facilities in order to take advantage of economies of scale and regional characteristics of water and land resources, and allow a more rational allocation of public funds to achieve more pollution control for the dollar.

2. *Secure better financing* of waste and water facilities than local governments can obtain.

3. *Guarantee compliance* with the state's water quality standards and solid waste regulations.

While the record of the new agency is too brief to be definitive on these points, several positive indicators have emerged.

BACKGROUND AND LEGISLATIVE HISTORY

MES has its historical roots in river basin planning in the United States[2] and comprehensive river basin management in other countries, particularly Germany. Its theoretical roots are the research and writings of American resource economists.[3]

The idea for a Maryland agency to construct and operate waste facilities was first developed by a study commission of state officials under the leadership (although not the chairmanship) of James B. Coulter.[4] Governor J. Millard Tawes appointed the commission in 1966 to study water pollution problems and the state's response. In its 1967 report, *A Program for Water Pollution Control in Maryland*.[5] the commission recommended a statewide Waste Acceptance Service (WAS), a state governmental organization to build and operate wastewater treatment facilities. Solid wastes and water supply were not covered in the commission's study.

Sanitary services in Maryland have historically been the responsibility of local governments, as in most other states. The commission believed that the existing waste control institutions were not using, and were not constituted to be capable of using, the best available waste management technology. Existing agencies lacked funds and their political jurisdictions were too limited to conform to the boundaries of water pollution problems—the river basin. The Patuxent River is an example. Eighteen wastewater treatment plants that handle over 50,000 gallons per day and several smaller ones line the river, when a few large plants could do the job much more cheaply.[6]

The state, in addition to being able to build bigger and cheaper facilities, could locate facilities and discharge points in the most advantageous spots, where receiving waters could best assimilate the waste material.

The commission also saw benefits to regional approaches to operations and maintenance of facilities. A statewide waste acceptance service could afford to use new monitoring techniques, mathematical modeling, computer-based maintenance systems, and other emerging new equipment that localities could not afford to buy and use. Although local governments can secure grants-in-aid to cover up to 80 percent of the funds needed to construct wastewater treatment plants, no state or federal aid is available to help finance operation of facilities.

Looking to Germany's experience with river basin institutions (Genossenschaften) on the Ruhr, Maryland analysts thought that if their state could handle wastes throughout a whole river basin, as well as manage other aspects of water, then low flow augmentation could be used to relieve pollution concentrations. Reaeration and other instream management techniques could also be used.

Proponents of the WAS system argued that while some Maryland communities had joined together in regional institutions, such as the Washington Suburban Sanitary Commission, these arrangements required a specific act of the General Assembly. Therefore, the process was difficult and inhibited large-scale systems.

The commission thought WAS could offer an economic incentive for better industrial waste management by structuring its fees like an effluent charge. The fee would reflect the volume and character of the discharge. This user fee idea was based on Ohio's experience with fee formulae. The commission report contended that this user fee would "internalize" the social costs of water pollution to industrial and municipal sources, motivating them to reduce pollution in the most efficient manner.

The commission report, with these findings, was submitted to newly elected Governor Spiro T. Agnew in 1967, who authorized a feasibility study of the WAS concept.[7]

In the meantime, the state's role in regulating pollution and subsidizing local control measures stimulated fresh interest on the part of legislators in better local waste management. State antipollution goals were being set in specific terms in water quality standards.

In January, 1969, a Legislative Council Committee report "Feasibility of Incentives for the Construction of Waste Treatment Facilities,"[8] endorsed the WAS concept as "the best hope for success in dealing with Maryland's pollution problems," and recommended its speedy adoption. This committee studied the WAS economic incentive mechanism and an industrial subsidy system and preferred the former.

By 1970, "the environment" boomed as a public issue and elected officials were supporting the environmental bills as never before. In his "honeymoon" period with the legislature, the new governor, Marvin Mandel, recommended legislation in 1970 to create the Maryland Environmental Service. The bill received sufficient support to pass, but not without a fight.

When the governor agreed to the state service idea on the eve of the 1970 legislative session, it had been discussed only in very general terms and never seriously considered by legislators or local officials. But then the concept was quickly translated into a bill for introduction in January. Senate Bill 382, as introduced, was based on the earlier WAS concept, but with one important last-minute addition—state authority to treat, recycle, and dispose of solid wastes. This provision was the most controversial with legislators. The proposed Maryland Environmental Service was to draft regional plans, and then, on its own initiative and without local governmental approval, proceed to construct the needed new facilities and eventually assume ownership of existing works.

Battle lines were quickly drawn. County officials and their lobby group, the Maryland Association of Counties, concerned about what they saw as a threat to local autonomy, actively opposed the measure. The original bill made no express provision for participation or control by local governing bodies, except for a clause that said the state needed to secure a contract with a locality or industry before commencing any kind of business. Amendments were added to require further local governmental approval in the following ways:

1. The five-year plans for solid and liquid waste management must be approved by the County Commissioners or other local governing bodies before they can be implemented. Only the General Assembly can override the local government's veto of the plan.[9] The biennial revisions of the plan, however, do not require local approval, but do require one public hearing in each county.[10]

2. Local government can veto the location within its jurisdiction of any solid waste disposal site.[11] Local governments control all land use decisions and set fees for refuse services and sewerage charged to homes and businesses in their communities.

On balance, the amendments turned the bill around from a state controlled program to more of a state/local "partnership" that requires local governments' concurrence on key decisions. While regional planning, construction, and operation remain the objective of the service, the method was changed in the legislature from a mandatory approach to a quasi-voluntary state program.

There was no organized opposition to the bill from industry. In fact, some industry spokesmen saw advantages to being able to turn the technical and management problems of waste treatment over to the state, even though the financial burden of this activity would remain with the waste generator. Other industry spokesmen felt that the state agency would have more legal and technical options available to it. For example, the state can condemn land for sites for treatment and disposal facilities.

In 1972 the General Assembly expanded MES' authority, effective July 1, to include powers to plan for and provide water supply facilities. These projects include supply and distribution networks and water treatment facilities. Another act that year authorized a $10-million state bond issue to finance capital facilities for the collection, transportation, recycling, and disposal of solid wastes built by MES.

HOW MES WORKS

The Maryland Environmental Service Law, as amended, provides for the new state entity to be located for administrative purposes within the

213

Department of Natural Resources. The secretary of the department appoints the service's Board of Directors—the director, the secretary and treasurer—with the concurrence of the governor and they serve at the secretary's pleasure. However, for all corporate functions, MES is independent. The secretary of Natural Resources cannot divert its staff or funds. It has powers, like those of a statewide sanitary district, to acquire, build, and operate liquid and solid waste treatment and disposal works, water supply facilities—all on a wholesale basis, —to Maryland's local subdivisions and industries. For purposes of the act, the city of Baltimore is considered a county, thus making the total of local subdivisions 24. MES conducts business as a corporation and, just as any other sanitary district, it must conform to environmental regulations. The service may extend all or any mix of its services, after securing a contract with the industry or locality. Upon request it may also collect wastes from some central locations, once the local garbage collection system has collected them. Like a public corporation and, just as any other sanitary district, it must conform to environmental regulations.

Planning

MES is to institute regional approaches to waste control and water supply by drafting and implementing areawide five-year plans in conjunction with localities. Approval of the plans by both state and affected local jurisdictions constitutes their commitment to implement all measures called for.

First, MES designated planning regions for liquid and solid wastes. River basins are the liquid waste regions. Solid waste management planning regions were selected on the basis of population concentrations, economic sectors, hydrological data, and other technical factors. The objective is to be able to understand the plans two ways: by "problem shed"—watersheds and solid waste management sheds—for technical planning purposes, and by political boundaries—the county—for purposes of actual presentation to the public and to local officials who must approve the final products. MES will also be designating planning regions for water supply, pursuant to its new authority.

After the regions were designated, MES began to draft the actual plans in cooperation with the local governmental engineers and waste management personnel. These plans will set forth the requirements for waste and water facilities in the regions for the next five years, although the actual planning horizon is longer. These projections are based, in part, on master plans for sewage and water that incorporate land use projections. When no local land use plan or data are available, state and local officials will make rough projections of growth in the area. However, MES is prohibited from deciding who will receive solid and liquid waste services and water supplies. These remain local decisions, along with all land use matters. However, MES sets its rates based on volume and character of collected wastes, providing an economic feedback to local land use decisions.

In addition to stating five-year needs, the regional plans designate those new and existing facilities or portions of them that will be built, expanded, and operated by municipalities or industries and that will be provided by the state.

The five-year regional plans may only be adopted by the service after the approval of affected local jurisdictions. A public hearing is required before local action is taken to allow for citizen comment. If the plan is not approved by all necessary counties within 120 days after it is submitted, the plan may only be approved or modified by a joint resolution of the General Assembly.

The law that created MES set no deadlines for completion of the plans, but other directives do. MES's liquid waste plans will fulfill the federal requirement for river basin plans, which must be completed by July 1, 1973 to receive federal construction funds. State law requires each county to prepare a solid waste plan by no later than January 1, 1974, and this will serve as the MES deadline for its solid waste plans.

Before fully launching river basin planning, MES drafted a plan for the Monocacy River, a small tributary of the Potomac, as a test case to perfect the planning technique. This work was completed in summer, 1972 by MES staff. The test plan will guide other river basin planning activities of the staff and consultants. Consultants will be used extensively in drafting the basin plans, and then the permanent MES staff will update and maintain the plans.

In drafting wastewater management plans, MES is relying in large part on the county sewer and water plans mandated by the legislature in 1966 and completed by the counties by January 1, 1970. These plans vary widely as to quality of data and recommendations and methodology of preparation, but all set out a schedule of actions for the county and state. The service must rationalize the differences among the plans for the same waterway, provide more detailed information when that submitted is sketchy or incorrect, and insure that authorized abatement actions will meet water quality standards. When county plans have missed opportunities for cost savings or better treatment through regional facilities or regional management, the service will revise the plans accordingly. Consultants will be used extensively in drafting the basin plans, and then the permanent MES staff will update and use them.

The 1970 session of the legislature that set up the Maryland Environmental Service and required it to draft regional solid waste plans also passed another law requiring counties to draft solid waste management plans on a county-by-county basis. Both will be completed by January, 1974. The Department of Health and Mental Hygiene administers a program of state grants to finance up to 50 percent of the cost of the counties' planning.

In an effort to tie its own and the counties' solid waste planning processes together, MES has been negotiating contracts with the counties to fund jointly and direct one solid waste planning effort. The state itself will be a solid waste planning region for MES activity. MES director, Thomas D. McKewen, has suggested that both governments hire one consultant to do the combined planning, splitting the costs.[12] Or the local government could draft plans for collection of solid wastes and MES could devise plans for their disposal.

Upon adoption of the five-year plans, a Service District will be designated to serve for financial and operational matters, and MES will proceed to acquire, extend, and construct those facilities set forth for it in the plans. Once MES builds a system, no competing facility can be built.

A MES Take-Over

The second way that MES proceeds to extend its services is when it is directed to do so by the secretary of Natural Resources or the secretary of Health and Mental Hygiene. In all these instances, the complete costs of providing the services are charged to the municipality or person involved. If an industry or municipality violates an order of the secretary of Health affecting sewerage systems or refuse disposal works, the secretary *must* direct the service to take over the violator's waste control problems. In this way, MES could become a unique implementing arm of the regulatory authority of the state. Specifically, the secretary of Health may issue orders to:

1. Municipalities to provide sewage systems of refuse disposal works, in which case the service must construct the ordered facilities and put them into operation, but then the service may turn the operations of these systems over to the local government.

2. Persons (individuals or corporations) to abate pollution, in which case the service must construct the ordered facilities and put them into operation, but then the service must provide the facilities and the person must discharge only to that system.

3. Municipalities or persons to operate their sewage or refuse disposal systems properly; if the municipalities or persons do not comply, the service shall take over these operations.

4. Municipalities or persons to extend or alter sewage or refuse disposal works, in which case the service shall extend or alter these facilities or install new ones, as ordered by the secretary of Health.

An industry discharging directly into a waterway instead of into a joint municipal/industrial system is under the jurisdiction of the director of the Department of Water Resources in the Department of Natural Resources. If that industry fails to comply with a previous order to abate pollution, then the director of the Department of Water Resources *may* ask the secretary of Natural Resources to direct MES to take over and operate those facilities. If the director of Water Resources does not direct the service to move in, then he *must* take court action against the industry.

The director of Water Resources is given an option, which is not available to the secretary of Health and Mental Hygiene. This was designed to prevent the service from being forced to operate major waste control facilities for large industries.[13] The director is to select the option that achieves water pollution abatement as quickly and cheaply as possible. The director of the Department of Water Resources may prefer to achieve industrial pollution abatement through legal action in the courts. This may be particularly advantageous when industrial process changes or the use of different raw materials are the most efficient waste control techniques. In providing wastewater treatment and disposal services to an industry, the Maryland Environmental Service can provide only "end-of-the-line" treatment facilities. It cannot operate within a company's plant, and cannot, therefore, institute waste reduction through in-process changes, switching to different raw materials, and treating wastes along the production line.

Even when MES is required to provide facilities to a recalcitrant industry or town, it must first have a contract. If the two concerned parties cannot agree to charges or other aspects of the contract, the Public Service Commission, upon petition from either party, will solve the predicament by binding arbitration.[14]

This provision for MES to respond to a directive has not been used yet. In the future, this unique authority may be able to solve the political and financial difficulties of enforcing environmental standards on local governments. Officials in many states find that their traditional regulatory procedures are better suited to securing industrial compliance than that of local government.

However, at this time, MES officials have a more conservative view of the use of this provision. MES Director McKewen described the power this way:

This provision is intended to be used in instances where imminent hazard to public health or natural resources exists and is not or cannot be resolved by responsible local authorities or individuals. It also expresses the state's commitment to use its power wherever and whenever needed to abate pollution if other responsible authorities are unable to do so.[15]

Mandatory Response to Requests

A third way MES can assume the responsibility for liquid or solid waste management or water supply is when it is requested to do so by any governmental entity or privately owned concern in Maryland. Then MES *must* provide the requested service. The only two negotiable items are the rates and starting dates for service. MES does not have to assume responsibility for the entire system. For example, it may contract only to finance new construction, or just to do the design work, or just perform the actual construction.

McKewen believes this mandatory response to requests provision was included

to remove temptation for MES to pick and choose among the needs existing within the state and concentrate exclusively on those which were financially attractive or environmentally glamorous. The provision also ensures local government and industry that they will

217

receive uniform treatment from the Service. This uniformity does not extend to rates since these must reflect operation costs which will vary from place to place and from time to time.[16]

Financing

MES activity is funded by revenue bonds, general obligation bonds, appropriations, and grants. MES is expected to become self-supporting within five years, except for planning costs, which are covered by a $4-million bond authorization approved by the legislature in 1968 for river basic planning. Until MES can sustain itself, it receives an appropriation from the legislature. MES could not become self-supporting until a substantial number of revenue-producing projects are in operation.[17] In fiscal year 1971, MES received $200,000 from the legislature and in fiscal year 1972, $444,982. In fiscal year 1973, MES was appropriated almost $400,000, but total expenditures are anticipated at $870,695.

The charge agreed upon in a waste management contract will reflect at least the full costs of the actual transportation, purification, final disposal, or recycling of the wastes, as well as overhead costs for MES. While the service currently plans to structure its fees to reflect only these costs, the Environmental Service Act allows the service to set its charges in such a way as to have the effect of an effluent charge. The effluent charge would reflect not just the cost of waste treatment, but also accounts for the ultimate pollution that results. An effluent charge to an industry or two increases as the amount or character of waste becomes more severe.

While both the current Maryland fee structure and the effluent charge are intended to give the waste generator an economic incentive to reduce his residues in an efficient manner, the effluent charge is intended to "internalize" the full social and economic costs of his pollution. Setting such effluent charges would require a great deal of technical, scientific, and economic data, which would need to be frequently updated.

The service can finance its capital expenditures with the state's general obligation bonds, its own revenue bonds, and grants from state and local governments. The primary financing technique will be the issuance of revenue bonds by the service. No other state agency must approve these issues. It is hoped that MES revenue bonds will have a significant financial advantage over other revenue bonds, because MES bonds are backed by contracts and a guarantee. The law directs that if a locality fails to meet conditions of the contract, the Maryland comptroller shall divert five types of state-shared revenues to the MES: the racing tax; the state corporate income surtax; the recordation tax; the tax on amusements; and the license tax.[18] These funds sometimes amount to as much as 20 percent of some local governments' revenues. An industry or other person must pay his bill for contracted services, or the amount becomes a lien against his property. MES bonded indebtedness does not accrue to local or state indebtedness, giving local governments another incentive to use MES financing services.

MES bonds have been given an AA rating, but none have been sold to date. Thus, more time will be needed to show the actual financing benefits MES will provide.

Staff and Budget

The philosophy of MES is to limit its management and planning staff and to contract out planning, design, and construction work to private firms. The fiscal 1973 budget allows for 33 positions. The rationale is to avoid hiring people that the organization will not continue to need. The work load of the service will fluctuate greatly with the number of requests it receives for aid. Also after the initial waste management plans are completed, MES's planning activities will be minimal. By hiring only a core headquarters staff and contracting for the remaining work, MES intends to meet its five-year deadline for self-support. Table 8.1 shows the funds and staff levels for fiscal years 1971 through 1973.

TABLE 8.1

Maryland Environmental Service Budget Estimates and Staff

	Fiscal 1971	Fiscal 1972	Fiscal 1973	
	Actual	Appropriation	Request	Allowance
Total number of authorized positions	27	29	33	33
Salaries and wages	$160,823	$270,093	$401,704	$400,368
Technical and special fees	5,911	85,000	108,000	97,500
Operating expenses	123,550	89,889	279,769	372,827
Total general fund appropriation	200,000	444,982	557,189	390,327
Add: Reimbursable portion of maintenance and operation cost			126,733	232,274
gross requirement			683,922	
Less: general fund reversion	49,761			
Net general fund expenditure	150,239	444,982		
Federal fund expenditure				29,541
Add: special fund expenditure	140,055		105,551	218,553
Total expenditure	290,294	444,982	789,473	870,695

Source: Maryland Environmental Service, Department of Natural Resources, Budget Form No. 1 "Budget Bureau Estimates Fiscal Year 1973."

The Environmental Service relates to other state agencies in three ways: its facilities and discharges to the environment are regulated by two state agencies; it receives state and federal grants for the construction of wastewater treatment plants and state loans for collection lines, administered by the Department of Health and Mental Hygiene; and its planning work is supplemented by the Department of Health for sewers, water systems, solid waste disposal sites, and by the Department of Water Resources in the case of river basin planning.

MES must comply with regulations administered by the Departments of Health and Water Resources, and this raises the question of the proper administrative location of the public utility agency.

The Department of Health and Mental Hygiene regulates solid waste disposal facilities, whether privately or publicly owned. Open burning and open dumps are prohibited. Other rules and permit systems govern construction of sewers and wastewater discharges from municipal systems, including industrial wastes discharged to joint municipal/industrial facilities. The department's air quality standards can be affected by incineration of solid wastes.

The Department of Water Resources administers the water quality standards program and issues permits for industrial wastes discharged directly to waterways. To a limited extent, this department also can require certain pretreatment by industries discharging to municipal sewers.

MES must also secure a permit from its sister agency, the Department of Water Resources, in order to change the course, current, or cross-section of any state waterway. This would be necessary, for example, to run a sewer across or under a stream. It must also secure approval for any plan for sediment control before construction of facilities anywhere in the state.

The administrative location of MES, a possible polluter, within the Department of Natural Resources (DNR) thus creates a potential conflict of functions. The DNR is both the *regulator* of water quality and the *regulated*. The regulator is concerned with the highest possible water quality that can reasonably be attained, while the regulated (MES) is concerned with keeping down costs of construction and operations in order to keep within the local governments' increasingly stringent budget and avoid raising user charges for sewerage and trash services. When spokesmen, or advocates, for these two points of view are housed within the same administrative agency, past experience shows that at least one of the two advocacy roles is compromised. Usually, this is the "regulator" role.

The MES record is still too brief to demonstrate any conflict or to prove the countertheory—that the MES waste management function and the DNR regulatory responsibilities are mutually supportive. This second point of view might be labeled the "management efficiency" position. This theory holds that by locating together the several programs affecting water quality or land quality, program efficiencies could result and environmental quality be enhanced. Environmental controls could be selected after analysis of a wide range of management alternatives and the best and cheapest one selected.

Spokesmen for this point of view cite Blair Bower: "Efficient management of wastes requires analysis of the entire waste management system. . . ."[19] Bower's waste management system includes:

-facilities for handling, treating and disposing of wastes, which is the MES function;
-facilities for modifying the assimilative capacity of the environment, notably reservoirs to store and release water during periods of low stream-flows, mechanical devices for re-aerating rivers, dredging up the polluted residues on bottoms and disposing of spoil on shore. The Department of Water Resources can implement some of these approaches, particularly regulating water quantity by its permits for water withdrawals;
-regulations for modifying the generation and discharge of wastes, such as standards, charges and controls over location of industries and other waste sources. The Department of Water Resources administers the water quality standards program. MES can also structure its user fees for waste treatment and disposal to have the effect of an effluent charge. However, a notable omission, is that MES is prohibited from making land use decisions, such as where industries will be located;
-facilities and procedures for collection and analysis of data necessary to monitor environmental quality or particular waste sources and treatment facilities. The Department of Water Resources conducts the state's water quality monitoring activities.[20]

Allen Kneese and Blair Bower cite the benefits of such comprehensive water quality institutions, as they witnessed them in Germany (the Ruhr Genossenschoften), in England (English River Authorities, created in 1963), in France (river basin agencies authorized in 1964) and for the Delaware River (the Delaware River Basin Commission, established by interstate-federal compact in 1961). The Ruhr river basin institution, for example, can construct domestic and industrial waste treatment works and reservoirs, manage water flows, conduct chemical and biological lab work and has financial, judicial, rate assessment, and other functional responsibilities relating to management of water in the basin.

Concluding from these studies, Kneese and Bower say:

If regional agencies were to be able to achieve economic efficiency, they should have power to: analyze and implement a wide range of alternatives, influence the pattern of land use as it relates to the water management program; and articulate private and local government decisions with their own operations through regulation or charges.[21]

221

A third position on the administrative location of MES is that MES may operate wholly independently within the DNR, and, therefore, no conflict or benefits will occur. MES does have a large measure of independence within the DNR. The secretary cannot divert its funds or staff. MES decisions are not subject to review by the department's Board of Review that oversees the other agencies in the department. It issues bonds on its own motion and acts in many other ways as an independent public corporation. Furthermore, the director of the service has indicated that he will keep his agency separate from the water quality regulatory program as much as possible. For instance, MES officials will not serve on DNR task forces recommending water quality standards, thereby retaining their right to complain about any overly stringent standards. However, it is still unclear how independent MES can be as long as its director serves at the pleasure of the DNR's secretary.

THE OHIO AND NEW YORK APPROACHES

The New York Environmental Facilities Corporation and the Ohio Water Development Authority are similar to MES in that each is a public utility corporation within its respective state government.[22] Each provides service for the treatment and disposal of liquid and solid waste. While Maryland and Ohio treat both industrial and municipal wastes, wherever they are discharged, New York handles only municipal wastes. New York will, however, accept industrial wastes discharged into a municipal system. New York can also handle air pollutants, but only those discharged by municipal sources. Only Maryland provides water supply services.

Maryland is unique in providing specific authority and funds to draft five-year plans, which, when implemented, are intended to institutionalize regional waste management. In this way, Maryland's program is designed as a systematic, long-range strategy for regional controls.

However, while New York and Ohio are not explicitly forbidden to do such planning, no funds are made available for this purpose. Further, there is no signing by county governing bodies to agreements in these states. The New York and Ohio agencies are not designed as implementers of a grand strategy, but rather as service organizations to local governments once the community itself has assessed its own needs and priorities. Nor do Ohio or New York have the involuntary take-over provision when standards are violated.

New York and Ohio were intended to be self-supporting from their conception, and consequently were only loaned money from their respective state treasuries. These funds must be paid back from their first revenues. The Ohio Water Development Authority was charged with the responsibility of administering monies received from the federal government under Section 8 of the Federal Water Pollution Control Act, from a $120-million bond issue passed in 1968, and from the issuance of revenue bonds. New York and Ohio have the authority to provide financing to municipalities and, in the case of Ohio, to industries as well.

222

CURRENT PROJECTS AND FUTURE HOPES

In addition to its planning work, MES has taken over responsibility for waste control operations at state governmental facilities and is developing some specific physical projects for local governments and commercial enterprises.

The only facilities that MES actually operates today are those for state institutions. MES operates 14 state-owned sewage treatment plants, supervises 5 others, and provides supervisory service for another 10.[23] The agency is investigating the recycling of solid wastes in state parks and surveying the solid waste disposal practices of state institutions.

Specific projects under study for localities and industries include a regional sewage treatment plant to replace one proposed and four existing plants that are scheduled for replacement, upgrading, or expansion. On another project, MES has a contract to build a sewage treatment plant to serve a community and replace two inadequate plants nearby that serve public institutions. MES is also investigating ways to dispose of urban solid wastes and sewage sludge and provide statewide collection for reprocessing or safe disposal of waste oils, tires, paper, fly ash, and waste sludges and is examining ways to dispose of toxic materials and hazardous substances. The $10-million bond money approved in 1972 will be used to demonstrate and implement some of the innovative approaches. Chart 8.1 shows the location of MES-owned facilities and project areas. It is hoped that recycling solid wastes and sewage sludge may be economical on a regional scale where it is inefficient on a purely local level.

Most of the projects under current investigation deal with more than one local jurisdiction, thus showing MES's capability to pull together separate governmental and commercial entities. MES officials hope to link those jurisdictions that have excessive wastes and no disposal sites (the highly urbanized areas), with those that could supply a proper disposal site (usually rural areas). For instance, sewage sludge could be used to reclaim barren soils and mined-out areas. As MES Director McKewen states: "The existence of an agency which has equal responsibility to both the jurisdiction that generates waste and the one which may offer to receive it should be valuable for accepting such projects in the future."[24] However, past experience in Maryland and other states does not warrant such optimism. Some of the most bitter opposition to the Environmental Service Act of 1970 came from rural counties, including those in western Maryland, that feared the new law would allow Baltimore to dump its garbage in their area.

The key unanswered question about the Maryland Environmental Service is whether it will be able to implement regional approaches to waste management and water supply when local governments can veto particular disposal sites as well as the general plans for solid and liquid wastes and water supply. As long as counties and Baltimore City do not violate air or water quality standards or regulations governing solid waste disposal, they are free to treat and dispose of their wastes independent of MES. MES will only be able to carry out regional strategies by convincing local officials that they can benefit from a

CHART 8.1

Maryland Environmental Service
Owned Facilities and Project Areas

State Owned Facilities

MES OPERATES	MES SUPERVISES	MES MONITORS
Bridewell House of Correction	Hugesville Correctional Camp	Cumberland-State Road
Crownsville State Hospital	New Germany State Park	Admin.
Montrose School for Girls	Swallow Falls State Park	Sandy Point State Park
Henryton State Hospital	Eastern Correctional Camp	Waxter Detention
Springfield State Hospital	Poplar Hill Correctional Camp	Center
Victor Cullen School for Boys		Maryland Training
Deep Creek Lake State Park		School for Boys
Bowie State College		Brooklandville State
Cheltenham Boys Village		Roads Admin.
Point Lookout State Park		Chesapeake Biological
St. Mary's State College		Lab
Md. Correctional Institution		Benson-State Police
Greenbrier State Park		Central Farm (U. of
Elk Neck State Park		Md.)
		U. of Md. Seafood Lab
		Salisbury - State Police

Feasibility Study and Project Areas

Hagerstown	Princess Anne
Burkittsville	Crisfield
Brunswick	Girdletree - Stockton
Frederick - Cannery	Snow Hill
Freedom District	West Ocean City
Little Gunpowder River Basin	Salisbury
Baltimore City - solid waste	St. Michael's
Patuxent River Basin	Kent Island - Queenstown
Blue Plains - sludge disposal	Swan Creek Basin
Battawoman Creek Basin	Perryville
La Plata	Port Deposit
Cobb Island, Swan Point	Conowingo Dam
	Upper Deer Creek Basin

Source: Based on Thomas D. McKewen, "Wholesaling Environmental Services," *Environmental Science and Technology* 6, no. 4 (April, 1972), p. 325.

state facility, either because construction and operating costs will go down, or because the state can secure better financing, or to relieve local officials of the political burden of locating waste facilities. There are some spokesmen for the state agency who feel that the economies of scale will lead in the long run to a fully state-operated system of waste control and water supply. However, others see the service, at best, as only an implementing instrument of continuing local policies.

What is clear to date is that neither local governments nor industries have rushed to take advantage of the service. This is due, in part, to the lack of information around the state about the service's benefits. A difficulty is that the MES advantages result from centralizing facilities and management systems, and localities fear such centralization means loss of local control. McKewen admits "there is a natural [inclination], on the part of local government in particular, to look on MES as just another regulatory agency. There is also a predictable concern by local governments over becoming captives of the state without adequate control to protect their interests in matters relating to charges and rate structures."[25]

To allay these local officials' fears, MES was prohibited from making land use decisions. This restriction generates the second vital, but unanswered, question: Can the service draft and implement effective environmental protection strategies while being prohibited from affecting land use? The direct and substantial interactions between land use and water/air/land quality have been extensively documented.[26] As people and industries concentrate, their waste discharges place more demands on the limited assimilative capacity of the environment. Costs and impacts on people of polluted streams or landfills and dumps can be minimized if the waste facilities are located away from populated areas, water intakes, or fishing grounds.

The future record of the Maryland Environmental Service will supply answers to these questions.

NOTES

1. Maryland Code Ann. Article 33B, Sec. 1-32 (1972). (Hereinafter referred to as MES law.)

2. See, for example, U.S. Department of the Interior, Federal Water Pollution Control Administration, *Delaware Estuary Comprehensive Study: Report on Alternative Water Quality Improvement Programs* (Washington, D.C.: FWPCA, February, 1966); U.S. Department of the Interior, Federal Water Pollution Control Administration, *Lake Erie Report: A Plan for Water Pollution Control* (Washington, D.C.: FWPCA, August 1, 1968), and Robert K. Davis, *The Range of Choice in Water Management, A Study of Dissolved Oxygen in the Potomac Estuary* (Baltimore: Johns Hopkins Press, 1968).

3. See, for example, Allen V. Knesse and Blair T. Bower, *Managing Water Quality: Economics, Technology, Institutions* (Baltimore: Johns Hopkins Press, 1968); and Blair T. Bower *et. al.*, *Waste Management*, a report prepared for the Regional Plan Association, (New York: The Association, March, 1968).

4. James B. Coulter is presently secretary of the Department of Natural Resources, was formerly its deputy secretary, and at the time he was a member of the study commission, was assistant commissioner of environmental health, Department of Health and Mental Hygiene. Andrew Huebeck served as chairman of the commission and was also secretary of the Board of Public Works. Other members were Paul McKee, director, State Planning Department and now director of the Department of Water Resources, and Donald Pritchard, director of Chesapeake Bay Institute.

5. Maryland Study Commission Report to Investigate the Problems of Water Pollution Control, *A Program for Water Pollution Control in Maryland* (Annapolis: Department of Health, 1967).

6. U.S. Department of the Interior, Federal Water Quality Administration, *Water Quality Management in the Patuxent River Basin* (Washington, D.C.: FWQA, 1970).

7. Trident Engineering Associates, Inc., *Feasibility and Planning Study for a Waste Acceptance Service*, prepared for the Governor's Commission to Investigate Water Pollution Control in conjunction with the Department of Health, State of Maryland (Annapolis: Department of Health, 1968).

8. Maryland, Legislative Council, Committee on Studying the Feasibility of Incentives for Construction of Waste Treatment Facilities, *Report* (Annapolis: Legislative Council, 1969).

9. MES Law, Sec. 5 (e).

10. MES Law, Sec. 5 (i).

11. MES Law, Sec. 4 (t).

12. Interview with Thomas McKewen, Director, Maryland Environmental Service, December, 1970.

13. Paul W. McKee and Thomas C. Andrews, *The Maryland Environmental Services Act of 1970*, Paper prepared for delivery at the 9th Annual Environmental and Water Resources Engineering Conference, Nashville, Tenn., June 4-5, 1970.

14. MES Law, Sec. 26.

15. Thomas D. McKewen, "Wholesaling Environmental Services," *Environmental Science and Technology*, 6, no. 4 (April, 1972), p. 327.

16. *Ibid*.

17. *Ibid*., p. 329.

18. MES Law, Sec. 7 (b).

19. Bower *et. al., op. cit.*, p. 9.

20. *Ibid*, p. 23.

21. Kneese and Bower, *op. cit.*, p. 281. For a more detailed statement of the six criteria for effective regional water quality management agencies see also p. 304.:

Regional agency should be able to internalize the major externalities associated with waste discharges.

Regional agency should be able to implement measures of all types to improve water quality.

Regional agency should be able to take adequate account of the interrelationship between water quality and other aspects of water systems.

Regional agency should be able to take into account through specific communication channels the interrelationship between water quality management and land use management.

Regional agency should be able to take into account through specific communication channels the interrelationships between water and other activities having impacts on environmental quality.

Regional agency should: (a) delineate the wide range of choice possible—costs and consequences of different combinations of measures and of different levels of quality; (b) reflect or consider adequately the views of those affected by water quality management activities.

22. For more detailed information on New York's, Ohio's, and Ontario's waste management public utilities, see John M. Armstrong, *Progress Report on the Feasibility of Regional Waste Treatment Facilities*, a report submitted under Project Number 100 26 0036 to the Upper Great Lakes Regional Commission, November 11, 1970.

23. McKewen, "Wholesaling Environmental Services," *op. cit.*, p. 327-28.

24. *Ibid.*

25. *Ibid.*

26. *Ibid.*, p. 329.

CHAPTER 9

The Michigan Environmental Protection Act (EPA) of 1970[1] guarantees the right of every public and private entity to sue any other public or private entity in state courts to protect the environment. This Michigan statute, sometimes referred to as the "Sax Law" for Joseph Sax, the University of Michigan law professor who first drafted the bill, relies on the judicial branch and private citizens to be watchdogs over executive agencies and private polluters.

The Environmental Protection Act gives everyone the right to sue, whether or not an administrative agency has established a specific environmental standard for the problem. Courts are then given wide latitude as to the issues they may consider. Judges can decide the appropriateness of any existing administrative standard and even direct the executive agency to adopt a new, court-specified rule. Indeed, the 1970 Michigan Act overturns the entire traditional process by which courts review actions of administrative agencies. Thus, in addition to increasing private initiative and expanding judicial involvement, the act seeks to restrict regulatory agency discretion. These agencies, which previously could set and enforce environmental standards with judicial review only for arbitrary action, now must be able to prove they are adequately protecting the environment.

The law also provides that an individual can sue as a member of the public—on a "class-action" basis—and employs the public trust doctrine. This assumes that the government possesses the state's natural resources in trust for the proper use and enjoyment of the citizenry. This fiduciary obligation, when abused, can be enforced in the courts by a private citizen who sues in his role as a member of the beneficiary class—the public.

228

BACKGROUND

Supporters of the Michigan Environmental Protection Act saw court action as a way to remedy what they considered flaws in the traditional governmental mechanisms that control pollution. In Michigan, as in most other states, the regulation and control of environmental damage is conducted chiefly by the executive and legislative branches of government. Usually legislative rule-making powers are delegated to an administrative agency. These agencies then establish specific standards for particular problems and create and maintain the machinery to enforce these standards. These regulatory programs are usually combined with subsidy and technical assistance activities. The administrative decisions to set and enforce standards are usually not reviewed by the courts for their substance, but the agency must demonstrate that its decisions are not arbitrary, an abusive use of its powers, or a violation of explicit statutory language.

While backers of the EPA considered the legislative/executive regulatory mechanism vital to environmental control, they felt there were limits to this system. They pointed out that the administrative agency, for example, is charged with the duty of dealing with specific problems foreseen by the legislature. When an unanticipated environmental problem arises, established procedures often do not apply. The result may be a lack of corrective action, because the agency may not have authority to move on the problem without further specific authorization from the legislature. Or, the agency, which is geared to implementing established procedures on a day-to-day basis, may not be able to move fast enough to cope with a new type of environmental emergency. Passing remedial legislation and devising new administrative procedures may be too time-consuming to halt effectively a potential disaster. Extensive damage to people and natural resources may occur in the interim.

Some critics feel that these problems are inherent in administrative structures, because legislators and program officials will never be able to anticipate all the varied environmental problems that can emerge. By contrast, they believe the courts are particularly adapted to patching the holes in the administrative framework and filling the gaps between programs established by the legislature. They see the courts as having a quick response capability needed to cope with specific, but unanticipated, problems. Such a capability would fill out Michigan's environmental protection package.

Two points are clear. First, the EPA reflects a feeling that the efforts of administrative agencies have sometimes failed in the past, have limits to what they can accomplish without court action, and are unable to deal adequately with many unanticipated problems. Second, the act embodies a considerable faith in the courts and the common law system of legal development, both to remedy a specific problem and to act as a more general motivational force on executive agencies.

Citizen suits under EPA can challenge the substance of public agency policies, not just their enforcement or procedural genesis. Such active citizen participation in rule-making is expected to help remedy the problem of administrative agencies becoming overly sympathetic to the problems of industries, cities, and agriculture and failing to regulate them vigorously. Michigan strategists felt that public officials would not be as motivated to bring action against polluters as a private citizen would be who suffers from the environmental damage. Sax notes that an aim of the law is to create uncertainty for all polluters, actual or potential. "The point is that it takes some uncertainty to keep those people on their toes."[2]

In testifying in support of his proposal, Sax stated:

> Without citizen participation important issues will sometimes go unexamined and unchallenged.
>
> Moreover, citizen prodding may be required to encourage an agency, busy with its routine work, to take a careful look at all the implications of a program which it is promoting or regulating.
>
> We ought not to forget how useful it can be—indeed how essential—to ventilate important issues of policy outside the often confining traditional channels of the bureaucracy; particularly is this so when a bill like H.R. 3055 is under attack on the grounds that it might shake up the well established formal channels of government a little bit. It might—and it should.[3]

The principal purpose of the Michigan EPA was to limit administrative discretion and insure that regulatory decisions were defensible on the merits from an environmental standpoint.[4]

The Michigan attorney general, testifying in opposition to the EPA legislation, said the measure was unnecessary, that current laws provided all the remedies that Michigan needed to protect the environment.[5] He indicated that provisions were made for citizens to file complaints with state agencies, and that this traditional channel was best equipped to consider the many sides of complex environmental issues.

But the bill's supporters countered that these agencies were not required to take any action on the complaints. Further, in those limited instances where judicial review was provided, a person must be specially aggrieved, and those who could complain to an agency could not equally seek redress in court.[6]

The EPA is intended to facilitate citizen suits by eliminating the need for the individual to show that he had suffered special harm from pollution. This right to sue to protect a public interest, rather than an individual one, has been increasingly used in other states on environmental matters and was used in Michigan to abate other types of problems.

In Massachusetts, Wisconsin, Tennessee, Minnesota, California, Colorado, and New York, courts have allowed private citizens to sue on behalf of the general public, challenging misuse of natural resources. Suits have been files against private industries and against government agencies themselves, particularly those that construct highways and dams.

Michigan citizens were permitted to sue on behalf of the public to enjoin certain kinds of public nuisances, such as houses of prostitution and gambling. However, before 1970 there was no such guarantee of standing to sue to protect the public interest in natural resources.

In Michigan prior to the 1970 act, as in many other states today, when environmentally concerned citizens have sought court remedies, help has not always been readily available. A lawsuit in the public interest against an air or water polluter or a proposed land development does not fit the usual judicial idea of what a lawsuit should be. Law in the United States has grown out of private disputes where one side has allegedly harmed another. This harm could be redressed by a judgment ordering money paid to the aggrieved party, or by the use of an injunction whereby the defendant would be ordered to take some action, affirmative or negative, that would right the wrong suffered by the plaintiff in a situation where the payment of money would not suffice. But injunctions have usually been private matters, not dealing with large segments of the economy. Thus, our law has grown up around the general situation of individual plaintiff's suing to redress private injuries. This doctrine has been supported by many on the grounds that concrete controversies between parties whose interests are vitally and immediately affected give more "shape" to a lawsuit. This inductive method of law-making is intended to make the emerging law more solidly grounded in reality.

Therefore, courts have been reluctant to entertain lawsuits on behalf of the broader public interest because of this historic emphasis upon a distinguishable private harm suffered specifically by a particular plaintiff. Where the courts do not find an apparent private injury in the traditional sense, they are likely to dismiss the lawsuit on the grounds that the plaintiff lacks what is called "standing to sue." Invocation of this doctrine presents a severe obstacle to lawsuits brought by private citizens to protect the public interest in a clean environment. Those who criticize the application of the "standing to sue" doctrine in connection with environmental problems feel it makes no sense to say that an individual cannot sue a polluter just because that polluter is harming many people instead of just one. In general, the law of standing is being eroded both by judicial decisions and by statutes.

Michigan's EPA, which does away with considerations of standing to sue on environmental matters in that state, as well as defining broadly an environmental policy, has been described as "almost radical"[7] and by Sax as a "dramatic legal breakthrough."[8]

Sax drafted the bill at the request of the Western Michigan Environmental Action Council, and it was dropped into the hopper of the 75th legislature in April, 1969. In January, 1970, when the bill was scheduled for routine consideration at public hearing, hundreds of persons turned out to support its enactment. A strong alliance, mostly of conservationists and the United Auto Workers, undertook to make passage the *cause celebre* of the legislative session. Industrial spokesmen opposed the bill on grounds that a flood of harassing lawsuits would result. However, the legislation passed, without significant amendments.

231

One opposing legislator attributed the EPA's passage to ". . . rapid public reaction, aided and abetted by political grandstanding. . . . The sex appeal of the environmental crises peaked during consideration of the bill, thereby causing a typical knee-jerk 'boobus americanus' reaction."[9]

THE EPA AND RESULTING LITIGATION

The EPA provides that a suit to protect the "air, water and other natural resources and the public trust therein from pollution, impairment or destruction," may be initiated by the attorney general, any municipal corporation, any person, business association, organization, or other legal entity.[10]

Judges can decide if pollution or other types of environmental damage exist to violate the act, whether or not an administrative agency has established a specific standard on the matter under litigation. If an agency has adopted a standard, judges can determine its "validity, applicability, and reasonableness." These terms are not defined in the statute. There is no need to show that the existing standards are "arbitrary, capricious, or unreasonable," as is usually the case when the court examines an administrative standard. Furthermore, if the court decides that a standard does not meet these very general criteria, it may direct the administrative agency to adopt a new standard, which the court specifies.

The plaintiff has the burden of establishing a prima facie case of existent or potential pollution whereupon the burden shifts to the defendant to submit evidence to the contrary. The defendant may also show, by way of an affirmative defense, that there is "no feasible and prudent alternative" to his conduct. Presumably this means economically, technologically, and perhaps socially "feasible and prudent," although the statute does not say.

If the suit involves administrative action, the court may grant whatever temporary relief it sees fit and remit the case to the agency. After action by the agency, the court must review the adjudication to see that it conforms with the legal standard established by the act.

The court's review is not limited to matters considered by the administrative agency, and additional evidence may be taken at the court's discretion. The requirements contained in most states' administrative procedure acts to not apply. For unlike most judicial review of administrative action, these proceedings are "de novo," that is, not confined by or limited to the record made in any administrative proceeding.

A master or referee may be appointed by the court to take testimony dealing with technical matters. In this way, judges are supposed to be supplied with sufficient scientific, economic, and engineering information on which to make a decision. The act does not specify how the master will go about his task or how he will be paid.

Where an administrative proceeding occurs from which there is judicial review, any person, organization, or other legal entity may intervene simply by alleging that the procedure involves conduct likely to have the effect of "polluting, impairing, or destroying the air, water, or other natural resources or the public trust therein."

The act contains two features that are intended to deter vexatious litigation. Plaintiffs are required to present a prima facie case at the outset, so that cases of no merit can be sorted out at an early point. Second, the courts can allocate costs among the parties, the traditional deterrent to lawsuits of insufficient merit. The courts may require the plaintiff to post a $500 security bond if his solvency is in doubt. These funds are forfeited to cover the defendant's costs if a preliminary injunction is issued that proves later to have been wrongfully granted.

The Michigan EPA has not produced the rash of harassing lawsuits feared by public agencies and corporations at the time of its enactment. In fact, the number has been too few to have had the measurable impact on the environment that the act's proponents had hoped. From October, 1970, when the act took effect, to March 1, 1972, only 36 suits have been filed.[11] These cases have been monitored and reported on by Joseph Sax and Roger L. Conner, who is a University of Michigan Law School student and a member of the Michigan Air Pollution Control Commission.[12]

The cases have been evenly distributed over time, with two or three cases filed each month. State and local agencies were sued in about one-half the cases, and such public agencies used the new act to bring suit or intervene in one-third of the cases, a surprisingly high number according to the act's proponents who see the law mainly as a limit to agencies' discretion.[13] Corporations were defendants in 13 cases. Thirteen of the suits involved class actions; 12 of which had class plaintiffs and one involved a class defendant.

In their status report on the law, Sax and Conner report that the average private citizen used the act most and that in almost every instance he received fair and intelligent treatment from the courts.[14]

The subject matter of the cases filed breaks down this way:

12 relate to air pollution
10 relate to water pollution
10 relate to land use (such as land drainage, pipeline location, solid
     waste disposal, dam and homesite development)
 2 concern fish and game management
 1 relates to pesticides
 1 affects water management.

In nine cases, hearings were held on the plaintiffs request for restraining orders or injunctions. Preliminary relief was granted in four instances and denied in five.

Thirteen cases were concluded by March, 1972; each disposed of in an average of six months. As of that date, no case had reached either the court of appeals or the supreme court, leaving all legal issues unresolved by the courts.

In eight cases the plaintiffs were successful and in five they failed. Most of the cases were settled out of court, supporting the claim of Sax and Conner that the statute is serving as a prod to negotiated settlements.

In agreeing that there has been no rash of lawsuits, a spokesman for the U.S. Chamber of Commerce was quoted as saying, "I don't think the Michigan law turned out as badly as some people thought, but there have been some wierd suits."[15]

Roberts v. *Michigan* is an example of a kooky case.[16] Roberts, an inventor of automotive air pollution control equipment, filed suit in October, 1970 on behalf of the citizens of Michigan to bring "under control the major cause of air pollution in the United States, namely, automotive vehicles." But he did not choose to sue the Michigan Air Pollution Control Commission for inadequate policies and lax enforcement. Rather, he chose the much more radical route of suing the state, the secretary of state for granting licenses to operate motor vehicles, and the State Highway Department for using public funds to construct and maintain highways, which contribute to air pollution. He sought to have the court impose standards for motor vehicles and highway construction, and until these were enforced, enjoin the licensing and operation of vehicles and the construction of roads. He asked money damages in the amount of $570 million.

The judge ruled against the plaintiff and declared the EPA, in part, an unconstitutional overdelegation of legislative power to the judiciary. Judge Warren observed that the Vehicle Code outlawed "excessive smoke and fumes," and interpreted that to mean that this was the extent of regulation desired by the legislature. He did not think that the EPA had the authority to consider other automotive pollution problems. Therefore, he would take no evidence on these other emissions. While saying the standards from the legislature were deficient, he ruled that the court could not direct the legislature to set better standards and that if he proceeded further he would be doing just that. He concluded that the act "so far as it pertains to pollution arising from operation of motor vehicles is unconstitutional."[17]

This case potentially raised the question of which governmental agencies are responsible for environmental protection. However, the suit never directly addressed whether the highway department and secretary of state were the proper defendants. Their primary missions are highway construction and proper operating condition of vehicles. While the EPA requires all agencies to consider air pollution and other environmental problems, the specific relief sought in the *Roberts* case may be the responsibility of the Air Pollution Control Commission, whom the legislature directly assigned the job of protecting air quality.

In evaluating the effects of the *Roberts* case, Sax and Conner wrote:

Roberts demonstrates one of the most troublesome issues arising out of the enactment of a law designed to benefit what may loosely be called a movement or a cause—the inability of any leadership to control the kinds of cases brought or the manner in which they are

234

litigated. Ironically, the real problem is quite the opposite of that feared by those who opposed the EPA's enactment; these critics had been worried that overzealous environmentalists might concertedly organize to tie the hands of regulatory agencies or to attack in overwhelming fashion certain agricultural or business interests. Instead, the danger is that inadequately planned litigation will produce damaging legal precedents and will generally impair the reputation of plaintiffs who use the statute.[18]

Cases that provide the best use of the Michigan Environmental Protection Act, according to Sax and Conner, are those that are the opposite of the grand-scale *Roberts* case—they call these "natural small-scale cases."[19] An example of such a case is *Wayne County Health Department* v. *Chrysler Corporation*.[20] Chrysler's Huber Avenue foundry in Detroit had been polluting the air for years because its abatement equipment broke down frequently. Negotiations between the county antipollution agency and the corporation had stalemated until several hundred local residents, who had damage suits pending against the corporation under the common law of nuisance, intervened as plaintiffs in the case. The new plaintiffs made the county agency seem moderate by comparison, for the private citizens were insisting that Chrysler admit its wrongdoing. This provided the company the necessary incentive to settle. In the settlement, Chrysler was required to close down the foundry if air pollution control equipment malfunctioned and could not be repaired within 24 hours. Also, to prevent having to close down the automobile production lines if the foundry were closed, the company was required to carry a ten-day inventory.

In general, Sax and Conner believe that lawsuits instituted under the EPA and the threat of additional ones have applied pressures to both government agencies and regulated parties, bringing about four types of positive effects:

1. freed environmental agencies to be as tough as they wanted to be, but had felt constrained from being, because of political and legal pressures from regulated parties; in these cases, the lawsuits equalize the pressure on the regulatory agency, allowing them to be more aggressive;

2. motivated recalcitrant environmental agencies into pursuing more stringent regulatory policies;

3. encouraged resource development agencies to give higher priority to environmental protection;

4. required private polluters to halt or prevent environmental damage.

An example of the first of these effects is shown in *Trout Unlimited* v. *Milliken*.[21] The sport fishermen's group, along with several property owners and the Board of County Commissions, successfully secured protections of the Au Sable River, one of the most famous trout streams in Michigan. The threat posed was rapid drainage of a nearby lake for flood control purposes. The project had considerable political support after heavy rains and much flooding. The Natural Resources Commission had agreed to the project, after securing only limited controls and despite the opposition of a staff report. The EPA-based suit ultimately secured for the Department of Natural Resources (DNR)

235

a detailed monitoring provision, as well as a reduction in maximum rate of flow adequate to protect nearby cottage owners and the fishery. A DNR official was reported later to have said: "The settlement definitely strengthens our hand with respect to controlling any possible adverse effects. . . . I am certain that without the order, we would not have (been able) to completely control the situation."[22]

In another instance, *Water Resources Commission v. Chippewa County*,[23] the state agency went directly to court in February, 1971, charging a violation of the EPA instead of following its usual administrative procedures. The state agency claimed that the Board of County Road Commissioners was storing salt for winter road clearing that was sweeping into ground waters and polluting well water supplies of local residents.

Sax and Conner contend that *West Michigan Environmental Action Council v. Betz Foundry, Inc.*,[24] is an example of an environmental agency being forced to upgrade policies. This case, in which the Air Pollution Control Commission was a defendant, "apparently caused" the commission to revise its policy of granting variances liberally.[25] They report that Commissioner Stanley Quackenbush said that "applications [for variances] would be scrutinized with greater care lest the commission be brought into court again."[26] The EPA is said to be at least partly responsible for "a new procedure under which the commission increasingly issued complaints and pressed for orders, rather than the informal agreements embodied in a variance."

Sax and Conner also say they have "every reason to believe" that *Tanton v. Department of Natural Resources*[27] caused the Natural Resources Commission to draft its "potent new land use policy."[28] In this case, the defendant had granted a developer a permit to dam Monroe Creek to create a lake for recreational homesites. The plaintiff showed the dam would damage trout fisheries and asked the department to demonstrate that it had developed a policy against which the appropriateness of proposals, such as the one in question, could be tested. The case is still pending. After *Tanton* had been initiated, but before the trial, the Natural Resources Commission unanimously pledged that it would not in any way abet new water or land uses that could damage the environment. However, the EPA suit was not the only incentive for a new policy. This policy came after the Governor's Special Commission on Land Use urged statewide controls.

The EPA put pressure on a development agency to give higher priority to environmental protection when the Michigan Consolidated Gas Company petitioned the Michigan Public Service Commission to authorize it to set up a priority scheme for rationing natural gas.[29] It proposed to put gas use to control air pollution near the bottom on the list. The attorney general and the Wayne County Health Department intervened, asking that clean air be given a higher priority. The state commission said that while its own authority said it *could* consider air pollution, that it was not *required* to do so. To the contrary, the attorney general said that the EPA was a source of new authority that *required* the commission to give equal attention to antipollution as to industrial uses. The commission did not resolve this question, but did move antipollution higher up the list of priorities.

The cases filed to date do not show the act's total effect, since proponents believe that the mere threat of an EPA authorized suit deters polluters and spurs public agencies into better enforcement of antipollution laws.[30]

ISSUES TO WATCH

The class action environmental lawsuit is receiving increasing support from conservationists across the nation. At least three other states have enacted laws similar to Michigan's—Connecticut, Minnesota, and Indiana—while New Jersey, California, and Massachusetts have it under very active consideration. Altogether, about 25 states and Congress are considering such legislation.

While interest in the Michigan law grows, the issues it raises are receiving increased and more heated debate. These issues relate to the EPA's constitutionality; to the ability of judges to cope with the highly technical nature of pollution abatement; and to the political question of whether judges who cannot be held accountable by the public should be so involved in environmental policy. While the brief experiences to date does not decide these issues, the future record of the Michigan Act will help answer some of these questions.

Constitutionality

Some of the act's opponents in the legal community charge that the act is unconstitutional on two grounds. The first is that the law is unconstitutionally vague as to what the courts can and cannot do. The second is that the act authorizes an improper delegation of legislative authority to the judiciary, violating the separation of powers doctrine. In three cases, Michigan judges have ruled on the question of unconstitutional delegation of legislative authority. This issue arises from Section 2 of the EPA which states:

(2) In granting relief provided by subsection (1) where there is involved a standard for pollution or for an anti-pollution device or procedure, fixed by rule or otherwise, by an instrumentality or agency of the state or a political subdivision thereof, the court may:
    (a) Determine the validity, applicability and reasonableness of the standard.
    (b) When a court finds a standard to be deficient, direct the adoption of a standard approved and specified by the court.

Sax and Conner make two points in defense of this section: First, that the court is not being asked to reexamine a legislatively set standard, but only those set by regulatory agencies and political subdivisions. Second, the EPA itself sets an environmental policy, albeit broadly defined, against which the courts merely evaluate administrative actions. Thus, the courts are not usurping legislative authority, but enforcing it.

Two judges have seen it differently. In *Crandall* v. *Biergans*[31] neighbors brought suit against the operator of a hog-finishing barn for odors emitted. The defendant proved that his activities were not a nuisance, and also that he had no "feasible and prudent" alternative. Regarding the constitutional question, Judge Corkin stated:

> Here the Court, of necessity, must determine that standards relating to the raising and maintaining of livestock are deficient because none exist. It is being asked to create standards, direct their adoption and proceed to enforcement. The Court would regard this as making law and thus an unconstitutional delegation of legislative power so far as the raising of livestock is concerned. The Court does not think the Environmental Protection Act, as it now stands, can serve as a basis for any relief to plaintiffs.[32]

Yet, Sax and Conner contend that in his overall decision, the court did set a specific standard—balancing the goal of no pollution against the need to carry on activities necessary to human existence that necessarily cause some odors.

The second "unconstitutional" ruling came from the judge in the *Roberts* v. *Michigan* case discussed earlier.

In the third case, *Lakeland Property Owners Assn.* v. *Township of Northfield*,[33] Judge Mahinske decided on February 29, 1972 that the EPA was constitutional. The property owners had challenged the expansion of a sewage treatment plant that was discharging in their vicinity and allegedly causing pollution. They sought to change the discharge point and to require tougher effluent standards than those contained in the Water Resources Commission's (WRC) order to the township. The township lost the argument that the case should be referred to the Water Resources Commission for administrative action, and then received a new and tougher WRC order. The court found that even if the township conformed to existing effluent standards, pollution would still result. Compliance with WRC standards was no defense against violation of the EPA, because the WRC's administrative standards were inadequate to meet the requirements of the EPA. As to constitutionality, he said:

> Defendant, in its Brief, relies heavily on the opinion of Judge Warren . . . in the matter of *Roberts* v. *State of Michigan*. . . . This court is of the opinion that it is not controlled by the opinion set out in *Roberts* by the learned Ingham County Circuit Court Judge and further finds that any dispute between circuits must be resolved by a higher tribunal.
>
> This Court does not believe [the EPA] is unconstitutional by virtue of it having contained therein a prohibited delegation of powers. Said Act simply states that when a Court finds a standard to

be unreasonable or deficient the Court may set an acceptable standard which the Court may enforce directly or order the agency involved to enforce such standard.[34]

In response to complaints that the EPA is too generally worded, Sax responds that similar complaints about "broadness" were made against the Sherman Antitrust Act, but the U.S. Supreme Court upheld that law as having a "charter of generality." He continues, "Unless you know in advance exactly what you want people to do, you've got to pass a broad statute."[35]

Higher Michigan courts have not ruled on constitutionality and the matter is by no means settled. Other legal scholars, such as Professor Louis Jaffe of the Harvard Law School, think that there is a point at which courts are constitutionally without power to intervene where the legislature has properly delegated power to an executive officer and that officer has fairly and substantially met the burdens imposed for protection of the environment. Jaffe believes the Michigan act goes beyond this point and that the courts are not constitutionally authorized to exercise the broad discretionary powers that are not clearly defined by the Michigan act.[36]

Those who believe that the Michigan act overdelegates to the court think the issue is not whether the administrative agency is thought to be acting in the best interests of the environment, but whether the power to so act has been properly delegated to that agency by the legislature. If such is the case, the courts should feel restrained.

The extent to which the Michigan act provides for judicial preemption of administrative tasks must be interpreted by the courts. As Jaffe indicates, a line will have to be drawn—and that line has not yet been identified.

It will be interesting to note the extent to which Michigan courts choose to rely on the record established by the administrative agencies, which are supposed to have the technical expertise in pollution matters. It is hard to imagine that courts will not at least scrutinize the testimony taken by these agencies, which is often extensive. But the degree to which the courts will be bound by the record is another matter. While the courts have been given carte blanche on environmental matters by the legislature, they may not choose to use it fully.

Some supporters of more limited citizen-suit provisions, while not supporting the sweeping provisions of the Michigan law, would permit suits on those matters where standards have been set by administrative action. A citizen could sue an offender for failure to meet the specific environmental standard or the agency that failed to enforce it. In this case, if a citizen is dissatisfied with established standards, he can challenge them only indirectly, for example by testing the agency's procedures against laws governing rule-making. And, if no standard exists, such as for noise or some exotic chemicals, no suits would be possible. This is the position of the Nixon administration on class-action-suit bills pending in Congress. The rationale for this position is that the courts need the technical guidance of the executive branch and the policy guidance of the legislature in authorizing specific standards.[37]

In addition to the legal question, others have inquired whether judges, who are legally trained, will be able to gather and evaluate the necessary technical information to define a proper environmental standard. It will be interesting to see whether the provision for a referee to aid the court will provide judges with the knowledge of a considerable amount of scientific, engineering, and economic data in order to set effective standards.

There are others who oppose the courts being given power to devise specific environmental standards when none were explicitly authorized by the legislature. These critics feel that such decisions involve trading-off several fundamental values of society—environmental and economic, as well as social. They say that the weighing of these varied public interests should be done by the legislature, whose members can be held accountable by the public through the electoral process. In this way, political responsiveness can be built into environmental decision-making. The courts, which are not subject to this review and control by the general public, cannot, it is contended, be sufficiently responsive to the public's wishes.

Other analysts of the Michigan law point out that court action is basically a reactive strategy, activated only after an environmental problem has become apparent. Court suits cannot substitute for planning and management procedures that constitute a preventive environmental strategy. Nor can the courts coordinate various actions. They must deal with one case, one specific type of a particular pollution problem at a time. Courts may treat differently two companies within a particular industry in different parts of the state.

However, supporters of the Michigan law do not envision that the courts will ever substitute for executive action except in very limited circumstances. Primarily, the court will be a motivational force to encourage more effective executive decisions. Also, court decisions can check an arbitrary administrative action.

The Public Trust Doctrine

Because the public trust doctrine has lain dormant for some time in the American common law, reservatons have been expressed about the Michigan attempt to reactivate it. The question is asked whether this is still a vital theory. This does not seem to be much of a problem in Michigan, however, for that state's statutes commonly refer to the public trust. Other states considering this measure will need to explore carefully the meaning of the "public trust" in their own state's law.

In his book, *Defending the Environment*,[38] Sax explains his idea of the environment as a public trust. The following excerpts from that book help illuminate the theory:

If an individual comes into court to protest the government-approved construction or operation of a factory on the ground that it will degrade the ambient air to an unreasonable degree and asserts that he is entitled to protection against such degradation as a matter of legal right—the same right he would have to enforce against a neighbor keeping pigs in the backyard—he could turn to no body of law that would support such a claim. He does not have a legal right . . . whereby he may get a court to consider the harm to him as a member of the public and hear evidence of the reasonable alternatives which would accommodate both his asserted right to environmental quality in clean air and the factory's asserted interest in producing its product. . . .

There is no good reason why we should hesitate to adopt a theory of public rights to environmental quality, enforceable at law, nor is there any reason to think we cannot adjudicate the reasonable accommodations needed to protect against unnecessary threats to the environment.

If the courts viewed the public interest in the Alaskan environment or the Hudson River as they do private property, they could go straight to the merits of the claims which citizens want to make. The same questions asked in private cases apply to public complaints: Is the activity necessary? Is there enough information to support the allegations that it can be carried on without undue harm to the environment? Are there better alternatives, or is there a reason to delay until we know more or have done better experimental work?

NOTES

1. Michigan Environmental Protection Act of 1970 (House Bill 3055, 75th Legislature); Mich. Comp. Laws Ann. Secs. 691.1201 *et seq.* (Supp. 1971).

2. *National Journal*, June 12, 1971, p. 1249.

3. Joseph L. Sax, in testimony before the Committee on Conservation and Recreation, Michigan House of Representatives on House Bill 3055, January 21, 1970, as reported in "An Environmental Common Law for Michigan," 14 Mich. *Law Quadrangle Notes* 27 (University of Michigan Law School) (1970), p. 31.

4. Joseph L. Sax and Roger L. Conner, "Michigan's Environmental Protection Act of 1970: A Progress Report," *Michigan Law Review*, 70, no. 6 (May, 1972), p. 1061.

5. Attorney General's memorandum of April 29, 1969, to the Michigan legislature, as reported in "An Environmental Common Law for Michigan," *op. cit.*, p. 29.

6. Sax, "An Environmental Common Law for Michigan," *op. cit.*

241

7. *Congressional Record,* September 22, 1970, p. S 16246.

8. Joseph L. Sax, *"An Environment in the Courts,"* *Saturday Review,* October 3, 1970, p. 56.

9. *Congressional Record*, September 22, 1970, p. S 16247.

10. Mich. Comp. Laws Ann. Sec. 691.1203 (Supp. 1972).

11. Sax and Conner, *op. cit.,* p. 1003.

12. *Ibid.*

13. *Ibid.*, p. 1008.

14. *Ibid.*, p. 1081.

15. *National Journal,* June 12, 1971, p. 1249.

16. File No. 12428-C, filed October 23, 1970 in Ingham County.

17. *Roberts* v. *Michigan,* Opinion Judge Warren, May 4, 1971, pp. 4-5.

18. Sax and Conner, *op. cit.,* p. 1018.

19. *Ibid.,* p. 1010.

20. File No. 166-223, filed October 1, 1970 in Wayne County.

21. File No. 13243-C, filed June 18, 1971 in Ingham County.

22. Letter from A. Gene Gazley, Assistant Director, DNR, to Roger Conner, August 2, 1971; as reported in Sax and Conner, *op. cit.,* p. 1014.

23. File No. 1255, filed February 10, 1971 in Chippewa County.

24. File No. 11409, filed March 2, 1971 in Kent County.

25. Sax and Conner, *op. cit.,* p. 1051.

26. *Ibid.*

27. File No. 13859-C, filed December 8, 1971 in Ingham County.

28. Sax and Conner, *op. cit.,* p. 1052.

29. No. U-3802 (Michigan Public Service Commission, 1971).

30. Senator Philip A. Hart, as reported in *National Journal,* June 12, 1971, p. 1249.

31. File No. 844, filed June 11, 1969, amended complaint September 3, 1971, in Clinton County.

32. *Crandall* v. *Biergans,* Opinion of Judge Corkin, February 14, 1972, p. 13.

33. File No. 1453, filed August 27, 1970 in Livingston County.

34. *Lakeland* opinion of February 29, 1972, pp. 19-20.

35. *National Journal,* June 12, 1971, p. 1250.

36. Louis Jaffe, Speech to the American Law Institute—American Bar Association Symposium on Environmental Law, Smithsonian Institution, January 29, 1971.

37. For a full explanation of the Nixon administration position on citizen suits, see the testimony of Timothy B. Atkeson, General Counsel to the Council on Environmental Quality, to the Senate Committee on Commerce, Subcommittee on Environmental Protection, Washington, D.C., April 15, 1971; and to the House Committee on Merchant Marines and Fisheries, Subcommittee on Fisheries and Wildlife Conservation, Washington, D.C., June 9, 1971.

38. Joseph L. Sax, *Defending the Environment,* (New York: Alfred A. Knopf, 1971).

10

RECOMMENDATIONS

Governments' ability to solve social problems has lagged far behind the public's demands. State governments' attempts to cure environmental ills are no exception. Legal authorities and funding have been inadequate and organizational patterns have thwarted the best use of even these meager assets.

Now state governments are moving to remedy this institutional lag, and one of their steps has been to reorganize antipollution and resource programs so that governmental organization can address current environmental needs.

The recommendations in this chapter seek to help states design an effective and responsive organizational structure for environmental programs. This structure, along with strengthened regulatory and resource management authority and adequate program funding, will allow state governments to meet their citizens' demands for healthier and satisfying surroundings.

States' institutional difficulties have been, in part, a lack of *motivation* to act aggressively enough against polluters and, in part, a lack of legal, financial, and analytical *capability* to solve waste management and resource problems. The two parts may, in fact, be one. History shows that when governments are fully motivated to cure a social problem, the ways and means are usually found to do so.

State governmental agencies, responding to powerful industrial, agricultural, and local governmental interests, have been reluctant to use what regulatory authority they had. Legislators, responding to similar interests, have not given agencies effective tools, funds, and swift, effective enforcement devices. Until the late 1960s and early 1970s, a clear majority of most states' voters was not perceived to support strong environmental controls. Now public wishes have changed, but the power of the regulated parties over many states' governments continues disproportionate to their interest in public decisions.

Now, a great many individuals are concerned with conservation and environmental protection, but they lack control over governmental action that their numbers and interest warrant. Consequently, the democratic precept is violated that each individual should have power over his government commensurate with his stake in the outcome of decisions. The assumption here is that each individual can best evaluate his own interests.

The imbalance of pressures on government arises because environmentalists, in contrast to regulated parties, are poorly organized for political action and underfunded, depending on donations from individuals and foundations. Consequently, many environmental and conservation organizations lack adequate staff and the professional and political skills needed to participate effectively in administrative and legislative proceedings. These organizations are reluctant to lobby legislators for fear of losing their tax-exempt status.

Organizing environmentalists is difficult, in general, because the benefits of environmental protection are widely dispersed over a large population with each being affected incrementally, while the costs of clean-up are concentrated at a high level to a far fewer number.

With much at stake, companies and local governments can assign their highly skilled lawyers, economists, scientists, engineers, public relations experts, and lobbyists to work full time promoting their positions with governmental officials. Economic interest groups can also make large, influencing political campaign contributions to elected state officials.

As a result, cozy relationships have sometimes developed between state officials and the polluters they are supposed to regulate. Regulators become overly sympathetic to the technological and financial problems of those they regulate and relax enforcement.

A major element in lax regulation has been the role of part-time, policy-making state boards, populated by the very industrialists, agriculturalists, and local governmental people who are the subject of controls. This is a type of "fox in charge of the chicken coop" strategy. In most states, these five-to-nine-member boards or commissions are appointed by the governor for a term to make the major policy decisions for pollution and resource management programs. Interest group membership is usually specified by statute (industry, labor, agriculture, local government, conservation) and while one or two conservation or "public" members are included, they are outnumbered by economic development interests. State departmental directors may also serve, to represent the interests of their constituencies. Theoretically, the board's make-up is designed to guarantee a broad and representative mix of views in state environmental policy, but in practice these bodies have been run as the private clubs of the regulated interests.

In the pollution field, these boards set air and water quality standards, issue waste control permits, set fines, issue enforcement orders, and recommend enforcement cases to be taken to court by the attorney general. The boards also approve budgets and sometimes hire the director of the full-time state agency that carries out the board's policy on a day-to-day basis.

244

The public has no direct control over board members who serve an appointive term and cannot be removed except for malfeasance. Many members were chosen by previous governors and are unresponsive to the wishes of a newly elected chief executive.

There have been many of these antipollution and resource boards and administrative agencies in each state, which create an organizational tangle, preventing policy-makers from having a comprehensive view of environmental problems. Public programs have developed piecemeal over the years as problems impinged on public awareness and a new organization was established for each new program. Consequently, a different board and administrative agency have existed for water pollution, air pollution, conservation, water use management, and many more natural resource activities. If program integration occurs anywhere for pollution control, it is in the state health department, which was the agency in many states that administered on a daily basis policies set by the air and water control boards. Often, health officials also administered a small solid waste planning effort, too meager an activity to be governed by a board. In many cases, the state health departments had consolidated pollution control staff responsibilities into one division. Often the part-time policy boards merely rubber-stamped the technical recommendations of the health department staff, but they could and often did veto any aggressive pollution abatement actions.

In the health department, pollution control programs had to compete with a large number of other health programs, unrelated to waste management, for staff time, funds, and public attention. Furthermore, location in the health department meant a very limited focus for pollution issues. Programs were staffed mainly by sanitary engineers and pollution was examined and controlled mainly for its health effects. There was little consideration of the other critical resource, economic, recreational, and aesthetic impacts. The administrative style of these officials was to emphasize friendly negotiations with polluters and voluntary compliance, rather than legal actions.

CRITERIA FOR EVALUATING PUBLIC ENVIRONMENTAL INSTITUTIONS

The criteria for evaluating public environmental institutions relate to the two sets of difficulties just discussed: governmental *motivation* and *capability* to solve publicly agreed upon environmental problems. We believe government should be evaluated as to whether it is motivated to respond to a majority of the public. Such responsiveness can be increased by guaranteeing meaningful public participation in decision-making for everyone affected by the outcome, with each having power over the decision commensurate with his stake in the outcome. This is a requirement in a democracy where the individual is assumed to be the best judge of his own interests and where government is established to protect the public interest. However, there must be a relative equity of access of individuals with various interests so that each person's interests are met at some time and some place.

Secondly, state government must be capable of carrying out, economically and quickly, the public's wishes for environmental protection, once these are established by maximum public participation.

Responsive Government

The following conditions will increase a government's motivation to respond to the wishes of a majority of individuals affected by environmental measures:

1. *The individual citizen must know the environmental policy options and the effect each will have on him.* An ideal state agency system will ensure that public issues are defined and discussed publicly, prior to decision-making. This does not mean that purely technical matters need to be aired, but only those significant ones that have a major effect on programs. To do this, the organization must first generate information on the costs and benefits of the major available alternatives, translate the highly technical terms into laymen's language, and then ensure that the findings are publicly articulated in a timely and meaningful manner to private individuals, interest groups, and elected representatives.

2. *Individuals and interest groups should have meaningful access to public decision-makers, either directly or through their elected representatives, and have sufficient power over these decision-makers to protect their own interests.* Access means knowing who will make a particular environmental decision and having a means to express preference in a way that will be recognized by the decision-maker. The system should work so that all interests are weighed in a decision in proportion to their stake in the outcome, with minority viewpoints heard and sometimes prevailing.

3. *Public decision-makers should be accountable to the citizens of the state.* The institutional structure should include a mechanism whereby the key public decision-makers can be recalled by the public or the public's elected representative if the effects of environmental decisions are unacceptable to enough people. Accountability can be established without potential replacement on a daily basis. Review and public evaluation through the electoral process every three or four years is adequate.

Effective Policies

Government institutions also need to be evaluated on their ability to make and carry out effective environmental policies, within the framework of goals set by maximum public participation. Effective policies are those that meet public objectives speedily and with the lowest cost to the total society—both public and private sectors.

Criteria in this category, as in the first, are necessarily qualitative, but quantitative measures of effectiveness can and should be used also when cost and reliability of the data can be assured.

Capability to perform effectively is influenced by the following conditions:

1. *Environmental institutions must have a clear analytical perspective on the major environmental problems as they occur in the natural world and be able to relate policies and programs to this perspective.* The analytical perspective of state organizations should match the relationships of resources and pollutants in the environment. Some pollutants, such as pesticides, travel through the soil, air, and water, and thus environmental agency staff need to be able to study their transport in all environmental media. Similarly, various living and nonliving resources interact in ecological systems in an intricate web of actions. To interdict wastes and protect resources effectively, the analyst must study the full chain of actions and devise program alternatives based on that knowledge. Proper perspective for an antipollution agency would include relations between land use and waste discharge, concentration, and treatment. The state's total set of environmental institutions needs a view of the total energy cycle in the state. An effective analytical perspective also includes an ability to see the economic and social consequences of policy alternatives, as well as the physical and biological interactions.

However, since it is a truism that everything relates to everything else in the natural environment, it is necessary to break down the interrelating whole, which may be seen by those at the top of state government, into two parts that are rational and manageable for operational program administration. The structure must be able to address the major environmental problems as they are perceived by the people of each state, because responsive governments will devise programs along these lines. Identifying an environmental agency's analytical perspective is best done by examining its planning perspective and products, by assessing the view of problems taken at the director's level, and by examining the integration or nonintegration of programs and how standards and other agency goals are devised.

2. *Effective environmental organizations must have the capacity to innovate.* A public agency should be flexible and creative in perceiving environmental problems, researching remedies, listening to suggestions from a wide variety of sources, and devising new techniques to solve them. Some ways to measure innovation include identifying the number of new programs initiated by an agency and the time it takes to devise a new program, once the need has been perceived.

3. *The institutional network must have sufficient power to carry out the missions assigned to it.* In the pollution control field this includes authority and funding to plan, regulate, do research and monitoring, give financial and technical assistance, and conduct public information programs.

4. *An effective institutional structure will evaluate its own performance and feed back such information to decision-makers in the agency, in the governor's office, to the legislature, and to the public.* Evaluation should be

carried out by formal studies and informal assessment, and each should occur regularly.

5. *Making and carrying out public decisions should proceed with reasonable speed and at the lowest possible governmental cost*. In large measure, this means administrative efficiency. This can be measured in many ways, including an assessment of the numbers and kinds of environmental standards set and enforced within a specific time period. The question of whether those standards are set at proper levels and for correct sources or needed at all is the broader question of total policy effectiveness.

Some of the criteria outlined for responsive government and effective environmental policies may seem at first glance to make countervailing demands on an institutional structure. For instance, increasing governmental discussion in public of environmental programs prior to decisions and guaranteeing greater citizen participation may in fact slow down public processes and raise the public costs of administering programs, at least in the short run. However, if government is to set policies that meet the needs of all the people in the long run, such participation is the most effective and efficient means to ensure this. Thus, both sets of evaluative criteria, those that concern adequate processes for citizen participation and those that measure the effective products of state agencies, are important and must be viewed in terms of one another.

RECOMMENDATIONS FOR A MODEL
STATE ENVIRONMENTAL STRUCTURE

This section recommends an organization of state environmental activities that we believe will meet the preceding criteria. Of course, not all criteria will apply to organizational patterns. Our objective is to describe a governmental structure that will raise the level of importance of critical environmental programs, create a highly visible unit of government that can act as a strong public advocate of major environmental concerns, encourage all citizens to participate meaningfully to affect decisions, give each agency all the powers it needs to do an effective job, and then make its director accountable to the governor, the legislature, and the public for its performance.

Such a structure will encourage, but of course cannot guarantee, effective policies and responsive government. Ultimately the success of government will depend on the quality of elected officials, the officials they appoint and technical staff they hire, the laws they pass, and the levels of funding, which are the products of the political process.

Each state's environmental problems and citizens' wishes for remedies are unique and, consequently, this model must be adjusted from state to state. Each state will need to examine its own resource needs, statutory authorities, and existing organizations before undertaking reorganization.

248

If the state decides to reorganize, any new department should be created to implement a clear and agreed-upon policy objective, because an organization, such as for pollution control or conservation, institutionalizes the pursuit of that goal. An organization has an organic quality and will seek to survive and grow. Each year it will propose legislation and ask for funds, usually at increasing levels. Private interest groups will realign themselves to relate to the new department and new legislative alliances will be welded.

A state will have to determine whether the benefits of restructuring outweigh the costs. States should realize that reorganizations may cost much in terms of time, political resistance, continuity or programming, and morale of transferred personnel. Reorganizations always upset the status quo and may lead to shifting political alliances and, in some cases, a temporary loss of political support for programs. Reorganizations also cost money. Although most are sold on economy grounds—the funds that will be saved by reducing overlaps and program duplication—new departments usually will receive more public money rather than less. While it is hoped that the new organization will be more efficient in spending each dollar, increased demands on the new agency, based on increased expectations for action, require higher legislative funding. Additional funds are also needed to provide a building for the new department, new forms and procedures, and more personnel.

On the positive side, reorganizations create a chance to change environmental policies by changing key agency officials and power structures both within an agency and between agency staff and regulated parties. The new personnel hired often have fresher ideas and a more vigorous sense of commitment to the programs and new policies than seasoned bureaucrats. New program mixes give new perspectives on problems and policies and can thereby increase responsiveness and effectiveness in government. Discussed below are three major reorganization issues and the major options examined for each.

1. What environmental programs are to be included in the new department? Pollution control? The traditional conservation programs for parks, wildlife, wilderness, forests, and fish? The management of water quantity or water use?

2. Should the use of boards or commissions be continued? If so, should they have policy-making powers or be only advisory? Should they be full time or part time? Our recommendations are based on the experience of the states studies in this book, findings in pertinent literature, and our personal perspective.

3. Which agency of state government should conduct broad environmental planning? Who should administer any program to assess and control environmental impacts from governmental development programs?

What Programs to Combine?

We believe that in most states a responsive and effective environmental organizational structure will include a separate new cabinet level department for all pollution control programs, rather than the major alternative, a larger environmental "superdepartment" combining pollution controls with conservation and resource management programs.

The new antipollution agency should carry out the full range of pollution control functions and administer programs for the control of water pollution, including drinking water, air pollution, solid wastes, pesticides, noise, oil pollution, acid-mine drainage, vessel pollution, power plant pollution, and radiation, and should also participate in power plant siting decisions. Centralization of principal pollution controls does not mean that all overlapping activities among state agencies should be rigidly eliminated, but only that the pollution control agency should have clear authority and be the lead agency. Some duplication of work among state agencies, particularly research, may be beneficial.

Pollution is a serious environmental problem now confronting many states, one lacking adequate governmental attention and most concerning voters and legislators. While pollution control is only one among many environmental objectives states should seek over the next decade (indeed, other problems such as land use management may be more significant), many new pollution control laws will likely be enacted in the immediate future and demand effective implementation. Pollution control is a significant and separate purpose of government and a department just for that purpose can concentrate all its time and energies solely on program implementation, unhampered by competing activities. The new organization will likely bring added prestige, attention, and a new professionalism to the effort. The person directing these programs can become a strong, vigorous advocate for tough antipollution measures in the state's budgeting, programming, and legislative processes. Similarly, a separate department for conservation and natural resource management can then maintain its unique advocacy role.

Creating a new, single-purpose pollution control agency may well encourage the adoption of a new, tougher regulatory approach, extending beyond merely pollution health effects. The state's analytical perspective on waste management problems will be sharply focused, concentrating on a small number of highly related, clearly defined phenomena—the generation, transportation, treatment, and disposal of physical-chemical pollutants that travel through air, water, and land successively and can interchange forms in the environment. These often come from the same source and can be similarly managed. From a functional point of view, various pollution control programs proceed by similar legal and engineering techniques and thus a co-location can be mutually supportive.

Consolidating pollution control work allows the public to hold one state organization accountable for a pollution problem of any type, and makes it easier for the public to know where to go with complaints. Also, single agencies for pollution control can most effectively encourage the development of strong antipollution interest groups to support the state program, so that the current imbalance of pressures on the state from environmentalists and regulated parties can begin to be restored.

250

While some environmentalists have feared that creation of a single anti-pollution department may make the regulatory program easier for polluters to ⸗ "capture," the reverse is more likely to be the case. The programs and its leadership will be increasingly visible to the public. The setting of standards and initiation of enforcement proceedings, or lack of them, will attract more press attention. Of course, such an agency may also be especially vulnerable to budget cuts and any environmental "backlash" from the public in times of economic downturn.

Regulated parties may find less red tape and confusion in dealing with a single agency for pollution control, and for this reason they have often supported such reorganizations. State governments, in turn, will find it easier to do business with their increasingly power federal partner, which has also centralized antipollution work in its Environmental Protection Agency (EPA).

The experience of the two states examined that created new pollution control agencies—Minnesota and Illinois—has shown some benefits of limiting environmental consolidations to just pollution controls. Because reorganizations occurred within the limited and defined area of pollution control, the new agencies in Minnesota and Illinois began with a clear analytical focus and less program disruption than in states creating superdepartments. Leaders were able to devote full attention to pollution regulation and become highly visible, tough environmental advocates. Minnesota's Pollution Control Agency has been especially successful in giving focus to environmental interest groups statewide and increasing public enthusiasm for the pollution control effort.

We recommend a consolidation of the water use management program with pollution controls in a new environmental department in those states where water is a particularly valuable state asset, as in Washington, or water shortages are a severe problem, as in the Southwest. Water resource management in many states is closely related to water pollution control and the two may be mutually supportive. Both programs' officials do river basin planning, issue permits for waste discharge or water use, and set and enforce regulations. Water quality and quantity are two parts of the same water problem in the environment and data can be shared effectively. The objectives of the water resource management are compatible with pollution control, unlike many other conservation and natural resource programs.

The new antipollution agency will need power to set standards governing emissions and effluents as well as environmental quality, enforce laws, have faster emergency powers, issue permits for installation and operation of abatement equipment and discharges, extend financial aid to localities, offer technical assistance to environmental pollution sources, conduct public information and planning relating to these programs, do research and statewide monitoring and surveillance.

States have differing views as to which pollution control functions, if any, conflict when administered by a single agency. We believe the main conflict of functions occurs between enforcement prosecution and adjudication of disputes. An agency cannot be a strong and effective adversary of an alleged polluter, initiating and even prosecuting enforcement cases in court, and an

251

unbiased judge in the same situation. To make adjudication credible and fair, we suggest that this responsibility not be located in the new pollution control department. It may be located in the regular courts, or assigned to a special adjudicative organization such as Washington State's Pollution Control Hearings Board or Illinois' Pollution Control Board. The Illinois board, however, has another function that conflicts with adjudication—the setting of environmental standards and regulations.

The question is increasingly debated of whether a pollution control agency should prosecute alleged law violators in court, rather than leave the matter exclusively to the attorney general. The typical division of authority between environmental agencies and justice department has caused two problems. First, since the attorney general is usually elected, he may be of a different political party than the governor. Agencies may limit referrals on political grounds or the attorney general may fail to forcefully prosecute for similar considerations. Second, environmental agencies also complain that justice department lawyers are inexpert on matters of pollution control and may also, as a result, lack interest and commitment to such cases.

If an environmental agency is given authority to prosecute polluters, the attorney general must continue to have this power as well, and a competitive situation may result. This was the case in Illinois. Competition may result in more and improved enforcement, but only if each agency has all the legal and scientific expertise needed to handle cases. Each must be able to act independently and the attorney general will need authority and funds to proceed without agency referrals. If the traditional route is continued, with the attorney general doing all prosecuting, we recommend that one or more state assistant attorneys general be assigned to and physically located in a state environmental agency, such as occurs in Minnesota and Washington. Then, state attorneys can gain competence, expertise, and increased enthusiasm for pollution control matters.

Environmental Superdepartments Rejected

Although major benefits accrue to new antipollution departments, we have not found that environmental superdepartments, which consolidate more types of conservation and natural resource programs, are even better.* In matters of program combination, if a little is good, a lot is not necessarily better. In fact, there is a point of counterproductivity that is reached when too many programs are mixed within one operational department. This principle has been borne out by Wisconsin's Department of Natural Resources and New York's Department of Environmental Conservation, departments that mix pollution controls with conservation and resource programs such as water, fish and wildlife, forests, and parks and recreation management.

*We have not examined another organizational pattern—the one used in Great Britain but not the United States. This is to combine pollution control and some aesthetic environmental programs with programs for housing and transportation. Great Britain's environmental superdepartment is a national ministry.

252

As executive departments get larger, they tend to become more unwieldy, reducing administrative efficiency. The greater the staff size and diversity of programs combined, the more time and energy must be devoted to getting the larger department set up and its many component programs operating smoothly in their new location.

Advocacy and emphasis on pollution control is diminished when pollution abatement is located in large department that must address many other environmental and conservation concerns. These programs will naturally and continuously compete for the director's attention, staff time, and public funds, and also for public attention and support. The opportunity for the emergence of a strong, highly visible pollution control advocate in government may be lost, since the environmental superdepartment's director will be compelled to take views that synthesize various competing environmental demands.

It is also likely that one program will dominate the other within a large environmental department. It is not easy to find a director with broad expertise and sufficient interest in all a superdepartment's programs. In Wisconsin's superdepartment, conservation programs such as parks, forests, fish, and wildlife have dominated the pollution control work from the outset. The secretary and his top management staff were chosen from the former Conservation Department, as a peace offering to conservationists who opposed the merger, and have failed to give adequate emphasis to the fledgling pollution control effort. Consequently, the state has no strong public antipollution advocate, and this work has lagged. In New York's superdepartment, pollution control receives greater internal emphasis than the conservation work, but both share the director's attention.

Superdepartments seem to have a negative effect on environmental and conservation interest groups, at least in the short run. Conservationists—sportsmen and wilderness buffs—have typically objected to the merging of the state's conservation and antipollution work on grounds that they may lose control over the consolidated department and that the popular antipollution work may dominate the mix. Pollution control interest groups have often protested that resource management programs such as forest cutting, dams, and park developments compromise tough pollution regulation. Instead of uniting, both interest groups are less likely to form alliances for political strength. Focusing on the same department has turned normal competition among these groups into more direct conflict, thus undercutting the base of political support for both antipollution and traditional conservation work. Such conflicts have been a constant factor with which the departments' directors have had to contend.

One theory in support of superdepartments, argued particularly in support of New York's action, is that this neutralizing of environmental groups is useful, that no one client group will be able to dominate a department that has many varied concerns. Thus, government officials can be more objective and make decisions based on rational analysis, instead of political pressuring. If this occurred, "rational analysis" would be only a substitute for the values of government planners for those of the public. Furthermore, this is not likely to occur, for while environmental groups' political strength may be weakened,

253

regulated interests will not likely be affected, thus increasing even more their relative control over government decisions. Rather than try to eliminate interest group pressures, a better approach is to insure that all individual preferences are fully represented in the process by which government's decisions are made. Such representation is more likely to occur when a state has several environmental departments focusing on different major public goals. Pollution control and conservation interest groups differ on goals and political style and each group will be strengthened by having two major environmental departments rather than one.

The principal reason cited to support environmental superdepartments is the improved analytical perspective they will bring to policy officials and staff in the long run. It is argued that when there is a broad environmental program mix, state officials will be able to develop a broad "ecological" perspective on resource management and a preventive approach to pollution control. Policy planners will be able to take account of the many interactions in nature of all programs relating to water, air, land, forests, minerals, fisheries, and wildlife. Thus, environmental superdepartments may be useful in the long run if they result in a new kind of integrated environmental policy-making and new ways of administering programs.

While this logic makes sense theoretically, it has proven almost impossible to implement in practice, at least in the short run, and thus these benefits are only potential. Despite all the energy devoted to linking pollution control and conservation work, close integration of these programs in the Wisconsin and New York superdepartments has not yet occurred. Basically, these states have found that the two sets of personnel have vastly different backgrounds and focus, and program objectives and functions are dissimilar. Only limited facilities and personnel can be shared, most of this in field work, and not much administrative cost-saving has resulted. The two sets of programs remain located in separate divisions, and usually act independently. We have not yet found extensive common resource planning or programming, and few, if any, signs of "ecological" thinking.

In general, environmental superdepartments seem to be more trouble than they are worth, at least in the short run. Big new departments have lacked a sharply defined mission and suffered considerable administrative confusion. Their directors have spent much time resolving problems arising between the pollution control and conservation components, but this conflict resolution has not been a conscious integrating force. It occurs on an ad hoc, case-by-case basis and often merely is a settling of staff squabbles. Time that might have been spent on needed antipollution or conservation work had to be focused on setting up an organizational pattern satisfactory to both the pollution control and conservation components, solving jurisdictional and program disputes, and overcoming internal and external opposition. Internal organization may become even a more major problem in the future for environmental superdepartments, and if the consolidated units have sufficiently strong political constituencies and histories of autonomous operations, integration may never occur. Rather, a series of bureaucratic fiefdoms may be set up, the most extreme example of which is the U.S. Department of Health, Education and Welfare.

A final argument offered to support an environmental superdepartment is that it will reduce the number of officials reporting to the governor and set up appointed directors who can make basic trade-offs among all environmental programs. Many governors favor this strategy, since it may free the governor of making many decisions and reduce embarrassing public feuding among state officials. Many departmental directors and some organizational specialists believe that an advocacy process, whereby many different, single-purpose agencies argue out their views in a public and political arena, is wasteful.

However, we believe that considerable public debate on policy issues will increase citizen participation. Also elected governors, and not appointed departmental directors and state bureaucrats, should make basic policy decisions, trading-off different public goals. These are not administrative matters but political ones, and they need to be articulated and debated in public. The public can then hold these elected officials fully responsible and recall them at election time if displeased. Within superdepartments, conflicts and trade-offs between component programs tend to be made internally and unilaterally, by the department head. It has, unfortunately, been considered by departmental directors a sign of poor management if subordinate program officials state opposing views in public. Thus, decisions are not as likely to be subject to direct public scrutiny and control. Separate agencies for pollution control and conservation or resource management work encourages greater public advocacy, citizen understanding of forthcoming issues, and executive accountability.

A word might be said here about the type of program mix found in environmental superdepartments. Within the superdepartments in Wisconsin and New York, there have been no conflicts of basic program orientation so serious as to actually bias or weaken a tough antipollution posture. However, this might occur in an environmental superdepartment that contained resource programs with strong developmental, promotional, or resource "exploitive" objectives, as well as pollution control. Examples of these might be the department of mines or the public utilities commission. A potential conflict occurs in Maryland's Department of Natural Resources where the Environmental Service that builds and operates waste management facilities and discharges wastes is housed along with the water pollution regulatory program. Experience points to the fact that when a public agency contains programs that are charged with both promoting and regulating an activity, the promotional side tends to dominate and bias the regulatory work, as the program is "captured" by those strong, well-organized, and well-financed private interests that are suppose to be regulated. This was the case when the U.S. Department of Agriculture completely regulated pesticides and the Atomic Energy Commission had exclusive control of radiation regulation.

What Type of Policy Leadership Should an Environmental Department Have?

The most effective and responsive policy leadership for a new pollution control agency is a single director, appointed by the governor and directly accountable and responsible to him. Part-time boards or commissions that set policy should be abolished but could usefully be replaced by a citizen advisory group. This was the approach of Washington's reorganization. The departmental director should have full authority to make all decisions, within statutory limits, for his department and then be held responsible for them.

The most important advantage of the single leader, rather than policy leadership by a board, is that this increases a department's responsiveness and accountability to the governor, legislature, and public. There is no intervening, part-time, appointive organization between the governor and the department giving orders and often blocking a governor's wishes. As a state's chief elected official, the governor should have adequate control over his executive branch. New governors, not preexisting commissions, should be able to hire and fire departmental directors according to their own ideas of how executive programs should be run. Otherwise, the wishes of the voters expressed in their election of a governor cannot be implemented. If the popular demand is for a new type of leader and new policy thrust for an agency, a new director can be brought in. If the governor appoints an ineffective leader or adopts inadequate policies, he can be voted out at the next election. Some people fear this system of direct control by the governor will overpoliticize department decisions, resulting in actions based on short-term voters' whims rather than long-range needs. This is a risk in a responsive political system and can only be overcome by the election and appointment of high-quality officials. Another fear is that the director, who will have considerable power, will be ineffective or unsympathetic to pollution control. This is another chance one takes in a responsive system. The probability, however, is that if the environment is a real concern of a great many voters, the governor will see it to be in his own interests to appoint a strong and committed pollution fighter.

A single director, rather than board leadership, also eases the accessibility to decision-making for citizens and the legislature. Interest groups and legislators can go straight to one decision-maker to offer criticisms and demand solutions instead of having to deal with a group of persons, which is just another layer of decision-making.

A single leader can most effectively act as a strong public advocate for his program mission in dealing with other state agencies and the private sector. And, if a dynamic and aggressive leader is chosen, he can help to create an image of energy, strength, and forward movement for the agency that group leadership can rarely generate. He can act as a highly visible rallying point for public interest in his agency's programs, and steadily work to build a political and legislative base of support.

A single policy director can take prompt, vigorous actions, unencumbered by first having to gain consensus from a group with built-in conflicting interests. Speed may be particularly important in times of pollution crises and in meeting statutory deadlines. Single directors can implement and articulate more consistent and less confusing policies to the public and regulated parties.

Washington State's environmental reorganization successfully eliminated policy-making boards, replacing them with a citizen advisory Ecological Commission. While the commission has a vague and limited veto power over regulations, this power has never been used and the body, in effect, is purely advisory. The Department of Ecology's director is appointed by and is directly responsible to the governor. The effect has been to give the director a sounding board to gather public opinion or publicize his own views, without reducing his ability to move swiftly or deal directly with the governor. New York's Department of Environmental Conservation is reviewed by a State Environmental Board, which is mostly advisory, but must approve major pollution control standards proposed by the department's director. In contrast to Washington's Ecological Commission, this board is an increasingly influential force in departmental decision-making, which slows down the department's policy-setting processes until a consensus is reached by the board, and may dilute environmental standards.

Illinois' Pollution Control Board is a group of five appointed full-time members who serve a term and has its own staff, research capability, and budget. This policy leadership concept is a compromise between eliminating or limiting boards as in Washington and New York, and continuing part-time citizen boards that set all major policy, as in other states. If a state decides to continue with a board that has significant powers, that body should serve full time and have its own resources, such as in Illinois.

A full-time board is more knowledgeable and competent as an environmental policy-maker than a part-time board, and by making membership a job it may reduce the conflicts of interest that members have with outside business concerns. If a board works full time and has its own staff and investigatory powers it is more likely to make decisions independently of the state administrative agency. Thus, the board will not appear to be making decisions that are really those of the state agency, a situation that conceals the real locus of decisions from the public. However, we do not recommend that a board have the dual responsibility of standards-setting and adjudication that the Illinois board has, since these functions may be conflicting. While pollution control standards-setting requires an advocacy role, fair-minded adjudication of pollution cases requires an uncommitted posture.

Part-Time Policy Boards Rejected

Part-time policy-making boards representing special interests have been traditionally used by many state governments, such as Wisconsin and Minnesota, in hopes of incorporating diverse public values into environmental policies and increasing direct citizen participation. They are particularly prevalent in states operating under the "weak governor" administrative system, where there is fear of centralized political power, and boards are established to check the chief executive's power. A newly elected governor cannot easily gain a majority of members of these citizen-composed policy boards, whose members are usually appointed for overlapping four- or five-year terms, and cannot be dismissed except usually for malfeasance. Many policy boards, such as Wisconsin's Natural Resources Board, have the power to appoint the departmental director, which even further removes the department from a governor's direct line of control. This "third" layer of government is not directly accountable to anyone. Hence, a situation may develop whereby an executive agency acts very much under the control of a group of men whom the public has no way to control.

The alleged benefits of part-time policy-making boards have failed to materialize in many states, such as Wisconsin and Minnesota. While group decisions are meant to be broadly representative of a variety of interests, distinctly removed from the bureaucracy and political allegiances, one or two interests may dominate decisions. These may be biased in favor of the polluters the agency is attempting to regulate, such as are some members of Minnesota's Pollution Control Board. Even if board members are not obviously biased, or if this bias is not a majority, special interests will be present. Thus, usually board decision-making represents not so much a compromise or balancing of interests, but more a potential veto power for special interests. In any event, it is difficult to find a balanced membership producing balanced judgments. Decisions are often inconsistent—tough in one instance, weak in another—thus presenting no consistent policy or clear, united front to the public. On a highly controversial issue the board may be deadlocked, preventing needed action.

In theory, a board is supposed to act as a decision-making body, higher than the full-time agency, and have a long-range view of problems, separated from day-to-day crises. But, in practice, they rarely add much that is new to decision-making or act as higher decision-making bodies. Serving part-time, board members meet only once a month or less. Typically they have little technical expertise in environmental matters, since they were chosen to represent different viewpoints or for political purposes. Often board members merely react to what the agency puts before them, rather than initiating discussions on their own, and they are forced to rely on the expertise and opinions of the agency's staff. Even so, board deliberations take up a lot of time, slowing down the entire decision-making process. Special interest lobbying before boards is also time-consuming, and agency directors are forced to spend time and energy keeping board members abreast of activities, often with no productive results. If boards do not effectively exert their powers, they may serve to confuse the public as to the real locus of decision-making. For example, while many citizens in Wisconsin believe that the Natural Resources Board has power and focus their attention there, the secretary of the Department of Natural Resources usually makes the real decisions, with the board merely acting as a rubber stamp. Thus, the board actually serves to disguise the real decision-making, thus reducing meaningful citizen participation.

In contrast, Minnesota's Pollution Control Board is a powerful decision-making body and its meetings are controversial, lengthy, and well-attended by the public. Here, citizen access to decision-making is increased. However, the question here is access to what kind of decision-making, to what kind of people? If the board did not exist, no doubt interest groups and individuals would double their efforts to gain increased access to the agency and make it more directly responsive to them.

258

In addition to consolidating pollution control programs, there are two broad environmental functions that any state seriously launching on a program of environmental management ought to undertake. The first is comprehensive environmental planning, which not only ties all environmental programs together but also links these with other state programs and objectives. A comprehensive and long-range view of environmental problems is necessary in state government, particularly at the governor's level, while operational programs are administered in several, manageably sized departments. The environmental planning should have both long-range problem prevention perspectives, as well as shorter-range policy and program planning goals. It should include land use planning. This kind of planning seeks to protect and systematically allocate the state's land and related water resources to a variety of competing demands and private claims on it, such as for agriculture, industry, transportation, housing, fisheries and wildlife, and recreation. While pollution control is a serious objective of state government, and one demanding a separate operational department, the pollution crisis is but a symptom of society's failure to account for and manage energy and resources in ecological systems. These broad and long-term issues should be the mission of the environmental planning unit.

The second function is what may be termed environmental impact analysis. This is the task of defining and assessing the likely impact on the environment that proposed state development projects will have. The objective is to instill environmental objectives in all state agencies, but particularly resource development ones, by requiring them to make detailed environmental observations on their programs at all stages. Environmental impact analysis is also intended to be an informational device to aid public decision-makers at all levels by setting out the environmental costs and benefits of a state activity. This task would require all state agencies to submit statements on the adverse environmental impact of their proposed projects to a state authority for review. This is now required of all federal agencies by the National Environmental Policy Act of 1969, and several states also have similar requirements.* Environmental impact review authority may or may not be accompanied by a veto power but will be a stronger function if it is. The federal Council on Environmental Quality, which reviews the proposed projects of federal agencies on environmental grounds, does not have veto power.

We believe that the two functions of comprehensive environmental planning and the assessment and control of environmental impacts from other state programs are mutually supportive and should be administered together. We also recommend that the planning and impact authority be administered separately

---

*As of the end of 1972, environmental impact statements were required in California, Hawaii, Indiana, Massachusetts, Montana, Minnesota, New Mexico, North Carolina, Wisconsin, and Puerto Rico. Delaware requires them for matters affecting its coastal region. Bills providing for such requirements were vetoed by the governors of New York and Connecticut.

from a state's day-to-day operational environment agencies, carried out at the top of the state's organizational structure—in the office of the governor. This will give the state a broad view of environmental problems and policies, while allowing implementation of those policies to be carried out by several manageably sized environmental departments.

The organization to do the two jobs might be a state planning office if that unit has a strong multipurpose planning capability and if the planning process is linked to a program-budgeting system as an implementation tool. In other states, a central management and budgeting office might do the work if it had a planning component. In many states, planning agencies or the central administration agency are within the governor's office, are considered part of his staff, and are directly responsible to him. They are distinguished in this way from other executive-line agencies with operational programs.

However, if the planning and/or administration office focuses mainly on economic development work, as happens in many states, environmental planning should not be performed there unless steps can be taken to insure that it is not dominated or biased by the economic development objectives. Alternatively, environmental planning could be conducted by a small permanent staff in the governor's office.

To arrive at this conclusion on the location of environmental planning and impact authority, we asked these questions:

1. How can planning and impact control be done so that it affects all agencies of state government and balances all interests fairly? How can environmental plans and impact decisions be implemented?

2. How can the unique advocacy roles of the several environmental and other agencies be preserved?

3. How can environmental planning be brought down from its ivory tower to become useful to operational programs, but with the long-range perspective retained?

4. How can accountability be built into a planning and environmental impact control program that necessarily involves trading-off different public values?

5. How can environmental planning be related to other state planning efforts?

Both comprehensive environmental planning and impact analysis involve resolving many conflicting state goals. Each process must balance environmental objectives against other social and economic ones statewide, and sometimes they go against one another. These activities should seek to incorporate environmental objectives into governmental decision-making on a systematic basis, but weighing them fairly against other concerns in specific cases. Adjudication involves a broad assessment of everyone's interest, and then a firm, unbiased decision for or against one interest depending on the situation. This is particularly true when the environmental impact statement is backed up by a veto power over state agency programs.

The advantage of the governor's office as the locus for environmental planning and impact adjudication is that this office is supposed to have a broad view of the entire executive branch, and also the highest decision-making power needed to settle interagency disputes. Environmental impact adjudication is a fundamental policy function that should be made by the governor or his immediate staff in the executive branch or in the legislature. The governor can be held directly accountable to the voters, and thus is more likely to be responsive to the full range of individual preferences in society. The governor should not be shielded from the clash of environmental and other state objectives, such as economic development. These clashes are some of the most significant statewide issues today.

As the final adjudicator in the executive branch of various state missions, the governor should be immediately involved in the settlement of such basic disputes. The governor's office also has the most power and prestige to implement comprehensive environmental plans and to make environmental impact decisions stick in various state agencies.

The joint administration of the planning and impact authority is likely to benefit both programs, since the work of one can bring information to the other. Both are highly technical, time-consuming, and thoughtful functions that should be carried out by staff specially hired for these purposes. Environmental planning and impact analysis need not necessarily be performed by the same persons; but if not, they should respond to the same direction and have continuous contact with one another.

The environmental impact analysis function involves making short-term, hard, day-to-day decisions on whether and how state agencies should proceed with their proposed projects. However, these decisions must be based on some clear-cut guidelines for evaluating the trade-offs between environmental and other state programs and objectives, and these guidelines must have some long-term vision. The existing planning staff may have important experience in statewide interdepartmental planning, and could be helpful here. Also, because planning staff are oriented toward the longer-run, they should have some contact with day-to-day problems, choices, and trade-offs involved in environmental impact statements lest they begin to operate in an ivory tower and political/economic vacuum.

These comprehensive environmental functions do not belong in an environmental department because these jobs are basically adjudicative in nature. Environmental superdepartments, as well as antipollution agencies, have usually been set up to perform as advocacy agencies, and this role is urgently needed at present. They should actively lobby for strong environmental clean-up measures, and serve as public spokesmen and rallying points for the public's environmental interests. However, an agency cannot be an advocate and an unbiased adjudicator at the same time. Both jobs would suffer.

Also, whenever comprehensive planning functions are assigned to line-executive agencies involved in day-to-day operations and crises, there is a strong tendency for the planning staff to lose their long-term analytical perspective as they are increasingly drawn into daily problems. The natural tendency, particularly for new agencies, is to rely more and more on the planning staff to help the agency out of immediate crises. It is especially difficult to initiate and sustain a planning effort that is supposed to go beyond the scope of the agency's immediate jurisdiction, and comprehensive environmental planning is meant to do just this.

New York's Department of Environmental Conservation is a good case in point. It is one of the few state environmental departments that is actually charged with broad environmental planning functions. However, in its first year the department had only a handful of planning staff and concentrated all its efforts on pollution regulation. The statutorily required environmental plan will be a year and half behind its originally required date, September, 1971, and even so will concentrate mainly on the department's own programs.

The administration and review of environmental impact statements is also a highly time-consuming function, particularly if it is to be performed well. This job would be in constant competition with an environmental agency's other major activities and might cause a slowdown in these. The experience of the federal advisory Council on Environmental Quality (CEQ), charged with broad environmental policy development and program coordination as well as the impact analysis authority, bears this out. Swamped with environmental impact statements arriving daily from federal agencies, CEQ has had to spread its small staff very thinly over many tasks.

If a state decides to locate comprehensive environmental planning and impact analysis in its central planning agency and/or budget and administrative offices, some new professional planning staff may have to be hired. If these central units do exist, they are better locations for the two broad environmental functions than a new, full-time special council in the governor's office. A special council, such as the CEQ, represents just one objective rather than all state aims and still does not tie in with ongoing programs. Comprehensive environmental planning and impact adjudication efforts are important and just-emerging activities for state government and it is hoped that they will be systematically incorporated into all governmental processes from the beginning. Furthermore, such councils usually take on an advocacy approach on environmental issues and so lose credibility as unbiased adjudicative bodies, able to weigh fairly the varied interests of the states' citizens. A new council might also simply duplicate existing skills and staff in a state's planning and budgeting offices.

One traditional method used to solve interagency disputes is an interagency council, composed of the heads of the affected agencies. Minnesota has just set up such a five-member council in the governor's office to review environmental impacts. We do not recommend this kind of institution for environmental planning or impact adjudication. The experience with special interagency councils is that they are not consensus-producing bodies. Typically, interagency councils can discuss unbiasedly only those matters that will not adversely affect any of their members. The final decision is usually decided by the board's composition, which will be either stacked "for the environment" or, more likely, "for economic development" from the start.

262

THE ROLE OF THE PRIVATE CITIZEN

One of the main considerations of all preceding recommendations has been to open up the processes of state government to all private citizens. The aim is to create a structure that will generate more information for the public and make decision-makers visible, accessible, and responsive to the public.

Organizational improvements need to be accompanied in most states by stronger statutory guarantees for citizen participation. The typical token gestures, such as public hearings, have fallen into widespread and justified disrepute. These public meetings are usually held after key governmental decisions are made, but may give the impression that the public has endorsed the agency's decisions.

We recommend that states examine and adopt new techniques, such as guaranteeing private citizens' right to sue private and public entities in state courts on a class-action basis, such as in Michigan. However, the legislature needs to accompany such authority with more specific policy guidelines for the courts to follow than in the Michigan law. Through court actions, the private citizen can be a watchdog on the performance of executive agencies, as well as a supplement to public enforcement actions. Environmentalists should also have the right to participate as parties in regulatory proceedings and to appeal departmental decisions, just as regulated parties do. Groups of conservationists should be able to initiate standards-setting proceedings, as in Illinois. In fact, we commend the state's attention to the list of rights to participate in administrative proceedings included in the Illinois Environmental Protection Act of 1970, as outlined in Chapter 1.

A NOTE TO THE LEGISLATURE

State legislatures, even more than the U.S. Congress, have increasingly abdicated many significant powers to the executive branches of government. Now, with the creation of streamlined and aggressive administrative environmental agencies, the domination of the state legislatures will increase unless these bodies take steps to reassert their authority.

In nearly every legislature in the country, members serve only part time, some meeting only biennially. They lack their own staff and research funds, and have come either to depend on special interest groups for information and assistance or merely to take the word of executive agencies and the governor as to what new laws are needed and how existing ones are being administered.

Even the New York legislature, which has been rated second best in the nation,[1] was recently described as "an auxiliary to the Governor's office."[2] It certainly was such an auxiliary when enacting the legislation creating the Department of Environmental Conservation.

In addition to underfunding their own powers to investigate and draft bills, legislatures have willingly overdelegated to the executive branch their state constitutional powers to set policy by enacting vague and open-ended laws. Environmental bills rarely include significant, specific policy guidance to the administering agencies or the courts. Rather, laws are loaded with platitudes about beautifying everyone's environment in all ways, for all uses, all the time. Instead of making policy choices and setting priorities, these bills sound like campaign speeches, which they often become.

The vaguely written laws are dumped in the lap of appointed executive officials or state bureaucrats, who then make the basic policy decisions. In this way, legislators abdicate their responsibility to make fundamental value judgments affecting their constituents and trade-offs among environmental and other competing public goals. These are properly legislative functions, because only legislators and not administrative agency officials can be held accountable by the voters. This, of course, is what legislators fear—that they will offend some voters in the process of setting priorities and lose some votes at the next election. But legislative priority-setting is a necessary concomitant of the democratic process. If legislatures are going to reassert their policy powers and approach a coequal status with the newly efficient and popular environmental agencies, they will need to take several measures.

We recommend that specific policy statements accompany laws that create new environmental departments, setting out their specific purpose and strategy. Then, when enacting new statutory authority for these agencies, the laws should be more specific than in the past and also be accompanied by definitive policy statements.

We further recommend that legislative hearings and investigations be conducted annually to oversee and evaluate the programs and expenditures of the new environmental agency.

To accomplish these tasks effectively, legislatures will need to equip themselves with funds and able, full-time staff to investigate environmental bills and problems of the state and oversee the executive administration of laws. They should also be able to contract for analyses outside the legislature and have a permanent, formal means of securing the analytical aid of their states' universities.

Committee structures need to be sufficiently parallel to the executive departmental divisions to facilitate legislative overview and allow bills to come from committees in a manner that relates to the new department's structure.

Additional changes needed to strengthen state legislatures generally are recommended in the report of the Citizens' Conference on State Legislatures.[3]

NOTES

1. John Burns, *The Sometimes Governments, A Critical Study of the 50 American Legislatures by the Citizens Conference on State Legislatures* (New York: Bantam Books, 1971), p. 51.

2. David H. Beetle, "How Can We Improve Legislative Operation in New York State," *Monitor*, September-October, 1969.

3. Burns, *op. cit*

THE NEW FEDERAL ENVIRONMENTAL ORGANIZATIONS

Recognizing some of the same institutional fragmentation and gaps that have troubled many states, the federal government created three new agencies for environmental protection in 1970. The genesis of each organization was different, and the main motives for their creation ranged from highly political to more analytical. However, each move was designed to redirect and integrate federal policy formation and implementation in order to focus on environmental problems in a more comprehensive and interrelated manner. By this structuring, it was hoped that federal activities would more closely match the environment, which had come to be perceived as a single interconnected system.

The Council on Environmental Quality (CEQ)

Early in 1970, Congressional initiative resulted in the National Environmental Policy Act of 1969, which among other things established a three-member advisory Council on Environmental Quality in the Executive Office of the President to act as an overall planning and coordinative unit for environmental policy and to increase concern for environmental protection in other federal agencies.

The CEQ has a very broad environmental focus, but few day-to-day operational "line" responsibilities. Its mission is to help develop broad policies and coordinate environmental programs, and its purview ranges across pollution controls, resource and conservation programs, open space and recreation, land use, population control, urban quality, and everything else that makes up the environmental package. With a small, highly professional staff, the CEQ was meant to be the federal government's broad environmental quality spokesman, thinker, and gadfly. It is responsible for advising both the president and Congress, and prepares an annual report on the state of environmental quality in the country. It is also meant to oversee environmental research in all federal agencies.

One daily responsibility of the CEQ is to develop guidelines for, and review, the mandatory environmental impact statements accompanying all federal agencies' legislative and project proposals that are expected to have a major environmental effect. These statements, known as "102 statements," are authorized by the National Environmental Policy Act of 1969. However, the CEQ has no veto power over federal agency proposals, but rather can enforce its recommendations only through persuasion and political pressures.

The CEQ's location in the president's office was considered appropriate for the overview, prestige, and executive access necessary for these tasks. However, some persons feel that CEQ is no longer needed since the creation of the Environmental Protection Agency because many of their responsibilities for planning, research, and policy formation overlap.

The Environmental Protection Agency (EPA)

Created in the fall of 1970 by Reorganization Plan No. 3 of 1970, the Environmental Protection Agency consolidates the major federal pollution control programs. It was a product of President Nixon's Advisory Council on Executive Organization, also known as the Ash Council for its director, Roy L. Ash, then president of Litton Industries. The primary objective of EPA is to integrate pollution control planning and standards-setting to avoid federal actions that merely traded one form of pollution for another variety in the environment. Centralizing antipollution regulation was also expected to increase the political visibility and viability of that effort.

The major antipollution programs consolidated into EPA were previously scattered among three cabinet departments, one independent agency, and one interagency council. These were:

1. water pollution control, formerly located in HEW and in the Interior Department just prior to reorganization, and drinking water quality from HEW;
2. air pollution control from HEW;
3. solid wastes management from HEW;
4. control of pesticides in food from HEW, Agriculture's pesticides licensing activities, and Interior's pesticides research;
5. radiation protection from HEW, environmental radiation standards-setting from the Atomic Energy Commission, and the interagency Federal Radiation Council;
6. ecological systems research from the newly created CEQ.

EPA was meant to be a strong and largely single-purpose independent agency, focusing mainly on the regulation of harmful physical-chemical contaminants in the water, air, and land. It was meant to be a highly visible and aggressive national advocate for tough antipollution measures, and to serve as a focal point for increased public interest and political support for these. Its creation was meant to signal a new era of federal commitment to pollution clean-up.

Because of its substantial regulatory and financial assistance programs EPA is the federal agency that has the greatest impact on state environmental efforts. Through new legislation and its own initiatives, EPA is assuming an

266

increasingly large role over the setting of air and water quality standards. Many state governments' water, air, and solid waste pollution control programs have been, and are, given sizable financial support from EPA—both general program support and aid for particular functions such as planning. A considerably larger amount of funds aid the construction of municipal wastewater disposal facilities and these funds are channeled through the states that allocate amounts to localities. At the present time, EPA is organized largely on a program basis, e.g., air and water pollution, but the agency is moving incrementally toward a functional internal structure. In 1971, EPA had close to 6,800 staff, including 9 main regional offices and regional administrators.

The National Oceanic and Atmospheric Agency (NOAA)

A separate reorganization process, begun earlier in the Johnson administration, culminated in the National Oceanic and Atmospheric Agency, which consolidates atmospheric monitoring and smaller marine science programs. The agency was set up in the fall of 1970, by Reorganization Plan No. 4 of 1970. NOAA reflects, in large part, the recommendations of the Commission on Marine Science, Engineering and Resources set up in 1966, and better known as the Stratton Commission for its chairman, Julius A. Stratton, then chairman of the Ford Foundation. The Stratton Commission wanted NOAA as an independent agency to pursue long-range scientific research on our marine and atmospheric environments and their interactions. However, after much debate NOAA was located in the Commerce Department, where its principal component, the Environmental Sciences Services Administration (ESSA), was already located. ESSA's staff of 9,600 was at that time 80 percent of the new NOAA's staff and 40 percent of Commerce's personnel.

With the exception of the Weather Bureau, which is part of ESSA, NOAA has a more limited, basic research mission and has not had much interaction with EPA and the CEQ. Other components of NOAA are elements of the Bureau of Commercial Fisheries, the marine sport fish program, and the Marine Minerals Technology Center (from the Interior Department); the Office of Sea Grant Programs (from the National Science Foundation); and elements of the U.S. Lake Survey (from the Department of the Army). The following programs were also to be transferred to NOAA by executive action: the National Oceanographic Data Center and the National Oceanographic Instrumentation Center (from the Department of the Navy) and the National Data Buoy Project (from the Department of Transportation).

STATE ORGANIZATIONS FOR POLLUTION CONTROL, 1972

A. ADMINISTRATIVE LOCATION OF POLLUTION CONTROL PROGRAMS

Model I: *Separate agency for major pollution control programs (11 states)*

Alaska	Department of Environmental Conservation (water and air pollution, solid waste, land use and coastal zone management)
Arkansas	Department of Pollution Control and Ecology (pollution control and strip mine regulation)
Florida	Department of Pollution Control
Illinois	Pollution Control Board, Environmental Protection Agency, and Institute for Environmental Quality
Maine	Environmental Improvement Commission (air and water pollution, land use control, and water development regulation)
Minnesota	Pollution Control Agency
Mississippi	Air and Water Pollution Control Commission (no solid waste)
Nebraska	Department of Environmental Control (air and water pollution and land use regulation)
North Carolina	Department of Water and Air Resources
Oregon	Department of Environmental Quality
South Carolina	Pollution Control Authority

Model II: *Separate agency for major pollution control and water use program (2 states)*

Washington	Department of Ecology

New Mexico	Environmental Improvement Agency (all pollution controls and also administers consumer protection and occupational and migrant health)

Model III: *Superdepartment for major pollution control and conservation/resource management programs (9 states)*

California	Resources Agency
Connecticut	Department of Environmental Protection
Delaware	Department of Natural Resources and Environmental Control
New Jersey	Department of Environmental Protection
New York	Department of Environmental Conservation
Massachusetts	Executive Office of Environmental Affairs*
Pennsylvania	Department of Environmental Resources
Vermont	Agency of Environmental Conservation
Wisconsin	Department of Natural Resources

Model IV: *State agencies or commissions specializing predominantly in water pollution control and possibly some water resources management and other resource programs. Remaining pollution controls are usually administered by the State Health Department (9 states)*

Alabama	Water Improvement Commission (water pollution only)
California	Resources Agency (both water pollution and management). (Reorganized. If an integrated pollution division, this should be moved to Model III)
Louisiana	Stream Control Commission; Wildlife and Fish Commission
Maryland	Department of Natural Resources (both water pollution control and management)

---

*A cabinet-level office administering the Departments of Natural Resources, and Metropolitan District Commission. An "open planning" approach involving the participation of private citizens is studying the reorganization of these departments and will recommend changes by early 1973.

Michigan	Department of Natural Resources (both water pollution and management)
New Hampshire	Water Supply and Pollution Control Commission (both water pollution and management)
Texas	Water Control Board (water pollution only)
West Virginia	Department of Natural Resources (both water pollution and management)
Virginia	Water Control Board (water pollution only)

Model V: *State agencies locating water pollution control, and possibly other pollution control programs, in State Health Department (remaining 19 states)*

B. TYPE OF POLICY LEADERSHIP FOR POLLUTION CONTROL

Model I: *Single departmental director, appointed by the governor, with advisory board or no board (9 states)*

Alaska	Board advises only
Connecticut	Board advises only
Maryland	Board advises only
New Jersey	Advisory boards
New York	Environmental Board approves pollution control standards but in practice is mostly advisory
Pennsylvania	Board advises only
Rhode Island	
Washington	Ecological Commission may veto standards of Department of Ecology but in practice is mostly advisory
Wyoming	Board advises only

Model II: *Full-time board for policy-making (1 state)*

Illinois	Full-time board, with funds and staff, sets environmental standards and regulates and adjudicates pollution cases

Model III: *Part-time, citizen or interagency board to set policy (40 states)*

a. Board governs pollution control agency

Arkansas	Nebraska
Florida	New Mexico

Maine	North Carolina
Minnesota	Oregon
Mississippi	South Carolina

    b.   Board governs environmental superdepartment
           Delaware
           Vermont
           Wisconsin

    c.   Board governs the water pollution control program, which may be located in larger resources department

Alabama	New Hampshire
California	Texas
Louisiana	Virginia
Massachusetts	West Virginia
Michigan	

    d.   State board of health and/or one or more special boards govern all pollution control programs, located in state health department (18 others states).

C.   STATES ALSO HAVING SPECIAL POLLUTION CONTROL ADJUDICATIVE BODIES IN EXECUTIVE BRANCH (either an administrative court or an appeals forum)

Arizona	State board of health hears appeals from state agency
Delaware	Hearing appeals council
Illinois	The Pollution Control Board acts as an administrative court, adjudicating antipollution enforcement cases; sets fines and substitutes for lower Illinois court, with appeals from the board going to the appellate courts
Nebraska	Hearing appeals council
Pennsylvania	Hearing appeals council
Washington	Hearings Appeals Board hears appeals from decisions of Department of Ecology and regional air pollution control agencies

PERSONS INTERVIEWED

Illinois

William L. Blaser, former Director, Environmental Protection Agency, Springfield.

✓ Lee Bot⁄ Open Lands Project, Chicago.

Carol Cowgill, University of Chicago School of Law, Chicago.

David P. Currie, former Chairman, Pollution Control Board, Chicago.

Jacob D. Dumelle, Member of the Pollution Control Board, Chicago.

Paul Engelhart, Bureau of the Budget, State of Illinois, Springfield.

Ace Extrom, President, Illinois Wildlife Association, Blue Island.

Richard Kates, Attorney at Law, Chicago.

Jim D. Keehner, Assistant Attorney General, Chief of the Southern Division, Air and Water Pollution Control Board, Springfield.

John Kirkwood, Tuberculosis Institute of Chicago, Chicago.

✔ Clarence Klassen, former Director, Environmental Protection Agency, Springfield.

Steve Klein, Assistant to the Chairman, Pollution Control Board, Chicago.

Samuel T. Lawton, Jr., Member of the Pollution Control Board, Chicago.

Mary Lee Leahy, Attorney at Law, Chicago, Illinois (a delegate to the convention to draft amendments to the Illinois Constitution and author of the Environmental Amendment) Appointed Director Environmental Protection Agency in 1973

Joseph J. Magsamen, former Chief, Bureau of Administration, Environmental Protection Agency, Springfield.

William J. Nettles, Administrative Assistant to the Attorney General, Springfield.

Preston Peden, Director, Governmental Affairs Division of Chicago Association of Commerce and Industry, Chicago.

Wally Poston, Director of Environmental Control, City of Chicago.

Louise Rome, President, Illinois League of Women Voters, Chicago.

Michael Scheiderman, Director, Environmental Institute, Chicago.

Thomas W. Scheuneman, Chief of the Bureau of Enforcement, Environmental Protection Agency, Springfield.

M. P. Venema, President, Universal Oil Products Company, Des Plaines.

Phillip T. Zeni, Environmental Protection Agency, Springfield.

Minnesota

John Badalich, former Executive Director, Minnesota Pollution Control Agency, Minneapolis.

Dr. John Borscher, former member of the Minnesota Pollution Control Board, Chairman of Urban and Regional Planning and Geography Department, University of Minnesota, Minneapolis.

Mary Brascugli, State Chairman for Environmental Quality, League of Women Voters, and member of the Minneapolis-St. Paul League of Women Voters.

Lawrence Carlson, President (1971), Minnesota Conservation Federation, Minneapolis.

Dr. Chuck Carson, Assistant to Executive Director of the Minnesota Pollution Control Agency, and Director of the Special Services Division, Minneapolis.

Donald Cleveland, Research Staff, Water Resources and Pollution Subcommittee of the Minnesota House Land and Water Resources Committee, St. Paul.

Hon. Lloyd Duxbury, former State Representative and Speaker of the House in Minnesota, lawyer, Washington, D.C.

F. Robert Edman, Management Consultant, and Consultant to the Minnesota Resources Commission, St. Paul.

Dr. Paul Engstrom, President, Minnesota Environmental Citizen Control Association, St. Paul.

Dale Fetherling, environmental staff writer, *Minneapolis Tribune,* Minneapolis.

Hon. Alfred France, Environmental Coordinator, Dayton-Hudson Corporation, former member of the Minnesota House of Representatives and former Federal Co-Chairman of the Upper Great Lakes Regional Commission, St. Paul.

Steve Gadler, member, Minnesota Pollution Control Board, St. Paul.

Paul Gilje, Director, Citizens League, Minneapolis.

Robert Goligoski, environmental staff writer, *Pioneer Press,* St. Paul.

Paul Gove, environmental liaison to Governor Wendall Anderson, Governor's Office, St. Paul.

David Hamernick, Assistant to the Director of Environmental Planning, Minnesota State Planning Agency, St. Paul.

Robert Herbst, Commissioner, Minnesota Department of Natural Resources, and former President of the Isaac Walton League, St. Paul.

David Hills, Water Resources Research Center, University of Minnesota, Minneapolis.

Theodore Kolderie, Director, Citizens League, Minneapolis.

Lawrence Koll, former environmental liaison to Governor LeVander, Governor's Office, St. Paul.

273

Jerry Kuehn, Assistant to Director of Environmental Planning, Minnesota State Planning Agency, St. Paul.

Michael Link, Public Relations, Sierra Club, Minneapolis.

✔ Grant Merritt, Executive Director of the Minnesota Pollution Control Agency, Minneapolis.

Hon. Gordon Rosenmeier, former Minnesota State Senator and President of the State Senate, lawyer, Little Falls.

Theodore Shields, President, Minnesota Association of Commerce and Industry, St. Paul.

William Sizer, Director of Environmental Planning, Minnesota State Planning Agency, St. Paul.

Dr. William Walton, Director, Water Resources Research Center, University of Minnesota, and member of the Water Resources Coordinating Committee of the State Planning Agency, St. Paul.

Douglas Young, former administrative assistant to Governor LeVander, Governor's Office, St. Paul.

Washington

David Ackerman, Stanford Research Institute, Palo Alto, California.

George Barlow, Department of Ecology, Olympia.

Jim Behlke, Executive Assistant Director, Public Service Branch, Department of Ecology, Olympia.

John Biggs, Director, Department of Ecology, Olympia.

Sam Billingsley, Manager, Environmental and Utility Liaison, Washington Public Power Supply System, Olympia.

Jerry Bollen, Assistant Director, Office of Operations, Department of Ecology, Olympia.

Lawrence B. Bradley, Executive Director, Industrial Development Division, Department of Commerce and Economic Development, Olympia.

Lyle Burt, reporter, *Seattle Times*, Olympia.

Bert Cole, Director, Department of Natural Resources, Olympia.

Arthur Dammkohler, Air Pollution Control Officer, Puget Sound Air Pollution Control Agency, Seattle.

Brewster Denny, University of Washington Professor, Seattle.

James Dolliver, Special Assistant to the Governor, Olympia.

Marvin B. Durning, Attorney at Law, Seattle.

Brock Evans, Attorney at Law, counsel for northwest Sierra Club and Federation of Western Outdoor Clubs, Seattle.

Oswald H. Greager, Chairman, Thermal Power Plant Site Evaluation Council, Olympia.

Matthew W. Hill, Chairman, Pollution Control Hearings Board, Olympia.

Fred Hahn, Assistant Director, Office of Planning & Program Development, Department of Ecology, Olympia.

George Hansen, Department of Ecology, Olympia.
Pete Hildebrandt, Assistant Director, Office of Technical Services, Department of Ecology, Olympia.
Wes Hunter, Deputy Director, Department of Ecology, Olympia.
Emil Jensen, Director, Department of Social and Health Services, Olympia.
Ralph Johnson, University of Washington Professor, Seattle.
Dan Keller, Program Coordinator for Natural Resources and Recreation and DOE, Office of Program Planning & Fiscal Management, Olympia.
Robert Lane, environmental reporter, *Seattle Times*, Seattle.
Joseph F. Lightfoot, Executive Secretary, Thermal Power Plant Site Evaluation Council.
John McGregor, Eastern Washington feed lot owner, Ecological Commission, Walla Walla.
Bertram L. Metzger, Jr. of Houghton, Cluck, Coughlin & Riley, Attorneys at Law, counsel for Washington Public Power Supply System.
John R. Miller, Attorney at Law, Washington Environmental Council board.
Dr. Gordon H. Orians, Seattle, Professor of Zoology, University of Washington, Ecological Commission, Seattle.
Carl Pratt, Department of Ecology, Olympia.
Steve Raymond, Assistant Editor, *Seattle Times*, Seattle.
John W. Riley of Houghton, Cluck, Coughlin & Riley, Attorneys at Law, counsel for Washington Public Power Supply System.
William H. Rodgers, Jr., Professor of Law, University of Washington, Seattle.
Charles Roe, Assistant Attorney General assigned to the Department of Ecology, Olympia.
Richard A. Schmidt, Stanford Research Institute.
David Skellenger, of Houghton, Cluck, Coughlin & Riley, Attorneys at Law, counsel for Washington Public Power Supply System.
✓ Richard Slavin, Director, Planning and Community Affairs, Office of Program Planning and Fiscal Management.
Ed Standish, Department of Ecology, Olympia.
Robert Stockman, Executive Assistant Director, Administration & Planning Branch, Department of Ecology, Olympia.
✓ Joan Thomas, Vice President, Washington Environmental Council.
Thor Tollefson, Director, Fisheries Department, Olympia.
Howard M. Vollmer, Stanford Research Institute, Palo Alto, California.
Avery Wells, Department of Ecology, Olympia.
Ann Widditsch, Washington Environmental Council, League of Women Voters, member Ecological Commission, Seattle.
Tom Wimmer, Washington Environmental Council board, Seattle.
Dick Young, environmental writer, *Seattle Post Intelligencer,* Seattle.

Wisconsin

Hon. Norman Anderson, Wisconsin State Senator, Chairman of the Senate Conservation Committee, Madison.

Bruce Braun, Coordinator of Budget Operations, Office of the Director of the Bureau of Budget and Management, Wisconsin Department of Administration, and also member of the former Governor's Committee on Water Resources and Kellett Reorganization Commission, Madison.

Robert Brumder, environmental assistant to Governor Patrick Lucey, Governor's Office, Madison.

Gary Carlson, former budget analyst for natural resource and environmental programs, Bureau of Budget and Management, Wisconsin Department of Administration, Madison.

Andrew Damon, Legal Counsel Bureau, Wisconsin Department of Natural Resources, Madison.

Prof. Irving Fox, former Associate Director, Water Resources Center, and former Chairman of the Department of Urban and Regional Planning, University of Wisconsin, Madison.

Thomas Frangos, Director, Division of Environmental Protection, Wisconsin Department of Natural Resources, Madison.

Paul Gossens, Assistant Attorney General for the Environment, Attorney General's Office, Madison.

Whitney Gould, environmental staff writer, *Capital Times,* Madison.

Prof. Matthew Holden, Political Science Department, University of Wisconsin, Madison.

Emil Kaminski, Director, Legal Services Bureau, Wisconsin Department of Natural Resources, Madison.

Prof. James Kerrigan, Assistant Director, Water Resources Center, University of Wisconsin, Madison.

Paul Keshishian, Environmental Director, Wisconsin Power and Light Company, Madison.

Michael Lovejoy, current budget analyst for natural resource and environmental programs, Bureau of Budget and Management, Wisconsin Department of Administration, Madison.

Mrs. James MacDonald, Chairman for Environmental Quality, Wisconsin League of Women Voters, Madison.

Wayne McGown, Secretary, Wisconsin Department of Administration, Madison.

Paul Olsen, Chairman, Nature Conservancy, Madison.

John Potter, current member of the Wisconsin Natural Resources Board and former Chairman of the Natural Resources Board, Wisconsin Rapids.

Prof. David Ranney, formerly with the Department of Political Science, University of Wisconsin, Madison.

Prof. Gerald Rohlich, current member of the Wisconsin Natural Resources Board, Director, Water Resources Center, University of Wisconsin, and member of the former Governor's Committee on Water Resources and Kellett Reorganization Committee.

J. Robert Smith, Director, Division of Forestry, Wildlife and Recreation, Wisconsin Department of Natural Resources, Madison.

Stan Welch, Director, Field Division, and former Director of the Forestry Division, Wisconsin Department of Natural Resources, Madison.

Theodore Wiesniski, Assistant to the Director, Division of Environmental Protection, Wisconsin Department of Natural Resources, Madison.

Oliver Williams, Assistant to the Director, Division of Environmental Protection, Wisconsin Department of Natural Resources, Madison.

Wisconsin Resource Conservation Council, members, Madison.

Lester Voigt, Secretary, Wisconsin Department of Natural Resources, Madison.

New York

John Allen, Finance Director, New York Department of Environmental Conservation, Albany.

Breck Arrington, former Assistant to the Commissioner, New York Department of Environmental Conservation, Albany.

Nicholas Barth, Planning and Research, New York Department of Environmental Conservation, Albany.

Peter Berle, member of the New York State Assembly, Conservation Committee, lawyer, New York City.

James Biggane, Executive Deputy, New York Department of Environmental Conservation, and former Executive Secretary, State Environmental Board, Albany.

Holt Bodinson, Director, Environmental Education Services, Communications and Education Division, New York Department of Environmental Conservation, Albany.

Blair Corning, Assistant to the Commissioner, New York Department of Environmental Conservation, Albany.

Henry Diamond, Commissioner, New York Department of Environmental Conservation, Albany.

Stan Fishman, Assistant Attorney General for the Environment, State Attorney General's Office, Albany.

Russ Gladieux, senior budget analyst, Organization and Management, Division of the Budget, State Executive Department, Albany.

Alexander Grannis, Director of Enforcement, Legal Counsel's Office, New York Department of Environmental Conservation, Albany.

Frederick Howell, Director, Planning and Research, New York Department of Environmental Conservation, Albany.

George Humphries, Regional Director for New York City and Acting Regional Director for Nassau and Suffolk Counties, New York Department of Environmental Conservation, New York City.

Peter Kahn, Citizens for Clean Air, New York City.

Irwin King, Executive Secretary, State Environmental Board, former Director of Communications and Education, New York Department of Environmental Conservation, Albany.

Charles LaBelle, Legal Counsel, New York Department of Environmental Conservation, Albany.

Robert Lahrman, Vice President for Public Relations, Consolidated Edison Co., New York City.

Dr. Mason Lawrence, Deputy Commissioner, Environmental Management Section, New York Department of Environmental Conservation, Albany.

William Lawrence, senior budget analyst, Division of the Budget, State Executive Department, Albany.

League of Women Voters, members, New York City.

Stanley Legg, Deputy Commissioner, Field Services, New York Department of Environmental Conservation, Albany.

Robert McMannis, Director, Communications and Education, New York Department of Environmental Conservation, Albany.

Mark Messing, Friends of the Earth, New York City.

Dwight Metzler, Deputy Commissioner, Environmental Quality Section, New York Department of Environmental Conservation, Albany.

Ronald Redersen, First Deputy Commissioner, New York Department of Environmental Conservation, Albany.

Steven Rice, Assistant Counsel to the Governor, Governor's Office, Albany.

Alexander Rihm, Director, Air Resources, Environmental Quality Section, New York Department of Environmental Conservation, Albany.

Eric Rubin, former Assistant to the Public Service Commissioner, Albany.

David Sive, environmental lawyer, Environmental Planning Lobby, Sierra Club and other interest groups, New York City.

William Whyte, member of the State Environmental Board, New York City.

Vermont

Schuyler Jackson, Assistant Secretary, Agency of Environmental Conservation, Montpelier.

Arthur Ristau, Director, Environmental Planning Information Center, Montpelier.

Kenneth E. Senecal, Executive Officer, Environmental Board, Montpelier.

Maine

Robert Coakley, Finance Officer, Department of Environmental Protection, State of Maine, Augusta.

Orlando DeLogu, Member, Environmental Improvement Commission, Portland.

Donaldson Koons, Chairman, Environmental Improvement Commission, Waterville.

Henry Warren, Director, Bureau of Land Quality, Department of Environmental Protection, State of Maine, Augusta.

278

Maryland

Thomas Andrews, Chief of Administrative Services, Maryland Environmental Service, Annapolis.

James B. Coulter, Secretary, Department of Natural Resources, Annapolis.

Thomas Downs, Special Assistant Attorney General, Maryland Environmental Service, Annapolis.

Reed W. McDonagh, Deputy Director, Maryland Environmental Service, Annapolis.

Paul W. McKee, Director, Department of Water Resources, Annapolis.

Thomas D. McKewen, Director, Maryland Environmental Service, Annapolis.

Joseph J. Murnane, Executive Secretary, Maryland Association of Counties, Annapolis.

Michigan

Joseph Sax, Professor, School of Law, University of Michigan, Ann Arbor.

American Law Institute. "A Model Land Development Code: Tentative Draft No. 3." Philadelphia: Institute, mimeographed, April, 1971.

Baldwin, Malcolm F., and James K. Page, eds. *Law and the Environment.* New York: Walker and Co., 1970.

Burch, William, Neil Cheek, and Lee Taylor, eds. *Social Behavior, Natural Resources and the Environment.* New York: Harper and Row, 1972.

Bosselman, Fred, and David Callies. *The Quiet Revolution in Land Use Control.* Prepared for the U.S. Council on Environmental Quality. Washington, D.C.: U.S. Government Printing Office, 1972.

Burns, John. *The Sometimes Government: A Critical Study of the 50 American Legislatures by the Citizens Conference on State Legislatures.* New York: Bantam Books, 1971.

Caldwell, Lynton Keith. *Environment: A Challenge For Modern Society.* New York: Natural History Press, 1970.

Clawson, Marion. *Suburban Land Conversion in the United States: An Economic and Governmental Process.* Baltimore: Johns Hopkins Press, 1971.

Cooley, Richard A., and Geoffrey Wandesforde-Smith. *Congress and the Environment.* Seattle: University of Washington Press, 1970.

Davies, J. Clarence, III. *The Politics of Pollution.* New York: Pegasus, 1970.

Downs, Anthony, *Inside Bureaucracy.* Boston: Little, Brown, 1967.

Fortune Editors, eds. *Environment: National Mission for the Seventies.* New York: Harper and Row, 1970.

"The Greening of Public Policy: Planning the National Environment," *Journal of the American Institute of Planners.* Vol. 37 (July 1971).

Hagman, Donald G. *Urban Planning and Land Development Control Law.* St. Paul: West Publishing Co., 1971.

Harrison, Gordon. *Earth Keeping: The War with Nature and A Proposal for Peace.* Boston: Houghton Mifflin, 1971.

Haskell, Elizabeth H. *Quality of the Urban Environment: The Federal Role.* Washington, D.C.: The Urban Institute, February, 1970.

Klausner, Samuel Z., ed. *Society and Its Physical Environment.* Annals of the American Academy of Political and Social Science, 389 (May 1970), 1-115.

Kneese, Allen V., and Blair T. Bower. *Managing Water Quality: Economics, Technology, Institutions.* Baltimore: Johns Hopkins Press, 1968.

_____ , eds. *Environmental Quality Analysis: Theory and Method in the Social Sciences.* Baltimore: Johns Hopkins Press, 1972.

Landsberg, Hans H., Leonard L. Fischman, and Joseph L. Fisher. *Resources in America's Future: Patterns of Requirements and Availabilities, 1960-2000*. Baltimore: Johns Hopkins Press, 1963.

"Law and the Environment: A Symposium." Cornell Law Review, 55,663 (May 1970).

McHarg, Ian. L. *Design With Nature*. Garden City, N.Y.: Natural History Press, 1969.

Meadows, Donella, et al. *The Limits to Growth: A Report for the Club of Rome's Project on the Predicament of Mankind*. New York: Universe Books, 1972.

Mosher, Frederick C., ed. *Government Reorganizations: Cases and Commentary*. A joint project of the Inter-University Case Program, Inc., and the Institute of Government Studies. Indianapolis: Bobbs-Merrill, 1967.

Nader, Ralph. Power and Land in California. Washington, D.C.: Center for the Study of Responsive Law, mimeographed, 1972.

National Academy of Sciences, National Research Council, Committee on Pollution. *Waste Management and Control*. Washington, D.C.: National Academy of Sciences, 1966.

Perloff, Harvey, ed. *The Quality of the Urban Environment*. Baltimore: Johns Hopkins Press, 1969.

Roos, Leslie L., Jr., and Norlou R. Roos. *Pollution, Regulation and Evaluation*. Working Paper 76-71. Evanston, Illinois: Northwestern University, Graduate School of Management, 1971.

Rubino, Richard A., and William R. Wagner. *The State's Role in Land Resource Management*. Lexington, Kentucky: Council of State Governments, 1972.

Schmid, A. Allan. *Federal Decision-Making for Water Resource Development*. Arlington, Va: National Water Commission, December, 1971.

Seidman, Harold. *Politics, Position and Power*. New York: Oxford University Press, 1970.

Sive, David. "Some Thoughts of an Environmental Lawyer in the Wilderness of Administrative Law." *Columbia Law Review*. (April 1970) 70-4.

Thompson, James D. *Organizations in Action*. New York: McGraw-Hill, 1967.

U.S. Congress. Conference Committees, 1969. *National Environmental Policy Act of 1969*. Conference Report to accompany S. 1075. 91st Congress, 1st Session, House Report No. 91-765. Washington, D.C.: U.S. Government Printing Office, 1969.

U.S. Congress. House Committee on Government Operations. Subcommittee on Executive and Legislature Reorganization. *Reorganization Plan No. 3 of 1970* (Environmental Protection Agency). Hearings. 91st Congress, 2nd Session. July 22-August 4, 1970. Washington, D.C.: U.S. Government Printing Office, 1970.

U.S. Congress. House Committee on Government Operations. Subcommittee on Executive and Legislative Reorganization. *Reorganization Plan No. 4 of 1970* (National Oceanic and Atmospheric Administration). Hearings. 91st Congress, 2nd Session. July 28-29, 1970. Washington, D.C.: U.S. Government Printing Office, 1970.

281

U.S. Congress. Senate Committee on Government Operations. Subcommittee on Executive Reorganization and Government Research. *Reorganization Plans No's. 3 and 4 of 1970.* Hearings. 91st Congress, 2nd Session. July 28-September 1, 1970. Washington, D.C.: U.S. Government Printing Office, 1970.

U.S. Congress. Senate Committee on Interior and Insular Affairs. *National Environmental Policy Act of 1960.* Report to accompany S. 1075. 91st Congress, 1st Session. Senate Report No. 91-296. Washington, D.C.: U.S. Government Printing Office, 1969.

U.S. Congress. Senate Committee on Interior and Insular Affairs. *National Land Use Policy: Background Papers.* Washington, D.C.: U.S. Government Printing Office, April 1972.

U.S. Congress. *National Environmental Policy Act of 1969: National Environmental Policy.* Hearings on S. 1975, S. 237 and S. 1752. 91st Congress, First Session, April 19, 1969. Washington, D.C.: U.S. Government Printing Office, 1969.

U.S. Citizens' Advisory Committee on Environmental Quality. *Report of the Task Force on Land Utilization and Urban Growth*, Washington, D.C. Forthcoming.

U.S. Council on Environmental Quality. *Environmental Quality—1970; -1971; and -1972.* Washington, D.C.: U.S. Government Printing Office, 1970, 1971 and 1972.

U.S. Environmental Protection Agency. 1972 Compendium of State Water Pollution Control Agencies with Regulatory/Policy-Making Responsibility. Washington, D.C.: Environmental Protection Agency, 1972. Mimeographed.

U.S. Government. Domestic Council. The White House. *Report on National Growth, 1972.* Washington, D.C.: U.S. Government Printing Office, February, 1972.

U.S. Government. National Goals Research Staff. The White House. *Toward Balanced Growth: Quantity With Quality.* Washington, D.C.: U.S. Government Printing Office, July, 1970.

U.S. Government. The President's Advisory Council on Executive Organization. Executive Office of the President. *Establishment of a Department of Natural Resources; Organization for Social and Economic Programs.* Memoranda for the President. Washington, D.C.: U.S. Government Printing Office, February, 1970.

ABOUT THE AUTHORS

ELIZABETH H. HASKELL, an analyst of environmental public policy and organizations, has been legislative assistant to U.S. Senator Henry M. Jackson, Chairman of the Senate Committee on Interior and Insular Affairs, and to U.S. Congressman Richard C. White of Texas, dealing specifically with natural-resource and environmental policies. She was also legislative specialist to the Assistant Secretary of the Interior for Water Quality and Research.

After leaving public service, Mrs. Haskell studied and wrote extensively on federal and state environmental activities and organizations. Until 1970 she was a member of the research staff of the Urban Institute of Washington, D.C. and completed a two-volume compendium and evaluation of federal programs involved in urban waste management and other aspects of quality of the urban environment. More recently, Mrs. Haskell directed a research group funded by the Ford Foundation in a study of the pollution control, land use, and conservation efforts of state governments. In 1970-71 she was a Fellow of the Woodrow Wilson International Center for Scholars at the Smithsonian Institution and also served as an environmental adviser and consultant to federal and state legislatures and executive agencies.

Mrs. Haskell studied political science at the University of Pennsylvania and international affairs at the University of Vienna in Austria.

VICTORIA S. PRICE was a staff member of President Nixon's Council on Executive Organization (the Ash Council) and helped to write the memorandum leading to the creation of the federal Environmental Protection Agency in 1970; she also worked on the internal design of the agency. Mrs. Price has traveled and spoken widely on new state environmental management programs. She is now a consultant on environmental problems to local groups in New York City and Long Island.

Mrs. Price was an analyst for three years in the Social Science Division of RAND Corporation in Santa Monica, California, where she did research and writing on Southeast Asia, including analyses of the 1968 TET offensive in South Vietnam and negotiations with the North.

Mrs. Price studied international relations at the University of Wisconsin and received a master's degree in public administration from the University of California at Berkeley.